Hallmark Keepsake Ornaments

HALLMARK KEEPSAKE ORNAMENT VALUE GUIDE

Tracker Edition 1973 - 2005

Includes Miniature Ornaments, Easter/Spring Ornaments, Special Issue Ornaments, Halloween Ornaments, and Tree Toppers

Hallmark

KEEPSAKE ORNAMENTS

Hallmark Keepsake Ornament Value Guide

This publication is not affiliated with Hallmark Cards, Inc. or any of its affiliates, subsidiaries, distributors, or representatives. Product names and designs are the property of Hallmark Cards, Inc. Any opinions expressed are solely those of the authors and do not necessarily reflect those of Hallmark Cards, Inc.

PUBLISHER
Jim Kelley

MANAGING EDITOR
Nicki Pierce

BUSINESS AND PRODUCTION
Peter Custer – Vice President
Lee Sherry – Production Director
Tom Demeter – Art Director
Sharen Forsyth – Operations Manager
Chuck Barnard – Sales and Service Manager
Gloria Kelley – Photo and copy editing
Jocelyn Kelley – Photo and copy editing
Megan Hall – Photo and copy editing

SPECIAL THANKS
Jane Bigham
Rhonda Cline
David Hamrick
Tim Kline
Sara Motsinger
Frank Williams

CONTRIBUTORS
Jay Brown
Nancy Copeland
Kathleen Earls
Terri Legrand
Lee Schooler
Linda Wilson

Bangzoom Publishers
(A Division of Bangzoom Software, Inc.)
14 Storrs Avenue
Braintree, MA 02184
www.bangzoom.com

dedicated to the memory of

Meredith DeGood

Table of Contents

Editorials

So Much To Do!
Reach Promotion
2004

40th Anniversary
BARBIE™
1999

Keepsake Christmas Ornaments

Nesting Nativity
Club Item
2001

Frosty Friends #26
2005

Table of Contents

Crystal Claus
Miniature
1999

Brass Nativity
Hall Family
1982

Graceful Angel
Miniature
Tree Topper

Blessed Nativity Collection
2000

Welcome to the Hallmark Value Guide

This is the first value guide fully licensed by Hallmark Cards, Inc. We started from scratch to create the most comprehensive book ever published on the subject. We hope you enjoy using it.

How Did We Get Our Prices?

Questions have been raised about the prices in this Guide. Much discussion with long-time collectors revealed the need for a value guide that is realistic in terms of the current market. Bangzoom does not arbitrarily decide how to price an item – this information is gathered from collectors, from auction web sites, from many other pieces of information available to us. Unfortunately, collectibles are not a static value item – values are driven by two main variables: supply and demand. When demand is high and supply is low, prices go up. When demand is low and supply is high, prices go down. No investment is guaranteed to continue to appreciate in value year after year. Some items grow in popularity while others may diminish. It is not an easy process to assign values to so many items and expect they will be accurate all of the time.

What Does The Overall Market Look Like?

The collectibles market overall has been hit very hard in recent years. The slowing of the economy, the lingering effects of the September 11th tragedy, unemployment, military action overseas, and uncertainty on the part of consumers means fewer dollars are being spent on items that are not necessities. The number of individuals selling their collections has also increased. While making the market for collectibles more global, eBay has also increased the number of sellers who can reach buyers. Buyers are getting more conservative and more patient with the increased supply of old and rare items showing up in the secondary market. Right now it is a great time to buy. In the not-to-distant future it will most likely be a great time to sell.

Summing It Up

The market is showing signs of improvement. Bangzoom feels that the values shown in this Guide are an accurate reflection of current market values. We will continue to monitor those values for any changes and will record these variations in future editions. Values should never drive a collector; rather, the love of the item collected should be the deciding factor in a purchase.

More About The Book

We list values in this guide for items in MIB (mint in box) condition. We observe prices at auctions, the Internet, retail stores, and "buy-sell" sections in collector magazines. We list all prices gathered, then arrive at a consensus. When a sound average price could not be established, the value is designated as N/E. N/A is used to signify there was no retail price (gift or prize) or that there is no official style number.

Series color-code — **4032.**

Mary's Angels 14: Chrysantha
Retail price and item number — 795QX6985 • $28
Value

4033. — Colorway color-code

Mary's Angels 14: — Series name and number
Chrysantha — Item name
($N/A)QX6985C • $89
Edition Size - 15000. — Notes

All series ornaments are listed by series name and number. In cases where the ornament also has its own name, that name has been added after the series name. For instance, "A Cool Yule" is listed as "Frosty Friends 1: A Cool Yule." The only times the ornaments' names aren't listed are on the "Miniature Harley-Davidson Motorcycle Milestones" and the "Winnie the Pooh and Christopher Robin, Too" series because there simply wasn't enough room to list both.

Collection names have been put before the ornament's name so when listed alphabetically, all collection items are together. The only time the full collection name isn't used is on the "Twas the Night Before the Night Before Christmas" which is abbreviated as "Twas the Night Before..."

Colorway, Club/Event, and Series items, in this order, have been color-coded for easy reference. For example, if an item is both a Colorway and an Event piece, it has been given the Colorway color.

1. Colorway **1.** Club/Event **1.** Series

We urge the reader to remember that this is a guide, and the actual selling price will always depend on a number of factors, including the motivation of the buyer and seller, the location, and the economic climate. It is impossible to arrive at one definitive price. This is why we call this book a *guide*.

Meredith DeGood

Pioneer Authority of the Hallmark Secondary Market

by Frank Williams

In the early 1980s, Hallmark Keepsake Ornaments and Merry Miniatures had reached the "ripe ol' age" of nearly ten years, often a benchmark to genuine collectibility. In its effort to emerge beyond a passing fad, Hallmark produced its first comprehensive picture book of ornaments. Yet, a collectible seeking legitimacy needs a trustworthy and recognizable "authority" willing to do research on behalf of all collectors. My dear friend, Meredith DeGood, became just that for Hallmark and its enthusiasts.

Meredith and Hal DeGood

Initially, in a small part of a store front antique mall in West Des Moines, Iowa, Meredith expanded the reach of her business, The Baggage Car, by pioneering the marketing of vintage Hallmark items in a "For Sale" list in 1983. The list grew to over forty, double-column pages in the 1990s and put her in touch with collectors nationwide. As her inventory grew, so did her expertise. While many endeavored to compile price guides at that time, she alone had amassed a spectrum of inventory which allowed her to determine by actual sales, not by hypothesis, an ornament's value.

Her knowledge spanned everything Hallmark, including the beloved Little Gallery with its pewter and sterling, pins, magnets, cookie cutters, and in later years, Tender Touches and Kiddie Car Classics. Her integrity added consistency to the Hallmark secondary market. She offered fair value when purchasing collectibles. She shared voluminous information through her newsletters, which were savored by "newbie" and seasoned collector alike.

Meredith understood collectors, as she was one herself. If the town had a water tower, Meredith found the Hallmark account there. And yes, when her car was filled to the brim, further treasures found were shipped home. She and her husband, Hal, delighted in the thrill of the hunt, just as we do. When Hal retired from the insurance industry, politically correct Meredith hired him and bestowed upon him the title, "International Traffic Manager/Shipping Clerk."

Meredith was one of a kind. A national tabloid exposed her as the woman with thousands of dollars worth of magnets on her refrigerator. She bought rare pieces as surprise gifts for Clara Johnson Scroggins, a well-known Hallmark expert, author, and collector. She did the same for countless others so they might have complete collections. And she kept Hallmark in good standing with collectors by loaning hundreds of Merry Miniatures to be photographed for Hallmark brochures. Because the Merry Miniatures were so valuable, UPS could not insure them fully, so Meredith had them driven to Kansas City. Who would have guessed that months later, Iowa native and Keepsake artist, Bob Siedler, would drive to Des Moines unannounced and walk into The Baggage Car to return them.

Meredith counseled us to find a secondary dealer we could trust and to stick with that person. And to rousing laughter, she warned us in a 1998 collecting seminar at Hallmark's 25th Anniversary Celebration that shipping costs from multiple sources add up, plus long distance calls can get expensive... unless, of course, you phone from work.

Meredith's passing in October of 2004 leaves a huge void in our collector community. It is fitting that the First Edition of the Bangzoom *Hallmark Keepsake Ornament Value Guide* is dedicated to Meredith DeGood, as she was our hobby's rare "First Edition."

History of the Christmas Ornament

Reprinted by permission Hallmark Cards, Inc.

For many people, decorating their home and Christmas trees with ornaments is one of the most enjoyable ways to capture the magic and excitement of the holidays.

Although Christmas trees first appeared in America in the 1700s, the emergence of the modern Christmas tree actually dates back to 15th and 16th century Germany.

Early German heavy glass kugel ornament

Evergreens were used first in church plays at Christmas and were hung with apples to symbolize a Paradise tree. Paradise trees later found their way into homes, where they were adorned with small white wafers, and later, small pastries cut into stars, angels, hearts and flowers.

During the next 200 years, this custom slowly spread throughout Germany and Europe. Decorated trees were brought to America by Hessians–German mercenaries–fighting in the Revolutionary War.

Christmas wasn't widely celebrated in the United States until the 1800s, however, because of the Puritans' influence. As a result, decorated trees did not become widely popular until people saw the ornaments brought to America by families emigrating from Germany and England in the 1840s.

Typical beaded Czech ornament.

Ornaments became a big hit. F.W. Woolworth of five-and-dime fame had reluctantly stocked his stores with German-made ornaments in 1880. By 1890, he was selling $25 million worth of ornaments at nickel and dime prices.

The ornaments available at that time primarily were German hand-cast lead and hand-blown glass decorations. As time passed, the ornaments became more elaborate – and expensive. Silk and wool thread, chenille and tinsel embellished many of them. Stiff spun glass appeared as angel and butterfly wings; tinsel was used on fancy flower baskets, vases, air balloons and egg zeppelins.

Germany faced virtually no competition until 1925. Then Japan began producing ornaments in large quantities for export to this country. Czechoslovakia also entered the field with many fancy ornaments. By 1935, more then 250 million Christmas tree ornaments were being imported to the United States.

Not until 1939 and the outbreak of World War II did an American company significantly enter the ornament business. Using a machine designed to make light bulbs, Corning engineers produced more than 2,000 ornament balls a minute.

In 1973, when Hallmark introduced six glass ball ornaments and 12 yarn figures as the first collection of Hallmark Keepsake Ornaments, a new tradition of Christmas decorating was started and a new collectible industry was born. When the first line was introduced, they were unique in design, year-dated and available only for a limited time – innovations in the world of ornaments. Since 1973, Hallmark has introduced more than 3,000 different Keepsakes Ornaments and more than 100 ornament series, groups of ornaments that share a specific theme.

The finished Keepsake Ornaments reflect the way styles, materials, formats and technology have expanded since the first ones appeared in Hallmark stores in 1973. Once a collection of decorated glass balls and yarn figures, Keepsake Ornaments now are made in a wide array of wood, acrylic, bone china, porcelain, and handcrafted formats.

But one thing hasn't changed. Their superior craftsmanship and high quality still ensure that Keepsake Ornaments will become family heirlooms and cherished collectibles.

One of Hallmark's first yarn ornaments, Mr. Santa.

The 2005 Hallmark Keepsake Ornament Line

Traditions of fun and family memories continue.

For more than 30 years, Hallmark Keepsake Ornaments have transformed Christmas trees everywhere into 3-D scrapbooks of memories that capture and preserve times, events and special occasions. Most Americans think of a Christmas tree as a memory tree, one adorned with ornaments representing life's special events. In a survey by Hallmark, 97 percent of the respondents display Christmas trees.

Hallmark unveils a brand new line of more than 280 handcrafted, dated ornaments every year. This season, Hallmark is making it easier and more enjoyable than ever to capture moments and commemorate milestones through holiday ornaments with a wider variety of themes and several new personalization options.

Cordelia
Joyful Tidings

Joyful Tidings Collection features angels in beautiful colors of the season. Each angel represents a color and its symbolic meaning. Cordelia in red symbolizes Love, Azura in blue represents Peace, Guilda in Gold stands for tradition, Arianne in silver symbolizes Beauty, and Esmeralda in green represents Generosity.

Fairy Messengers 1: Poinsettia Fairy

Three New Series begin this year for the avid ornament enthusiast. "Skylar A. Woolscarf" is the first in the Snowtop Lodge series that features delightful snow folk that wear scenes such as a cityscape. Northern Cardinal is first in the Beauty of Birds series which will feature a variety of feathered friends, each with a small gift of nature. First in the Fairy Messengers is the Poinsettia Fairy. Fairies that represent messages associated with various flowers will be featured in this colorful series.

Keepsake Kids Play Sets feature hand-painted wood character pieces designed to help children create a Christmas tradition. Both the Nativity and Santa's Workshop play sets feature seven character pieces plus a stable or workshop that doubles as a storage case. They're fun, they tell wonderful stores, and they give kids a bit of Christmas that's all their own.

"Countdown to Christmas" Keepsake Kids

Kids' Interests photo holder ornaments and stands capture the memories children have while chasing their dreams. Each photo holder displays a special moment in a child's life. A sticker sheet included with each ornament makes it easy to personalize with the child's name, activity, and year date. This is sure to become a family keepsake.

Darth Vader - Star Wars™

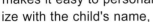

The return of many favorites including Disney™, Lionel Trains™, Looney Tunes™, Peanuts™, Star Wars™ and Star Trek™.

Ornaments as Gifts

Ornaments are viewed as personal gifts during the holiday season. They allow the sender to show the receiver how much "I know you" by picking out an ornament that addresses their special relationship. For example, this year there are Keepsake Ornaments for those who serve in the military, for those who enjoy fishing, or for those who have adopted children.

My First Christmas (Girl) Child's Age

Milestones are also acknowledged through ornament giving. For example, Baby's First Christmas, the child's age series, and first home ornaments are often given as gifts to help the recipient preserve the special event for years to come.

Design themes range from pop culture icons of yesteryear and today to ornaments commemorating special relationships. Ornaments reflect consumers' emotional and relationship-building interests and reinforce Hallmark's industry-leading position in products that help people celebrate and connect with one another. Consumers are traditionally drawn to Keepsake Ornaments that evoke emotions and feelings.

"People choose Hallmark Keepsake Ornaments as gifts, or for themselves because Keepsake Ornaments help them connect with others,

Our First Christmas

honor a special relationship, or reflect a person's interest," says Michael Jindrich, marketing manager for Keepsakes.

Keepsake Ornaments also help people who rely on Hallmark to help them express their feelings, mark milestones, such as weddings or births, and commemorate important relationships such as parents, children, siblings, and friends.

Ornaments as Collectibles

"Hallmark finds its collections are so well-liked because they represent something that captures the meaning of an important, memorable moment in time," says Jindrich. "Enthusiasts have a passion about Hallmark Keepsake Ornaments because of their sentimental value and their relevance from generation to generation."

Best Night of the Week - Wonderful World of Disney®

In 1973, when Hallmark introduced six glass ball ornaments and twelve yarn figures as the first collection of Hallmark Keepsake Ornaments, a new tradition of Christmas decorating was started and a new collectible industry was born. When the first line was introduced, they were unique in design, year-dated and available only for a limited time – innovations in the world of ornaments. Since 1973, Hallmark has introduced thousands of different Keepsakes Ornaments and more than 100 ornament series.

The Halloween Hauntington Collection

A Look Back at 2004

Cookie Doe

Every year, there are a few special ornaments that capture the imagination of Hallmark collectors everywhere. In 2004 the ornament "hits" were abundant. Here's a look at some of the ornaments that had collectors returning to their favorite stores over and over "on the hunt."
Hallmark reminded us all of our love for baking Holiday treats with several "baking theme" ornaments. Cookie Doe captured hearts with its creative way of using cooking utensils to form this clever, adorable reindeer. Christmas Cookies was also a favorite, as we could both see and smell those cookies baking.

Jack Skellington from the Nightmare Before Christmas proved to have fans nationwide snapping up this one of the more unusual hits of 2004.

The "Queens" were fun gifts to both give and receive. Many enjoyed The "Queen Of..." collection which celebrates the hobbies and interests of someone we all know–maybe even ourselves.

Journey of the Train - The Polar Express™

The Polar Express Movie created a huge demand for the Hallmark Polar Express Bells. And, it looks like the movie and ornaments will become a new part of our Holiday Traditions.

Queens of Gardening, Shoes, and Multi-Tasking

Carousel Ride Display

Three new series began in 2004. The Majestic Lion, the first in the Carousel Ride series, re-creates the elaborate carousel animals master wood-carvers once took great pride in creating. A battery-operated carousel ride is also available as a display for this series and is available again in 2005.

Father Christmas is a series of Santas inspired by classic images, and Downhill Delivery is first in the Nick and Christopher series which features two of Santa's favorite sidekicks enjoying a different winter activity each year.

Santas From Around The World

The colorful Santa Around The World collection of eight proved to be popular. Most of us "wanted them all" and found the Mexican and USA African American Santas were in short supply.

Although Wizard of Oz ornaments are always a collector favorite, the 2004 "I'm Melting! Melting!" was one of the most unique ornaments Hallmark has ever offered. With voice, motion and lights, just press the button and hear the Wicked Witch cry out a memorable line in film history as she really melts to the floor!

I'm Melting! Melting! The Wizard of Oz™

It looks like 2005 is filled with many unique Hallmark creations. So, which ornaments will be the "2005 biggest hits"? We'll just have to wait and see!

My Love of Collecting

By Kathleen Earls

Collecting Hallmark items is so addictive and so much fun. I still remember with fondness getting my first Merry Miniatures booklet in a Hallmark store. That was all it took to set me on a quest. Booklet in hand, my youngest daughter and I hit the stores in rural Michigan, checking off as we went along, eager to find another store, flea market or antique store to search for an elusive mini. At the stores, I also discovered lapel pins, and with a Rosie Wells book in hand, a new quest was on. This book had few pictures of pins and cookie cutters, which made collecting them even more challenging. Then I met a lady who had actually created a large notebook-style book with full size pictures just for cookie cutters.

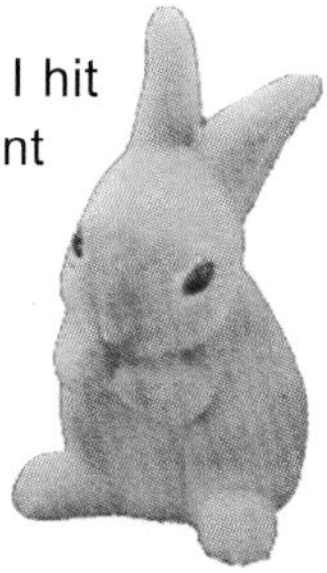

Flocked Bunny
Merry Miniature

My first Hallmark Expo really opened up the world of Hallmark. There I discovered a new love – trimmers. Again, another booklet with illustrations of Christmas items gave me another list to check off. Whenever we took trips, I found myself hitting all the Hallmark stores with the same zeal others reserve for art museums. There were so many fascinating collectibles and my desires kept growing as I learned of each one: candles, key chains, purses, Betsey Clark, various figurines, Tender Touches, mini pewter figurines and plates, stocking hangers and stockings. Of course, it only took finding a Clara Scroggins book of ornaments to set a quest for all of those. I was so thrilled when I finally added the last Keepsake Ornament to my collection that dated back to 1973.

You're Always Welcome
Tender Touches

Jane Bigham, a noted Hallmark collector, was instrumental in that acquisition. Along the way, I discovered there were other special ornament collections, including the

Pony for Christmas #1
Colorway

Mayor's ornaments for Kansas City, the Hall Family ornaments made for Hallmark employees, Ambassador ornaments made for other stores, and, more recently, Colorway ornaments won at Premiers and Expos.

Hallmark Pins

My latest venture is collecting lapel pins in their original packaging or on the original cards marked with their different prices. I am always discovering new ones and updating my files and pictorial inventory. The buttons have proven the most challenging, since some are marked and others are not. Several internet friends have helped me in my pursuit with information and pictures from their collections.

I have found Hallmark collecting a great source of enjoyment and have met many wonderful people with similar interests. Show and tell and trading are such fun – like kids with baseball cards. And, I constantly learn new information on the items I collect through the world of eBay.

My husband even got the Hallmark collecting fever with Kiddie Car Classics. I think that is what is so wonderful about the Hallmark Collections – there are so many varied items that have been made over the years that appeal to different collectors. Even the store displays become items to collect. Go to a show and catch the bug. Once you have one collectible, you feel the desire to find them all, and the quest is the most fun.

Don's Street Rod
Kiddie Car Classic

Special Issue Ornaments

by Tim Kline

If you're an extremely serious collector of Hallmark ornaments, some call us fanatics, your interest in Hallmark ornaments may have expanded beyond the regular and series issues to pursuing some of the more unusual items. Among these are the Colorways, Hall Family card ornaments, Mayor's ornaments, Ambassador, 25 Year Club, special retailer ornaments, prototypes, and other out-of-the-main-stream items. This article is for you.

Here Comes Santa #9: Santa's Woody Special Edition Colorway

Colorways and Event Pieces

1991 - present

What's a Colorway? Lots of collectors have asked this question, but they're also the ones who are responsible for this name in the first place.

In 1994 when Hallmark awarded door-prizes at their first regional event, they announced that the winners were going to receive "mis-takes." Of course these weren't really mistakes, but rather, extremely limited, special edition ornaments taken from the regular product line that were painted in different color schemes. Although the first Colorways were given away in 1994, the first one was actually a special gold plated KC Angel ornament given to noted ornament collector and spokesperson Clara Johnson Scroggins as a "Thank You" during the 1993 KC Convention.

Gold Plated K.C. Angel

Colorway, or Colourway in its British spelling, was borrowed from the collectors of porcelain figurines and character jugs, where the artist decides to change the coloring scheme for some special purpose. Although other terms such as "repaint" have surfaced, collectors seem to prefer the descriptiveness of "colorway" in its American spelling.

Since the first Hallmark Keepsake Ornament Collector's Club (KOCC) national event in Kansas City in 1991, periodic events have been held in various cities around the country and known as Conventions, Expo, Artists on Tour (AOT), Local Club Tour (LCT), Jubilee, and Art of Keepsakes (AOK). Each successive event has seen a growth in popularity, as it has moved from a one-time event at a single location to multiple regional events around the country. Later this year the club will hold its latest event, Keepsake Lane.

Santa's Favorite Stop
1993 Convention Item

As the popularity and notoriety of Colorways has increased, Hallmark has expanded its distribution, making special pieces available for purchase by KOCC members or as rewards for Member-Get-A-Member campaigns, and as gifts/prizes at Ornament Debut and Premier and Holiday Open House. The rarest by far are the prizes from national club events. In 1999 gold seals were added to the boxes to make the prizes more identifiable from the regular issue ornaments. Colorways and other Event pieces are noted throughout this guide are tabbed in gold.

Mayor's Ornaments

1981 - Present

The Mayor's Christmas Tree is a Kansas City tradition that began in 1908 when Mayor Thomas Crittenton erected the city's first official tree at City Hall. A charity drive to support the needy during the holidays accompanied that first tree. In 1973 the tree was relocated to Hallmark's Crown Center Square. A fresh tree is cut and decorated for each year's festivities which begin the day after Thanksgiving and run through the end of the year. The tree is quite a spectacle, standing 100 feet tall, decorated in 7,200 lights. It's become the symbol for the city-wide holiday charity, the Mayor's Christmas Tree Fund.

Five Pointed Acrylic Star
1981 Mayor's Tree
Ornament

Money donated to the Mayor's Christmas Tree Fund buys clothes and food for needy families, gifts for elderly shut-ins and hospitalized patients, parties for impoverished children and more. Beginning in 1981 Hallmark created an annual Mayor's Christmas Tree Ornament which is sold at Crown Center, proceeds going to the charity fund. From 1981 through 1986 the Mayor's ornaments utilized designs from the Hallmark line, but revised the inscriptions. Since 1987, the ornament has been a unique design from Hallmark artist, Fayrol Unverferth, utilizing the wood from the previous year's Christmas tree. These ornaments have become highly collectible, with several designs becoming quite rare and valuable. Hallmark commemorated the Mayor's tree on the 2003 Nostalgic Houses & Shops Town Hall, #20 in the series.

Here are some highlights of the Mayor's Christmas Tree Ornaments:

1981 Holiday Highlights: Christmas Star
(QX501-5)
The Mayor's Christmas Tree ornament has the words "Mayor's Christmas Tree 1981" and the Crown Center logo on it.

1982 First Christmas Together
(QX302-6)
Designed by Ed Seale.

1983 Holiday Highlights: Christmas Stocking
(QX303-9)
Mayor's version has the words "Mayor's Christmas Tree 1983" and the Crown Center logo on it.

1984 Baby's First Christmas
(QX340-1)
This has the words "Mayor's Christmas Tree 1984" and has no Crown Center logo on it.

Hall Family Christmas Cards/Ornaments

1974 - present

Beginning in 1974, Joyce C. Hall and, more recently, Donald Hall have selected an artist from Hallmark to create an ornament which is attached to their annual family Christmas card. Employees who have been with Hallmark for at least 25 years are included in the distribution. A similar card and ornament was distributed to members of the KOCC in 1992, 2000, and 2001. We have included a complete check list of Hall Family ornaments in this guide, the first time it has been published with photos.

Brass Filigree Stocking
2004 Hall Family Ornament

Ambassador Ornaments

1979 - 1982

The Holiday House Collection of ornaments was created by Hallmark for distribution through its subsidiary, Ambassador Cards, to F.W. Woolworth's, Ben Franklin Stores, card shops, supermarkets and drugstores from 1979 through 1982. The test ornaments distributed in 1979 were almost exclusively repackaged ornaments from Hallmark's regular ornament line, while designs in subsequent years were exclusive to the line. The only way to tell that some of these ornaments are from the Ambassador line is if the ornament is still in the box, otherwise they would be considered a no-box Hallmark ornament. We have included a complete check list of Ambassador ornaments in this guide, the first time one has been compiled.

Mouse on Moon
Ambassador Holiday House Collection

Hallmark Collectibles

by Jane Bigham

For Many It Reaches Far Beyond Ornaments

You've just found the last ornament to finish your series of Frosty Friends, and you are so happy to finally have your collection complete. But wait a minute. Did you know that Hallmark issued two Frosty Friends stocking hangers and a Christmas stocking with the Eskimo on it? Do you have the four reversible trimmers with the Frosty Friends characters in your collection? Have you ever seen the Snow Domes with the Frosty Friends ornaments inside or the Little Gallery paperweight with the Frosty Friends Eskimo etching? And don't forget the Frosty Friends lapel pin and magnet, too. Just when you think you have completed your collection, there are always other fun things to search for... and we all know that half of the fun is in the hunt.

When I started dealing in Hallmark fifteen years ago, I thought that Hallmark collectors either focused on Hallmark Ornaments or Hallmark Merry Miniatures. Now I realize that if something is marked "Hallmark," someone collects it. While the experienced Hallmark collectors are sure to recognize a favorite ornament, lapel pin or Betsey Clark figurine, Hallmark has introduced several new artists' lines such as Mary's Bears by Mary Hamilton, Jan Karon's Mitford designs and Marjolein Bastin's giftware. Just as Hallmark continues to introduce new collectible lines, collectors continue expanding their collections and are always searching for new display ideas (and storage space) to accommodate their ever-expanding treasures.

Merry Miniatures Debut in 1974

First issued as party favors, Merry Miniatures made their debut in 1974 and still are one of the most popular collections today. Some of these early favors are not listed in Hallmark publications and would be fun to add to any Merry Miniature collection. The blushing bride, the dancing ballerina, the elusive mushroom house container or even the plastic panorama eggs are sure to make even your closest Hallmark friends a little envious. In the 70s, many original

Mouse
Merry Miniature

Hallmark characters were introduced into the Hallmark designs, such as the Betsey Clark waif-like boy and girl, Joan Walsh Anglund's faceless children, Mary Hamilton's big-eyed Charmers, Shirt Tales animals with their big smiles, and even the ever popular Merry & Happy Snowmen. These popular characters, combined with other characters of the day, were featured in ornaments and other gift products such as Merry Miniatures, Lapel Pins, and Little Gallery. Who could resist purchasing a lapel pin with Little Lulu holding her ice cream cone or Winnie the Pooh with his pot of honey? The Raggedy Ann and Andy Merry Miniatures are still two of the most popular ornaments, and are sought out by a wide range of collectors.

Little Gallery Gift Introduced In 1976

Hallmark also carried over these characters into one of their most popular gift lines, Little Gallery, which was introduced in 1976. These gift items were issued in limited numbers and were made in pewter, bronze, porcelain and crystal. The creativity of the artists made these gifts more meaningful because they included heartfelt messages that related to the artist's drawings on each design. Some of the hardest to find treasures in the Little Gallery Collection are the sterling silver ornaments, which featured Muppet characters, and Joan Walsh Anglund children. These currently sell for several hundred dollars a piece.

Tender Touches and More In 1990

In 1990, Hallmark introduced a similar line, Hallmark Galleries, which included Mary Engelbreit giftware, Tobin Fraley carousels, Thomas Blackshear clowns and Norman Rockwell plates and music boxes. By far the most popular collection in this line were Ed Seale's Tender Touches figurines. This collection of charming woodland animals doing human activities contributes to Ed Seale being one of the most beloved Hallmark artists.

Easter Parade Bears
Tender Touches

Kiddie Car Classics, Legends in Flight, Great American Railroad & Road Rovers

When Hallmark introduced the Kiddie Car Classics in 1992, there was finally something for wives to purchase for their car fanatic husbands. To add to the excitement of the Kiddie Car Collection, Kiddie Cars were painted in different colors and offered as "Colorway" prizes at

Hallmark events. The introduction of the Legends in Flight and Great American Railways Collections in recent years has added additional enticements. Perhaps the Kiddie Car collector would find an interest in the die-cast metal cars that Hallmark issued in 1981 called the Road Rovers. These were issued four different years and had such cute names attached to them that a collector would just have to have them. Who could resist Firey Fred, Scoop Coup or the Fuzz Buzz?

Kiddie Car Classic

Collectors That "Want It All"

There are Hallmark collectors who own 10 or 20 ornaments and then there are those "Very Serious" collectors like my friends, Lee Schooler and Dean Oehlert, who really do "want it all" and collect EVERYTHING ever issued by Hallmark. I asked Lee to make a list of all her different Hallmark collections and the list contained over 100 categories. If it has "Hallmark" stamped on it, Lee and Dean collect it. Their ever-growing collection contains over 15,000 items beautifully displayed, floor to ceiling, in every room of their home. That's why we call their house the "Hallmark Museum."

Whether your collection is large or small, the most important thing is that it makes you smile. I have enjoyed tempting my collector friends with new Hallmark treasures that I find. And even after fifteen years, I'm still surprised to find things that I have never come across before.

Happy Collecting!

Hallmark: An American Dream

Becomes An American Institution

Reprinted by permission Hallmark Cards, Inc.

Telling the story of Hallmark Cards, Inc. is like flipping the pages of an American scrapbook. There are famous characters: Winston Churchill, Walt Disney, Norman Rockwell, and Maya Angelou... new product advancements... retailing innovations... and a set of timeless values: service, quality, caring, and innovation.

The story begins in 1910, when 18-year-old Joyce Clyde Hall stepped off a train in Kansas City, MO, with nothing but two shoeboxes of postcards under his arm. He had little money – not even enough to take a horse-drawn cab to his lodgings at the YMCA – but he had an entrepreneurial spirit and the determination of a pioneer.

Hall printed some invoices and started sending packets of a hundred postcards to dealers throughout the Midwest. A few of the dealers kept the cards without paying. Some returned the unsolicited merchandise with an angry note. But about a third sent a check. Within a couple of months, the teenage businessman had cleared $200 and opened a checking account. He was in business.

Hallmark Founder Joyce C. Hall

A Vision

With those two boxes and a vision, J.C. Hall pioneered a brand synonymous with integrity and gave birth to an industry that flourishes today. Some 6 billion greeting cards are sent each year in the United States alone. Hallmark is the industry leader – one of every two greeting cards sent is a Hallmark card – all beginning with the creativity and innovation of J.C. Hall.

Hall quickly made a name for himself with the picture postcards he sold, but he knew the future was more than postcards. In 1915, Hall Brothers, as the company was named when Rollie Hall joined his brother in business, saw the potential in high-quality valentines and

Christmas cards – mailed in envelopes – and began creating and printing their own cards.

Hall's instinct was right and greeting cards gained popularity. Armed with the success of the Hall Brothers greeting cards, J.C. Hall continued to innovate to keep his budding company growing. The first foray into other product lines came in 1917 when the Hall brothers invented modern gift wrap.

Traditionally, gifts were wrapped in brown paper or colored tissue, called "gift dressing." One chilly December night before Christmas, Hall Brothers ran out of their stock of gift dressing. The sibling entrepreneurs knew they had to meet the needs of hurried shoppers wrapping up their carefully selected purchases. Rollie Hall headed to the product plant to search for anything else customers could use to decorate their packages. He returned with a stack of fancy decorated envelope linings from France. They charged 10 cents a sheet for the linings and the pages flew off the shelves into shoppers' bags. The following year, Hall Brothers packaged the linings in sets of three and again sold out. It was enough to convince them to start designing and printing their own gift wrap. Other innovations followed and the Hallmark brand began to take form.

Building a Brand

Goldsmiths of 14th century London marked the gold and silver articles they crafted with a special symbol, signifying the purity and quality of their product. Each member of the Goldsmiths Hall had one of these symbols, called a "hall mark." J.C. Hall had read stories of the goldsmiths and was intrigued by the word. "Hallmark" not only said quality, it included the family name.

In 1928, the company began marketing its brand by using the Hallmark name on the back of every card. This marketing move was followed by an advertising first. That same year, Hallmark was the first in the greeting card industry to advertise nationally – the ad was written by J.C. Hall personally and appeared in *Ladies' Home Journal*. The move was called "Hall's Folly," and one advertising executive told Hall, "You'll never be able to advertise greeting cards if you expect people to turn them over and read the name."

Hall was convinced of the power of national advertising and next turned to radio, sponsoring "Tony Wons' Radio Scrapbook" in 1938. The program featured Tony Wons chatting with listeners, sharing sentiments from Hallmark cards, and ending the program with: "Look on the back for the identifying mark – a Hallmark card."

The burgeoning brand solidified its position in American history in 1944 with nine simple words. One of the most recognized slogans in advertising, "When You Care Enough to Send the Very Best," was born from a three-by-five-inch notecard. Ed Goodman, a sales and marketing executive at Hallmark, jotted down his thoughts on what Hallmark stood for – caring, quality, the best. And the best was about to get better with the first sponsorship of an hour-long television program.

The series of specials that would become the Hallmark Hall of Fame began in 1951 with Amahl and the Night Visitors, the first original opera created especially for television. NBC approached Hallmark about sponsoring the opera in early December. Hallmark's marketing department knew the sponsorship would be costly and the program's Christmas Eve air-date was after most Christmas shoppers had made their holiday purchases. They asked themselves, are Americans going to tune in to opera on television? The answer was a resounding "yes!" J.C. Hall decided to take the risk and sponsor the program to thank all the people who bought Hallmark cards. The opera moved viewers to send thousands of letters, cards, and telegrams thanking Hallmark for presenting it.

Hallmark saw the value in creating a series of dramatic specials produced with the highest standards of quality and taste. In the 50-plus years since, Hallmark Hall of Fame productions have won 78 Emmy Awards. In 1961, the National Academy of Television Arts and Sciences presented its first – and only – Emmy Award ever given to a sponsor when it said, "Thank you, Mr. Hall, for caring enough to send the very best in television."

J.C. Hall received the first Emmy ever awarded to a sponsor for the Hallmark Hall of Fame.

The Brand Flourishes

The Hallmark Hall of Fame was the right venue to showcase the values of Hallmark – quality, caring, and innovation. The sponsorship made Hallmark an American institution and brought the Hallmark brand alive for consumers by bringing it into their homes. Even the commercials were of the highest quality – 90-second or longer emotion-driven vignettes that required at least one box of tissues. Decades after its inception, Hallmark Hall of Fame continues to be "appointment television," a program families plan an evening around.

When the company name was officially changed from Hall Brothers to Hallmark Cards, Inc. in 1954, the tradition of entrepreneurship started by J.C. Hall was deeply ingrained. In nearly a century of product innovations and creative partnerships, the company:

- Developed retail advancements such as "Eye Vision," a display system that presented greeting cards in easy-to-view displays rather than out-of-sight in drawers, and an automated reorder and display control system that provided a record of what was selling and what was not, thus creating an accurate index of public tastes.
- Partnered with notable artists and personalities, from Charles Schulz to Saul Steinberg, and Winston Churchill to Dwight D. Eisenhower, who collaborated with Hallmark to develop the first Presidential Christmas cards.
- Pioneered decorative paper party products.
- Changed the way people decorate for Christmas by introducing Hallmark Keepsake Ornaments.
- Introduced a line of humorous cards called Shoebox Greetings (named for the two shoe boxes of postcards that started Hallmark) that has become one of consumers' favorite card brands.
- Developed culturally-relevant card lines for Jewish, African-American, and Hispanic consumers.
- Worked with software manufacturers to enable consumers to create personalized Hallmark greeting cards on their home computers.
- Extended its reputation for quality to the floral industry with Hallmark Flowers.

Partners in Quality

One of Hallmark's most creative partnerships is with its employees. Known as "Hallmarkers," employees own nearly one-fifth of the privately-held company through the Employee Profit-Sharing and Ownership plan. With around 800 writers and artists on its payroll,

Hallmark employs one of the world's biggest and best creative staffs. That staff includes painters and poets, but also editors, photographers, calligraphers, sculptors, designers, cartoonists, needlework artists, and specialists in various graphic techniques.

In 1932, Hallmark signed its first licensing agreement with one of the 20th century's most recognizable names – Walt Disney. And in 1960, the Peanuts® gang started appearing on Hallmark greeting cards. Partnerships and licensing agreements with top artists, writers and brands continue today. A new generation of Hallmark shoppers recognize famed poet Maya Angelou ... popular Dutch nature artist Marjolein Bastin ... kid sorcerer Harry Potter™ ... the ever-fashionable Barbie™ ... the irascible yet irresistible Maxine ... and Kaya, Felicity, Josefina, Kirsten, Addy, Samantha, Kit, and Molly from The American Girls Collection. Today, Hallmark has agreements with seven of the top 10 leading licensors for characters and entertainment properties.

As the leader of the greeting card industry, Hallmark leaves its mark on more than just cards. The legacy of quality family entertainment started with the Hallmark Hall of Fame lives on with Hallmark Entertainment, Inc., the world's leading producer of movies and miniseries for television. The Hallmark Channel television network reaches millions of households around the globe with Hallmark's family-oriented programming. Subsidiary Binney & Smith adds personal development products to Hallmark's business with quality brands like Crayola®, Silly Putty® and InkTank™.

Staying in Touch

Although the company is approaching its 100th year, the Hallmark brand continues to evolve. It has remained a household name by staying in touch with consumer tastes and trends to ensure Hallmark products are relevant to today's consumers. The company researches the latest consumer trends in color, fashion, design, and lifestyles. It also conducts focus groups and surveys, facilitates online consumer communities, and utilizes a sophisticated point-of-sale network to understand consumer needs today and in the future.

Hallmark trend experts research what's "en vogue," a practice marketing analysts praise. "They're never going to be 100 yards ahead, but they're never going to fall 100 yards behind, either. They're right there walking with us," said one analyst. Hallmark's creative staff then incorporates the research into designs and editorial to create timely and culturally-relevant products.

On the Corner, Around the Globe
Whenever, however, wherever people are communicating thoughts and feelings, connecting with each other, and celebrating milestones, Hallmark is there. Hallmark products can be found at more than 44,000 retail outlets domestically and online at Hallmark.com. Hallmark Gold Crown® stores, the company's flagship network of independently-owned card and gift specialty stores, carry the most extensive selection of gift and personal expression products. The Expressions From Hallmark and Ambassador lines of greeting cards serve customers in discount stores, supermarkets, drugstores, and other mass merchandise outlets.

Hallmark introduced its quality products and services to the world audience when it formed Hallmark International in 1966. Today, the company publishes in 30 languages and its products are available in more than 100 countries around the globe.

A Century of Leadership
J.C. Hall retired in 1966, leaving the company he built in the capable hands of his son, Donald J. Hall. Don Hall continued to expand Hallmark, and with his father, spearheaded the development of Crown Center, a mixed-use real estate development to halt decay around the headquarters neighborhood in Kansas City, Mo. Outside of headquarters, Hall looked internationally for expansion, increasing distribution worldwide.

Hallmark international headquarters are located in Kansas City, Mo.

When Don Hall retired as president and chief executive officer in 1986, Irvine O. Hockaday, Jr. took the reins of the privately-owned company. Hockaday is credited with complementing Hallmark's well-established personal expression business with new initiatives, including thriving businesses in family entertainment and personal development.

In 2002, Donald J. Hall, Jr., grandson of founder J.C. Hall, became the third-generation of the Hall family to take the helm of the American institution that is Hallmark today. He continues to build on the tradition that is the mark of excellence for the company.

"*It is an awesome responsibility, and an incredible privilege, to lead a company dedicated to enriching lives. At Hallmark, we are invited to give voice to people's feelings – of joy and grief, of compassion and healing. We provide ways for people to express themselves and are there when they celebrate life's seasons. We help them reach out with words of hope and encouragement every day. These are enduring human needs, which is why I have such confidence in the future of our company.*"
– Donald J. Hall, Jr.
President and CEO, Hallmark Cards, Inc.

Insuring Your Collection

by Nicki Pierce

You've enjoyed the Hallmark ornaments on your tree each holiday season and can't imagine Christmas without them. Each year your ornament collection has grown, and now the tree (and possibly your entire home) is full and overflowing. The ornaments are rich in sentimental value to you, but your collection may have a considerable dollar value as well.

What if you have a disastrous fire, water damage in your storage area, or a nasty burglary? Will your homeowner's insurance cover the loss? At what point do you need to add your collectibles to your homeowner's policy? Do you need a separate policy? What documentation do you need to make a claim should there be a loss?

Know Your Coverage

Many homeowner's or rental insurance policies will cover your collection as part of the normal policy. Depending on the insurance company and the value of your collection, an additional policy may be needed to be adequately covered. You should check with your insurance company to see if your collection has a level of coverage that is comfortable for you.

"There's no set time when you should go from homeowner's policy coverage to a separate policy," says Danforth Walker, founder and chief executive of Collectibles Insurance Agency in Westminster, MD, which provides coverage to 16,000 collectors and 2,000 dealers nationwide. We find it best to assess your collectibles' value. If you have more than $3,000 worth of collectibles, it's time to get separate insurance for them."

Document the Contents and Value of Your Collection and Determine Value

Many insurance companies will accept a reputable secondary market source such as this Hallmark Value Guide in determining the value.

In order to gauge how much coverage you need, you must first document your collection to calculate how much it would cost to replace your ornaments. Today, most insurance policies are written as replacement value, which would provide enough money to replace a or damaged collection. Replacement value policies pay out the amount needed to actually replace the items, which is especially important for collectibles because they appreciate in value.

The Hallmark Value Guide software available at **www.bangzoom.com** can aid in preparing the list quickly and will total the secondary market value for you. Simply print the listing once you've clicked on the items you have in your collection. Or, you can write or type your documentation list using this Hallmark Value Guide. This same documentation will aid you should you ever need to file a claim.

To ensure proper coverage, it is important that your agent understand the secondary market values. And, if you have particularly valuable ornaments or if you have an extensive collection, the carrier may want a professional appraisal. Again, find out what your insurance company requires.

Close-up photography and video footage of your ornaments are a good back-up in case of a claim. And, storing all documentation safely away from your home is critical.

Weigh the Risk

After you calculate the replacement cost of your collection, you can determine if you have adequate insurance to cover any losses. If you find you need additional coverage, you can purchase a "rider" to your policy, which provides broader coverage and insures your collection for specific dollar amounts.

As with all insurance, you must weigh the risk of loss against the cost of additional coverage, and make an informed decision with which you are comfortable.

The Keepsake Ornament Club

The 19-year-old Keepsake Ornament Club allows members to choose their ornaments and to enjoy members-only products and privileges.

For the $25 membership fee, members receive the following:

- Two Membership-Exclusive Keepsake Ornaments from a choice of four of the following ornaments (a $40 value):

(from left to right: Snow Day Magic, The Opening Game – A Fun Family Tradition, Christmas Window 2005 – 3rd in the Christmas Windows Series, Ruby Slippers The Wizard of Oz)

- The opportunity to purchase seven additional Club-Exclusive Keepsake Ornaments, including:

(from top-left to bottom-right: Santa Nutcracker, All Decked Out, It's Christmas Eve!, Barbie Designer Showcase, Muscle Cars, Peanuts Christmas Pageant, Countdown to Christmas)

- The Club magazine, *For Keeps*, filled with ornament news, decorating tips and more
- The next *Dream Book* - featuring the latest and greatest in Keepsake Ornaments

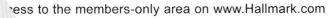

...ess to the members-only area on www.Hallmark.com

...Gold Crown Card points whenever they purchase Club-Exclusive products

- Opportunities to receive other members-only offers
- An invitation to special events throughout the year, including the 2005 National Events "Welcome to Keepsake Lane"

2005 "WELCOME TO KEEPSAKE LANE" National Club Member Events

You won't want to miss the six Club Member Events in 2005 in the following cities:

- August 27 - New York City, NY
- September 10 - St Louis, MO
- September 17 - Dallas, TX
- October 8 - Orlando, FL
- October 22 - Detroit, MI
- November 5 - San Jose, CA

- Meet fellow collectors that share your love for Keepsake Ornaments
- Learn new ways to display and decorate with your ornaments
- Meet six Keepsake Ornament studio artists who will sign your favorite ornaments
- Enjoy fun activities and attend informative "insider" seminars
- Register to win special prizes
- Shop the special offerings created just for the event
- Get a free surprise bag just for attending
- Shop with Secondary Market dealers that offer a wide selection of past year ornaments

The best news is that it's not too late to join the Keepsake Ornament Club and get in on the fun! To join, or to give a Club membership as a gift, call the toll-free number 1-800-HALLMARK, or pick up an application at any of the 4,200 Hallmark Gold Crown® stores across the country. Registration is $30 per member (member guest $20).

Hallmark Collecting 101

The Language of Hallmark Collectors

by Rhonda Cline

In the Beginning

It began simply when the first Keepsake ornaments were produced in 1973. Over the years Hallmark collecting has grown, evolved, and without even realizing it, Hallmark collectors have developed a language all their own, full of terms and acronyms. Let's try to pin-it-all down with this Hallmark Collecting 101 lesson in understanding the language of Hallmark collectors.

Buying Ornaments

Hallmark ornaments are unveiled each year in July and are available for purchase at your local Hallmark stores through December. For some reason or another, you will eventually come across an item that you desire, but are unable to purchase locally. Perhaps it came out earlier than you expected; maybe it was only available to club members; or perhaps, it was just an item that you forgot. If you can't find the item at your local Hallmark store – where do you go? Welcome to the fun and exciting world of the secondary market.

The Secondary Market

The source for buying and selling collectibles according to basic supply-and-demand principles. Popular pieces which have been retired can appreciate in value far above the original prices. Secondary market dealers sell past year Hallmark collectibles at collectible shows, Hallmark Club Events, and in antique mall showcases. However, most of today's secondary market buying and selling occurs via the internet. Every internet search engine will direct you to web sites that offer large selections, on line auctions, and collector bulletin boards, all of which are very active in the Hallmark secondary market.

Box Condition

Box condition is an important factor. Unfortunately, box condition, like beauty, is in the eye of the beholder. Everyone's concept of Mint in Box will be similar, but never exactly the same. Often, extreme age is taken into consideration, allowing ornaments from the 1970's and 80's that have very slight box damage to be considered Mint in Box. If you are a collector who expects perfection in the box – let the dealer know. This will help you get what you expect.

The following are the primary box conditions and their abbreviations. Note that in all instances the ornament is expected to be in mint condition:

- **Mint in Box** – (box is in undamaged condition) – MIB, MINB, MIMB, NRFB, NIB
- **Box, No Tag** – (box is undamaged, but missing price tag) – BNT
- **Slightly Damaged Box** – (slightly or very slightly damaged box) SDB, VSDB
- **Damaged Box** – DB
- **No Box** – NB

All values in this guide are based on a mint ornament in a mint box. Box condition will affect the secondary market value of your collection. The degree of damage to the box will decrease the value incrementally. In general, an ornament with no box loses approximately 30-50% of it's value.

Series and Collections

Each year collectors look forward to the release of the *Dream Book*, the annual catalog unveiling the ornaments to be available for that year. The most popular aspects of the Hallmark Keepsake Ornaments are the series and collections. Collectors are always excited to see the unveiling of the new series each year as well as discovering what new editions are being added and what series are ending.

Series ornaments are ornaments that are released as part of an official Hallmark series. Each year of the series, there is one edition piece released. These series edition ornaments are often marked on the bottom of the ornament with their edition number. Christmas series ornaments are identified by the edition number inside a Christmas tree and Easter/Spring series use an Easter egg. Since 2002, the series ornaments are also specially packaged in blue boxes. Series complements are pieces that are meant to be displayed with the series, but are not edition pieces. They are as their name implies: complements to the series. Like the series edition pieces, series complements are packaged in blue boxes as well. In this guide Series ornaments are tabbed in blue. Hallmark has stated that an official series will always last at least three years; beyond that, there is no way of predicting how long a series may last.

There are also a number of "unofficial" series or collections. These are groups of ornaments that are not officially recognized as a series by Hallmark, and the ornaments are not marked or packaged as series ornaments. However, each year a new ornament has been added to the line-up during the life of the "series." Some examples of "unofficial" series are Star Trek, Wizard of Oz, Feliz Navidad and Hershey's Chocolate.

Collections are different because they are not limited to one piece per year. Yearly collections such as Looney Tunes and Disney are popular with a wide range of collectors. There are also collections that focus on particular artistic styles such as Marjolein Bastin's Nature's Sketchbook, and Folk Art Americana. More recently the Frostlight Faeries have become a very popular collection.

More Ornament Types

- **Club Ornaments** – Each year Hallmark Keepsake Ornament Collector Club (KOCC) members receive club edition ornaments with their membership, as well as the opportunity to purchase special club edition ornaments. In this guide, club ornament pictures are tabbed in gold (see page 2).

- **Colorways** – Specially painted ornaments. In this guide, Colorway ornament pictures are tabbed in pink (see page 2).

- **Crown Reflections** – Blown glass ornaments offered from 1998 - 2001. Li'l Blown Glass were smaller versions issued in 1999.

- **Event Exclusives** – Ornaments available only during a specific Hallmark event. These ornaments may be available for purchase, awarded as prizes, or given as a participation gift. Most event items are highly sought after and higher in secondary market value because the production numbers are much lower than the regular Keepsake line of ornaments. These are also reffered to as Expo or Artist on Tour (AOT) exclusives, as the different events have had different names over the years.

- **Laser Gallery** – Delicate ornaments made with archival paper, cut by a tiny, precise laser beam. The patterns were assembled by hand and most come equipped with light clips to allow the tree lights to showcase the intricate designs. Offered in 1999 and 2000.

- **Magic Ornaments** – Ornaments featuring light, sound, music and/or motion. Vastly popular with Hallmark Collectors.

- **Personalized Ornaments** – Offered between 1993 and 1995,

Hallmark Personalized ornaments allowed collectors to convey a personal message to someone they loved. Collectors could select an ornament and write their message on a form. The Hallmark Gold Crown store would then order the ornament directly from Hallmark imprinted with the personal message.

- **Premier Ornaments** – As the name indicates, ornaments that are intended to be sold only during the July Hallmark Ornament Premier Weekend.

- **Reach Program** – Ran from 1989 to 2002 and consisted of several pieces that could be purchased for a special price, often with a minimum store purchase. The individual pieces made up a themed set, such as the 1989 Christmas Carrousel, 1992 Santa and His Reindeer, 2000 Snoopy Christmas, and 2002 Snow Cub Club.

- **Showcase Ornaments** – Offered from 1993 to 1996 and were a separate collection within the Keepsake line. Available only in Gold Crown Stores, these creative ornaments were distinct for their unique designs and materials.

- **Trimmers** – Holiday tree decorations and package trimmers were offered in the 1980's. They were sold without boxes and are not part of the Keepsake Ornament Collection.

- **Collector Cards** – Hallmark first included collector cards (similar to baseball cards) inside a few sports ornaments in 1995. Since 2002, the cards have been included in all ornament boxes.

Whew... we may have missed a few phrases from the Language of Hallmark (will have to catch them in Hallmark 102), but we hope this Hallmark 101 lesson will help you navigate and enjoy the Wonderful World of Hallmark Collecting!

Hallmark Keepsake Ornament Museum

The only Hallmark Keepsake Ornament museum that contains virtually every ornament Hallmark produced from 1973 to the present is not located in Hallmark Cards home office in Kansas City, Missouri. Rather, it is located at The Party Shop in Warsaw, Indiana. This project has been a labor of love by The Party Shop's owner and museum curator, David Hamrick, who opened the 1500 square foot museum in 1996 in his Hallmark Gold Crown store.

David and his family have owned Hallmark stores for twenty-six years, and he started collecting and selling retired and rare Hallmark Keepsake Ornaments in 1984. When The Party Shop moved to its present 12,000 square foot location almost ten years ago, he started displaying these collectible ornaments. Thus began the museum that today has over 4,000 ornaments on display. Along with every Hallmark Keepsake Ornament from 1973 to today, the museum exhibits Hallmark's Easter and Halloween ornaments, miniatures, lighted ornaments, and Collector Club pieces.

In addition to rare ornaments like the first Frosty Friends or Star Trek items, the museum has ornaments produced only in prototypes and never sold. About the thousands of people who visit The Party Shop's Keepsake Ornament Museum each year, Hamrick comments, "We have something for everyone to see, whether you are an avid Hallmark collector or you are just someone who enjoys ornaments."

The Party Shop offers free, conducted tours of the museum seven days a week to groups of 1 or 100. If you cannot make it to Northern Indiana, you may view the museum online at www.thepartyshop.com.

The Party Shop, One Ornament Place, 3418 Lake City Highway, Warsaw, Indiana 46580, Tel: 574-267-8787

Top Websites

Top Hallmark Related Websites

The Official Hallmark Cards, Inc site...
www.hallmark.com
The Hallmark Website will keep you in tune with what‘s new and what‘s happening. Free e-cards, a dealer store locator, Collector Club bulletin board, new products, artist profiles, and much more. This should be your first stop when travelin' on the internet!

Looking for Past Year ornaments...
www.hookedonhallmark.com
A favorite site for shopping and learning about your collection. You'll enjoy the frequent sales as well as the great selection of thousands of ornaments, 1973 to present. A fun and friendly site to visit and shop! (not officially related to Hallmark Cards, Inc.)

The Favorite Hallmark Collectors gathering place...
www.yulelog.com
You'll want to stop by YuleLog often. Buy, sell, trade, and chat on bulletin boards dedicated to Hallmark collecting. Sponsored by the YuleLog Ornament Collection DataBase. (not officially related to Hallmark Cards, Inc.)

Stop and Shop Kiddie Car Classics and more...
www.ornament-shop.com
A large selection of Kiddie Car Classics and ornaments, with a picture gallery for shopping ease. The Ornament Shop also buys and trades ornament collections. (not officially related to Hallmark Cards, Inc.)

Looking for an Unusual Hallmark Collectible?...
www.janesholidaykeepsakes.com
In addition to past year ornaments, Jane has vast knowledge and a large selection of unusual Hallmark collectibles. If it's not listed on the site, send an email...she's likely to have it available! (not officially related to Hallmark Cards, Inc.)

Keep Up-to-Date...
http://pressroom.hallmark.com
Get the latest information on the newest ornaments directly from Hallmark. Also learn about upcoming events and even read artist profiles.

FREE BONUS DOWNLOADS

We know this is one of the most comprehesive books ever published on Hallmark Keepsake Ornaments.

We know we gave you over 6,000 full color images and the current up-to-date information you want.

We know we've gathered some of the world's top authorities to give you their unique perspectives in creating this price guide.

We know you got a lot when you purchased this book.

WE WANT TO GIVE YOU MORE!

Because we love Hallmark Keepsake Ornaments as much as you do, we would like to welcome you to sign-up for our free bonus internet download. We offer you a plethora of special bonus materials which you cannot find in the book, and we offer this for FREE. You'll get:

- Special articles and news flashes by the industry's top authorities
- Special indexes and collector checklists you cannot find elsewhere
- Discounts on the software and other merchandise

http://www.bangzoom.com/hallmark

Keepsake Christmas Ornaments

While for some, Hallmark Keepsake Ornaments may be merely Christmas decorations, Hallmark Keepsake Ornament collectors consider them little works of art that often are full of special memories and sentimental value. Clearly they are special treasures.

1973

1.
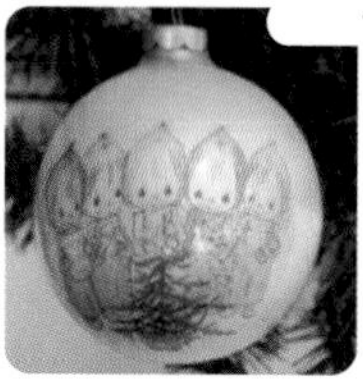
Betsey Clark
250XHD1002 • $97

2.

Betsey Clark 1: Christmas 1973
250XHD1102 • $125

3.

Christmas Is Love
250XHD1062 • $82

4.

Elves
250XHD1035 • $65

5.

Manger Scene
250XHD1022 • $95

6.

Santa With Elves
250XHD1015 • $40

7.

Yarn Angel
125XHD785 • $24
Re-issued in 1974 as QX1031.

8.

Yarn Blue Girl
125XHD852 • $22

9.

Yarn Boy Caroler
125XHD832 • $23

10.
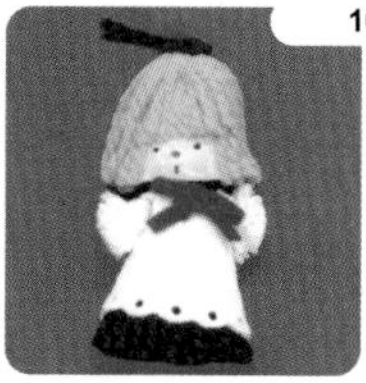
Yarn Choir Boy
125XHD805 • $24

11.

Yarn Elf
125XHD792 • $30
Re-issued in 1974 as QX1011.

12.
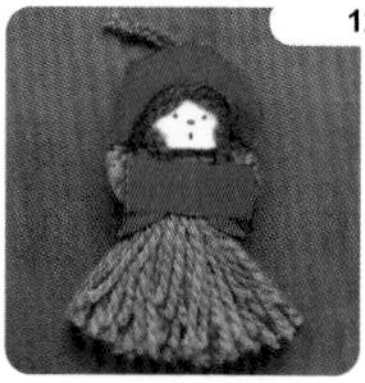
Yarn Green Girl
125XHD845 • $22

13.

Yarn Little Girl
125XHD825 • $31

14.

Yarn Mr. Santa
125XHD745 • $26
Re-issued in 1974 as QX1051.

15.
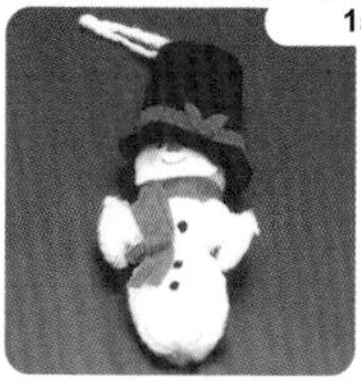
Yarn Mr. Snowman
125XHD765 • $25

16.
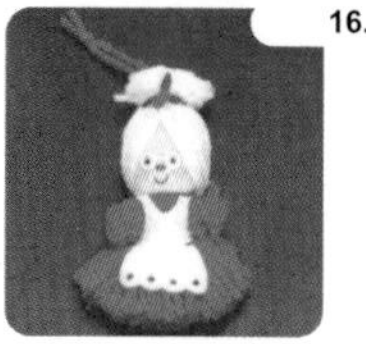
Yarn Mrs. Santa
125XHD752 • $30
Re-issued in 1974 as QX1001.

17.

Yarn Mrs. Snowman
125XHD772 • $28

18.

Yarn Soldier
100XHD812 • $25

1974

19.

Angel
250QX1101 • $70

20.

Betsey Clark 2: Musicians
250QX1081 • $71

21.

Buttons & Bo
350QX1131 • $56 • Set/2

22.
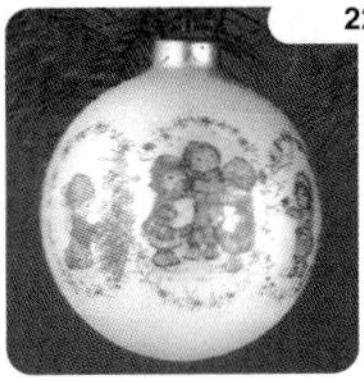
Charmers
250QX1091 • $52

23.

Currier & Ives
350QX1121 • $70 • Set/2

24.

Little Miracles
450QX1151 • $74 • Set/4

25.

Norman Rockwell
250QX1061 • $78

26.

Norman Rockwell
250QX1111 • $73

27.

Raggedy Ann and Raggedy Andy®
450QX1141 • $95 • Set/4

28.

Snowgoose
250QX1071 • $91

29.

Yarn Angel
150QX1031 • $31
Re-issue of 1973 XHD785.

30.

Yarn Elf
150QX1011 • $30
Re-issue of 1973 XHD792.

31.

Yarn Mr. Santa
150QX1051 • $26
Re-issue of 1973 XHD745.

32.

Yarn Mrs. Santa
150QX1001 • $30
Re-issue of 1973 XHD752.

33.

Yarn Snowman
150QX1041 • $30

34.

Yarn Soldier
150QX1021 • $31

1975

35.
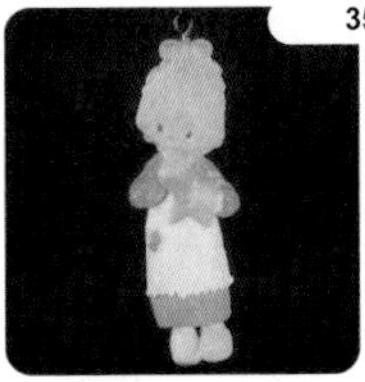
Betsey Clark
250QX1571 • $180

36.
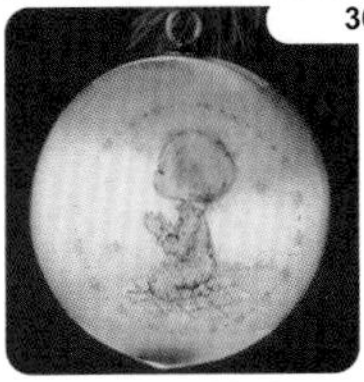
Betsey Clark
250QX1631 • $40

37.

Betsey Clark
350QX1671 • $58 • Set/2

38.

Betsey Clark
450QX1681 • $64 • Set/4

39.
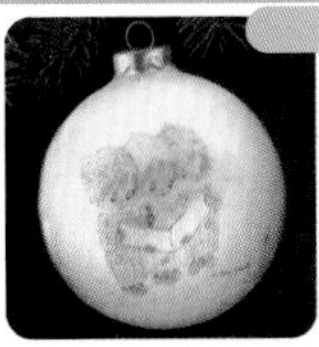
Betsey Clark 3: Caroling Trio
300QX1331 • $65

40.
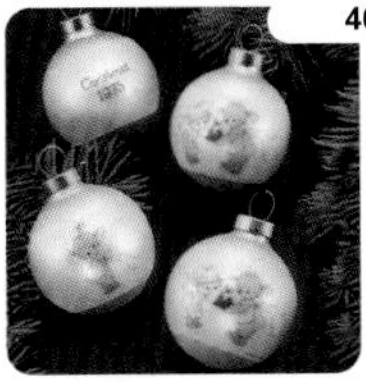
Buttons & Bo
500QX1391 • $61 • Set/4

41.
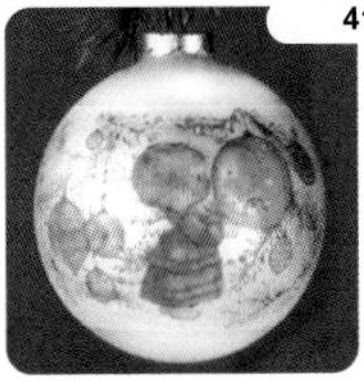
Charmers
300QX1351 • $43

42.

Currier & Ives
400QX1371 • $60 • Set/2

43.

Currier & Ives
250QX1641 • $35

44.

Drummer Boy
250QX1611 • $188

45.

Little Miracles
500QX1401 • $57 • Set/4

46.

Marty Links™
300QX1361 • $61

47.

Mrs. Santa
250QX1561 • $116

48.
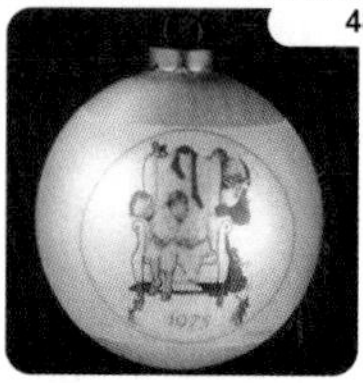
Norman Rockwell
300QX1341 • $65

49.

Norman Rockwell
250QX1661 • $65

50.

Nostalgia: Drummer Boy
350QX1301 • $210
Re-issued in 1976.

51.

Nostalgia: Joy
350QX1321 • $160

52.

Nostalgia: Locomotive
350QX1271 • $95

53.

Nostalgia: Peace On Earth
350QX1311 • $130

54.
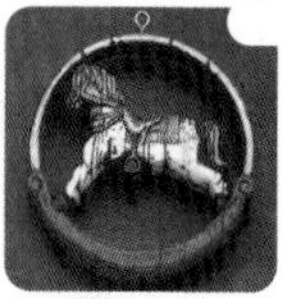
Nostalgia: Rocking Horse
350QX1281 • $99
Re-issued in 1976.

55.

Nostalgia: Santa and Sleigh
350QX1291 • $213

56.

Raggedy Andy®
250QX1601 • $300

57.

Raggedy Ann®
250QX1591 • $263

58.

Raggedy Ann®
250QX1651 • $70

59.

Raggedy Ann and Raggedy Andy®
400QX1381 • $65 • Set/2

60.

Santa
250QX1551 • $116

61.

Yarn Caroler
175QX1261 • $29
Re-issued in 1976, 1978 & 1979.

62.

Yarn Drummer Boy
175QX1231 • $27
Re-issued in 1976, 1978 & 1979.

63.

Yarn Mr. Santa
175QX1241 • $33
Re-issued in 1976, 1978 & 1979.

64.

Yarn Mrs. Santa
175QX1251 • $24
Re-issued in 1976, 1978 & 1979.

65.

Yarn Raggedy Andy®
175QX1221 • $55
Re-issued in 1976.

66.

Yarn Raggedy Ann®
175QX1211 • $40
Re-issued in 1976.

1976

67.

Angel
450QX1711 • $110
Twirl-About

68.
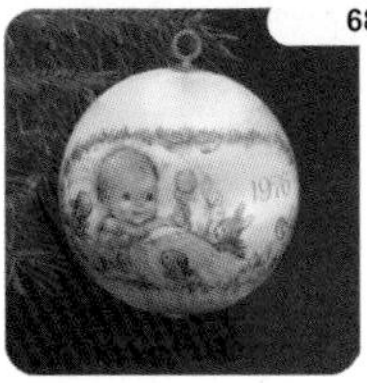
Baby's First Christmas
150QX2111 • $290

69.

Betsey Clark
250QX2101 • $36

70.

Betsey Clark
450QX2181 • $88 • Set/3

71.

Betsey Clark 4: Christmas 1976
300QX1951 • $49

72.

Bicentennial '76 Commemorative
250QX2031 • $46

73.

Bicentennial Charmers
300QX1981 • $59

74.

Cardinals
225QX2051 • $60

75.

Charmers
350QX2151 • $47 • Set/2

76.

Chickadees
225QX2041 • $48

77.

Colonial Children
400QX2081 • $83 • Set/2

78.

Currier & Ives
300QX1971 • $53

79.

Currier & Ives
250QX2091 • $47

80.

Happy The Snowman
350QX2161 • $46 • Set/2

81.

Marty Links™
400QX2071 • $51 • Set/2

82.

Norman Rockwell
300QX1961 • $70

83.

Nostalgia: Drummer Boy
400QX1301 • $210
Re-issued from 1975.

84.

Nostalgia: Locomotive
400QX2221 • $115

85.

Nostalgia: Peace On Earth
400QX2231 • $134

86.
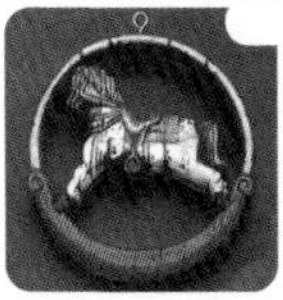
Nostalgia: Rocking Horse
400QX1281 • $99
Re-issued from 1975.

87.

Partridge
450QX1741 • $147
Twirl-About

88.
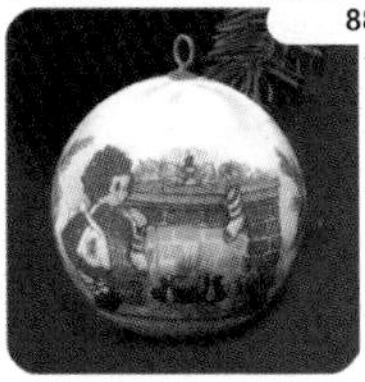
Raggedy Ann®
250QX2121 • $82

89.

Rudolph and Santa
250QX2131 • $95

90.
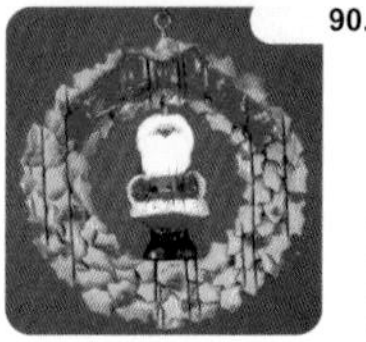
Santa
450QX1721 • $90
Twirl-About

91.

Soldier
450QX1731 • $66
Twirl-About

92.

Tree Treat: Angel
300QX1761 • $195

93.

Tree Treat: Reindeer
300QX1781 • $114

94.

Tree Treat: Santa
300QX1771 • $149

95.

Tree Treat: Shepherd
300QX1751 • $117

96.

Yarn Caroler
175QX1261 • $29
Also issued in 1975, 1978 & 1979.

97.

Yarn Drummer Boy
175QX1231 • $27
Also issued in 1975, 1978 & 1979.

98.

Yarn Mr. Santa
175QX1241 • $33
Also issued in 1975, 1978 & 1979.

99.

Yarn Mrs. Santa
175QX1251 • $24
Also issued in 1975, 1978 & 1979.

100.

Yarn Raggedy Andy®
175QX1221 • $55
Re-issued from 1975.

101.

Yarn Raggedy Ann®
175QX1211 • $40
Re-issued from 1975.

102.

Yesteryears: Drummer Boy
500QX1841 • $97

103.

Yesteryears: Partridge
500QX1831 • $92

104.

Yesteryears: Santa
500QX1821 • $108

105.

Yesteryears: Train
500QX1811 • $134

1977

106.

Angel
175QX2202 • $50

107.

Baby's First Christmas
350QX1315 • $122

108.

Beauty of America: Desert
250QX1595 • $65

109.

Beauty of America: Mountains
250QX1582 • $60

110.

Beauty of America: Seashore
250QX1602 • $64

111.

Beauty of America: Wharf
250QX1615 • $62

112.

Bell
350QX1542 • $55

113.

Bellringer
600QX1922 • $55
Twirl-About

114.

Betsey Clark 5: Truest Joys of Christmas
350QX2642 • $375
RARE

115.

Charmers
350QX1535 • $65

116.

Christmas Mouse
350QX1342 • $60

117.

Colors of Christmas: Bell
350QX2002 • $37

118.

Colors of Christmas: Candle
350QX2035 • $44

119.

Colors of Christmas: Joy
350QX2015 • $46

120.

Colors of Christmas: Wreath
350QX2022 • $48

121.

Currier & Ives
350QX1302 • $70

122.
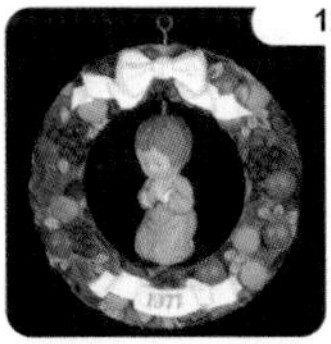
Della Robia Wreath
450QX1935 • $77
Twirl-About

123.

Disney
350QX1335 • $50

124.

Disney
400QX1375 • $67 • Set/2

125.
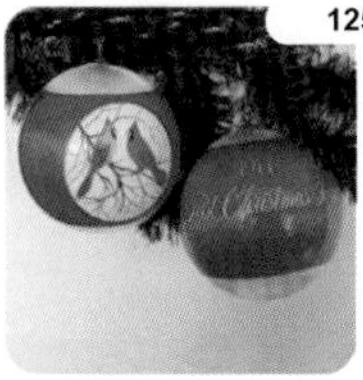
First Christmas Together
350QX1322 • $65

126.

For Your New Home
350QX2635 • $43

127.
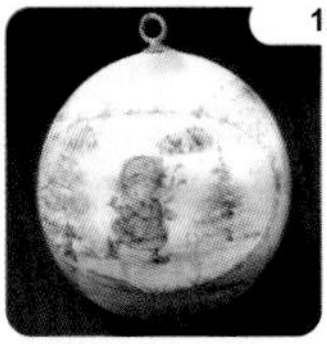
Granddaughter
350QX2082 • $198
RARE

128.
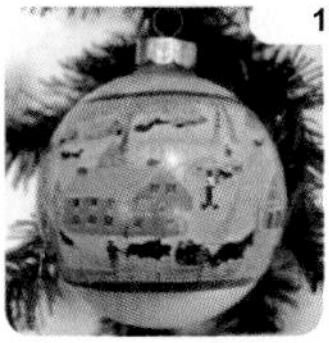
Grandma Moses
350QX1502 • $125
RARE

129.

Grandmother
350QX2602 • $115
RARE

130.
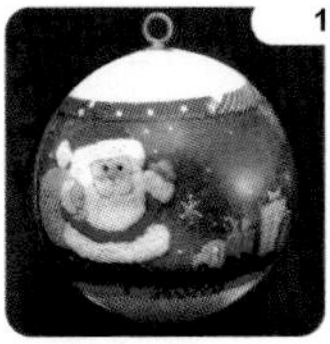
Grandson
350QX2095 • $247
RARE

131.

Holiday Highlights: Drummer Boy
350QX3122 • $45

132.

Holiday Highlights: Joy
350QX3102 • $53

133.
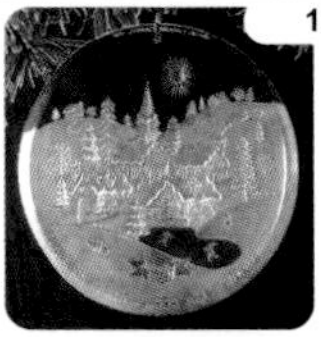
Holiday Highlights: Peace On Earth
350QX3115 • $52

134.

Holiday Highlights: Star
350QX3135 • $41

135.

Love
350QX2622 • $50

136.

Mandolin
350QX1575 • $50

137.
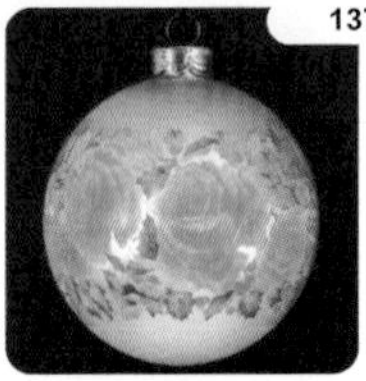
Mother
350QX2615 • $68

138.

Mr. and Mrs. Snowman Kissing Ball
500QX2252 • $60

139.

Norman Rockwell
350QX1515 • $55

140.

Nostalgia: Angel
500QX1822 • $97

141.

Nostalgia: Antique Car
500QX1802 • $63

142.

Nostalgia: Nativity
500QX1815 • $150

143.

Nostalgia: Toys
500QX1835 • $110

144.

Old Fashioned Customs Kissing Ball
500QX2255 • $60

145.

Ornaments
350QX1555 • $70

146.

PEANUTS®
350QX1355 • $75

147.

PEANUTS®
250QX1622 • $85

148.

PEANUTS®
400QX1635 • $95

149.
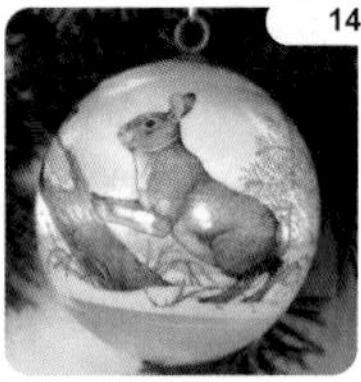
Rabbit
250QX1395 • $75

150.

Santa
175QX2215 • $55

151.

Snowflake Collection
500QX2102 • $175 • Set/4
RARE

152.

Snowman
450QX1902 • $65
Twirl-About

153.
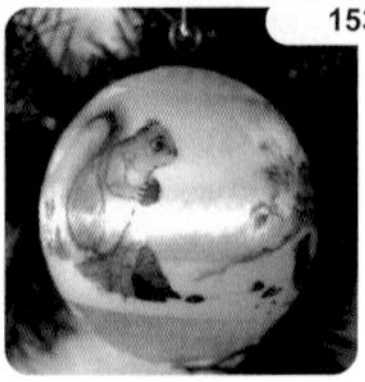
Squirrel
250QX1382 • $75

154.

Stained Glass
350QX1522 • $47

155.

Weather House
600QX1915 • $75
Twirl-About

156.

Wreath
350QX1562 • $60

157.

Yesteryears: Angel
600QX1722 • $95

158.

Yesteryears: House
600QX1702 • $95

159.

Yesteryears: Jack-in-the-Box
600QX1715 • $126

160.

Yesteryears: Reindeer
600QX1735 • $128

1978

161.

25th Christmas Together
350QX2696 • $41

162.

Angel
450QX1396 • $115
Re-issued in 1981.

163.
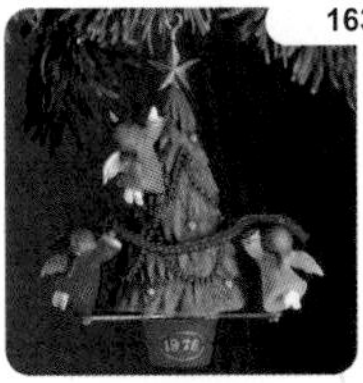
Angels
800QX1503 • $215

164.
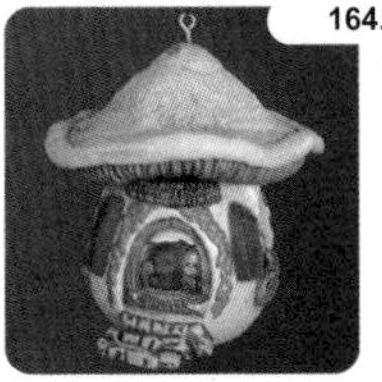
Animal Home
600QX1496 • $102

165.
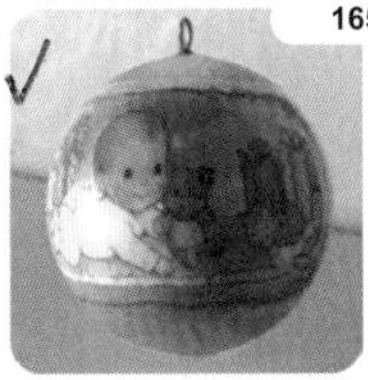
Baby's First Christmas
350QX2003 • $100

166.

Betsey Clark 6: Christmas Spirit
350QX2016 • $65

167.
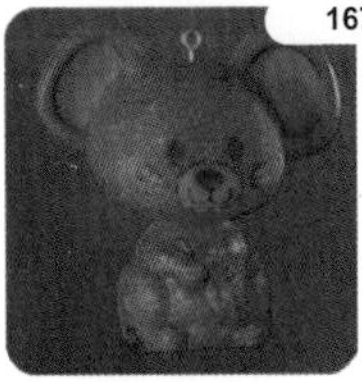
Calico Mouse
450QX1376 • $110

168.

Carousel 1: Antique Toys
600QX1463 • $290

169.

Colors of Christmas: Angel
350QX3543 • $50

170.

Colors of Christmas: Candle
350QX3576 • $47

171.

Colors of Christmas: Locomotive
350QX3563 • $79

172.

Colors of Christmas: Merry Christmas
350QX3556 • $45

173.

Disney
350QX2076 • $90

174.

Dove
450QX1903 • $54
Twirl-About

175.

Drummer Boy
350QX2523 • $45

176.

First Christmas Together
350QX2183 • $66

177.

For Your New Home
350QX2176 • $42

178.

Granddaughter
350QX2163 • $48

179.
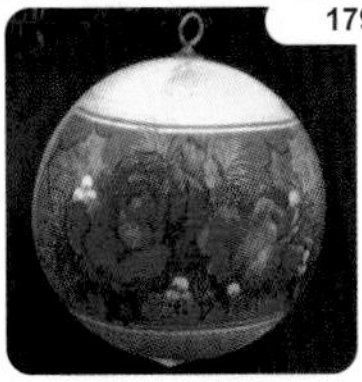
Grandmother
350QX2676 • $36

180.

Grandson
350QX2156 • $32

181.

Hallmark's Antique Card Collection Design
350QX2203 • $83

182.
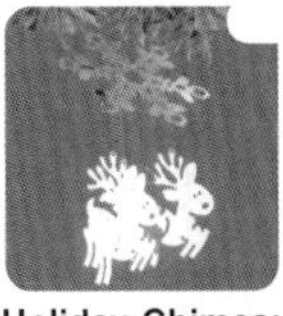
Holiday Chimes: Reindeer Chimes
450QX3203 • $62
Re-issued in 1979 & 1980.

183.

Holiday Highlights: Dove
350QX3103 • $112

184.

Holiday Highlights: Nativity
350QX3096 • $20

185.

Holiday Highlights: Santa
350QX3076 • $70

186.

Holiday Highlights: Snowflake
350QX3083 • $42

187.

Holiday Memories Kissing Ball
500QHD9003 • $115

188.

Holly and Poinsettia Ball
600QX1476 • $105

189.

Joan Walsh Anglund
350QX2216 • $52

190.
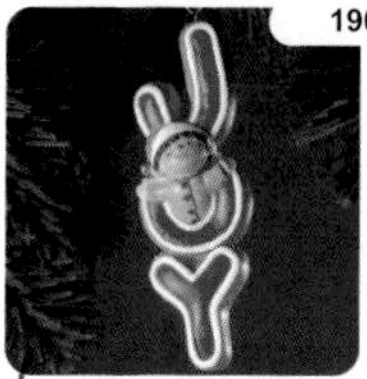
Joy
450QX1383 • $69

191.

Joy
350QX2543 • $38

192.

Little Trimmers: Collection
900QX1323 • $318 • Set/4

193.

Little Trimmers: Drummer Boy
250QX1363 • $60

194.
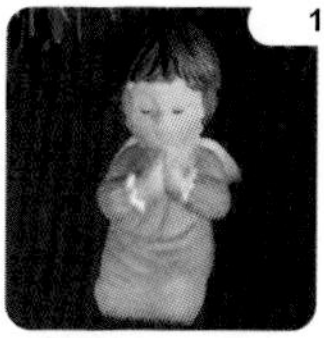
Little Trimmers: Praying Angel
250QX1343 • $65

195.

Little Trimmers: Santa
300QX1356 • $76
Re-issued in 1979.

196.

Love
350QX2683 • $47

197.

Merry Christmas (Santa)
350QX2023 • $54

198.

Mother
350QX2663 • $37

199.

Nativity
350QX2536 • $83

200.

Panorama Ball
600QX1456 • $95

201.

PEANUTS®
250QX2036 • $91

202.

PEANUTS®
250QX2043 • $64

203.
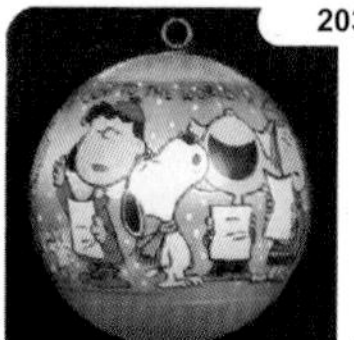
PEANUTS®
350QX2056 • $80

204.

PEANUTS®
350QX2063 • $84

205.
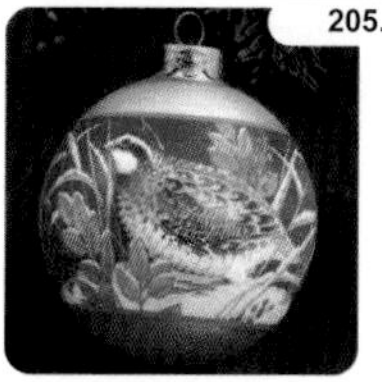
The Quail
350QX2516 • $47

206.

Red Cardinal
450QX1443 • $125

207.
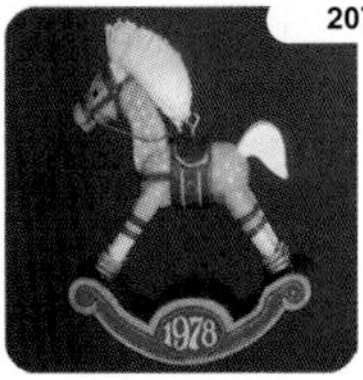

Rocking Horse
600QX1483 • $85

208.

Schneeberg Bell
800QX1523 • $152

209.

Skating Raccoon
600QX1423 • $102
Re-issued in 1979.

210.

Spencer Sparrow, Esq.
350QX2196 • $47

211.

Thimble 1: Mouse in Thimble
300QX1336 • $195
Re-issued in 1979.

212.

Yarn Caroler
200QX1261 • $29
Also issued in 1975, 1976 & 1979.

213.

Yarn Drummer Boy
200QX1231 • $27
Also issued in 1975, 1976 & 1979.

214.

Yarn Mr. Santa
200QX3403 • $33
Also issued in 1975, 1976 & 1979.

215.

Yarn Mrs. Santa
200QX1251 • $24
Also issued in 1975, 1976 & 1979.

216.

Yesterday's Toys
350QX2503 • $66

1979

217.
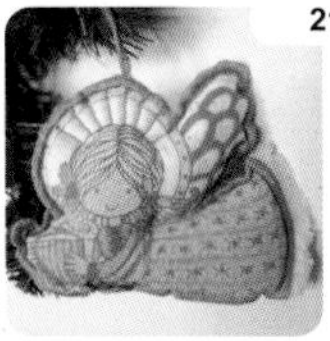
Angel Music
200QX3439 • $45
Re-issued in 1980.

218.

Baby's First Christmas
800QX1547 • $150

219.

Baby's First Christmas
350QX2087 • $55

220.

Behold The Star
350QX2559 • $67

221.

Bellringers 1: The Bellswinger
1000QX1479 • $295

222.

Betsey Clark 7: Holiday Fun
350QX2019 • $60

223.
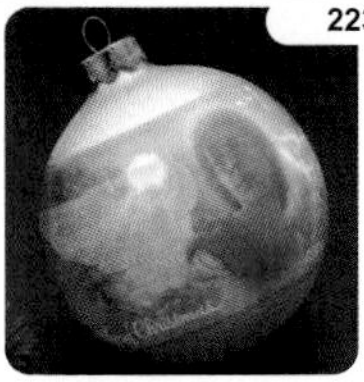
Black Angel
350QX2079 • $65

224.

Carousel 2: Christmas Carousel
650QX1467 • $190

225.

Christmas Chickadees
350QX2047 • $47

226.

Christmas Collage
350QX2579 • $38

227.

Christmas Eve Surprise
650QX1579 • $50

228.

Christmas Heart
650QX1407 • $95

229.

Christmas Is for Children
500QX1359 • $65
Re-issued in 1980.

230.

Christmas Traditions
350QX2539 • $53

231.

A Christmas Treat
500QX1347 • $76
Re-issued in 1980.

232.

Colors of Christmas: Holiday Wreath
350QX3539 • $44

233.

Colors of Christmas: Partridge in a Pear Tree
350QX3519 • $45

234.

Colors of Christmas: Star Over Bethlehem
350QX3527 • $71

235.

Colors of Christmas: Words Of Christmas
350QX3507 • $72

236.

The Downhill Run
650QX1459 • $160

237.

The Drummer Boy
800QX1439 • $95

238.

Friendship
350QX2039 • $38

239.

Granddaughter
350QX2119 • $53

240.

Grandmother
350QX2527 • $35

241.

Grandson
350QX2107 • $53

242.

Here Comes Santa 1: Santa's Motorcar
900QX1559 • $595

243.
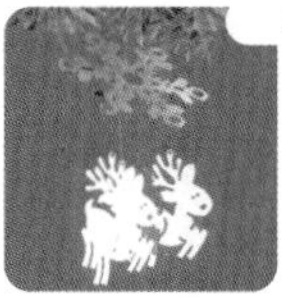
Holiday Chimes: Reindeer Chimes
450QX3203 • $62
Also issued in 1979 & 1980.

244.

Holiday Chimes: Star Chimes
450QX1379 • $39

245.
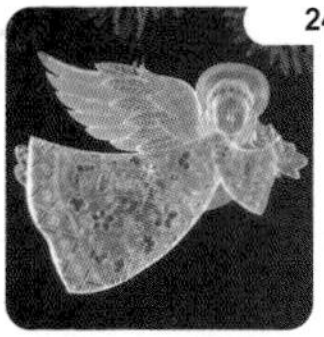
Holiday Highlights: Christmas Angel
350QX3007 • $118

246.
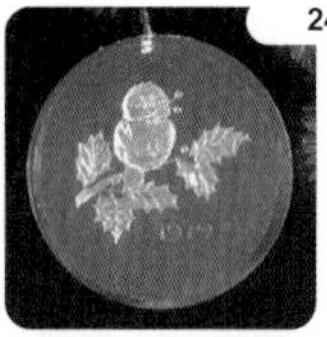
Holiday Highlights: Christmas Cheer
350QX3039 • $45

247.
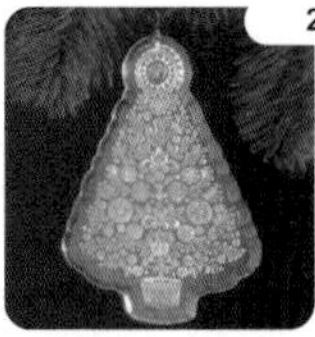
Holiday Highlights: Christmas Tree
350QX3027 • $85

248.

Holiday Highlights: Love
350QX3047 • $65

249.

Holiday Highlights: Snowflake
350QX3019 • $43

250.

Holiday Scrimshaw
400QX1527 • $150

251.

Joan Walsh Anglund
350QX2059 • $37

252.

The Light Of Christmas
350QX2567 • $41

253.

Little Trimmers: Angel Delight
300QX1307 • $75

254.
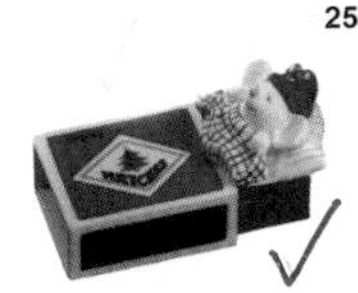
Little Trimmers: A Matchless Christmas
400QX1327 • $75

255.

Little Trimmers: Santa
300QX1356 • $76
Re-issued from 1978.

256.

Little Trimmers: Set
900QX1599 • $280 • Set/3

257.

Love
350QX2587 • $40

258.

Mary Hamilton
350QX2547 • $35

259.

Merry Santa
200QX3427 • $25
Re-issued in 1980.

260.

Mother
350QX2519 • $28

261.

New Home
350QX2127 • $59

262.

Night Before Christmas
350QX2147 • $40

263.

Our First Christmas Together
350QX2099 • $185

264.

Our Twenty-Fifth Anniversary
350QX2507 • $26

265.

Outdoor Fun
800QX1507 • $125

266.

PEANUTS® -Time to Trim
350QX2027 • $60

267.
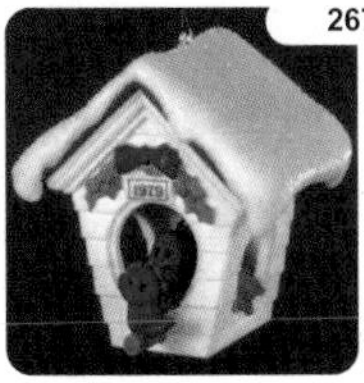
Ready For Christmas
650QX1339 • $95

268.

Rocking Horse
200QX3407 • $31
Re-issued in 1980.

269.

Santa's Here
500QX1387 • $64
Twirl-About

270.

Skating Raccoon
650QX1423 • $102
Re-issued from 1978.

271.

Skating Snowman
500QX1399 • $91
Re-issued in 1980.

272.
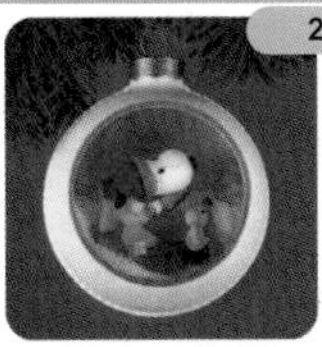
Snoopy® and Friends 1: Ice-Hockey Holiday
800QX1419 • $125

273.

Spencer Sparrow, Esq.
350QX2007 • $68

274.

Stuffed Full Stocking
200QX3419 • $30
Re-issued in 1980.

275.

Teacher
350QX2139 • $17

276.

Thimble 1: Mouse in Thimble
300QX1336 • $195
Re-issued from 1978.

277.

Thimble 2: A Chistmas Salute
300QX1319 • $125
Re-issued in 1980.

278.

Winnie the Pooh
350QX2067 • $85

279.

Yarn Caroler
200QX1261 • $29
Also issued in 1975, 1976 & 1978.

280.

Yarn Drummer Boy
200QX1231 • $27
Also issued in 1975, 1976 & 1978.

281.

Yarn Mr. Santa
200QX3403 • $33
Also issued in 1975, 1976 & 1978.

282.

Yarn Mrs. Santa
200QX1251 • $24
Also issued in 1975, 1976 & 1978.

1980

283.

25th Christmas Together
400QX2061 • $24

284.
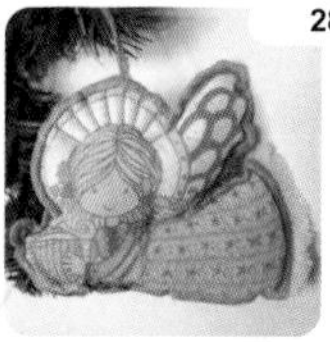
Angel Music
200QX3439 • $45
Re-issued from 1979.

285.

The Animals' Christmas
800QX1501 • $50

286.

Baby's First Christmas
1200QX1561 • $60

287.
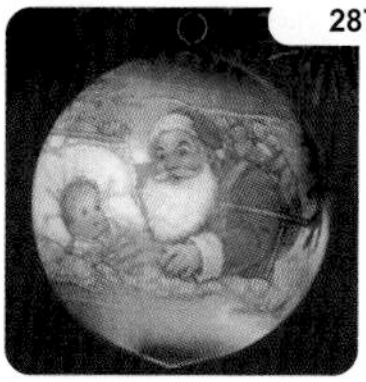
Baby's First Christmas
400QX2001 • $45

288.

Beauty Of Friendship
400QX3034 • $25

289.
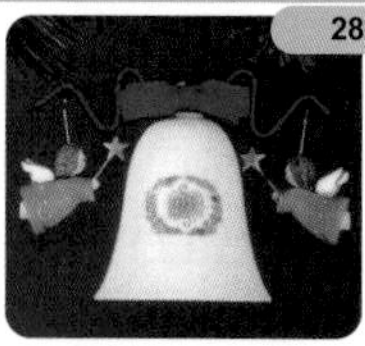
Bellringers 2: The Bellringers
1500QX1574 • $75

290.
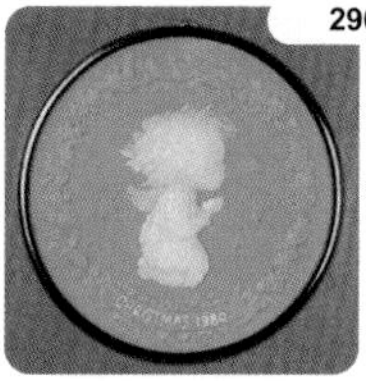
Betsey Clark
650QX3074 • $52

291.
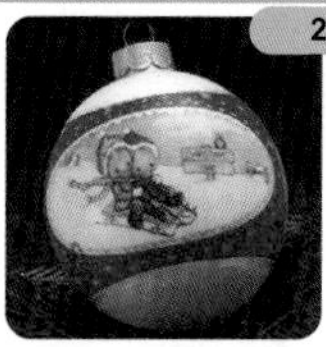
Betsey Clark 8: Joy-in-the-Air
400QX2154 • $32

292.

Betsey Clark's Christmas
750QX1494 • $27

293.
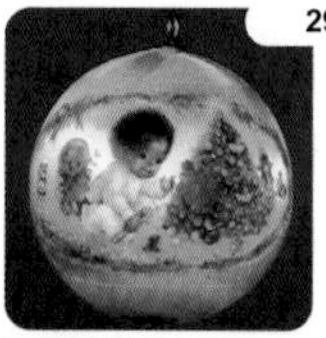
Black Baby's First Christmas
400QX2294 • $45

294.

Caroling Bear
750QX1401 • $95

295.

Carousel 3: Merry Carousel
750QX1414 • $122

296.

Checking It Twice
2000QX1584 • $125
Re-issued in 1981.

297.

Christmas At Home
400QX2101 • $25

298.

Christmas Cardinals
400QX2241 • $37

299.

Christmas Choir
400QX2281 • $137
RARE

300.

Christmas Is for Children
550QX1359 • $65
Re-issued from 1979.

301.

Christmas Kitten Test Ornament
400QX3534 • $318
RARE

302.

Christmas Love
400QX2074 • $37

303.

Christmas Time
400QX2261 • $37

304.
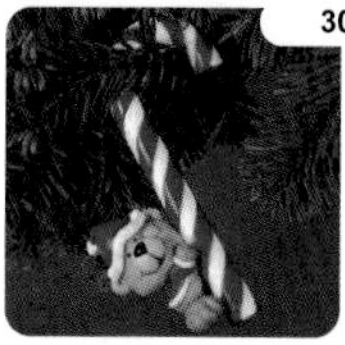
A Christmas Treat
550QX1347 • $76
Re-issued from 1979.

305.

A Christmas Vigil
900QX1441 • $144

306.

Colors of Christmas: Joy
400QX3501 • $35

307.

Dad
400QX2141 • $26

308.

Daughter
400QX2121 • $43

309.

Disney
400QX2181 • $41

310.
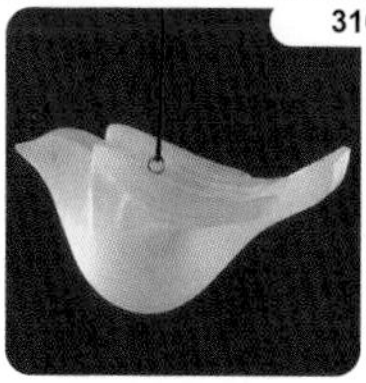
Dove
400QX3081 • $47

311.

Dove Test Ornament
400QX3521 • $412
VERY RARE. Shell only - $40.

312.

Drummer Boy
550QX1474 • $78

313.

Drummer Boy
400QX3094 • $40

314.

Elfin Antics
900QX1421 • $155

315.

First Christmas Together
400QX2054 • $48

316.

First Christmas Together
400QX3054 • $53

317.

Friendship
400QX2081 • $29

318.

Frosty Friends 1: A Cool Yule
650QX1374 • $500

319.

Granddaughter
400QX2021 • $41

320.

Grandfather
400QX2314 • $25

321.

Grandmother
400QX2041 • $32

322.

Grandparents
400QX2134 • $34

323.

Grandson
400QX2014 • $36

324.

Happy Christmas
400QX2221 • $28

325.

Heavenly Minstrel
1500QX1567 • $256

326.

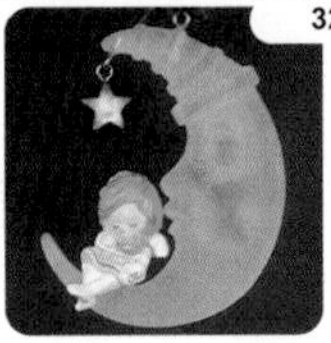

A Heavenly Nap
650QX1394 • $43
Re-issued in 1981.

327.

Heavenly Sounds
750QX1521 • $50
Twirl-About

328.

Here Comes Santa 2: Santa's Express
1200QX1434 • $160

329.

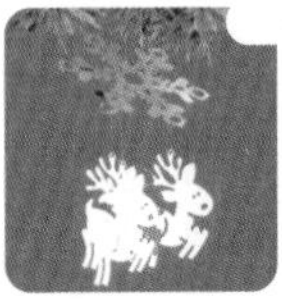

Holiday Chimes: Reindeer Chimes
550QX3203 • $62
Re-issued from 1978 & 1979.

330.

Holiday Chimes: Santa Mobile
550QX1361 • $54
Re-issued in 1981.

331.

Holiday Chimes: Snowflake Chimes
550QX1654 • $55
Re-issued in 1981.

332.

Holiday Highlights: Three Wise Men
400QX3001 • $25

333.

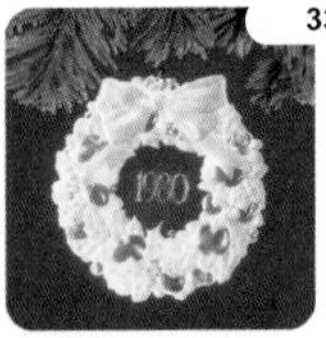

Holiday Highlights: Wreath
400QX3014 • $50

334.

Joan Walsh Anglund
400QX2174 • $31

335.

Jolly Santa
400QX2274 • $28

336.

Little Trimmers: Christmas Owl
400QX1314 • $35
Re-issued in 1982.

337.

Little Trimmers: Christmas Teddy
250QX1354 • $89

338.

Little Trimmers: Clothespin Soldier
350QX1341 • $37

339.

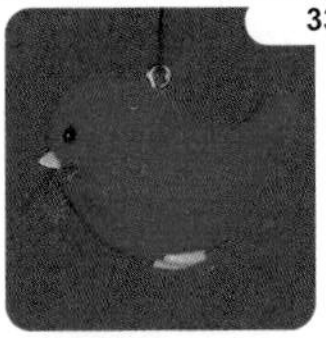

Little Trimmers: Merry Redbird
350QX1601 • $45

340.

Little Trimmers: Swingin' On A Star
400QX1301 • $67

341.

Love
400QX3021 • $40

342.

Marty Links™
400QX2214 • $18

343.

Mary Hamilton
400QX2194 • $30

344.

Merry Santa
200QX3427 • $25
Re-issued from 1979.

345.

Mother
400QX2034 • $26

346.

Mother
400QX3041 • $43

347.

Mother and Dad
400QX2301 • $25

348.

MUPPETS™
400QX2201 • $31

349.

Nativity
400QX2254 • $40

350.
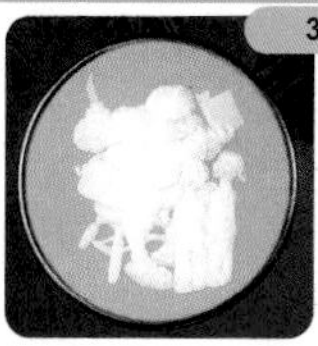
Norman Rockwell 1: Santa's Visitors
650QX3061 • $160

351.

PEANUTS®
400QX2161 • $53

352.
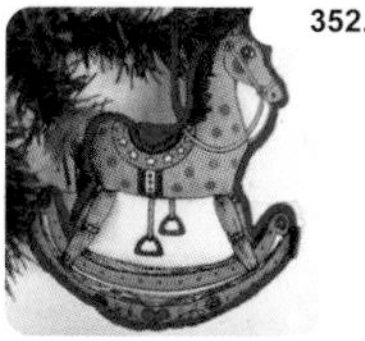
Rocking Horse
200QX3407 • $31
Re-issued from 1979.

353.
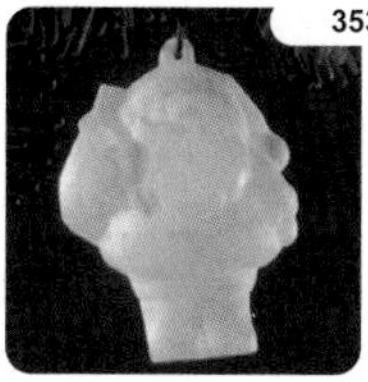
Santa
400QX3101 • $35

354.

Santa 1980
550QX1461 • $119

355.

Santa's Flight
550QX1381 • $78

356.

Santa's Workshop
400QX2234 • $37

357.

Skating Snowman
550QX1399 • $91
Re-issued from 1979.

358.

Snoopy® and Friends 2: Ski Holiday
900QX1541 • $95

359.
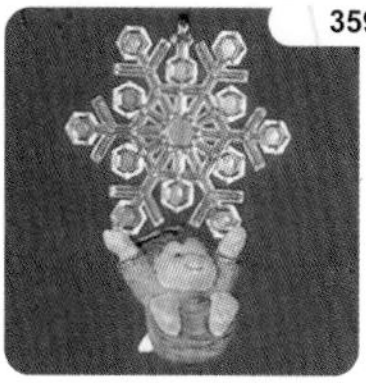
The Snowflake Swing
400QX1334 • $45

360.

Son
400QX2114 • $42

361.

A Spot Of Christmas Cheer
800QX1534 • $76

362.
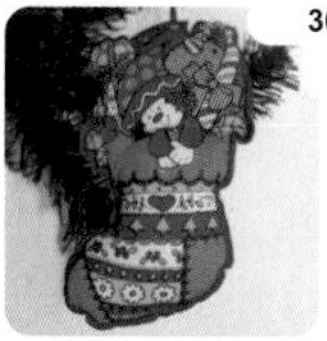
Stuffed Full Stocking
200QX3419 • $30
Re-issued from 1979.

363.

Teacher
400QX2094 • $13

364.

Thimble 2: A Christmas Salute
400QX1319 • $125
Re-issued from 1979.

365.
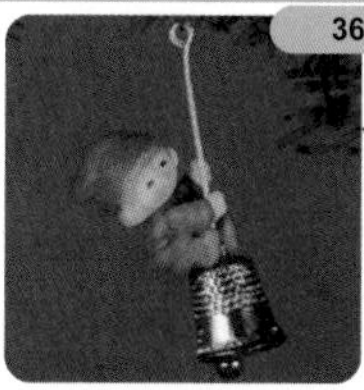
Thimble 3: Thimble Elf
400QX1321 • $192

366.

Yarn Angel
300QX1621 • $25
Re-issued in 1981.

367.

Yarn Santa
300QX1614 • $22
Re-issued in 1981.

368.

Yarn Snowman
300QX1634 • $22
Re-issued in 1981.

369.
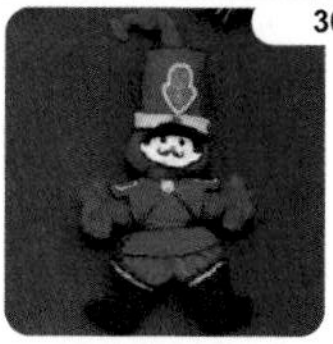
Yarn Soldier
300QX1641 • $20
Re-issued in 1981.

1981

370.

25th Christmas Together
550QX5042 • $29

371.

25th Christmas Together
450QX7075 • $50

372.

50th Christmas Together
450QX7082 • $14

373.

Angel
550QX1396 • $115
Re-issued from 1978.

374.

Angel
400QX5095 • $80

375.

Baby's First Christmas
1300QX4402 • $85

376.
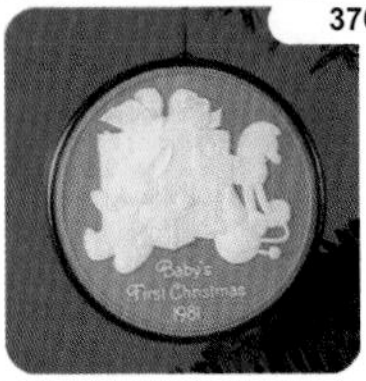
Baby's First Christmas
850QX5135 • $30

377.

Baby's First Christmas
550QX5162 • $47

378.

Baby's First Christmas
450QX6022 • $35

379.
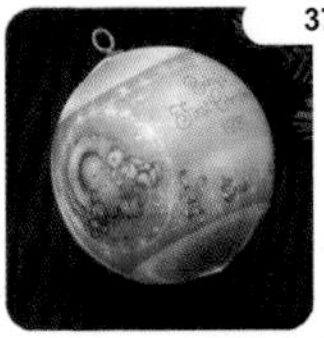
Baby's First Christmas (Boy)
450QX6015 • $40

380.
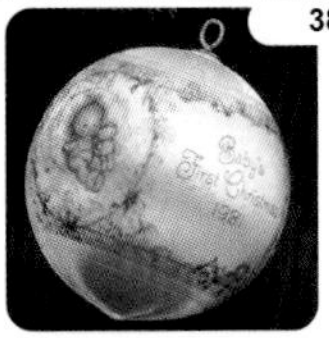
Baby's First Christmas (Girl)
450QX6002 • $40

381.

Bellringers 3: Swingin' Bellringer
1500QX4415 • $85

382.

Betsey Clark
900QX4235 • $75

383.

Betsey Clark
850QX5122 • $41

384.

Betsey Clark 9: Christmas 1981
450QX8022 • $31

385.

Calico Kitty
300QX4035 • $20

386.

Candyville Express
750QX4182 • $85

387.
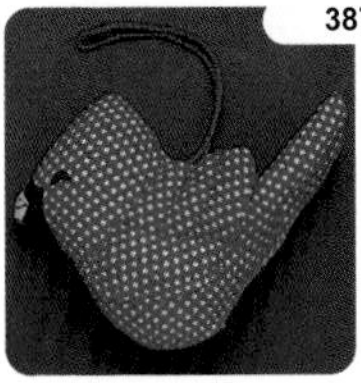
Cardinal Cutie
300QX4002 • $28

388.

Carousel 4: Skaters' Carousel
900QX4275 • $85

389.

Checking It Twice
2250QX1584 • $125
Re-issued from 1980.

390.

Christmas 1981 - Schneeberg
450QX8095 • $34

391.

Christmas Dreams
1200QX4375 • $95

392.
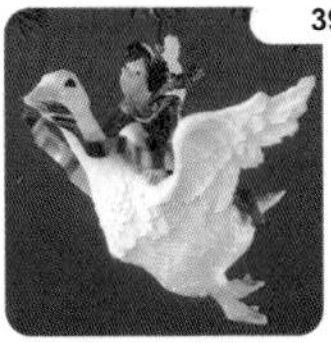
Christmas Fantasy
1300QX1554 • $108
Re-issued in 1982.

393.

Christmas In The Forest
450QX8135 • $150

394.

Christmas Magic
450QX8102 • $30

395.
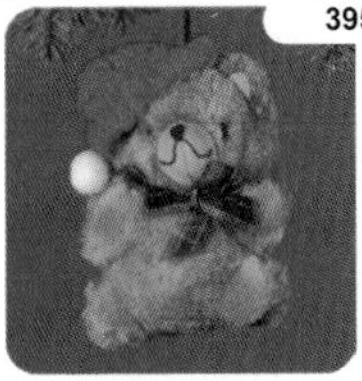
Christmas Teddy
550QX4042 • $30

396.
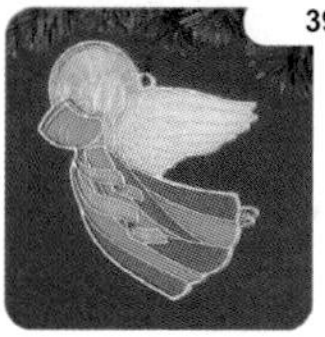
Crown Classics: Angel
450QX5075 • $25

397.

Crown Classics: Tree Photo Holder
550QX5155 • $32

398.

Crown Classics: Unicorn
850QX5165 • $28

399.

Daughter
450QX6075 • $50

400.

Disney
450QX8055 • $40

401.
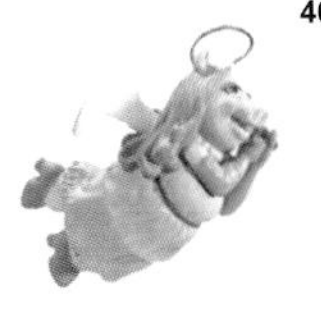
The Divine Miss Piggy™
1200QX4255 • $94
Re-issued in 1982.

402.

Drummer Boy
250QX1481 • $61

403.
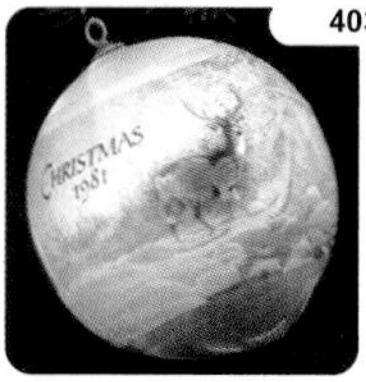
Father
450QX6095 • $26

404.

First Christmas Together
550QX5055 • $32

405.
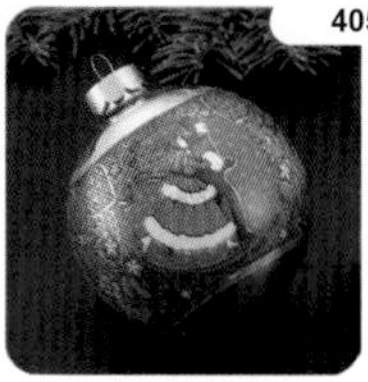
First Christmas Together
450QX7062 • $45

406.

The Friendly Fiddler
800QX4342 • $80

407.

Friendship
500QX5035 • $43

408.

Friendship
450QX7042 • $26

409.

Frosty Friends 2
800QX4335 • $395

410.

The Gift Of Love
450QX7055 • $41

411.

Gingham Dog
300QX4022 • $22

412.

Godchild
450QX6035 • $30

413.

Granddaughter
450QX6055 • $45

414.

Grandfather
450QX7015 • $26

415.

Grandmother
450QX7022 • $23

416.

Grandparents
450QX7035 • $25

417.

Grandson
450QX6042 • $45

418.
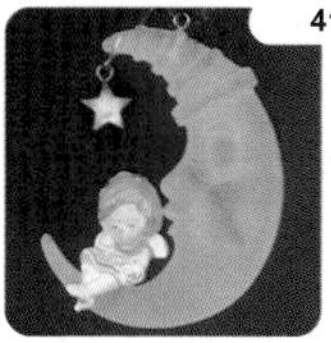
A Heavenly Nap
650QX1394 • $43
Re-issued from 1980.

419.

Here Comes Santa 3: Rooftop Deliveries
1300QX4382 • $220

420.

Holiday Chimes: Santa Mobile
550QX1361 • $54
Re-issued from 1980.

421.

Holiday Chimes: Snowflake Chimes
550QX1654 • $55
Re-issued from 1980.

422.

Holiday Chimes: Snowman Chimes
550QX4455 • $47

423.

Holiday Highlights: Christmas Star
550QX5015 • $34

424.

Holiday Highlights: Shepherd Scene
550QX5002 • $25

425.

Home
450QX7095 • $29

426.

Ice Fairy
650QX4315 • $95

427.
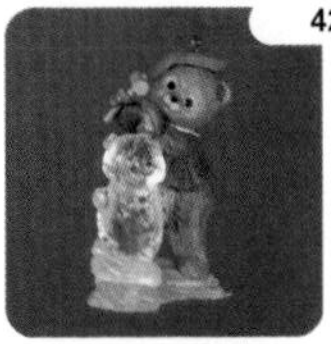
Ice Sculptor
800QX4322 • $93
Re-issued in 1982.

428.

Joan Walsh Anglund
450QX8042 • $34

429.

Kermit The Frog™
900QX4242 • $95

430.

Let Us Adore Him
450QX8115 • $55

431.

Little Trimmers: Clothespin Drummer Boy
450QX4082 • $55

432.

Little Trimmers: Jolly Snowman
350QX4075 • $58

433.

Little Trimmers: Perky Penguin
350QX4095 • $45
Re-issued in 1982.

434.

Little Trimmers: Puppy Love
350QX4062 • $42

435.
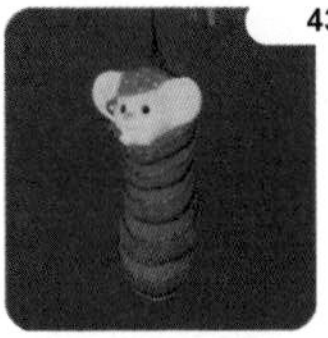
Little Trimmers: Stocking Mouse
450QX4122 • $79

436.

Love
550QX5022 • $35

437.
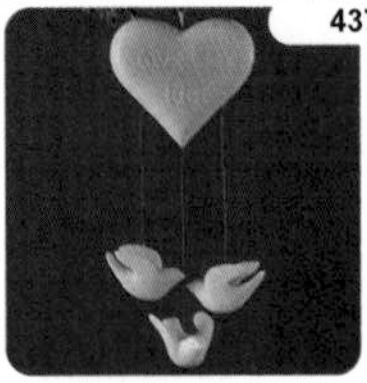
Love and Joy
900QX4252 • $125

438.

Marty Links™
450QX8082 • $29

439.

Mary Hamilton
450QX8062 • $26

440.

Merry Christmas
450QX8142 • $37

441.

Mother
450QX6082 • $28

442.

Mother and Dad
450QX7002 • $25

443.
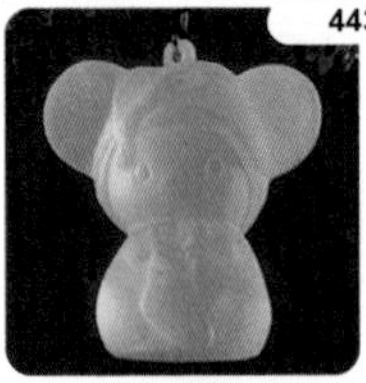
Mouse
400QX5082 • $30

444.

Mr. & Mrs. Claus
1200QX4485 • $140 • Set/2

445.

MUPPETS™
450QX8075 • $37

446.

Norman Rockwell 2: The Carolers
850QX5115 • $58

447.

PEANUTS®
450QX8035 • $46

448.
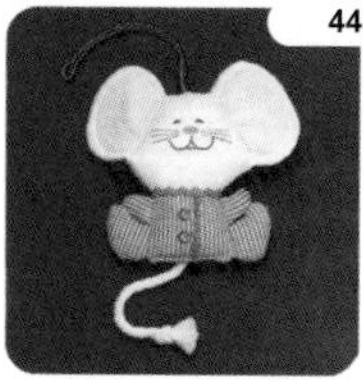
Peppermint Mouse
300QX4015 • $25

449.

Raccoon Tunes
550QX4055 • $31

450.
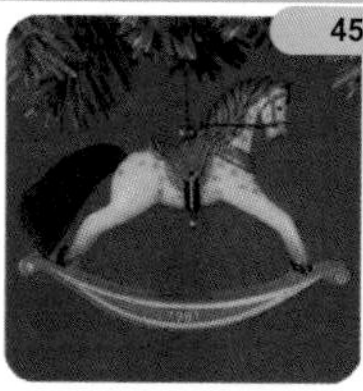
Rocking Horse 1
900QX4222 • $510

451.

Sailing Santa
1300QX4395 • $195

452.

Santa's Coming
450QX8122 • $35

453.
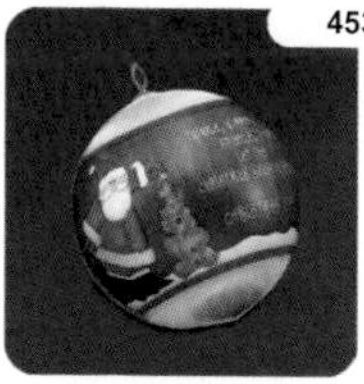
Santa's Surprise
450QX8155 • $29

454.

Snoopy® and Friends 3
1200QX4362 • $95

455.

Snowman
400QX5102 • $43

456.

Son
450QX6062 • $40

457.
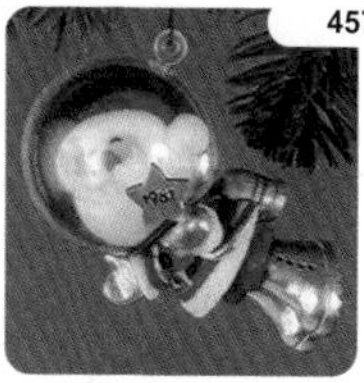
Space Santa
650QX4302 • $90

458.

St. Nicholas
550QX4462 • $69

459.

Star Swing
550QX4215 • $43

460.

Teacher
450QX8002 • $17

461.

Thimble 4: Thimble Angel
450QX4135 • $149

462.
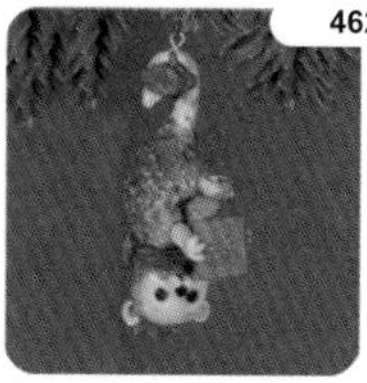
Topsy-Turvy Tunes
750QX4295 • $67

463.

Traditional - Black Santa
450QX8015 • $159

464.
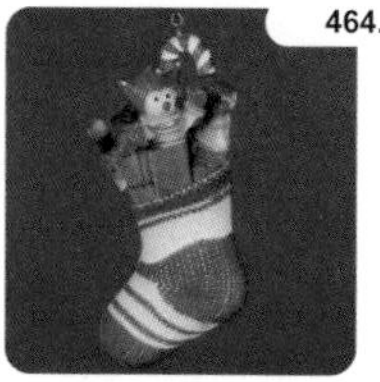
A Well-Stocked Stocking
900QX1547 • $76

465.

Yarn Angel
300QX1621 • $25
Re-issued from 1980.

466.

Yarn Santa
300QX1614 • $22
Re-issued from 1980.

467.

Yarn Snowman
300QX1634 • $22
Re-issued from 1980.

468.
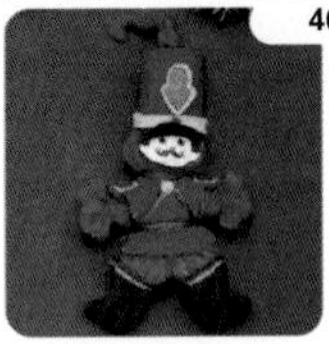
Yarn Soldier
300QX1641 • $20
Re-issued from 1980.

1982

469.

25th Christmas Together
450QX2116 • $26

470.

50th Christmas Together
450QX2123 • $19

471.
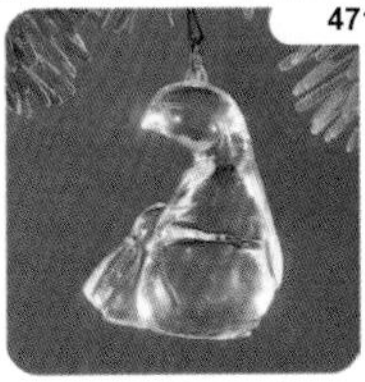
Arctic Penguin
400QX3003 • $32

472.
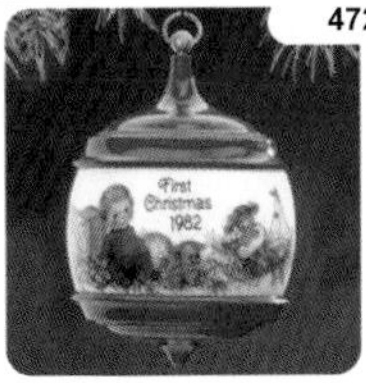
Baby's First Christmas
1600QMB9007 • $82

473.

Baby's First Christmas
550QX3023 • $49

474.

Baby's First Christmas
650QX3126 • $35

475.

Baby's First Christmas
1300QX4553 • $55

476.
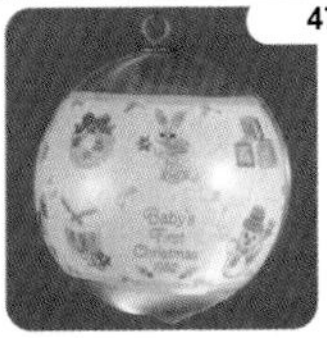
Baby's First Christmas (Boy)
450QX2163 • $32

477.
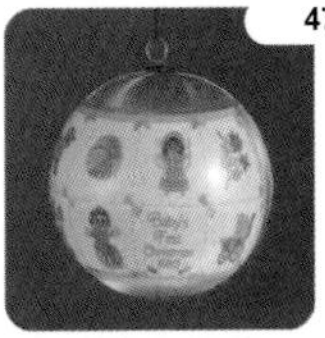
Baby's First Christmas (Girl)
450QX2073 • $32

478.

Baroque Angel
1500QX4566 • $130

479.

Bellringers 4: Angel Bellringer
1500QX4556 • $113

480.

Betsey Clark
850QX3056 • $35

481.

Betsey Clark 10: Joys of Christmas
450QX2156 • $38

482.

Brass Bell
1200QX4606 • $43

483.

Carousel 5: Snowman Carousel
1000QX4783 • $75

484.

Christmas Angel
450QX2206 • $45

485.

Christmas Fantasy
1300QX1554 • $108
Re-issued from 1981.

486.

Christmas Memories
650QX3116 • $34

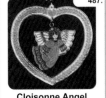

487.
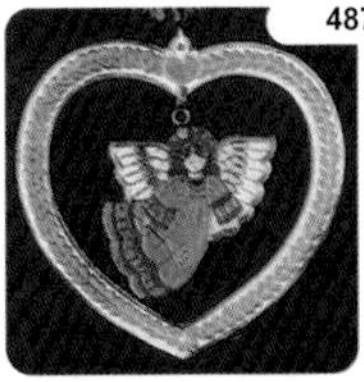
Cloisonne Angel
1200QX1454 • $127

488.

Clothespin Soldier 1: British
500QX4583 • $115

489.

Colors of Christmas: Nativity
450QX3083 • $59

490.

Colors of Christmas: Santa's Flight
450QX3086 • $47

491.

Cowboy Snowman
800QX4806 • $45

492.
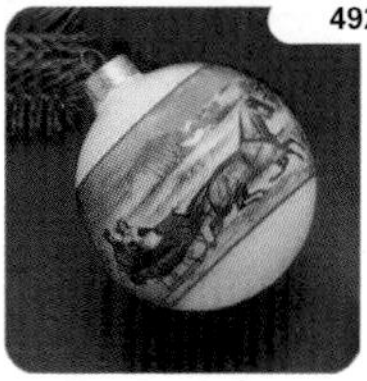
Currier & Ives
450QX2013 • $17

493.

Cycling Santa
2000QX4355 • $124
Re-issued in 1983.

494.
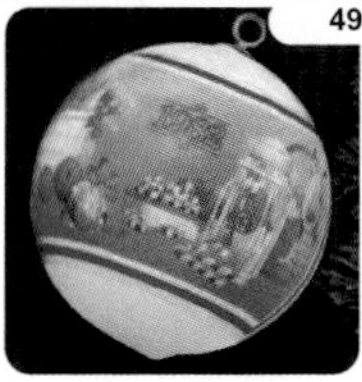
Daughter
450QX2046 • $49

495.

Disney
450QX2173 • $50

496.

The Divine Miss Piggy™
1200QX4255 • $94
Re-issued from 1981.

497.
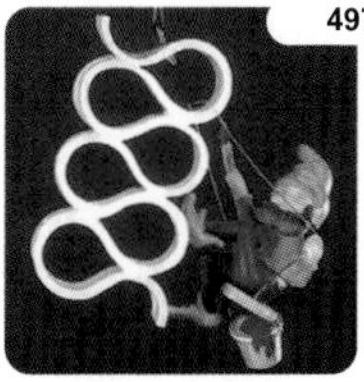
Elfin Artist
900QX4573 • $51

498.

Embroidered Tree
650QX4946 • $30

499.

Father
450QX2056 • $39

500.
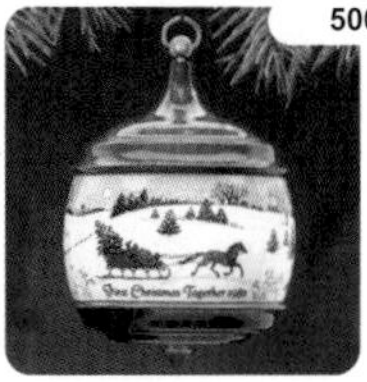
First Christmas Together
1600QMB9019 • $120

501.

First Christmas Together
450QX2113 • $43

502.

First Christmas Together
550QX3026 • $24

503.

First Christmas Together
850QX3066 • $45

504.
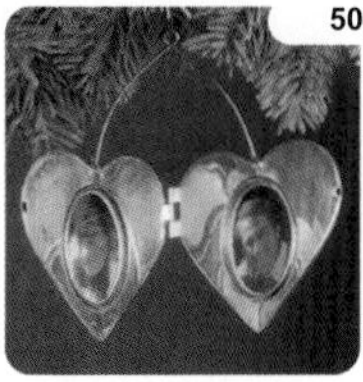
First Christmas Together
1500QX4563 • $29

505.

Friendship
450QX2086 • $24

506.
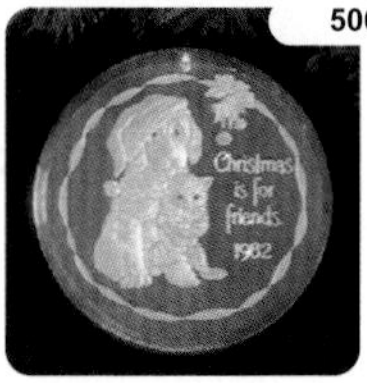

Friendship
550QX3046 • $24

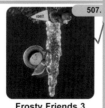

507.

Frosty Friends 3
800QX4523 • $300

508.

Godchild
450QX2226 • $29

509.

Granddaughter
450QX2243 • $35

510.
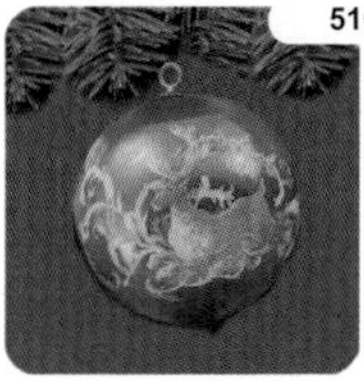
Grandfather
450QX2076 • $29

511.

Grandmother
450QX2003 • $29

512.

Grandparents
450QX2146 • $28

513.

Grandson
450QX2246 • $32

514.
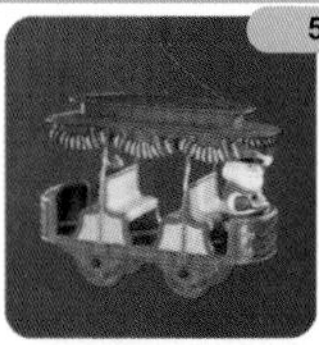
Here Comes Santa 4: Jolly Trolley
1500QX4643 • $118

515.

Holiday Chimes: Angel Chimes
550QX5026 • $550
RARE

516.

Holiday Chimes: Bell Chimes
550QX4943 • $41

517.

Holiday Chimes: Tree Chimes
550QX4846 • $42

518.
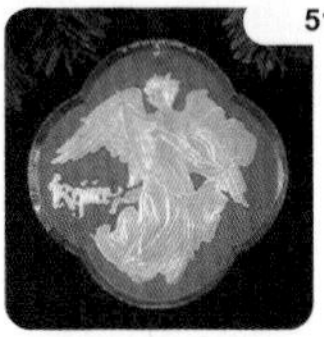
Holiday Highlights: Angel
550QX3096 • $113

519.

Holiday Highlights: Christmas Magic
550QX3113 • $26

520.

Holiday Highlights: Christmas Sleigh
550QX3093 • $59

521.

Holiday Wildlife 1: Cardinalis
700QX3133 • $282

522.
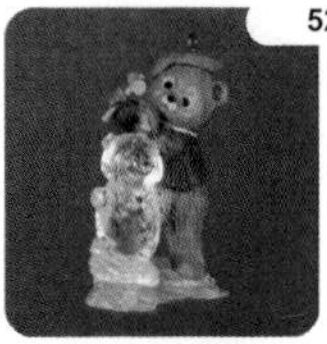
Ice Sculptor
800QX4322 • $93
Re-issued from 1981.

523.

Joan Walsh Anglund
450QX2193 • $34

524.
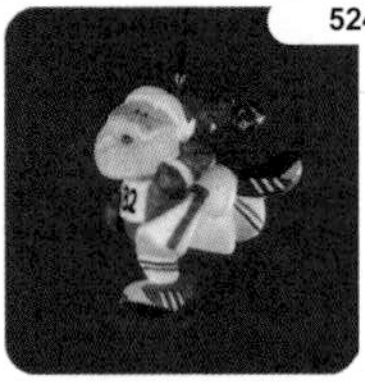
Jogging Santa
800QX4576 • $30

525.

Jolly Christmas Tree
650QX4653 • $101

526.
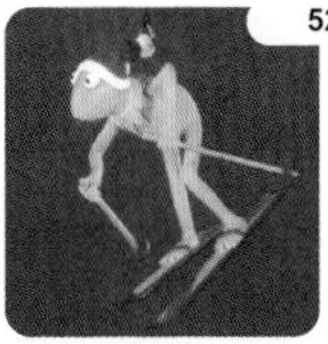
Kermit The Frog™
1100QX4956 • $105
Re-issued in 1983.

527.

Little Trimmers: Christmas Kitten
400QX4543 • $30
Re-issued in 1983.

528.

Little Trimmers: Christmas Owl
450QX1314 • $37
Re-issued from 1980.

529.

Little Trimmers: Cookie Mouse
450QX4546 • $45

530.
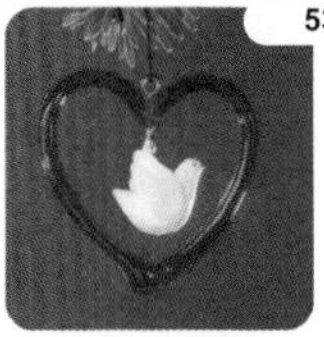
Little Trimmers: Dove Love
450QX4623 • $56

531.

Little Trimmers: Jingling Teddy
400QX4776 • $34

532.

Little Trimmers: Merry Moose
550QX4155 • $55

533.

Little Trimmers: Perky Penguin
400QX4095 • $45
Re-issued from 1981.

534.
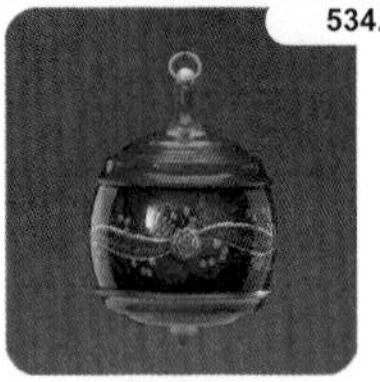
Love
1600QMB9009 • $101

535.

Love
450QX2096 • $34

536.

Love
550QX3043 • $31

537.

Mary Hamilton
450QX2176 • $32

538.

Merry Christmas
450QX2256 • $29

539.

Miss Piggy™ and Kermit™
450QX2183 • $55

540.

Moments Of Love
450QX2093 • $19

541.

Mother
450QX2053 • $24

542.

Mother and Dad
450QX2223 • $28

543.

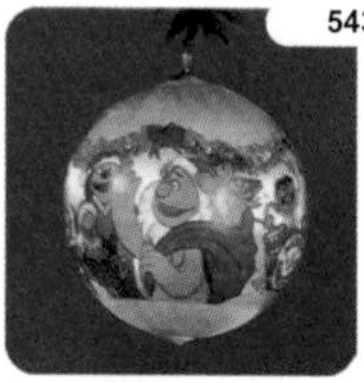

MUPPETS™ Party
450QX2186 • $42

544.

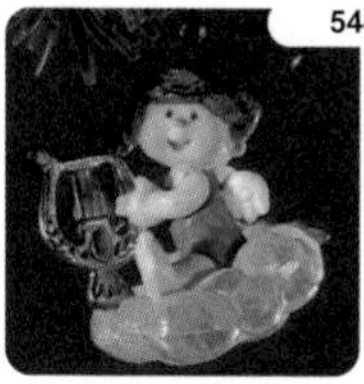

Musical Angel
550QX4596 • $115

545.

New Home
450QX2126 • $25

546.

Norman Rockwell
450QX2023 • $35

547.

Norman Rockwell 3: Filling the Stockings
850QX3053 • $34

548.

Old Fashioned Christmas
450QX2276 • $58

549.

Old World Angels
450QX2263 • $32

550.

Patterns Of Christmas
450QX2266 • $32

551.

PEANUTS®
450QX2006 • $34

552.

Peeking Elf
650QX4195 • $36

553.

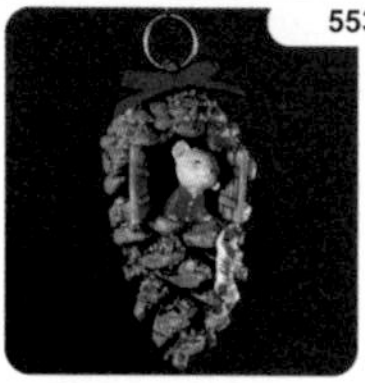

Pinecone Home
800QX4613 • $105

554.

Promotional Brass Ornament
350(N/A) • $24

555.

Raccoon Surprises
900QX4793 • $166

556.

Rocking Horse 2
1000QX5023 • $335

557.

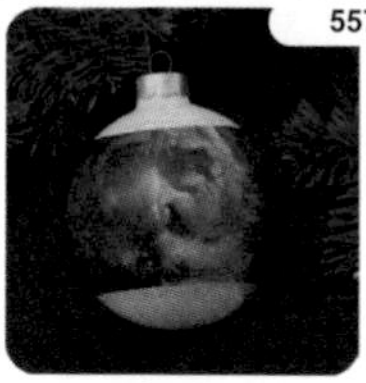

Santa
450QX2216 • $35

558.

Santa and Reindeer
900QX4676 • $73

559.

Santa Bell
1500QX1487 • $66

560.

Santa's Sleigh
900QX4786 • $34

561.

Santa's Workshop
1000QX4503 • $95
Re-issued in 1983.

562.

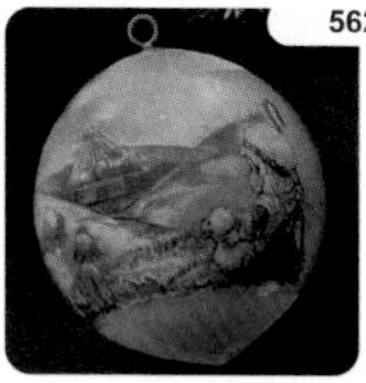

Season For Caring
450QX2213 • $35

563.

Sister
450QX2083 • $44

564.

Snoopy® and Friends 4
1300QX4803 • $122

565.

Snowy Seal
400QX3006 • $35

566.

Son
450QX2043 • $42

567.

The Spirit Of Christmas
1000QX4526 • $106

568.

Stained Glass
450QX2283 • $29

569.

Teacher
450QX2143 • $15

570.

Teacher
550QX3016 • $17

571.

Teacher
650QX3123 • $14

572.

Thimble 5: Thimble Mouse
500QX4513 • $61

573.
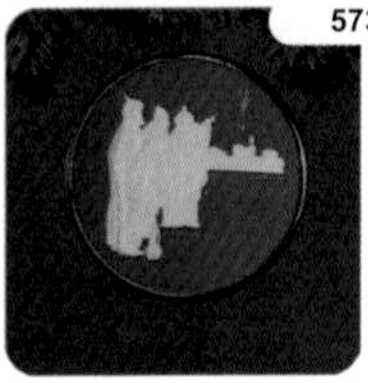
Three Kings
850QX3073 • $28

574.

Tin Locomotive 1
1300QX4603 • $462

575.

Tin Soldier
650QX4836 • $59

576.

Twelve Days of Christmas
450QX2036 • $33

1983

577.

1983
450QX2209 • $41

578.

25th Christmas Together
450QX2247 • $29

579.

Angel Messenger
650QX4087 • $106

580.

Angels
500QX2197 • $35

581.

The Annunciation
450QX2167 • $49

582.

Baby's First Christmas
1600QMB9039 • $95

583.

Baby's First Christmas
750QX3019 • $24

584.

Baby's First Christmas
700QX3029 • $29

585.

Baby's First Christmas
1400QX4027 • $40

586.

Baby's First Christmas (Boy)
450QX2009 • $38

587.

Baby's First Christmas (Girl)
450QX2007 • $36

588.

Baby's Second Christmas
450QX2267 • $46

589.

Baroque Angels
1300QX4229 • $85

590.
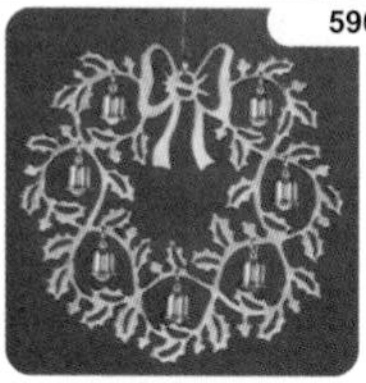
Bell Wreath
650QX4209 • $47

591.

Bellringers 5: Teddy Bellringer
1500QX4039 • $130

592.
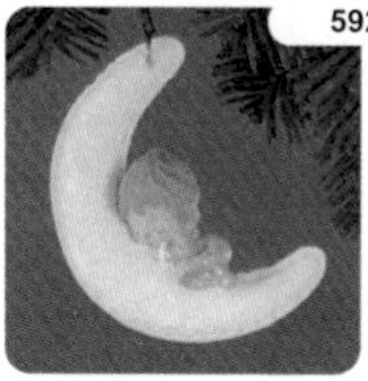
Betsey Clark
650QX4047 • $44

593.

Betsey Clark
900QX4401 • $43

594.

Betsey Clark 11: Christmas Happiness
450QX2119 • $37

595.
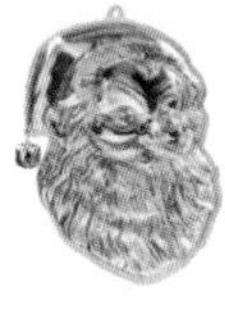
Brass Santa
900QX4239 • $32

596.
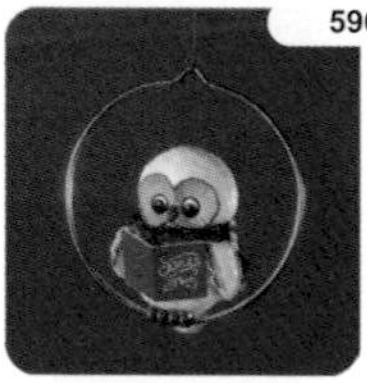
Caroling Owl
450QX4117 • $44

597.

Carousel 6: Santa and Friends
1100QX4019 • $59

598.

Child's Third Christmas
450QX2269 • $35

599.

Christmas Joy
450QX2169 • $42

600.
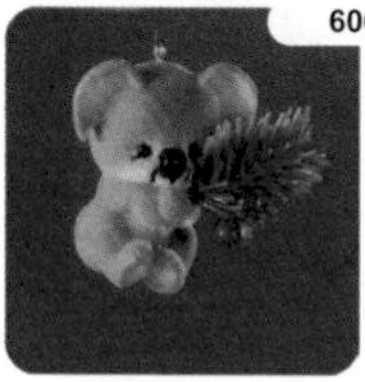
Christmas Koala
400QX4199 • $41

601.

Christmas Wonderland
450QX2219 • $150
RARE

602.

Clothespin Soldier 2: Early American
500QX4029 • $59

603.
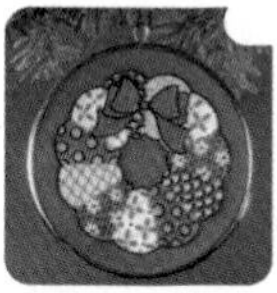
Crown Classics: Enameled Christmas Wreath
900QX3119 • $18

604.
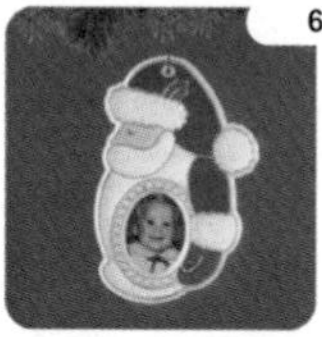
Crown Classics: Memories To Treasure
700QX3037 • $46

605.
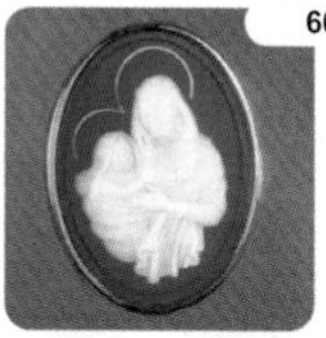
Crown Classics: Mother and Child
750QX3027 • $41

606.

Currier & Ives
450QX2159 • $31

607.

Cycling Santa
2000QX4355 • $124
Re-issued from 1982.

608.

Daughter
450QX2037 • $69

609.

Diana Doll
900QX4237 • $31

610.

Disney
450QX2129 • $65

611.

Embroidered Heart
650QX4217 • $28
Re-issued in 1984.

612.
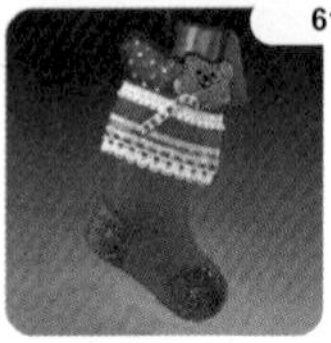
Embroidered Stocking
650QX4796 • $26
Re-issued in 1984.

613.

First Christmas Together
450QX2089 • $65

614.

First Christmas Together
750QX3017 • $28

615.

First Christmas Together
600QX3069 • $35

616.

First Christmas Together
600QX3107 • $42

617.

First Christmas Together
1500QX4329 • $40

618.

Friendship
1600QMB9047 • $129

619.

Friendship
450QX2077 • $45

620.

Friendship
600QX3059 • $23

621.
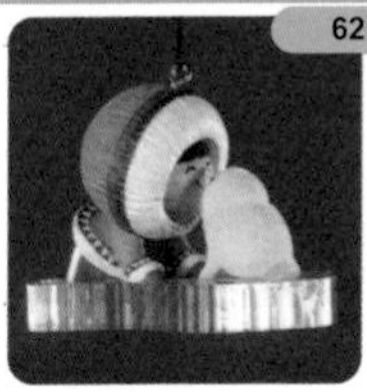
Frosty Friends 4
800QX4007 • $307

622.
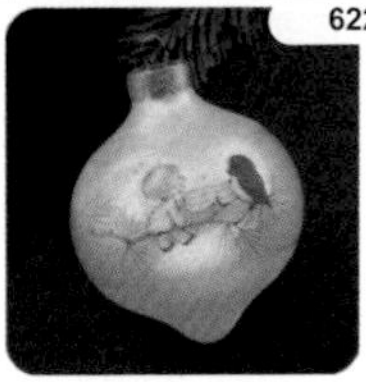
Godchild
450QX2017 • $19

623.

Grandchild's First Christmas
600QX3129 • $24

624.
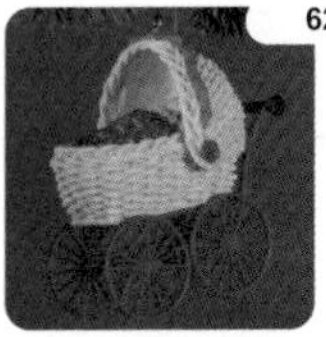
Grandchild's First Christmas
1400QX4309 • $36

625.

Granddaughter
450QX2027 • $53

626.

Grandmother
450QX2057 • $23

627.
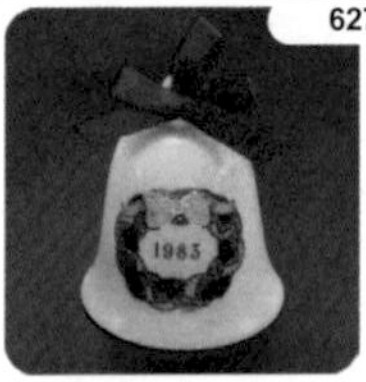

Grandparents
650QX4299 • $23

628.

Grandson
450QX2019 • $44

629.
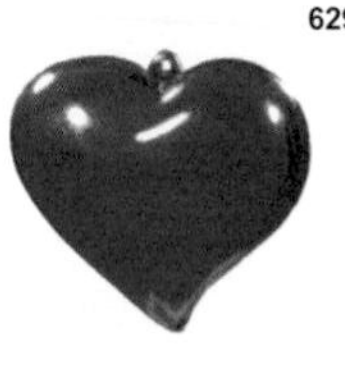
Heart
400QX3079 • $67

630.

Here Comes Santa
450QX2177 • $53

631.

Here Comes Santa 5: Santa Express
1300QX4037 • $338

632.

Hitchhiking Santa
800QX4247 • $43

633.
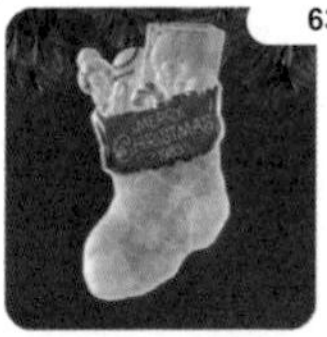
Holiday Highlights: Christmas Stocking
600QX3039 • $52

634.
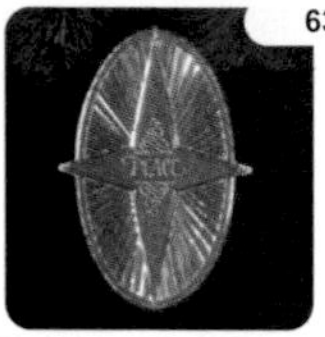
Holiday Highlights: Star Of Peace
600QX3047 • $30

635.
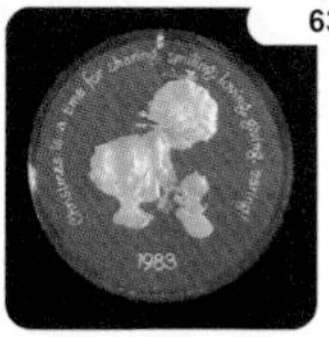

Holiday Highlights: Time For Sharing
600QX3077 • $40

636.

Holiday Puppy
350QX4127 • $31

637.

Holiday Wildlife 2: Black-Capped Chickadees
700QX3099 • $86

638.

Jack Frost
900QX4079 • $75

639.

Jolly Santa
350QX4259 • $40

640.
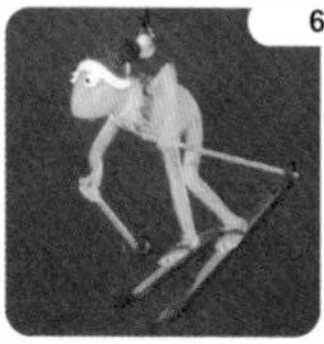
Kermit The Frog™
1100QX4956 • $105
Re-issued from 1982.

641.

Little Trimmers: Christmas Kitten
400QX4543 • $30
Re-issued from 1982.

642.

Love
450QX2079 • $80

643.

Love
600QX3057 • $17

644.

Love
600QX3109 • $50

645.

Love
1300QX4227 • $38

646.
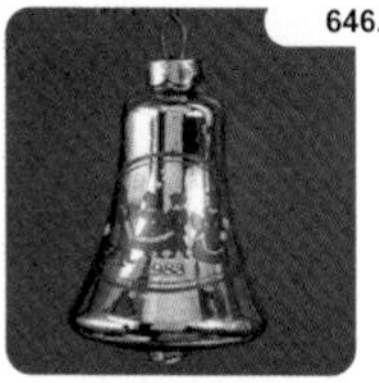
Love Is A Song
450QX2239 • $31

647.

Madonna and Child
1200QX4287 • $49

648.

Mailbox Kitten
650QX4157 • $70

649.

Mary Hamilton
450QX2137 • $47

650.
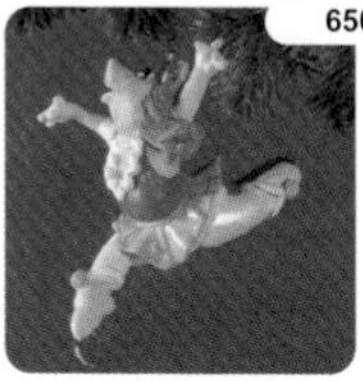
Miss Piggy™
1300QX4057 • $195

651.
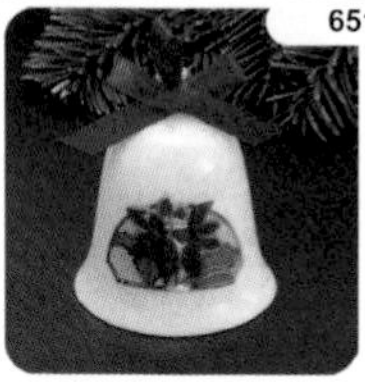
Mom and Dad
650QX4297 • $24

652.

Mother
600QX3067 • $29

653.

Mother's Day
1400QMB3407 • $189

654.

Mountain Climbing Santa
650QX4077 • $40
Re-issued in 1984.

655.

Mouse In Bell
1000QX4197 • $49

656.

Mouse On Cheese
650QX4137 • $49

657.

The MUPPETS™
450QX2147 • $46

658.
Nativity
1600QMB9049 • $149

659.
New Home
450QX2107 • $50

660.
Norman Rockwell
450QX2157 • $62

661.
Norman Rockwell 4: Dress Rehearsal
750QX3007 • $38

662.
An Old Fashioned Christmas
450QX2179 • $29

663.
Old-Fashioned Santa
1100QX4099 • $72

664.
Oriental Butterflies
450QX2187 • $35

665.
PEANUTS®
450QX2127 • $49

666.
Peppermint Penguin
650QX4089 • $52

667.
Porcelain Bear 1: Cinnamon Teddy
700QX4289 • $90

668.
Rainbow Angel
550QX4167 • $89

669.
Rocking Horse 3
1000QX4177 • $226

670.
Santa
400QX3087 • $37

671.
Santa's Many Faces
600QX3117 • $41

672.
Santa's On His Way
1000QX4269 • $48

673.
Santa's Workshop
1000QX4503 • $95
Re-issued from 1982.

674.
Scrimshaw Reindeer
800QX4249 • $34

675.
Season's Greetings
450QX2199 • $17

676.
Shirt Tales™
450QX2149 • $35

677.
Silver Bell
1200QX1109 • $50

678.
Sister
450QX2069 • $50

679.
Skating Rabbit
800QX4097 • $61

680.
Ski Lift Santa
800QX4187 • $65

681.
Skiing Fox
800QX4207 • $42

682.

Sneaker Mouse
450QX4009 • $48

683.

Snoopy® and Friends 5: Santa Snoopy™
1300QX4169 • $112

684.

Son
450QX2029 • $49

685.

Teacher
450QX2249 • $13

686.

Teacher
600QX3049 • $19

687.
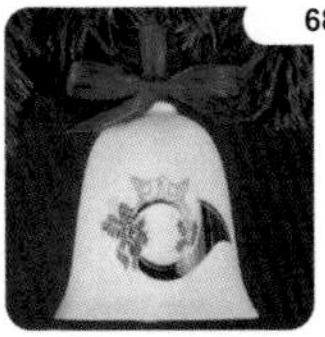
Tenth Christmas Together
650QX4307 • $47

688.

Thimble 6: Thimble Elf
500QX4017 • $41

689.

Tin Locomotive 2
1300QX4049 • $183

690.

Tin Rocking Horse
650QX4149 • $69

691.

Twelve Days Of Christmas
1500QMB4159 • $100
Re-issued in 1984.

692.

Unicorn
1000QX4267 • $82

693.

The Wise Men
450QX2207 • $65

1984

694.
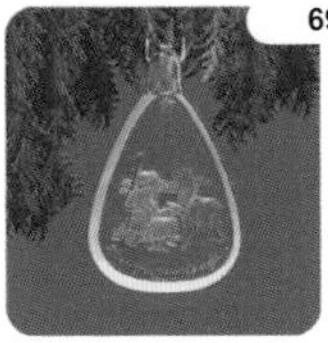
All Are Precious
800QLX7044 • $24
MAGIC. Re-issued in 1985.

695.

Alpine Elf
600QX4521 • $27

696.

Amanda
900QX4321 • $27

697.

Art Masterpiece 1: Madonna and Child and St. John
650QX3494 • $28

698.

Baby's First Christmas
700QX3001 • $30

699.

Baby's First Christmas
600QX3401 • $60

700.

Baby's First Christmas
1400QX4381 • $50

701.

Baby's First Christmas
1600QX9041 • $88

702.

Baby's First Christmas (Boy)
450QX2404 • $42

703.

Baby's First Christmas (Girl)
450QX2401 • $44

704.

Baby's Second Christmas
450QX2411 • $44

705.

Baby-sitter
450QX2531 • $16

706.

Bell Ringer Squirrel
1000QX4431 • $28

707.

Bellringers 6: Elfin Artist
1500QX4384 • $53

708.

Betsey Clark 12: Days are Merry
500QX2494 • $41

709.

Betsey Clark Angel
900QX4624 • $25

710.

Brass Carousel
900QLX7071 • $79
MAGIC.

711.

Chickadee
600QX4514 • $50

712.

Child's Third Christmas
450QX2611 • $32

713.

Christmas In The Forest
800QLX7034 • $35
MAGIC.

714.

Christmas Memories
650QX3004 • $21

715.

Christmas Owl
600QX4441 • $27

716.

A Christmas Prayer
450QX2461 • $35

717.

City Lights
1000QLX7014 • $56
MAGIC.

718.

Classical Angel
2750QX4591 • $97
Limited Edition - 24700.

719.

Clothespin Soldier 3: Canadian Mountie
500QX4471 • $32

720.
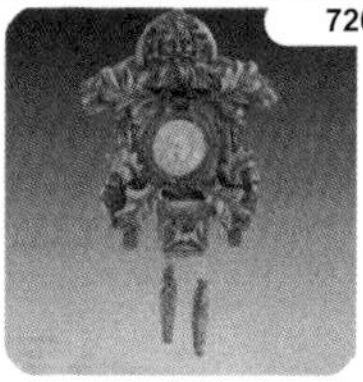
Cuckoo Clock
1000QX4551 • $49

721.

Currier & Ives
450QX2501 • $35

722.

Daughter √
450QX2444 • $49

723.

Disney
450QX2504 • $44

724.
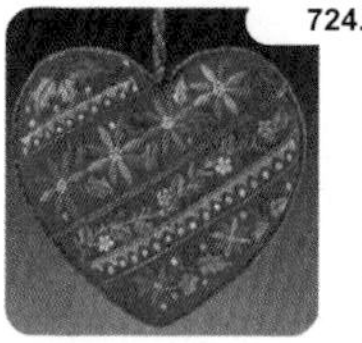
Embroidered Heart
650QX4217 • $28
Re-issued from 1983.

725.

Embroidered Stocking
650QX4796 • $26
Re-issued from 1983.

726.

Father
600QX2571 • $20

727.

First Christmas Together
450QX2451 • $28

728.

First Christmas Together
750QX3404 • $23

729.
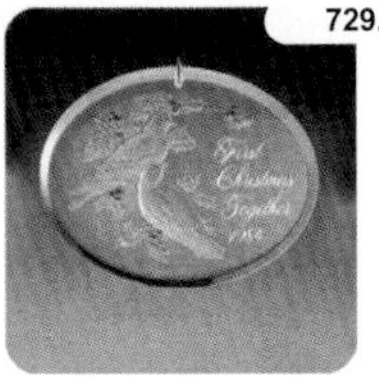
First Christmas Together
600QX3421 • $24

730.

First Christmas Together
1500QX4364 • $20

731.

First Christmas Together
1600QX9044 • $49

732.

Flights of Fantasy
450QX2564 • $35

733.

Fortune Cookie Elf
450QX4524 • $30

734.

Friendship
450QX2481 • $25

735.

Frisbee Puppy
500QX4444 • $37

736.

From Our Home to Yours
450QX2484 • $40

737.

Frosty Friends 5
800QX4371 • $112

738.
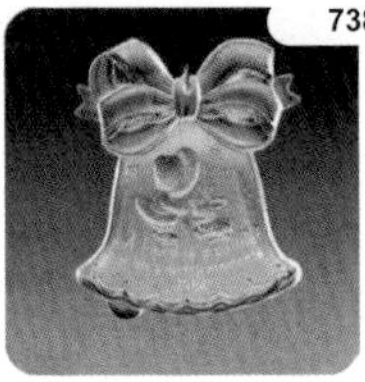
The Fun of Friendship
600QX3431 • $34

739.

A Gift of Friendship
450QX2604 • $21

740.

Gift of Music
1500QX4511 • $88

741.

Godchild
450QX2421 • $32

742.
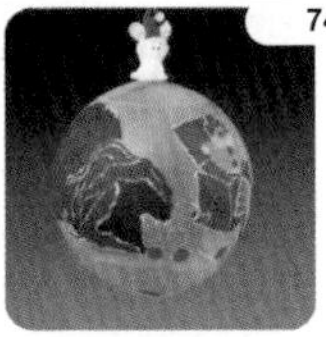
Grandchild's First Christmas
450QX2574 • $24

743.

Grandchild's First Christmas
1100QX4601 • $25

744.

Granddaughter
450QX2431 • $30

745.

Grandmother
450QX2441 • $29

746.

Grandparents
450QX2561 • $16

747.

Grandson
450QX2424 • $30

748.

Gratitude
600QX3444 • $14

749.

Heartful of Love
1000QX4434 • $38

750.

Here Comes Santa 6: Santa's Deliveries
1300QX4324 • $90

751.

Holiday Friendship
1300QX4451 • $38

752.

Holiday Jester
1100QX4374 • $40

753.

Holiday Starburst
500QX2534 • $29

754.

Holiday Wildlife 3: Ringed-Neck Pheasant
725QX3474 • $38

755.

Katybeth
900QX4631 • $29

756.

Kit
550QX4534 • $29

757.

Love
450QX2554 • $32

758.

Love...the Spirit of Christmas
450QX2474 • $49

759.
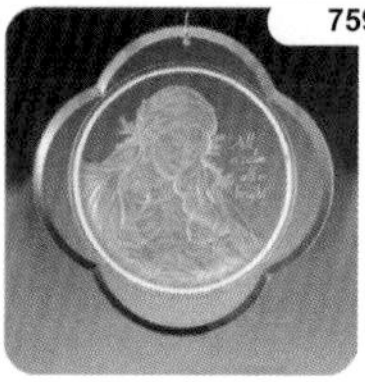
Madonna and Child
600QX3441 • $32

760.

Marathon Santa
800QX4564 • $34

761.

The Miracle of Love
600QX3424 • $24

762.

Mother
600QX3434 • $26

763.

Mother and Dad
650QX2581 • $25

764.

Mountain Climbing Santa
650QX4077 • $40
Re-issued from 1983.

765.

Muffin
550QX4421 • $25

766.

The MUPPETS™
450QX2514 • $41

767.

Musical Angel
550QX4344 • $82

768.

Napping Mouse
550QX4351 • $50

769.

Nativity
1200QLX7001 • $38
MAGIC. Re-issued in 1985.

770.

Needlepoint Wreath
650QX4594 • $14

771.

New Home
450QX2454 • $65

772.

Norman Rockwell
450QX2511 • $36

773.

Norman Rockwell 5: Caught Napping
750QX3411 • $41

774.

Nostalgic Houses & Shops 1: Victorian Doll House
1300QX4481 • $245

775.

Nostalgic Sled
600QX4424 • $28
Re-issued in 1985.

776.
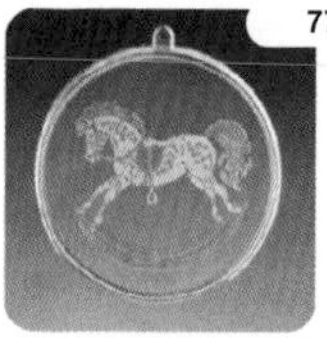
Old Fashioned Rocking Horse
750QX3464 • $16

777.
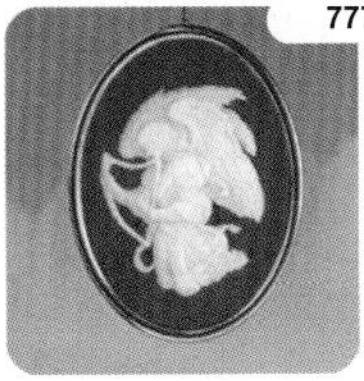
Peace on Earth
750QX3414 • $34

778.

PEANUTS®
450QX2521 • $37

779.

Peppermint 1984
450QX4561 • $30

780.

Polar Bear Drummer
450QX4301 • $41

781.

Porcelain Bear 2: Cinnamon Bear
700QX4541 • $48

782.

Raccoon's Christmas
900QX4474 • $68

783.

Reindeer Racetrack
450QX2544 • $35

784.

Rocking Horse 4
1000QX4354 • $106

785.

Roller Skating Rabbit
500QX4571 • $25
Re-issued in 1985.

786.

Santa
750QX4584 • $15

787.

Santa Mouse
450QX4334 • $41

788.

Santa Star
550QX4504 • $36

789.

Santa Sulky Driver
900QX4361 • $35

790.

Santa's Arrival
1300QLX7024 • $70
MAGIC.

791.

Santa's Workshop
1300QLX7004 • $58
MAGIC. Re-issued in 1985.

792.

A Savior is Born
450QX2541 • $38

793.

Shirt Tales™
450QX2524 • $18

794.
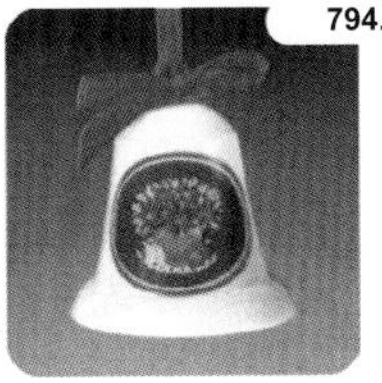
Sister
650QX2594 • $34

795.

Snoopy® and Woodstock™
750QX4391 • $83

796.

Snowmobile Santa
650QX4314 • $35

797.

Snowshoe Penguin
650QX4531 • $39

798.

Snowy Seal
400QX4501 • $28
Re-issued in 1985.

799.

Son
400QX2434 • $43

800.

Stained Glass
800QLX7031 • $29
MAGIC.

801.

Sugarplum Cottage
1100QLX7011 • $55
MAGIC. Re-issued in 1985/1986.

802.

Teacher
450QX2491 • $14

803.

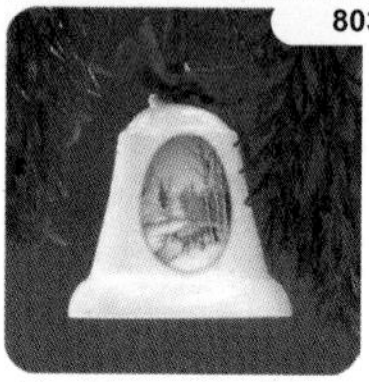

Ten Years Together
650QX2584 • $17

804.

Thimble 7: Thimble Angel
500QX4304 • $65

805.

Three Kittens in a Mitten
800QX4311 • $56
Re-issued in 1985.

806.

Tin Locomotive 3
1400QX4404 • $85

807.

Twelve Days of Christmas
1500QMB4159 • $100
Re-issued from 1983.

808.

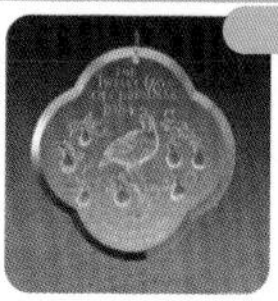

Twelve Days of Christmas 1: Partridge in a Pear Tree
600QX3484 • $335

809.

Twenty-Five Years Together
650QX2591 • $21

810.

Uncle Sam
600QX4491 • $44

811.

Village Church
1500QLX7021 • $52
MAGIC. Re-issued in 1985.

812.

White Christmas
1600QX9051 • $70

813.

Wood Childhood Ornaments 1: Lamb
650QX4394 • $49

1985

814.

All Are Precious
800QLX7044 • $24
MAGIC. Re-issued from 1984.

815.

Art Masterpiece 2: Madonna of the Pomegranate
675QX3772 • $20

816.

Baby Locket
1600QX4012 • $40

817.

Baby's First Christmas
1650QLX7005 • $55
MAGIC.

818.

Baby's First Christmas
500QX2602 • $45

819.

Baby's First Christmas
575QX3702 • $40

820.

Baby's First Christmas
700QX4782 • $20

821.

Baby's First Christmas
1500QX4992 • $80

822.

Baby's First Christmas
1600QX4995 • $50

823.

Baby's Second Christmas
600QX4785 • $41

824.

Babysitter
475QX2642 • $12

825.

Baker Elf
575QX4912 • $36

826.

Beary Smooth Ride
650QX4805 • $26
Re-issued in 1986.

827.

Betsey Clark
850QX5085 • $40

828.

Betsey Clark 13: Special Kind of Feeling
500QX2632 • $42

829.

Bottlecap Fun Bunnies
775QX4815 • $29

830.

Candle Cameo
675QX3742 • $13

831.
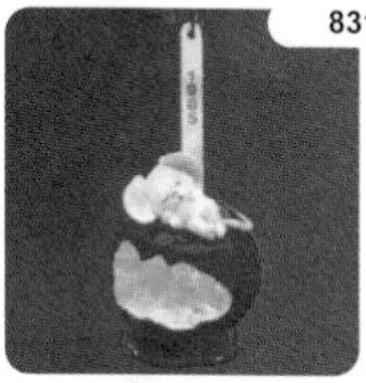
Candy Apple Mouse
650QX4705 • $64

832.

Charming Angel
975QX5125 • $28

833.

Children in the Shoe
950QX4905 • $50

834.

Child's Third Christmas
600QX4755 • $19

835.

Chris Mouse 1: Chris Mouse
1250QLX7032 • $98
MAGIC.

836.

Christmas Eve Visit
1200QLX7105 • $40
MAGIC.

837.
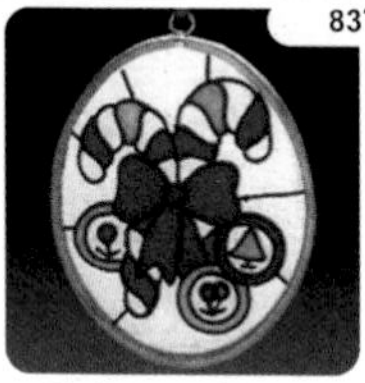
Christmas Treats
550QX5075 • $19

838.

Clothespin Soldier 4: Scottish Highlander
550QX4715 • $35

839.

Country Goose
775QX5185 • $14

840.

Dapper Penguin
500QX4772 • $30

841.

Daughter
550QX5032 • $29

842.

A Disney Christmas
475QX2712 • $44

843.

Do Not Disturb Bear
775QX4812 • $35
Re-issued in 1986.

844.
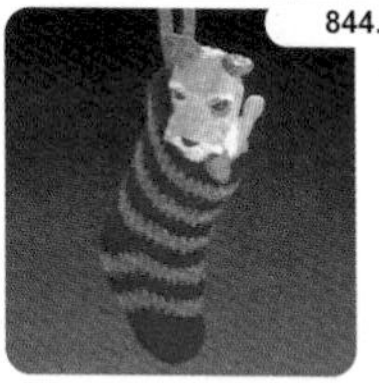
Doggy in a Stocking
550QX4742 • $41

845.

Engineering Mouse
550QX4735 • $24

846.

Father
650QX3762 • $12

847.

First Christmas Together
475QX2612 • $24

848.

First Christmas Together
675QX3705 • $22

849.

First Christmas Together
1675QX4005 • $25

850.

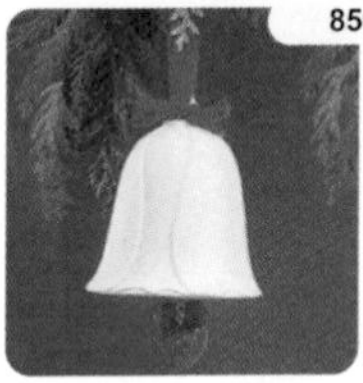

First Christmas Together
1300QX4935 • $69

851.

First Christmas Together
800QX5072 • $11

852.

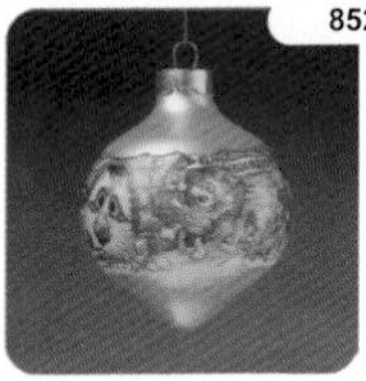

Fraggle Rock™ Holiday
475QX2655 • $31

853.

Friendship
675QX3785 • $17

854.

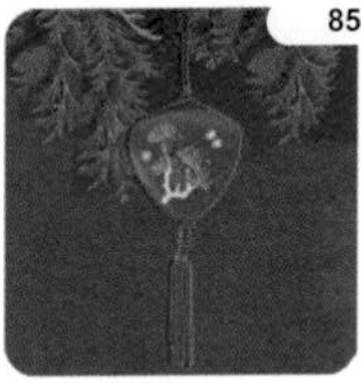

Friendship
775QX5062 • $18

855.

From Our House to Yours
775QX5202 • $14

856.

Frosty Friends 6
850QX4822 • $155

857.

Godchild
675QX3802 • $20

858.

Good Friends
475QX2652 • $50

859.

Grandchild's First Christmas
500QX2605 • $17

860.

Grandchild's First Christmas
1100QX4955 • $22

861.

Granddaughter
475QX2635 • $29

862.

Grandmother
475QX2625 • $24

863.

Grandparents
700QX3805 • $10

864.

Grandson
475QX2622 • $40

865.

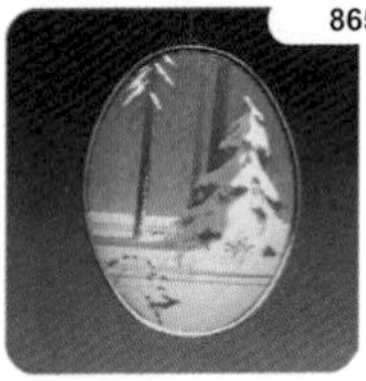

Heart Full of Love
675QX3782 • $18

866.

Heavenly Trumpeter
2750QX4052 • $60
Limited Edition - 24700.

867.

Here Comes Santa 7: Santa's Fire Engine
1400QX4965 • $80

868.

Holiday Heart
800QX4982 • $22

869.

Holiday Wildlife 4: California Partridge
750QX3765 • $35

870.

Hugga Bunch™
500QX2715 • $29

871.

Ice Skating Owl
500QX4765 • $23

872.
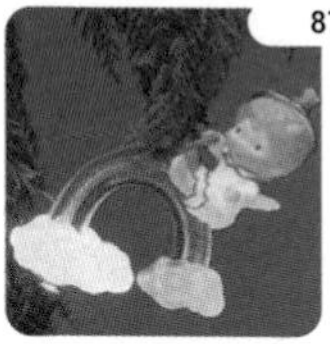
Katybeth
1075QLX7102 • $41
MAGIC.

873.
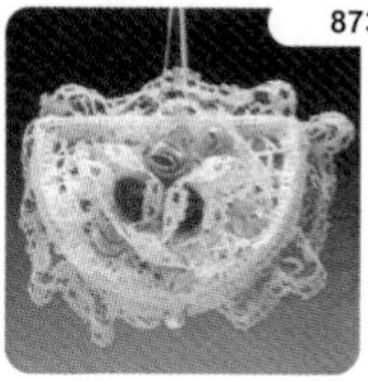
Keepsake Basket
1500QX5145 • $29

874.

Kit the Shepherd
575QX4845 • $27

875.

Kitty Mischief
500QX4745 • $30
Re-issued in 1986.

876.
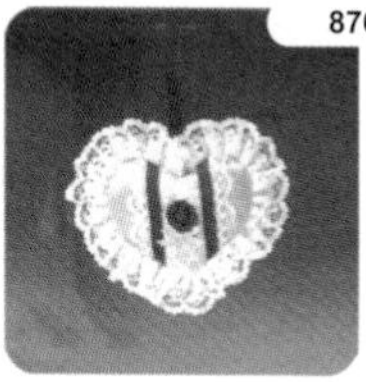
Lacy Heart
875QX5112 • $30

877.

Lamb in Legwarmers
700QX4802 • $26

878.

Little Red Schoolhouse
1575QLX7112 • $75
MAGIC.

879.

Love At Christmas
575QX3715 • $38

880.

Love Wreath
850QLX7025 • $22
MAGIC.

881.

Merry Mouse
450QX4032 • $28
Re-issued in 1986.

882.
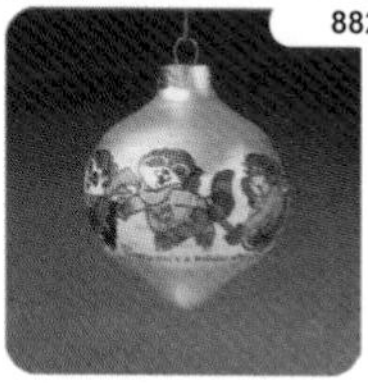
Merry Shirt Tales™
475QX2672 • $20

883.

Miniature Creche 1
875QX4825 • $25

884.

Mother
675QX3722 • $14

885.

Mother and Dad
775QX5092 • $28

886.

Mouse Wagon
575QX4762 • $64

887.

Mr. and Mrs. Santa
1450QLX7052 • $66
MAGIC. Re-issued in 1986.

888.

Muffin the Angel
575QX4835 • $32

889.

Nativity
1200QLX7001 • $38
MAGIC. Re-issued from 1984.

890.

Nativity Scene
475QX2645 • $54

891.

New Home
475QX2695 • $40

892.

Niece
575QX5205 • $30

893.

Night Before Christmas
1300QX4494 • $44

894.

Norman Rockwell
475QX2662 • $30

895.

Norman Rockwell 6: Jolly Postman
750QX3745 • $35

896.

Nostalgic Houses & Shops 2: Old Fashion Toy Shop
1375QX4975 • $129

897.

Nostalgic Sled
600QX4424 • $28
Re-issued from 1984.

898.

Old-Fashioned Doll
1450QX5195 • $42

899.

Old-Fashioned Wreath
750QX3735 • $24

900.

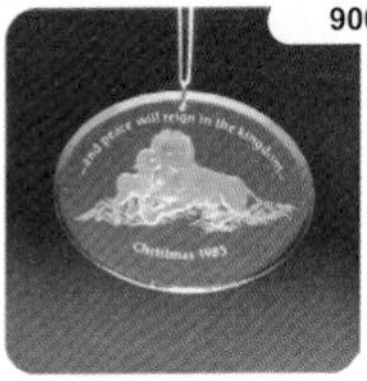

Peaceful Kingdom
575QX3732 • $41

901.

PEANUTS®
475QX2665 • $47

902.

Porcelain Bear 3
750QX4792 • $45

903.

Porcelain Bird
650QX4795 • $36

904.

Rainbow Brite™ and Friends
475QX2682 • $38

905.

Rocking Horse 5
1075QX4932 • $89

906.

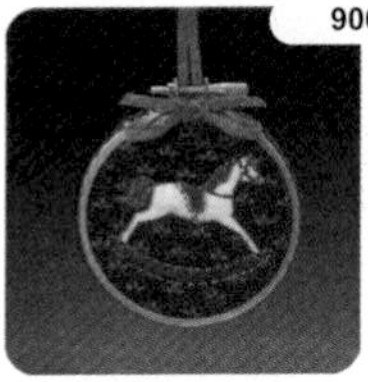

Rocking Horse Memories
1000QX5182 • $18

907.

Roller Skating Rabbit
500QX4571 • $25
Re-issued from 1984.

908.

Santa Claus
675QX3005 • $16

909.

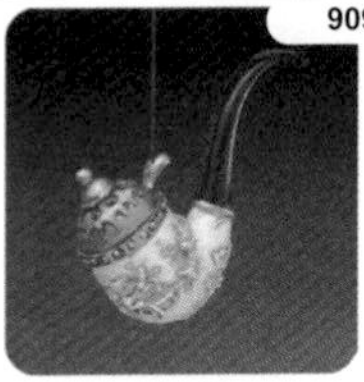

Santa Pipe
950QX4942 • $34

910.

Santa's Ski Trip
1200QX4962 • $77

911.

Santa's Village - Santa Claus the Movie™
675QX3002 • $16

912.

Santa's Workshop
1300QLX7004 • $58
MAGIC. Re-issued from 1984.

913.

Season of Beauty
800QLX7122 • $30
MAGIC.

914.

Sewn Photo Holder
700QX3795 • $20

915.

Sheep at Christmas
825QX5175 • $35

916.

Sister
725QX5065 • $26

917.

Skateboard Raccoon
650QX4732 • $45
Re-issued in 1986.

918.

Snoopy® and Woodstock™
750QX4915 • $65

919.

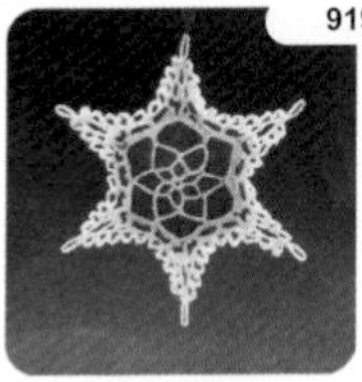

Snowflake
650QX5105 • $18

920.

Snow-Pitching Snowman
450QX4702 • $25
Re-issued in 1986.

921.

Snowy Seal
400QX4501 • $28
Re-issued from 1984.

922.

Soccer Beaver
650QX4775 • $24
Re-issued in 1986.

923.

Son
550QX5025 • $59

924.
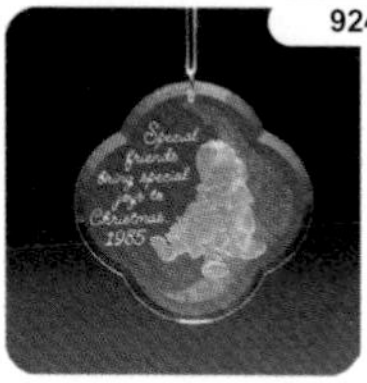
Special Friends
575QX3725 • $11

925.

The Spirit of Santa Claus
2250QX4985 • $95

926.
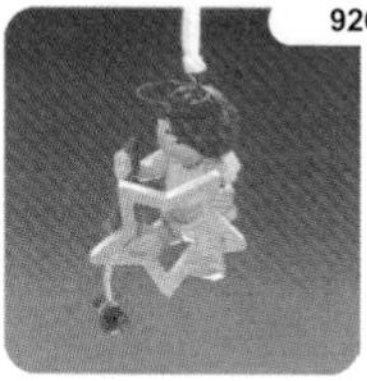
Stardust Angel
575QX4752 • $48

927.

Sugarplum Cottage
1100QLX7011 • $55
MAGIC. Also issued 1984 & 1986.

928.

Sun and Fun Santa
775QX4922 • $30

929.

Swinging Angel Bell
1100QX4925 • $41

930.

Swiss Cheese Lane
1300QLX7065 • $50
MAGIC.

931.

Teacher
600QX5052 • $22

932.

Thimble 8: Thimble Santa
550QX4725 • $49

933.

Three Kittens in a Mitten
800QX4311 • $56
Re-issued from 1984.

934.

Tin Locomotive 4
1475QX4972 • $70

935.

Trumpet Panda
450QX4712 • $24

936.

Twelve Days of Christmas 2: Two Turtle Doves
650QX3712 • $100

937.
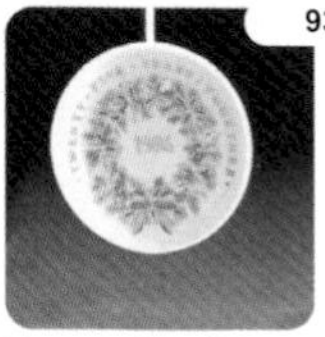
Twenty-Five Years Together
800QX5005 • $16

938.

Victorian Lady
950QX5132 • $21

939.

Village Church
1500QLX7021 • $52
MAGIC. Re-issued from 1984.

940.

Whirligig Santa
1250QX5192 • $35

941.

Windows of the World 1: Feliz Navidad
975QX4902 • $102

942.

With Appreciation
675QX3752 • $15

943.

Wood Childhood Ornaments 2: Train
700QX4722 • $59

1986

944.
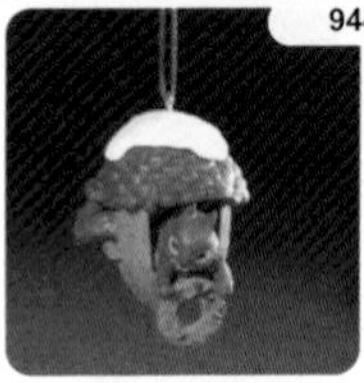
Acorn Inn
850QX4243 • $29

945.

Art Masterpiece 3: Madonna and Child with the Infant St. John
675QX3506 • $36

946.

Baby Locket
1600QX4123 • $36

947.

Baby's First Christmas
1950QLX7103 • $65
MAGIC.

948.

Baby's First Christmas
550QX2713 • $37

949.

Baby's First Christmas
800QX3792 • $34

950.
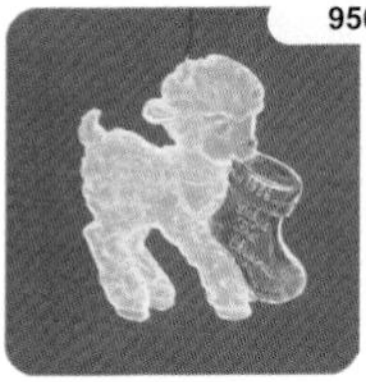
Baby's First Christmas
600QX3803 • $48

951.

Baby's First Christmas
900QX4126 • $58

952.

Baby's Second Christmas
650QX4133 • $37

953.

Baby-Sitter
475QX2756 • $16

954.

Beary Smooth Ride
650QX4805 • $26
Re-issued from 1985.

955.

Betsey Clark: Home for Christmas 1
500QX2776 • $32

956.

Bluebird
725QX4283 • $116

957.

Chatty Penguin
575QX4176 • $35

958.

Child's Third Christmas
650QX4136 • $22

959.

Chris Mouse 2: Chris Mouse Dreams
1300QLX7056 • $104
MAGIC.

960.

Christmas Beauty
600QX3223 • $17

961.

Christmas Classics 1: The Nutcracker Ballet - Sugarplum Fairy
1750QLX7043 • $97
MAGIC.

962.
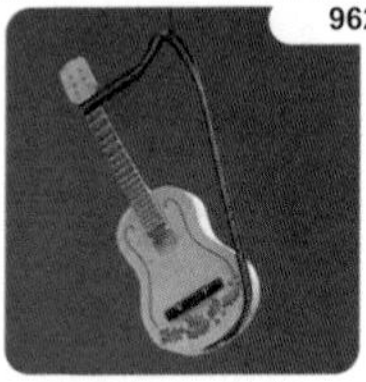
Christmas Guitar
700QX5126 • $26

963.

Christmas Sleigh Ride
2450QLX7012 • $75
MAGIC.

964.

Clothespin Soldier 5: French Officer
550QX4063 • $30

965.

Coca-Cola® Santa
475QXO2796 • $22

966.
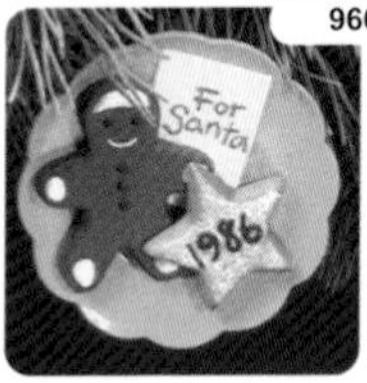

Cookies for Santa
450QX4146 • $30

967.

Country Sleigh
1000QX5113 • $24

968.
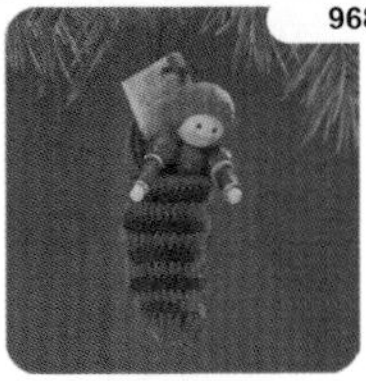
Daughter
575QX4306 • $50

969.

Do Not Disturb Bear
775QX4812 • $35
Re-issued from 1985.

970.
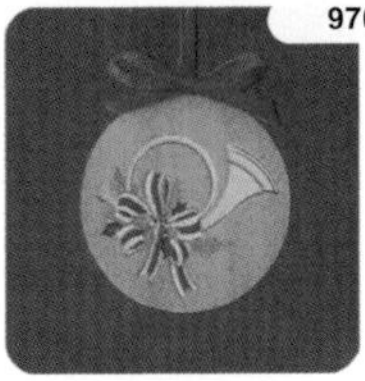
Father
650QX4313 • $15

971.
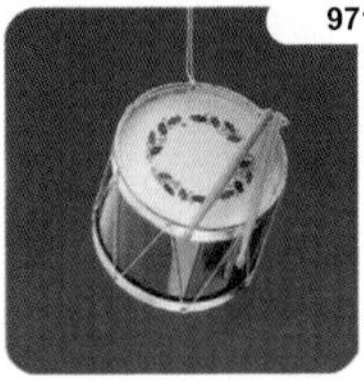
Favorite Tin Drum
850QX5143 • $31

972.
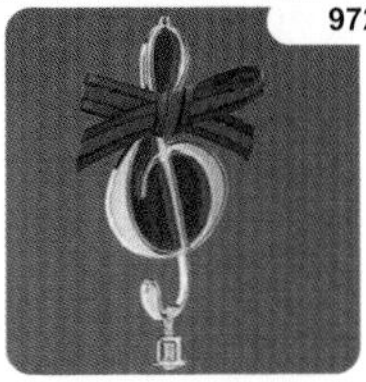
Festive Treble Clef
875QX5133 • $27

973.

Fifty Years Together
1000QX4006 • $15

974.

First Christmas Together
1400QLX7073 • $48
MAGIC.

975.

First Christmas Together
475QX2703 • $40

976.

First Christmas Together
700QX3793 • $24

977.

First Christmas Together
1600QX4003 • $32

978.

First Christmas Together
1200QX4096 • $29

979.

Friends Are Fun
475QX2723 • $68

980.
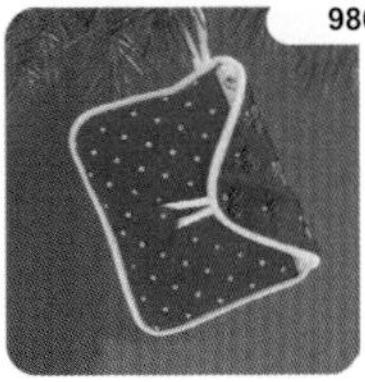
Friendship Greeting
800QX4273 • $12

981.
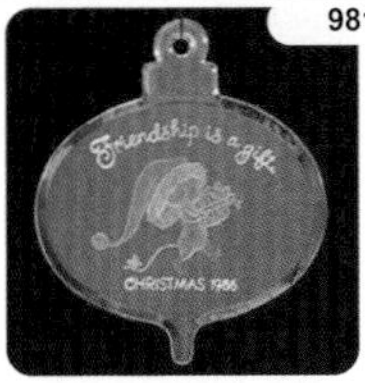

Friendship's Gift
600QX3816 • $12

982.

From Our Home to Yours
600QX3833 • $12

983.

Frosty Friends 7
850QX4053 • $89

984.

General Store
1575QLX7053 • $60
MAGIC.

985.

Gentle Blessings
1500QLX7083 • $118
MAGIC.

986.
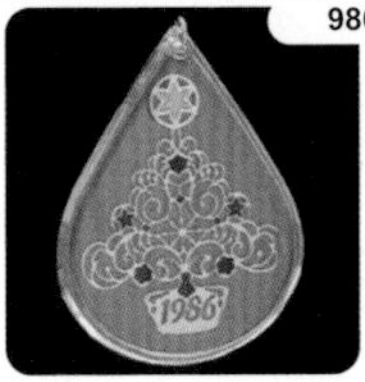

Glowing Christmas Tree
700QX4286 • $12

987.

Godchild
475QX2716 • $26

988.

Grandchild's First Christmas
1000QX4116 • $26

989.

Granddaughter
475QX2736 • $26

990.

Grandmother
475QX2743 • $24

991.

Grandparents
750QX4323 • $23

992.

Grandson
475QX2733 • $37

993.
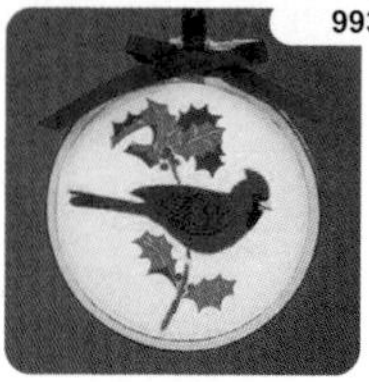
Gratitude
600QX4326 • $12

994.

Happy Christmas to Owl
600QX4183 • $24

995.
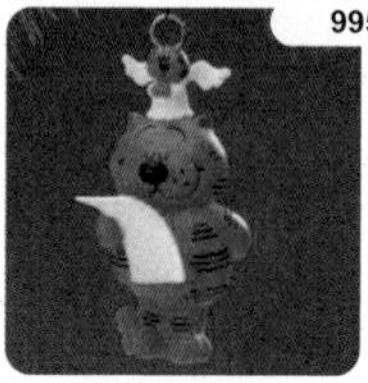
Heathcliff
750QX4386 • $24

996.
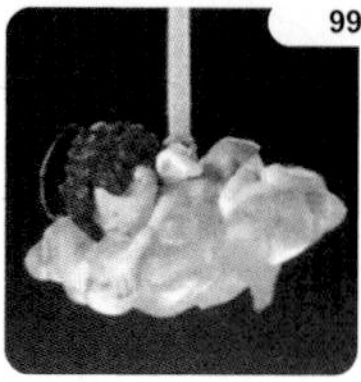
Heavenly Dreamer
575QX4173 • $42

997.

Heirloom Snowflake
675QX5153 • $14

998.

Here Comes Santa 8: Kringle's Kool Treats
1400QX4043 • $79

999.
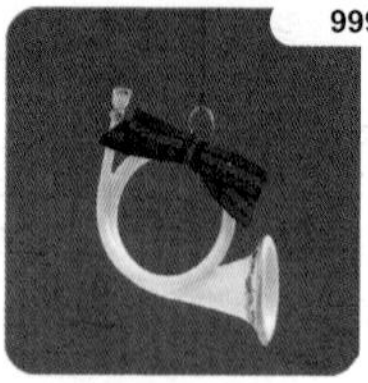
Holiday Horn
800QX5146 • $34

1000.

Holiday Jingle Bell
1600QX4046 • $70

1001.

Holiday Wildlife 5: Cedar Waxwing
750QX3216 • $26

1002.

Husband
800QX3836 • $12

1003.

Jolly Hiker
500QX4832 • $36
Re-issued in 1987.

1004.

Jolly St. Nick
2250QX4296 • $61

1005.
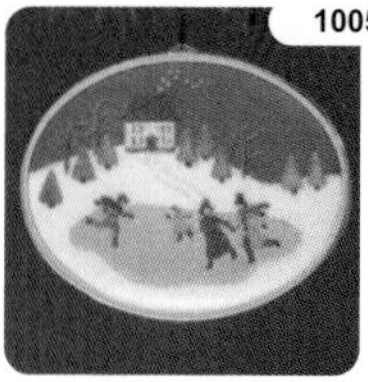
Joy of Friends
675QX3823 • $11

1006.

Joyful Carolers
975QX5136 • $36

1007.
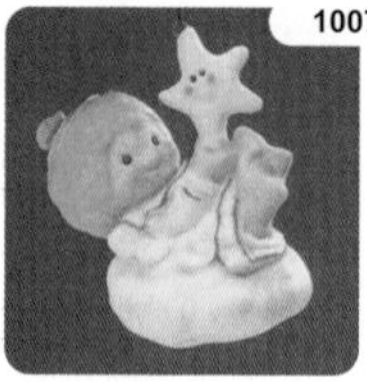
Katybeth
700QX4353 • $31

1008.

Keep On Glowin'!
1000QLX7076 • $46
MAGIC. Re-issued in 1987.

1009.

Kitty Mischief
500QX4745 • $30
Re-issued from 1985.

1010.

Li'l Jingler
675QX4193 • $50
Re-issued in 1987.

1011.

Little Drummers
1250QX5116 • $38

1012.

Loving Memories
900QX4093 • $37

1013.

The Magi
475QX2726 • $23

1014.

Magical Unicorn
2750QX4293 • $80
Limited Edition - 24700.

1015.
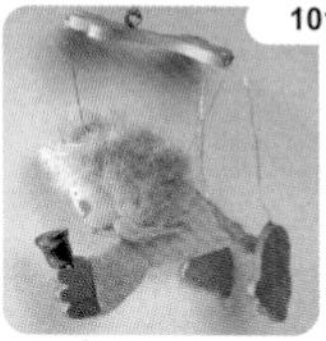
Marionette Angel
850QX4023 • $525
RARE

1016.

Mary Emmerling: American Country Collection
795QX2752 • $41

1017.

Memories to Cherish
750QX4276 • $41

1018.

Merry Christmas Bell
850QLX7093 • $25
MAGIC.

1019.

Merry Koala
500QX4153 • $28
Re-issued in 1987.

1020.

Merry Mouse
450QX4032 • $28
Re-issued from 1985.

1021.
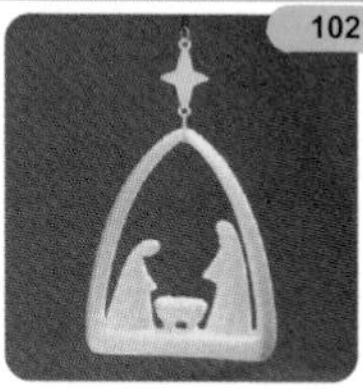
Miniature Creche 2
900QX4076 • $56

1022.

Mother
700QX3826 • $26

1023.
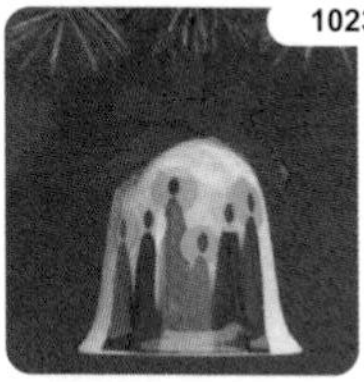
Mother and Dad
750QX4316 • $22

1024.

Mouse In The Moon
550QX4166 • $34
Re-issued in 1987.

1025.

Mr. and Mrs. Claus 1: Merry Mistletoe Time
1300QX4026 • $83

1026.

Mr. and Mrs. Santa
1450QLX7052 • $66
MAGIC. Re-issued from 1985.

1027.
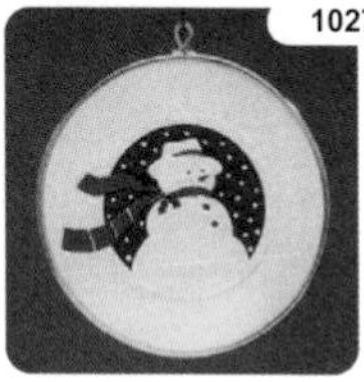
Nephew
625QX3813 • $14

1028.

New Home
475QX2746 • $78

1029.
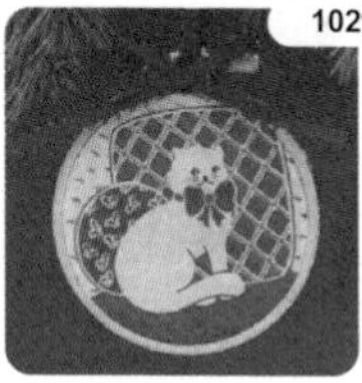
Niece
600QX4266 • $14

1030.

Norman Rockwell
475QX2763 • $41

1031.

Norman Rockwell 7: Checking Up
775QX3213 • $32

1032.

Nostalgic Houses & Shops 3: Christmas Candy Shoppe
1375QX4033 • $317

1033.

Nutcracker Santa
1000QX5123 • $48

1034.

Old-Fashioned Santa
1275QXO4403 • $52

1035.

On The Right Track
1500QSP4201 • $53

1036.

Open Me First
725QX4226 • $42

1037.
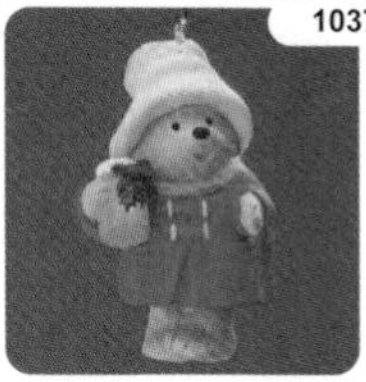
Paddington™ Bear
600QX4356 • $37

1038.
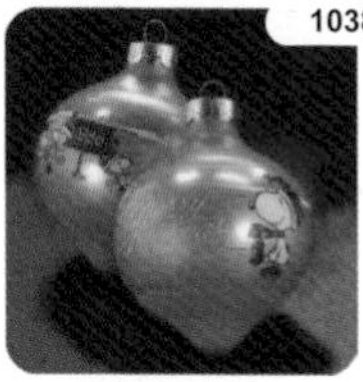
PEANUTS®
475QX2766 • $62

1039.
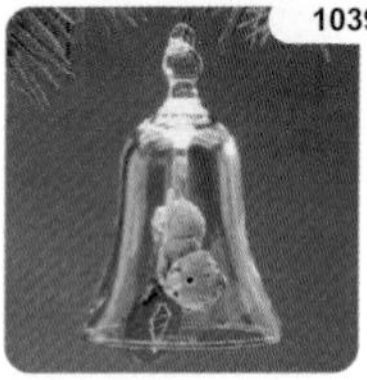
Playful Possum
1100QX4253 • $38

1040.

Popcorn Mouse
675QX4213 • $52

1041.

Porcelain Bear 4
775QX4056 • $41

1042.

Puppy's Best Friend
650QX4203 • $26

1043.

Rah Rah Rabbit
700QX4216 • $35

1044.

Reindeer Champs 1: Dasher
750QX4223 • $148

1045.
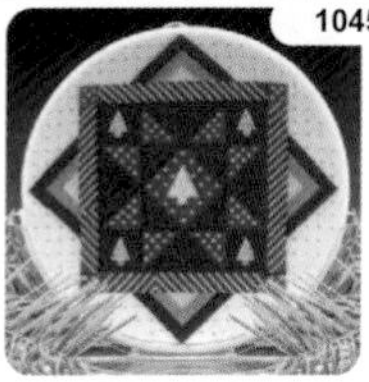
Remembering Christmas
875QX5106 • $18

1046.

Rocking Horse 6
1075QX4016 • $72

1047.

Santa and His Reindeer
975QXO4406 • $38

1048.

Santa and Sparky 1: Lighting the Tree
2200QLX7033 • $66
MAGIC.

1049.

Santa's Hot Tub
1200QX4263 • $59

1050.

Santa's On His Way
1500QLX7115 • $94
MAGIC.

1051.

Santa's Panda Pal
500QXO4413 • $20

1052.

Santa's Snack
1000QLX7066 • $56
MAGIC.

1053.

Season of the Heart
475QX2706 • $19

1054.

Sharing Friendship
850QLX7063 • $30
MAGIC.

1055.

Shirt Tales™ Parade
475QX2773 • $24

1056.

Sister
675QX3806 • $28

1057.

Skateboard Raccoon
650QX4732 • $45
Re-issued from 1985.

1058.

Ski Tripper
675QX4206 • $18

1059.

Snoopy® and Woodstock™
800QX4383 • $65

1060.

Snow Buddies
800QX4236 • $38

1061.

Snow-Pitching Snowman
450QX4702 • $25
Re-issued from 1985.

1062.

Soccer Beaver
650QX4775 • $24
Re-issued from 1985.

1063.

Son
575QX4303 • $42

1064.

Special Delivery
500QX4156 • $22

1065.

Star Brighteners
600QX3226 • $23

1066.
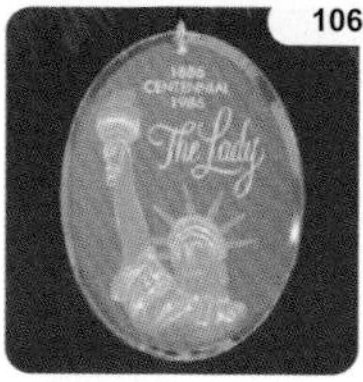
The Statue of Liberty
600QX3843 • $30

1067.

Sugarplum Cottage
1100QLX7011 • $55
MAGIC. Re-issued from 1984/85.

1068.

Sweetheart
1100QX4086 • $61

1069.

Teacher
475QX2753 • $14

1070.

Ten Years Together
750QX4013 • $29

1071.

Thimble 9: Thimble Partridge
575QX4066 • $26

1072.

Timeless Love
600QX3796 • $30

1073.

Tin Locomotive 5
1475QX4036 • $70

1074.

Tipping the Scales
675QX4186 • $22

1075.

Touchdown Santa
800QX4233 • $38

1076.

Treetop Trio
1100QX4256 • $39
Re-issued in 1987.

1077.
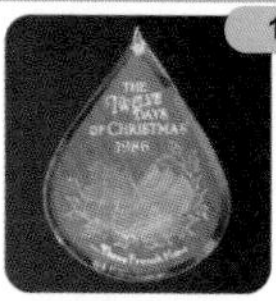
Twelve Days of Christmas 3: Three French Hens
650QX3786 • $58

1078.

Twenty-Five Years Together
800QX4103 • $30

1079.
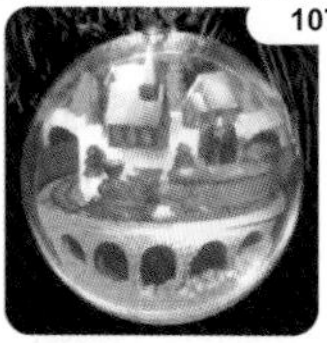
Village Express
2450QLX7072 • $87
MAGIC. Re-issued in 1987.

1080.

Walnut Shell Rider
600QX4196 • $31
Re-issued in 1987.

1081.

Welcome, Christmas
825QX5103 • $34

1082.

Windows of the World 2: Vrolyk Kerstfeest
1000QX4083 • $40

1083.

Wood Childhood Ornaments 3: Reindeer
750QX4073 • $26

1084.

Wynken, Blynken and Nod
975QX4246 • $43

1987

1085.

Angelic Messengers
1875QLX7113 • $101
MAGIC.

1086.

Baby Locket
1500QX4617 • $34

1087.

Baby's First Christmas
1350QLX7049 • $80
MAGIC.

1088.
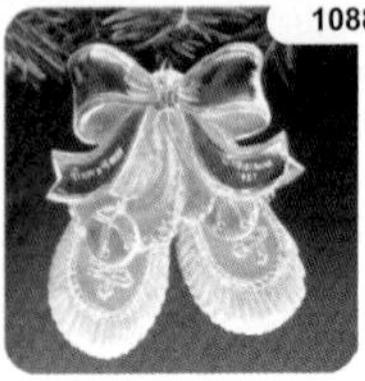
Baby's First Christmas
600QX3729 • $32

1089.
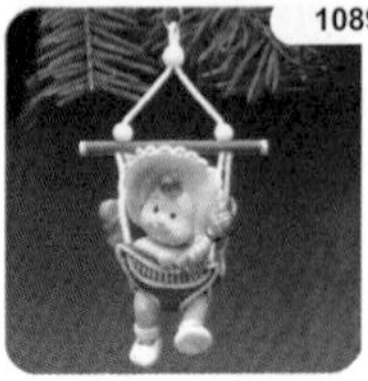
Baby's First Christmas
975QX4113 • $35

1090.

Baby's First Christmas
750QX4619 • $47

1091.

Baby's First Christmas (Boy)
475QX2749 • $36

1092.

Baby's First Christmas (Girl)
475QX2747 • $32

1093.

Baby's Second Christmas
575QX4607 • $36

1094.
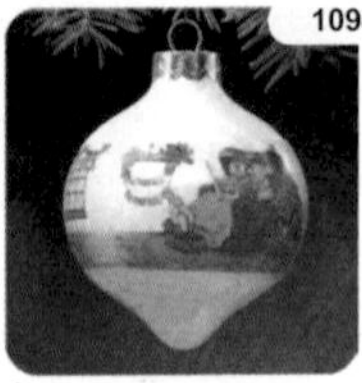
Babysitter
475QX2797 • $29

1095.

Beary Special
475QX4557 • $28

1096.

Betsey Clark: Home for Christmas 2
500QX2727 • $23

1097.

Bright Christmas Dreams
725QX4737 • $96

1098.
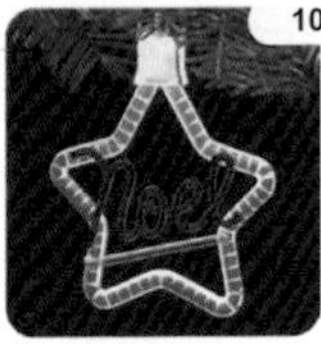
Bright Noel
700QLX7059 • $38
MAGIC.

1099.
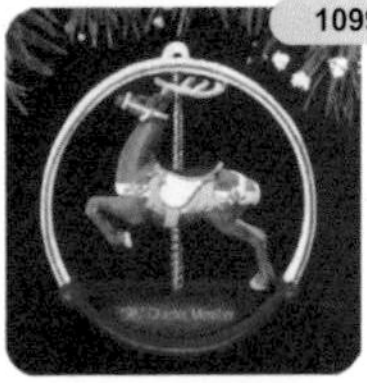
Carousel Reindeer
800QXC5817 • $49

1100.

Child's Third Christmas
575QX4599 • $36

1101.
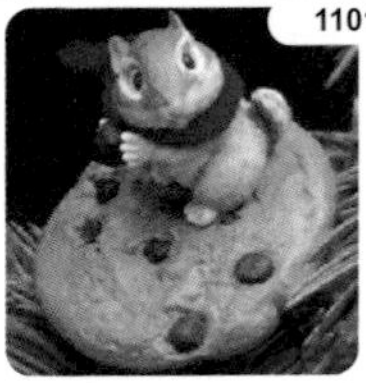
Chocolate Chipmunk
600QX4567 • $67

1102.

Chris Mouse 3: Chris Mouse Glow
1100QLX7057 • $78
MAGIC.

1103.

Christmas Classics 2: A Christmas Carol
1600QLX7029 • $58
MAGIC.

1104.

Christmas Cuddle
575QX4537 • $41

1105.

Christmas Fun Puzzle
800QX4679 • $31

1106.

Christmas Is Gentle
1750QX4449 • $50
Limited Edition - 24700.

1107.

Christmas Keys
575QX4739 • $29

1108.

Christmas Morning
2450QLX7013 • $48
MAGIC. Re-issued in 1988.

1109.
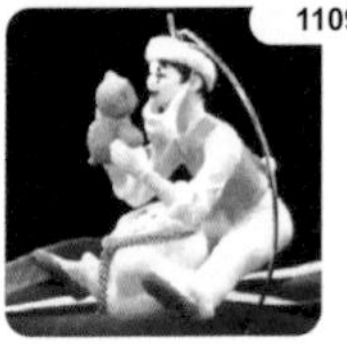
Christmas Time Mime
2750QX4429 • $30
Limited Edition - 24700.

1110.

Clothespin Soldier 6: Sailor
550QX4807 • $29

1111.

Collector's Plate 1: Light Shines at Christmas
800QX4817 • $69

1112.

The Constitution
650QX3777 • $19

1113.
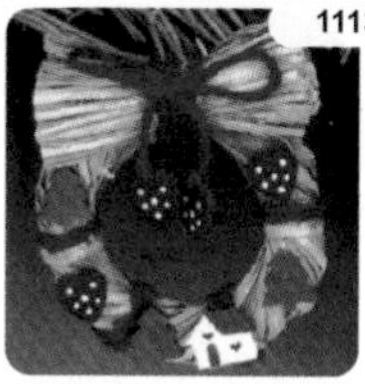
Country Wreath
575QX4709 • $19

1114.

Currier & Ives: American Farm Scene
475QX2829 • $41

1115.

Dad
600QX4629 • $35

1116.

Daughter
575QX4637 • $40

1117.

December Showers
550QX4487 • $31

1118.

Doc Holiday
800QX4677 • $44

1119.

Dr. Seuss®: The Grinch™'s Christmas
475QX2783 • $189

1120.

Favorite Santa
2250QX4457 • $38

1121.

Fifty Years Together
800QX4437 • $23

1122.
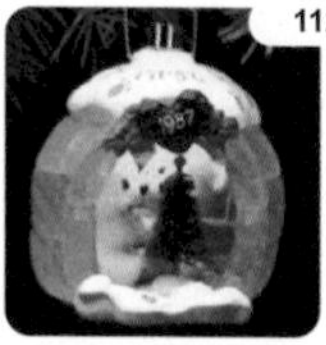
First Christmas Together
1150QLX7087 • $56
MAGIC.

1123.

First Christmas Together
475QX2729 • $31

1124.
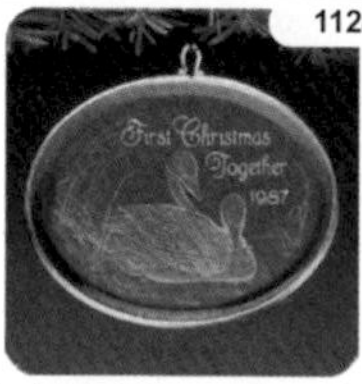
First Christmas Together
650QX3719 • $29

1125.
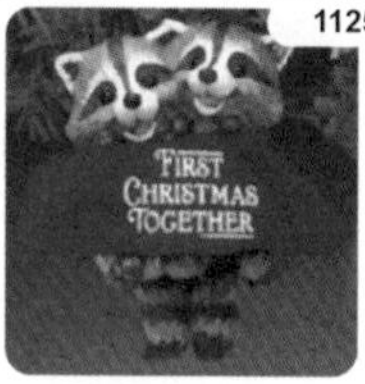
First Christmas Together
800QX4459 • $43

1126.

First Christmas Together
950QX4467 • $37

1127.

First Christmas Together
1500QX4469 • $35

1128.

Folk Art Santa
525QX4749 • $34

1129.

From Our Home to Yours
475QX2799 • $59

1130.
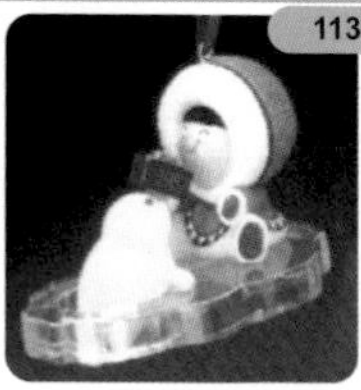
Frosty Friends 8
850QX4409 • $90

1131.

Fudge Forever
500QX4497 • $40

1132.
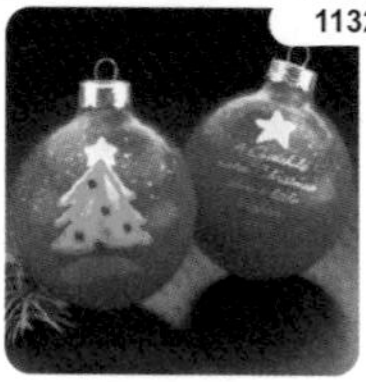
Godchild
475QX2767 • $29

1133.

Goldfinch
700QX4649 • $84

1134.

Good Cheer Blimp
1600QLX7046 • $71
MAGIC.

1135.

Grandchild's First Christmas
900QX4609 • $67

1136.

Granddaughter
600QX3747 • $16

1137.

Grandmother
475QX2779 • $17

1138.

Grandparents
475QX2777 • $22

1139.

Grandson
475QX2769 • $39

1140.

Happy Holidata
650QX4717 • $30
Re-issued in 1988.

1141.

Happy Santa
475QX4569 • $37

1142.

Heart in Blossom
600QX3727 • $29

1143.

Heavenly Harmony
1500QX4659 • $37

1144.

Here Comes Santa 9: Santa's Woody
1400QX4847 • $95

1145.

Holiday Greetings
600QX3757 • $10

1146.
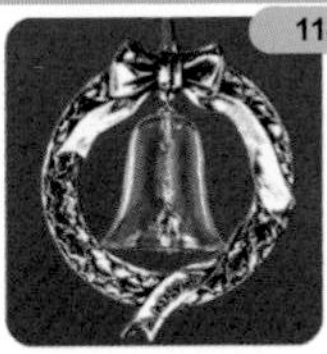
Holiday Heirloom 1
2500QX4857 • $34
Limited Edition - 34600.

1147.

Holiday Hourglass
800QX4707 • $36

1148.

Holiday Wildlife 6: Snow Goose
750QX3717 • $28

1149.

Hot Dogger
650QX4719 • $28

1150.

Husband
700QX3739 • $11

1151.

I Remember Santa
475QX2789 • $40

1152.
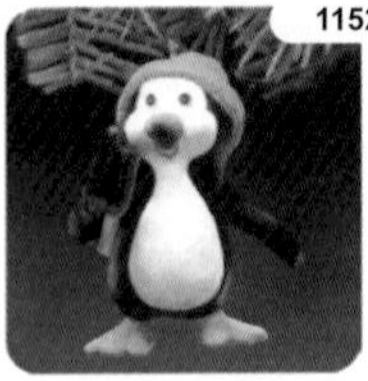
Icy Treat
450QX4509 • $35

1153.
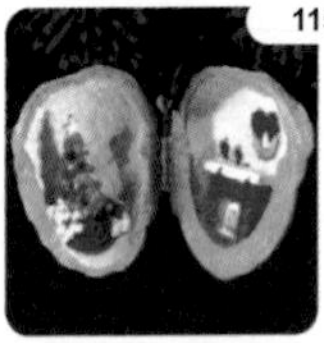
In a Nutshell
550QX4697 • $30
Re-issued in 1988.

1154.

Jack Frosting
700QX4499 • $53

1155.

Jammie Pies
475QX2839 • $18

1156.

Jogging Through The Snow
725QX4577 • $34

1157.
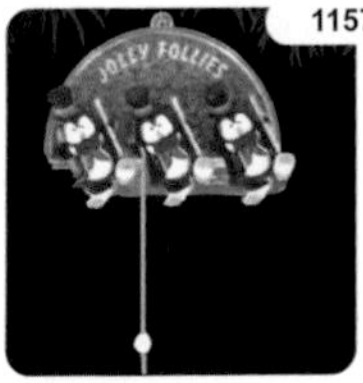

Jolly Follies
850QX4669 • $38

1158.

Jolly Hiker
500QX4832 • $36
Re-issued from 1986.

1159.

Joy Ride
1150QX4407 • $75

1160.
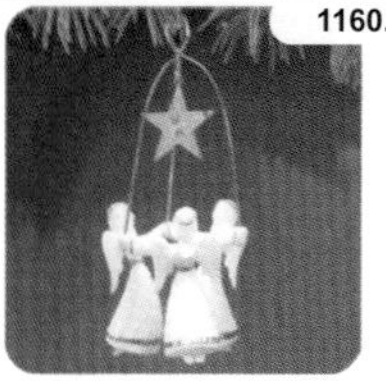
Joyous Angels
775QX4657 • $37

1161.

Keep On Glowin'!
1000QLX7076 • $46
MAGIC. Re-issued from 1986.

1162.

Keeping Cozy
1175QLX7047 • $40
MAGIC.

1163.
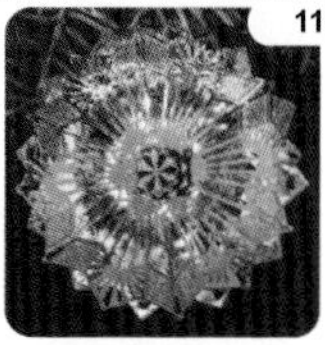
Lacy Brass Snowflake
1150QLX7097 • $23
MAGIC.

1164.

Let It Snow
650QX4589 • $28

1165.
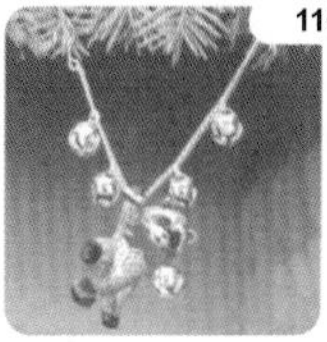
Li'l Jingler
675QX4193 • $50
Re-issued from 1986.

1166.

Little Whittler
600QX4699 • $35

1167.

Love Is Everywhere
475QX2787 • $29

1168.

Loving Holiday
2200QLX7016 • $59
MAGIC.

1169.

Memories Are Forever
850QLX7067 • $46
MAGIC.

1170.
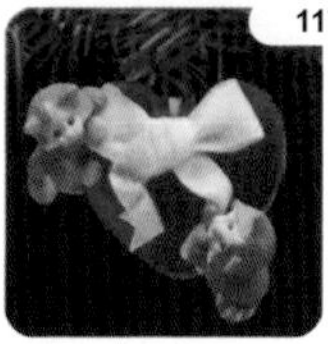
Meowy Christmas!
1000QLX7089 • $48
MAGIC.

1171.

Merry Koala
500QX4153 • $28
Re-issued from 1986.

1172.

Miniature Creche 3
900QX4819 • $41

1173.

Mistletoad
700QX4687 • $32
Re-issued in 1988.

1174.

Mother
650QX3737 • $22

1175.

Mother and Dad
700QX4627 • $20

1176.
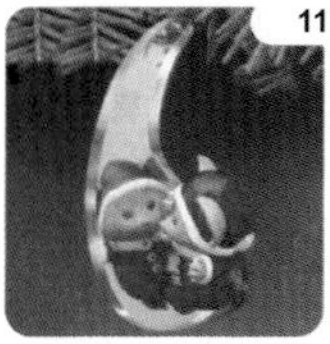
Mouse in the Moon
550QX4166 • $34
Re-issued from 1986.

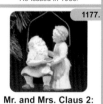

1177.

Mr. and Mrs. Claus 2: Home Cooking
1325QX4837 • $67

1178.

Nature's Decorations
475QX2739 • $38

1179.

New Home
600QX3767 • $34

1180.
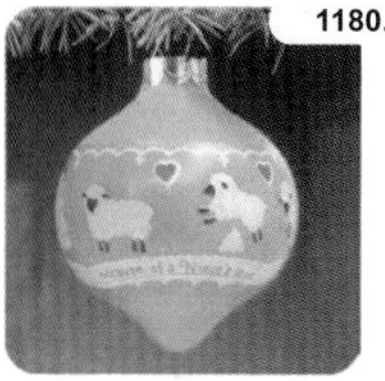
Niece
475QX2759 • $13

1181.

Night Before Christmas
650QX4517 • $42
Re-issued in 1988.

1182.

Norman Rockwell: Christmas Scenes
475QX2827 • $30

1183.

Norman Rockwell 8: The Christmas Dance
775QX3707 • $20

1184.
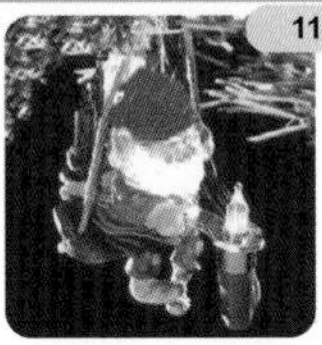
North Pole Power & Light
295XPR9333 • $22

1185.

Nostalgic Houses & Shops 4: House on Main Street
1400QX4839 • $103

1186.
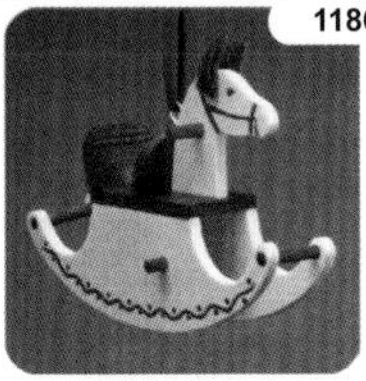
Nostalgic Rocker
650QX4689 • $23

1187.

Owliday Wish
650QX4559 • $24
Re-issued in 1988.

1188.

Paddington™ Bear
550QX4727 • $44

1189.

PEANUTS®
475QX2819 • $44

1190.
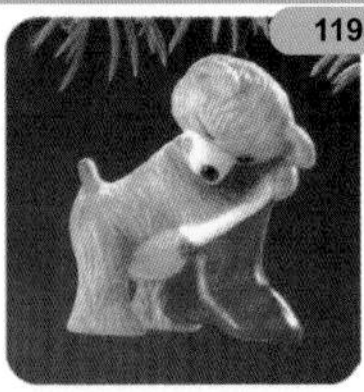
Porcelain Bear 5
775QX4427 • $22

1191.
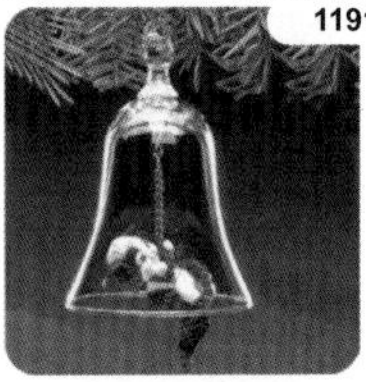
Pretty Kitty
1100QX4489 • $37

1192.
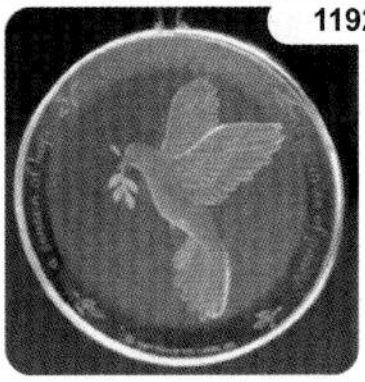
Promise of Peace
650QX3749 • $35

1193.

Raccoon Biker
700QX4587 • $35

1194.

Reindeer Champs 2: Dancer
750QX4809 • $44

1195.

Reindoggy
575QX4527 • $33
Re-issued in 1988.

1196.

Rocking Horse 7
1075QX4829 • $63

1197.

Santa and Sparky 2: Perfect Portrait
1950QLX7019 • $74
MAGIC.

1198.

Santa at the Bat
775QX4579 • $32

1199.
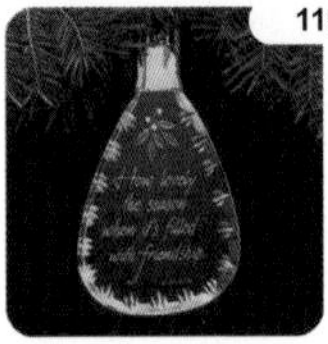
Season For Friendship
850QLX7069 • $20
MAGIC.

1200.

Seasoned Greetings
625QX4549 • $30

1201.

Sister
600QX4747 • $19

1202.

Sleepy Santa
625QX4507 • $41

1203.

Snoopy® and Woodstock™
725QX4729 • $61

1204.
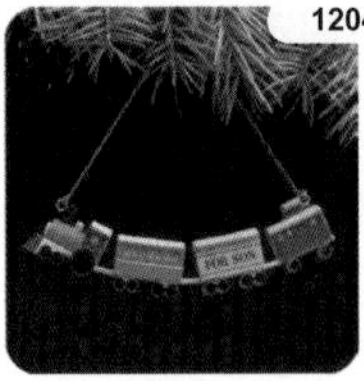
Son
575QX4639 • $79

1205.

Special Memories
675QX4647 • $36

1206.

Spots 'n Stripes
550QX4529 • $32

1207.

St. Louie Nick
775QX4539 • $34
Re-issued in 1988.

1208.

Sweetheart
1100QX4479 • $34

1209.

Teacher
575QX4667 • $29

1210.
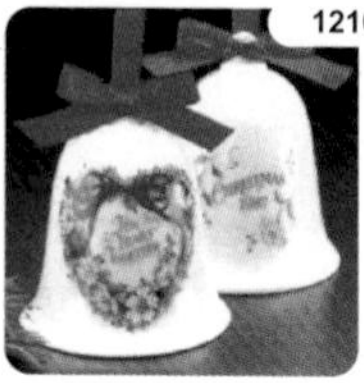
Ten Years Together
700QX4447 • $21

1211.

Thimble 10: Thimble Drummer
575QX4419 • $34

1212.

Three Men in a Tub
800QX4547 • $24

1213.

Time for Friends
475QX2807 • $30

1214.

Tin Locomotive 6
1475QX4849 • $47

1215.

Train Station
1275QLX7039 • $59
MAGIC.

1216.
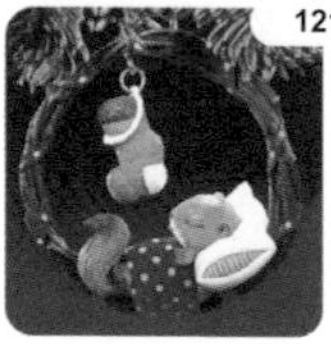
Treetop Dreams
675QX4597 • $30
Re-issued in 1988.

1217.

Treetop Trio
1100QX4256 • $39
Re-issued from 1986.

1218.

Twelve Days of Christmas 4: Four Colly Birds
650QX3709 • $40

1219.

Twenty-Five Years Together
750QX4439 • $20

1220.
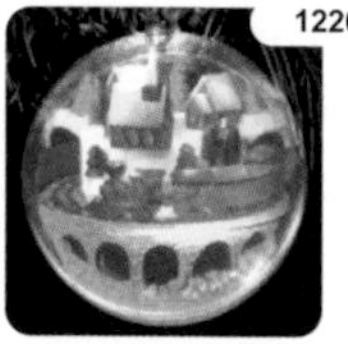
Village Express
2450QLX7072 • $87
MAGIC. Re-issued from 1986.

1221.

Walnut Shell Rider
600QX4196 • $31
Re-issued from 1986.

1222.

Warmth of Friendship
600QX3759 • $10

1223.

Wee Chimney Sweep
625QX4519 • $25

1224.

Windows of the World 3: Mele Kalikimaka
1000QX4827 • $30

1225.

Wood Childhood Ornaments 4: Horse
750QX4417 • $25

1226.

Word of Love
800QX4477 • $30

1227.

Wreath of Memories
($N/E)QXC5809 • $47

1988

1228.
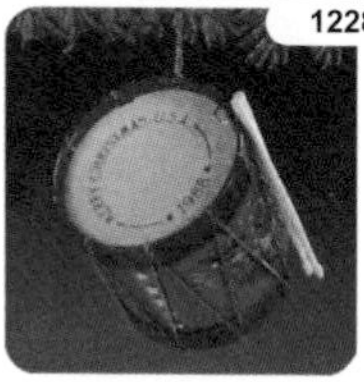
Americana Drum
775QX4881 • $30

1229.

Angelic Minstrel
2950QXC4084 • $42
Limited Edition - 49900.

1230.

Arctic Tenor
400QX4721 • $17

1231.

Baby Redbird
500QX4101 • $24

1232.

Baby's First Christmas
2400QLX7184 • $70
MAGIC.

1233.
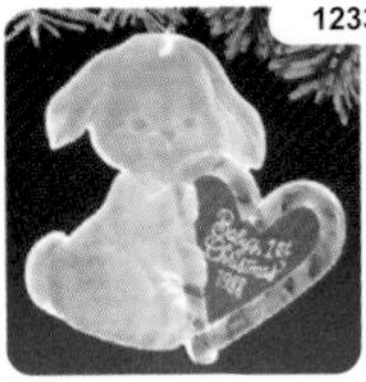
Baby's First Christmas
600QX3721 • $32

1234.

Baby's First Christmas
975QX4701 • $40

1235.

Baby's First Christmas
750QX4704 • $42

1236.

Baby's First Christmas (Boy)
475QX2721 • $32

1237.

Baby's First Christmas (Girl)
475QX2724 • $32

1238.

Baby's Second Christmas
600QX4711 • $43

1239.

Babysitter
475QX2791 • $17

1240.

Bearly Reaching
950QLX7151 • $38
MAGIC.

1241.

Betsey Clark: Home for Christmas 3
500QX2714 • $26

1242.

Child's Third Christmas
600QX4714 • $28

1243.

Chris Mouse 4: Chris Mouse Star
875QLX7154 • $98
MAGIC.

1244.
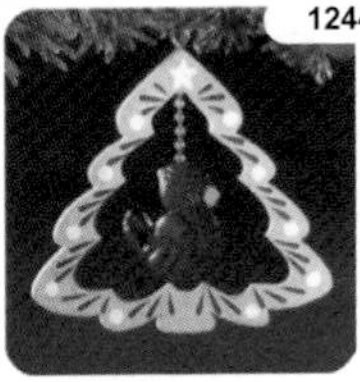
Christmas Cardinal
475QX4941 • $22

1245.

Christmas Classics 3: Night Before Christmas
1500QLX7161 • $43
MAGIC.

1246.

Christmas Cuckoo
800QX4801 • $31

1247.

Christmas Is Magic
1200QLX7171 • $54
MAGIC.

1248.

Christmas Is Sharing
1750QXC4071 • $48
Limited Edition - 49900.

1249.

Christmas Memories
650QX3724 • $35

1250.

Christmas Morning
2450QLX7013 • $48
MAGIC. Re-issued from 1987.

1251.

Circling The Globe
1050QLX7124 • $47
MAGIC.

1252.

Collector's Plate 2: Waiting for Santa
800QX4061 • $36

1253.

Cool Juggler
650QX4874 • $24

1254.

Country Express
2450QLX7211 • $68
MAGIC.

1255.

Cymbals of Christmas
550QX4111 • $49

1256.

Dad
700QX4141 • $28

1257.

Daughter
575QX4151 • $59

1258.

Feliz Navidad
675QX4161 • $53

1259.

Festive Feeder
1150QLX7204 • $61
MAGIC.

1260.

Fifty Years Together
675QX3741 • $15

1261.

Filled with Fudge
475QX4191 • $34

1262.
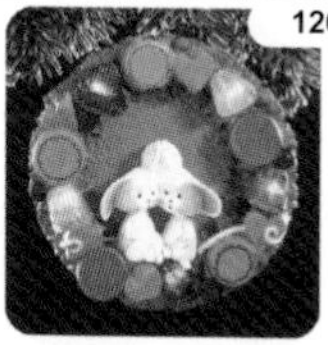
First Christmas Together
1200QLX7027 • $51
MAGIC.

1263.

First Christmas Together
475QX2741 • $28

1264.

First Christmas Together
675QX3731 • $28

1265.

First Christmas Together
900QX4894 • $32

1266.

Five Years Together
475QX2744 • $15

1267.

From Our Home To Yours
475QX2794 • $15

1268.

Frosty Friends 9
875QX4031 • $98

1269.

Glowing Wreath
600QX4921 • $19

1270.

Go For The Gold
800QX4174 • $25

1271.

Godchild
475QX2784 • $35

1272.

Goin' Cross Country
850QX4764 • $15

1273.

Gone Fishing
500QX4794 • $26
Re-issued in 1989.

1274.

Granddaughter
475QX2774 • $42

1275.

Grandmother
475QX2764 • $27

1276.

Grandparents
475QX2771 • $35

1277.

Grandson
475QX2781 • $36

1278.

Gratitude
600QX3754 • $12

1279.

Happy Holidata
650QX4717 • $30
Re-issued from 1987.

1280.
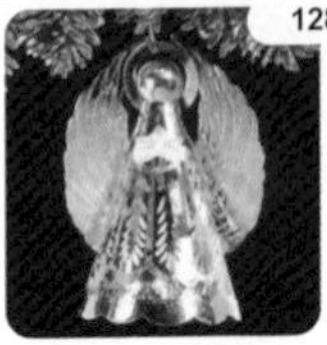
Heavenly Glow
1175QLX7114 • $34
MAGIC.

1281.

Here Comes Santa 10: Kringle Koach
1400QX4001 • $56

1282.

Hoe-Hoe-Hoe!
500QX4221 • $16

1283.
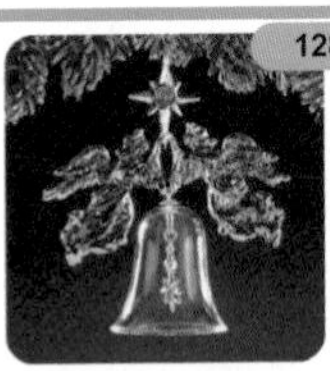
Holiday Heirloom 2
2500QX4064 • $30
Limited Edition - 34600.

1284.

Holiday Hero
500QX4231 • $27

1285.

Holiday Wildlife 7: Purple Finch
775QX3711 • $28

1286.
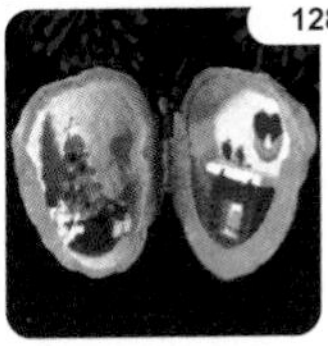
In a Nutshell
550QX4697 • $30
Re-issued from 1987.

1287.

Jingle Bell Clown
1500QX4774 • $32

1288.

Jolly Walrus
450QX4731 • $25

1289.

A Kiss From Santa
450QX4821 • $43
Re-issued in 1989.

1290.

Kiss the Claus
500QX4861 • $18

1291.

Kitty Capers
1300QLX7164 • $50
MAGIC.

1292.

Kringle Moon
550QX4951 • $32

1293.

Kringle Portrait
750QX4961 • $27

1294.

Kringle Tree
650QX4954 • $43

1295.

Kringle's Toy Shop
2450QLX7017 • $54
MAGIC. Re-issued in 1989.

1296.

Last-Minute Hug
2200QLX7181 • $52
MAGIC.

1297.

Little Jack Horner
800QX4081 • $24

1298.

Love Fills the Heart
600QX3744 • $25

1299.

Love Grows
475QX2754 • $53

1300.

Love Santa
500QX4864 • $18

1301.

Loving Bear
475QX4934 • $22
Twirl-About

1302.

Mary's Angels 1: Buttercup
500QX4074 • $130

1303.

Merry-Mint Unicorn
850QX4234 • $28

1304.
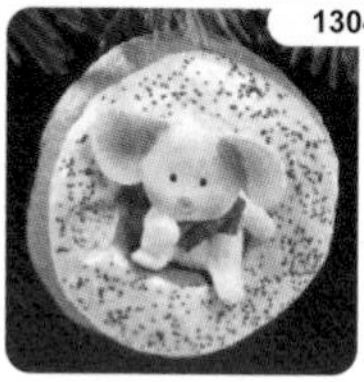
Midnight Snack
600QX4104 • $29

1305.

Miniature Creche 4
850QX4034 • $41

1306.

Mistletoad
700QX4687 • $32
Re-issued from 1987.

1307.

Moonlit Nap
875QLX7134 • $60
MAGIC. Re-issued in 1989.

1308.

Mother
650QX3751 • $24

1309.
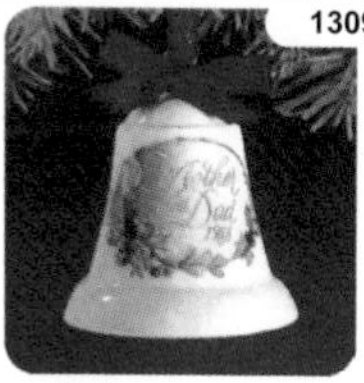
Mother and Dad
800QX4144 • $28

1310.

Mr. and Mrs. Claus 3: Shall We Dance
1300QX4011 • $65

1311.

New Home
600QX3761 • $26

1312.

Nick the Kick
500QX4224 • $22

1313.

Night Before Christmas
650QX4517 • $42
Re-issued from 1987.

1314.

Noah's Ark
850QX4904 • $60

1315.

Norman Rockwell: Christmas Scenes
475QX2731 • $34

1316.

Norman Rockwell 9: And To All a Good Night
775QX3704 • $23

1317.

Nostalgic Houses & Shops 5: Hall Bro's Card Shop
1450QX4014 • $65

1318.

Old-Fashioned Church
400QX4981 • $24

1319.

Old-Fashioned Schoolhouse
400QX4971 • $28

1320.

Oreo® Chocolate Sandwich Cookies
400QX4814 • $26
Re-issued in 1989.

1321.

Our Clubhouse
($N/E)QXC5804 • $34

1322.

Owliday Wish
650QX4559 • $24
Re-issued from 1987.

1323.

Par for Santa
500QX4791 • $22

1324.

Parade of theToys
2450QLX7194 • $53
MAGIC.

1325.

Party Line
875QX4761 • $26
Re-issued in 1989.

1326.

PEANUTS®
475QX2801 • $78

1327.

Peek-a-Boo Kitties
750QX4871 • $28
Re-issued in 1989.

1328.

Polar Bowler
500QX4784 • $20
Re-issued in 1989.

1329.
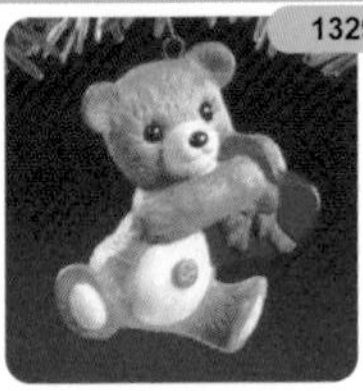
Porcelain Bear 6
800QX4044 • $31

1330.

Purrfect Snuggle
625QX4744 • $24

1331.
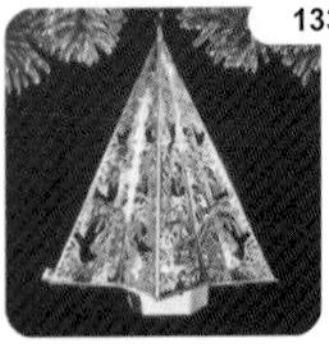
Radiant Tree
1175QLX7121 • $29
MAGIC.

1332.

Reindeer Champs 3: Prancer
750QX4051 • $32

1333.

Reindoggy
575QX4527 • $33
Re-issued from 1987.

1334.

Rocking Horse 8
1075QX4024 • $88

1335.

Sailing! Sailing!
850QX4911 • $28

1336.

Santa and Sparky 3: On With the Show
1950QLX7191 • $48
MAGIC.

1337.

Santa Flamingo
475QX4834 • $42

1338.

Shiny Sleigh
575QX4924 • $19

1339.
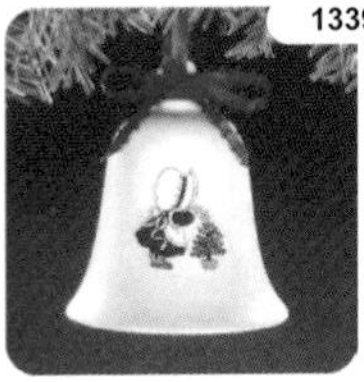
Sister
800QX4994 • $34

1340.

Skater's Waltz
2450QLX7201 • $65
MAGIC.

1341.

Sleighful Of Dreams
800QXC5801 • $32

1342.
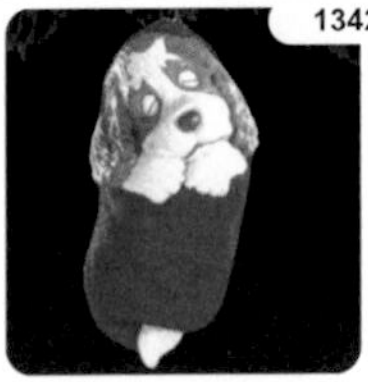
Slipper Spaniel
425QX4724 • $24

1343.
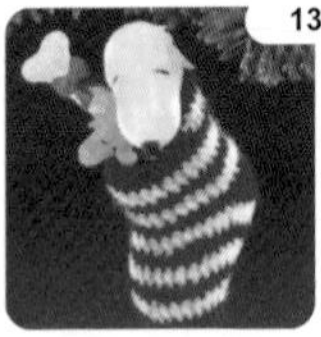
Snoopy® and Woodstock™
600QX4741 • $49

1344.

Soft Landing
700QX4751 • $23

1345.

Son
575QX4154 • $45

1346.

Song Of Christmas
850QLX7111 • $35
MAGIC.

1347.

Sparkling Tree
600QX4931 • $24

1348.

Spirit of Christmas
475QX2761 • $31

1349.

Squeaky Clean
675QX4754 • $34

1350.

St. Louie Nick
775QX4539 • $34
Re-issued from 1987.

1351.

Starry Angel
475QX4944 • $20

1352.

Sweet Star
500QX4184 • $36

1353.

Sweetheart
975QX4901 • $28

1354.

Teacher
625QX4171 • $30

1355.

Teeny Taster
475QX4181 • $30
Re-issued in 1989.

1356.

Ten Years Together
475QX2751 • $20

1357.

Thimble 11: Thimble Snowman
575QX4054 • $42

1358.

Tin Locomotive 7
1475QX4004 • $56

1359.

The Town Crier
550QX4734 • $20

1360.

Travels with Santa
1000QX4771 • $42

1361.

Tree Of Friendship
850QLX7104 • $15
MAGIC.

1362.
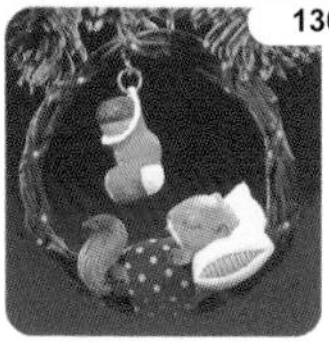
Treetop Dreams
675QX4597 • $30
Re-issued from 1987.

1363.
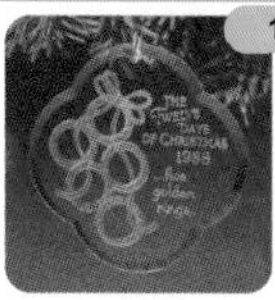
Twelve Days of Christmas 5: Five Golden Rings
650QX3714 • $39

1364.

Twenty-Five Years Together
675QX3734 • $24

1365.

Uncle Sam Nutcracker
700QX4884 • $37

1366.

Very Strawbeary
475QX4091 • $23

1367.

Windows of the World 4: Joyeaux Noel
1000QX4021 • $32

1368.

Winter Fun
850QX4781 • $40

1369.

The Wonderful Santacycle
2250QX4114 • $71

1370.

Wood Childhood Ornaments 5: Airplane
750QX4041 • $31

1371.

Year to Remember
700QX4164 • $22

1989

1372.
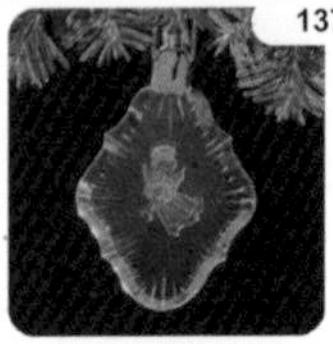
Angel Melody
950QLX7202 • $24
MAGIC.

1373.

The Animals Speak
1350QLX7232 • $95
MAGIC.

1374.
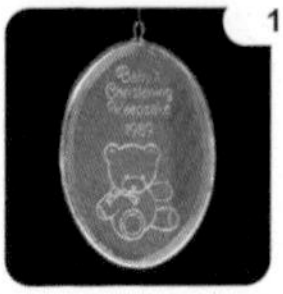
Baby Celebrations: Baby's Christening Keepsake
700BBY1325 • $40

1375.

Baby Celebrations: Baby's First Birthday
550BBY1729 • $30

1376.

Baby Partridge
675QX4525 • $16

1377.

Baby's First Christmas
3000QLX7272 • $60
MAGIC.

1378.
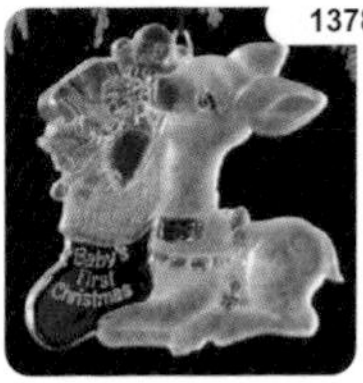
Baby's First Christmas
675QX3815 • $19

1379.

Baby's First Christmas
625QX4682 • $54

1380.

Baby's First Christmas (Boy)
475QX2725 • $30
Also issued as BBY1453.

1381.

Baby's First Christmas (Girl)
475QX2722 • $30
Also issued as BBY1553.

1382.

Backstage Bear
1350QLX7215 • $38
MAGIC.

1383.

Balancing Elf
675QX4895 • $24

1384.

Bear-i-Tone
475QX4542 • $17

1385.

Betsey Clark: Home for Christmas 4
500QX2302 • $36

1386.
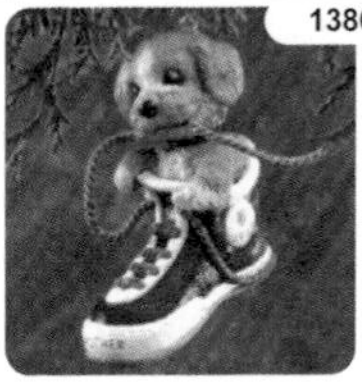
Brother
725QX4452 • $18

1387.

Busy Beaver
1750QLX7245 • $44
MAGIC.

1388.

Cactus Cowboy
675QX4112 • $38

1389.
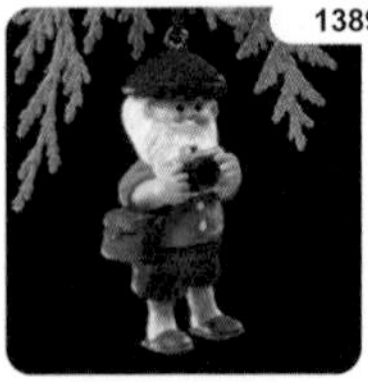
Camera Claus
575QX5465 • $14

1390.

Carousel Zebra
925QX4515 • $19

1391.
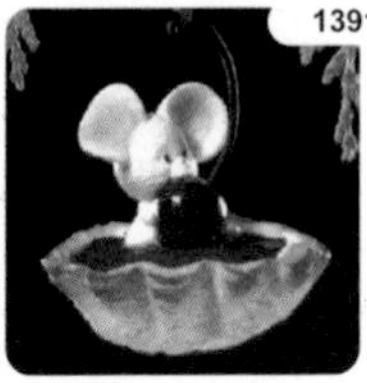
Cherry Jubilee
500QX4532 • $26

1392.

Child's Age: Baby's First Christmas
725QX4492 • $120

1393.

Child's Age: Baby's Second Christmas
675QX4495 • $40

1394.

Child's Age: Child's Third Christmas
675QX4695 • $34

1395.

Child's Age: Child's Fourth Christmas
675QX5432 • $24

1396.

Child's Age: Child's Fifth Christmas
675QX5435 • $24

1397.

Chris Mouse 5: Chris Mouse Cookout
950QLX7225 • $78
MAGIC.

1398.

Christmas Carousel Horse: Display Stand
100XPR9723 • $8

1399.

Christmas Carousel Horse: Ginger
395XPR9721 • $19

1400.

Christmas Carousel Horse: Holly
395XPR9722 • $19

1401.

Christmas Carousel Horse: Snow
395XPR9719 • $32

1402.

Christmas Carousel Horse: Star
395XPR9720 • $19

1403.

Christmas Classics 4: Little Drummer Boy
1350QLX7242 • $44
MAGIC.

1404.

Christmas Is Peaceful
1850QXC4512 • $40
Limited Edition - 49900.

1405.
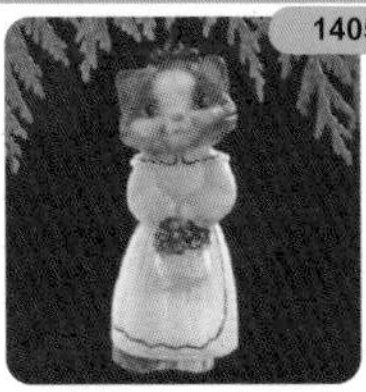
Christmas Kitty 1
1475QX5445 • $29

1406.

Claus Construction
775QX4885 • $35
Re-issued in 1990.

1407.

Collect A Dream
900QXC4285 • $35

1408.

Collector's Plate 3: Morning of Wonder
825QX4612 • $19

1409.

Cool Swing
625QX4875 • $37

1410.

Country Cat
625QX4672 • $22

1411.

Cranberry Bunny
575QX4262 • $25

1412.

Crayola® Crayon 1: Bright Journey
875QX4352 • $80

1413.

Dad
725QX4412 • $20

1414.

Daughter
625QX4432 • $24

1415.

Deer Disguise
575QX4265 • $28

1416.
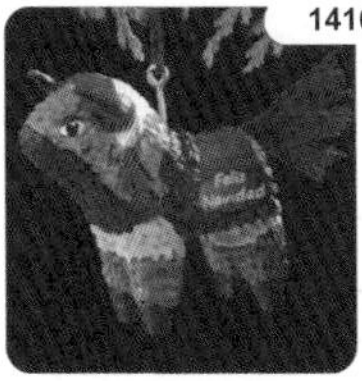
Feliz Navidad
675QX4392 • $60

1417.

Festive Angel
675QX4635 • $29

1418.

Festive Year
775QX3842 • $14

1419.

Fifty Years Together
875QX4862 • $14

1420.

The First Christmas
775QX5475 • $26

1421.

First Christmas Together
1750QLX7342 • $47
MAGIC.

1422.

First Christmas Together
475QX2732 • $29

1423.

First Christmas Together
675QX3832 • $26

1424.
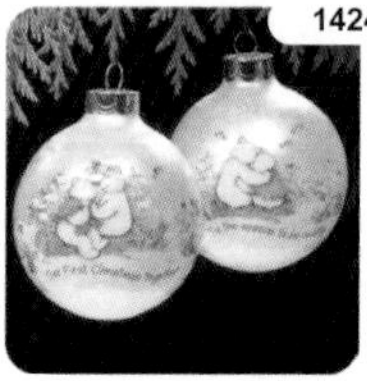
First Christmas Together
975QX4852 • $25

1425.

Five Years Together
475QX2735 • $19

1426.

Forest Frolics 1
2450QLX7282 • $86
MAGIC.

1427.

Forty Years Together
875QX5452 • $16

1428.

Friendship Time
975QX4132 • $29

1429.

From Our Home to Yours
625QX3845 • $20

1430.

Frosty Friends 10
925QX4572 • $58

1431.

Gentle Fawn
775QX5485 • $24

1432.

George Washington Bicentennial
625QX3862 • $15

1433.

Gift Bringers 1: St. Nicholas
500QX2795 • $23

1434.
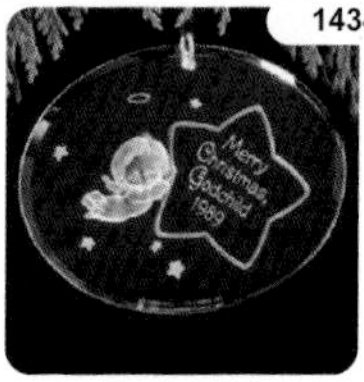
Godchild
625QX3112 • $14

1435.

Goin' South
425QX4105 • $24

1436.

Gone Fishing
575QX4794 • $26
Re-issued from 1988.

1437.
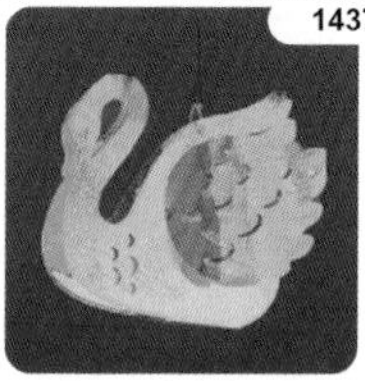
Graceful Swan
675QX4642 • $19

1438.

Granddaughter
475QX2782 • $29

1439.

Granddaughter's First Christmas
675QX3822 • $14

1440.

Grandmother
475QX2775 • $14

1441.

Grandparents
475QX2772 • $17

1442.

Grandson
475QX2785 • $29

1443.
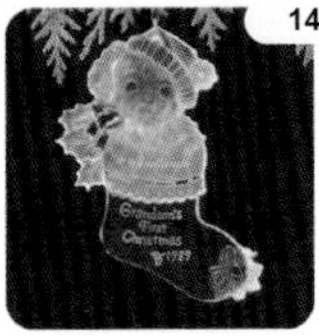
Grandson's First Christmas
675QX3825 • $13

1444.

Gratitude
675QX3852 • $11

1445.

Gym Dandy
575QX4185 • $16

1446.
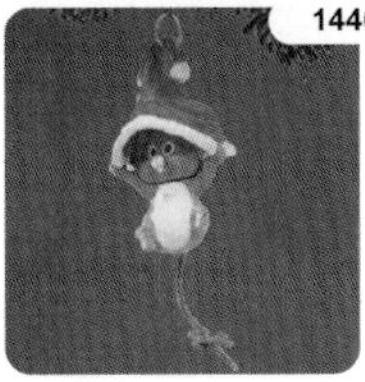
Hang in There
525QX4305 • $41

1447.
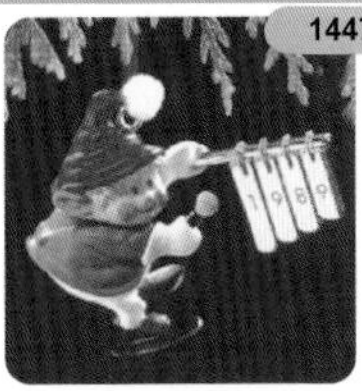
Hark! It's Herald 1
675QX4555 • $23

1448.

Here Comes Santa 11: Christmas Caboose
1475QX4585 • $59

1449.

Here's the Pitch
575QX5455 • $22

1450.

Holiday Bell
1750QLX7222 • $39
MAGIC.

1451.

Holiday Heirloom 3
2500QXC4605 • $40
Limited Edition - 34600.

1452.

Hoppy Holidays
775QX4692 • $19

1453.

Horse Weathervane
575QX4632 • $16

1454.

Joyful Trio
975QX4372 • $17

1455.

Joyous Carolers
3000QLX7295 • $77
MAGIC.

1456.

A Kiss From Santa
450QX4821 • $43
Re-issued from 1988.

1457.

Kringle's Toy Shop
2450QLX7017 • $54
MAGIC. Re-issued from 1988.

1458.

Kristy Claus
575QX4245 • $13

1459.

Language of Love
625QX3835 • $24

1460.

Let's Play
725QX4882 • $34

1461.

Loving Spoonful
1950QLX7262 • $45
MAGIC.

1462.

Mail Call
875QX4522 • $18

1463.

Mary's Angels 2: Bluebell
575QX4545 • $165

1464.

Merry-Go-Round Unicorn
1075QX4472 • $25

1465.

Metro Express
2800QLX7275 • $88
MAGIC.

1466.

Miniature Creche 5
925QX4592 • $20

1467.

Mom and Dad
975QX4425 • $28

1468.

Moonlit Nap
875QLX7134 • $60
MAGIC. Re-issued from 1988.

1469.

Mother
975QX4405 • $26

1470.

Mr. and Mrs. Claus 4: Holiday Duet
1325QX4575 • $58

1471.

New Home
475QX2755 • $24

1472.

Noelle
1975QXC4483 • $47
Limited Edition - 49900.

1473.

Norman Rockwell
475QX2762 • $22

1474.

North Pole Jogger
575QX5462 • $16

1475.

Nostalgic Houses & Shops 6: U.S. Post Office
1425QX4582 • $69

1476.

Nostalgic Lamb
675QX4665 • $18

1477.
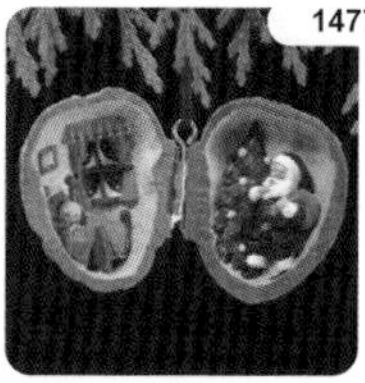
Nutshell Dreams
575QX4655 • $25

1478.
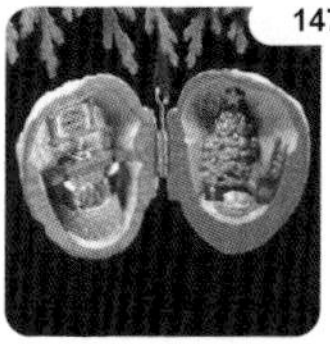
Nutshell Holiday
575QX4652 • $24
Re-issued in 1990.

1479.

Nutshell Workshop
575QX4872 • $24

1480.
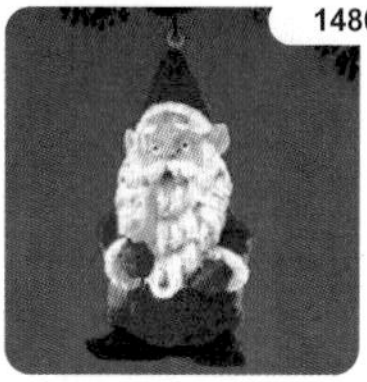
Old-World Gnome
775QX4345 • $20

1481.

On the Links
575QX4192 • $24

1482.
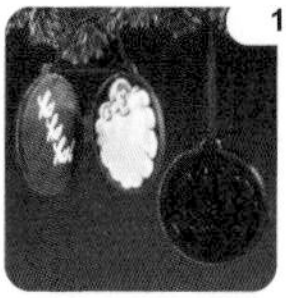
Oreo® Chocolate Sandwich Cookies
400QX4814 • $26
Re-issued from 1988.

1483.

The Ornament Express
2200QX5805 • $42 • Set/3

1484.

Owliday Greetings
400QX4365 • $17

1485.

Paddington™ Bear
575QX4292 • $32

1486.

Party Line
875QX4761 • $26
Re-issued from 1988.

1487.

PEANUTS®: A Charlie Brown® Christmas
475QX2765 • $70

1488.
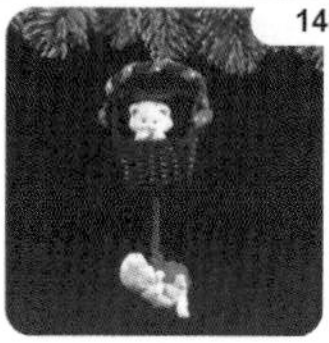
Peek-a-Boo Kitties
750QX4871 • $28
Re-issued from 1988.

1489.

Peppermint Clown
2475QX4505 • $58

1490.

Playful Angel
675QX4535 • $26

1491.

Polar Bowler
575QX4784 • $20
Re-issued from 1988.

1492.

Porcelain Bear 7
875QX4615 • $31

1493.

Reindeer Champs 4: Vixen
775QX4562 • $19

1494.

Rocking Horse 9
1075QX4622 • $62

1495.

Rodney Reindeer
675QX4072 • $14

1496.

Rooster Weathervane
575QX4675 • $14

1497.
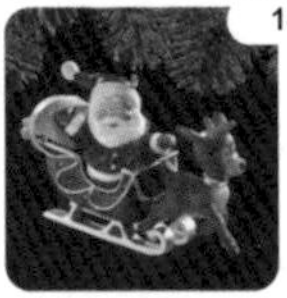
Rudolph The Red-Nosed Reindeer
1950QLX7252 • $45
MAGIC.

1498.

Sea Santa
575QX4152 • $29

1499.

Sister
475QX2792 • $17

1500.

Snoopy® and Woodstock™
675QX4332 • $38

1501.

Snowplow Santa
575QX4205 • $24

1502.

Son
625QX4445 • $30

1503.

Sparkling Snowflake
775QX5472 • $23

1504.

Special Delivery
575QX4325 • $18

1505.

Spencer® Sparrow, Esq.
675QX4312 • $26
Re-issued in 1990.

1506.

Spirit Of St. Nick
2450QLX7285 • $55
MAGIC.

1507.
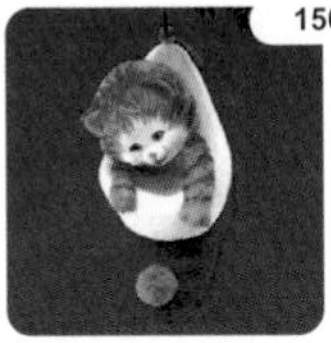
Stocking Kitten
675QX4565 • $17
Re-issued in 1990.

1508.

Sweet Memories
675QX4385 • $20

1509.

Sweetheart
975QX4865 • $35

1510.

Teacher
575QX4125 • $25

1511.

Teeny Taster
475QX4181 • $30
Re-issued from 1988.

1512.

Ten Years Together
475QX2742 • $29

1513.

Thimble 12: Thimble Puppy
575QX4552 • $30

1514.

Tin Locomotive 8
1475QX4602 • $45

1515.

Tiny Tinker
1950QLX7174 • $65
MAGIC.

1516.

TV Break
625QX4092 • $19

1517.

Twelve Days of Christmas 6: Six Geese A-Laying
675QX3812 • $20

1518.

Twenty-Five Years Together
875QX4855 • $13

1519.

Unicorn Fantasy
950QLX7235 • $30
MAGIC.

1520.

Visit From Santa
($N/E)QXC5802 • $52

1521.
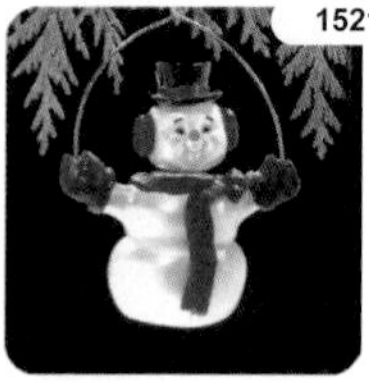
Wiggly Snowman
675QX4892 • $31

1522.

Windows of the World 5: Frohliche Weihnachten
1075QX4625 • $29

1523.
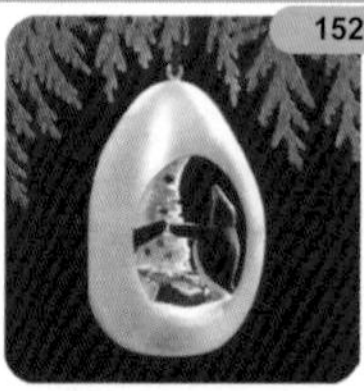
Winter Surprise 1
1075QX4272 • $25

1524.

Wood Childhood Ornaments 6: Truck
775QX4595 • $19

1525.

World of Love
475QX2745 • $38

1990

1526.
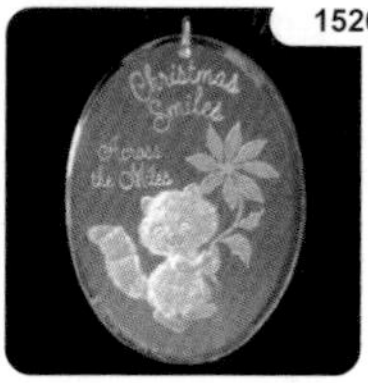
Across the Miles
675QX3173 • $14

1527.

Angel Kitty
875QX4746 • $24

1528.

Armful Of Joy
975QXC4453 • $32

1529.

Baby Celebrations: Baby's Christening
1000BBY1326 • $20

1530.

Baby Celebrations: Baby's First Christmas (Boy)
1000BBY1454 • $28

1531.

Baby Celebrations: Baby's First Christmas (Girl)
1000BBY1554 • $28

1532.
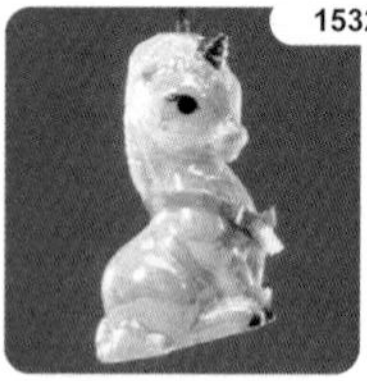
Baby Unicorn
975QX5486 • $20

1533.

Baby's First Christmas
2800QLX7246 • $65
MAGIC.

1534.

Baby's First Christmas
675QX3036 • $26

1535.
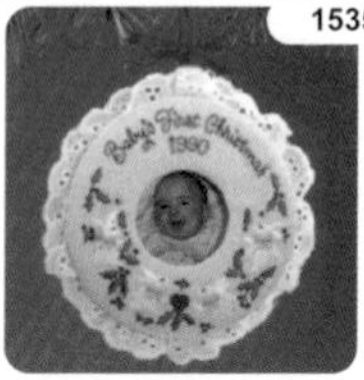
Baby's First Christmas
775QX4843 • $30

1536.
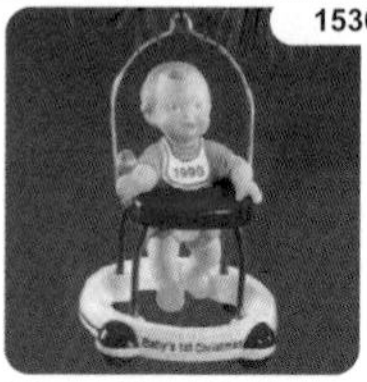
Baby's First Christmas
975QX4853 • $23

1537.

Baby's First Christmas (Boy)
475QX2063 • $26

1538.

Baby's First Christmas (Girl)
475QX2066 • $26

1539.

Bearback Rider
975QX5483 • $23

1540.
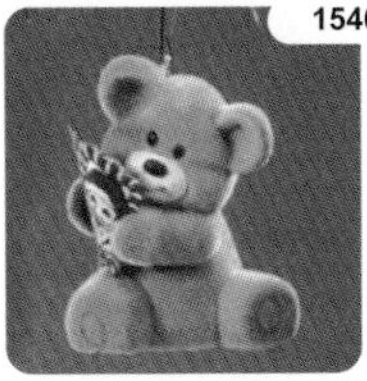
Beary Good Deal
675QX4733 • $17

1541.

Beary Short Nap
1000QLX7326 • $28
MAGIC.

1542.

Betsey Clark: Home for Christmas 5
500QX2033 • $24

1543.

Billboard Bunny
775QX5196 • $14

1544.

Blessings of Love
1400QLX7363 • $60
MAGIC.

1545.

Born to Dance
775QX5043 • $16

1546.

Brother
575QX4493 • $14

1547.
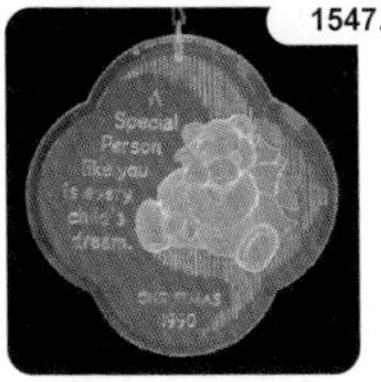
Child Care Giver
675QX3166 • $8

1548.

Child's Age: Baby's First Christmas
775QX4856 • $53

1549.

Child's Age: Baby's Second Christmas
675QX4863 • $46

1550.

Child's Age: Child's Third Christmas
675QX4866 • $28

1551.

Child's Age: Child's Fourth Christmas
675QX4873 • $18

1552.
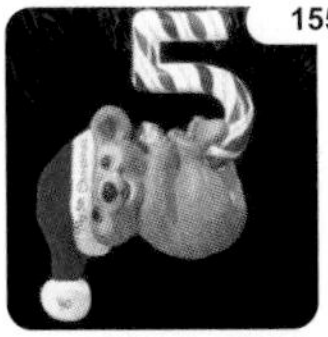
Child's Age: Child's Fifth Christmas
675QX4876 • $18

1553.

Children's Express
2800QLX7243 • $65
MAGIC.

1554.
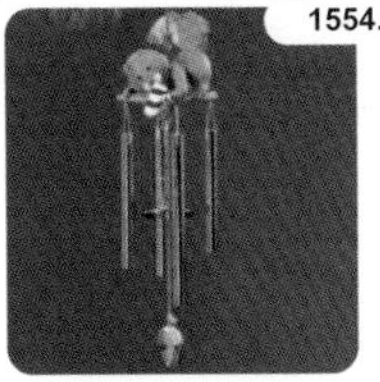
Chiming In
975QX4366 • $28

1555.

Chris Mouse 6: Chris Mouse Wreath
1000QLX7296 • $56
MAGIC.

1556.

Christmas Classics 5: The Littlest Angel
1400QLX7303 • $53
MAGIC.

1557.

Christmas Croc
775QX4373 • $23

1558.

Christmas Kitty 2
1475QX4506 • $29

1559.

Christmas Limited
1975QXC4766 • $108
Limited Edition - 38700.

1560.

Christmas Memories
2500QLX7276 • $50
MAGIC.

1561.
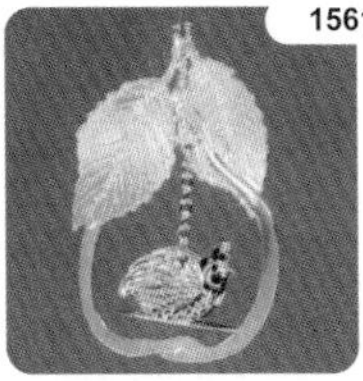
Christmas Partridge
775QX5246 • $17

1562.

Claus Construction
775QX4885 • $35
Re-issued from 1989.

1563.

Club Hollow
($N/E)QXC4456 • $32

1564.

Collector's Plate 4: Cookies for Santa
875QX4436 • $23

1565.
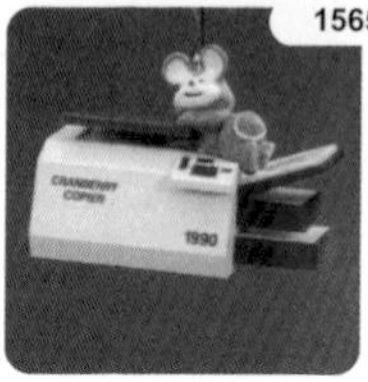

Copy of Cheer
775QX4486 • $14

1566.

Country Angel
675QX5046 • $127
Retailer display item only.

1567.

Coyote Carols
875QX4993 • $16

1568.

Cozy Goose
575QX4966 • $13

1569.

Crayola® Crayon 2: Bright Moving Colors
875QX4586 • $64

1570.

Dad
675QX4533 • $14

1571.

Dad-to-Be
575QX4913 • $19

1572.

Daughter
575QX4496 • $28

1573.

Deer Crossing
1800QLX7213 • $55
MAGIC.

1574.

Dickens Caroler Bell: Mr. Ashbourne
2175QX5056 • $22

1575.

Donder's Diner
1375QX4823 • $17

1576.
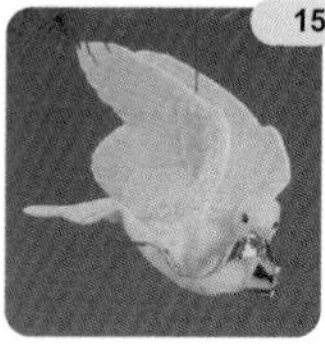

Dove Of Peace
2475QXC4476 • $65
Limited Edition - 25400.

1577.

Elf Of The Year
1000QLX7356 • $24
MAGIC.

1578.

Elfin Whittler
2000QLX7265 • $53
MAGIC.

1579.

Fabulous Decade 1
775QX4466 • $35

1580.

Feliz Navidad
675QX5173 • $32

1581.

Fifty Years Together
975QX4906 • $14

1582.

First Christmas Together
1800QLX7255 • $46
MAGIC.

1583.

First Christmas Together
475QX2136 • $28

1584.
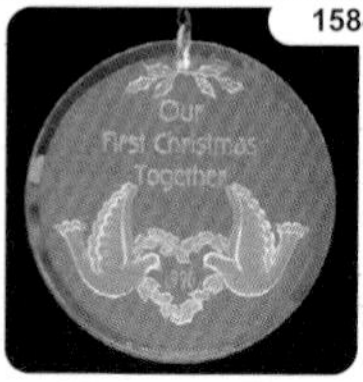

First Christmas Together
675QX3146 • $32

1585.
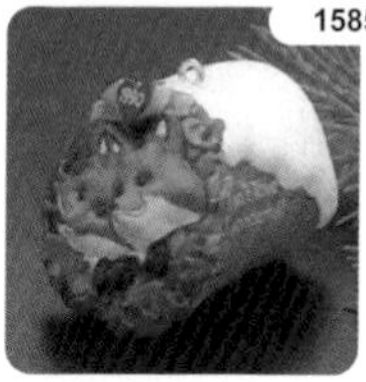

First Christmas Together
975QX4883 • $28

1586.
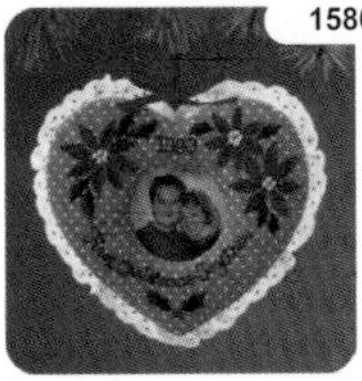
First Christmas Together
775QX4886 • $12

1587.
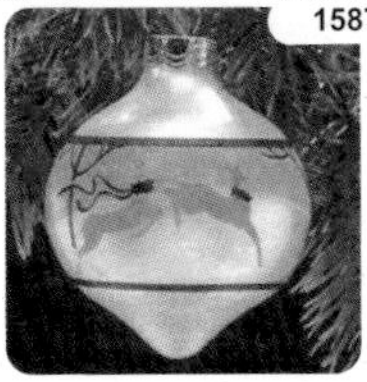
Five Years Together
475QX2103 • $15

1588.

Forest Frolics 2
2500QLX7236 • $70
MAGIC.

1589.
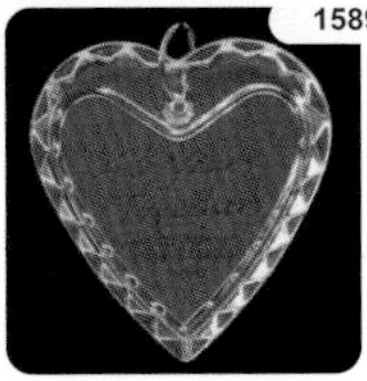
Forty Years Together
975QX4903 • $12

1590.

Friendship Kitten
675QX4143 • $26

1591.

From Our Home to Yours
475QX2166 • $12

1592.

Frosty Friends 11
975QX4396 • $42

1593.
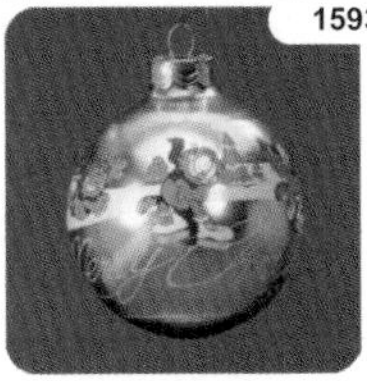
Garfield®
475QX2303 • $28

1594.

Gentle Dreamers
875QX4756 • $35

1595.

Gift Bringers 2: St. Lucia
500QX2803 • $20

1596.

Gingerbread Elf
575QX5033 • $24

1597.

Godchild
675QX3176 • $14

1598.

Golf's My Bag
775QX4963 • $28

1599.

Goose Cart
775QX5236 • $18

1600.

Granddaughter
475QX2286 • $28

1601.

Granddaughter's First Christmas
675QX3106 • $14

1602.

Grandmother
475QX2236 • $14

1603.

Grandparents
475QX2253 • $25

1604.

Grandson
475QX2293 • $35

1605.

Grandson's First Christmas
675QX3063 • $14

1606.
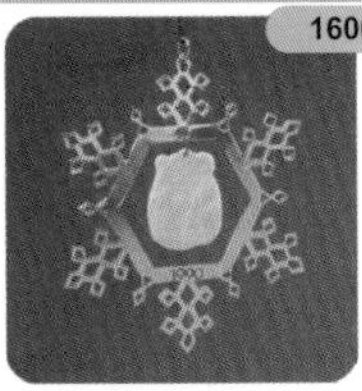
Greatest Story 1
1275QX4656 • $18

1607.

Hang in There
675QX4713 • $20

1608.

Happy Voices
675QX4645 • $15

1609.

Happy Woodcutter
975QX4763 • $24

1610.

Hark! It's Herald 2
675QX4463 • $18

1611.

Heart of Christmas 1
1375QX4726 • $45

1612.

Here Comes Santa 12: Festive Surrey
1475QX4923 • $65

1613.

Holiday Cardinals
775QX5243 • $22

1614.

Holiday Flash
1800QLX7333 • $42
MAGIC.

1615.

Home for the Owlidays
675QX5183 • $16

1616.

Hop 'N Pop Popper
2000QLX7353 • $118
MAGIC.

1617.

Hot Dogger
775QX4976 • $22

1618.

Jesus Loves Me
675QX3156 • $17

1619.

Jolly Dolphin
675QX4683 • $34

1620.

Joy is in the Air
775QX5503 • $29

1621.

King Klaus
775QX4106 • $22

1622.

Kitty's Best Pal
675QX4716 • $23

1623.

Letter To Santa
1400QLX7226 • $21
MAGIC.

1624.

Little Drummer Boy
775QX5233 • $22

1625.

Long Winter's Nap
675QX4703 • $29

1626.

Lovable Dears
875QX5476 • $19

1627.

Mary's Angels 3: Rosebud
575QX4423 • $114

1628.
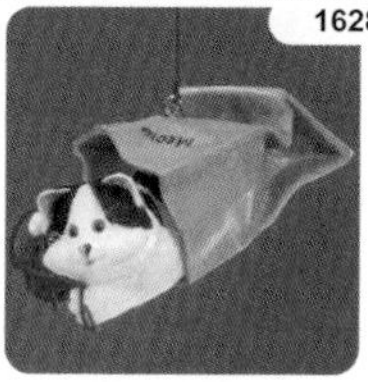
Meow Mart
775QX4446 • $25

1629.

Merry Olde Santa 1
1475QX4736 • $80

1630.

Mom and Dad
875QX4593 • $30

1631.

Mom-to-Be
575QX4916 • $32

1632.

Mooy Christmas
675QX4933 • $32

1633.

Mother
875QX4536 • $19

1634.

Mouseboat
775QX4753 • $17

1635.
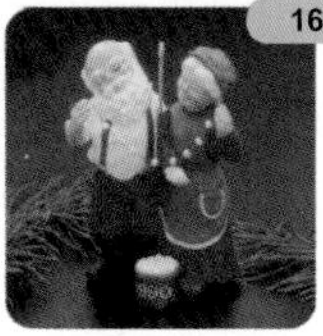
Mr. and Mrs. Claus 5: Popcorn Party
1375QX4393 • $79

1636.

Mrs. Santa's Kitchen
2500QLX7263 • $97
MAGIC.

1637.

New Home
675QX4343 • $29

1638.

Norman Rockwell Art
475QX2296 • $26

1639.

Nostalgic Houses & Shops 7: Holiday Home
1475QX4696 • $54

1640.
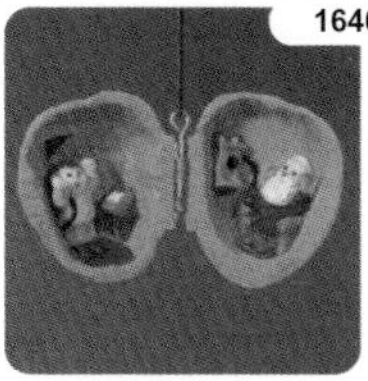
Nutshell Chat
675QX5193 • $22

1641.
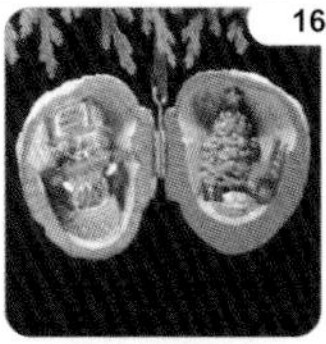
Nutshell Holiday
575QX4652 • $24
Re-issued from 1989.

1642.
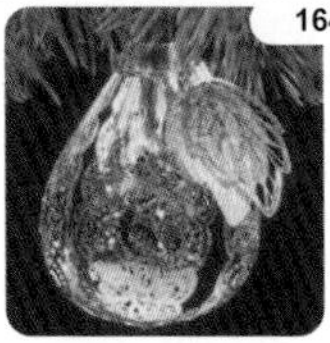
Partridges in a Pear
1400QLX7212 • $34
MAGIC.

1643.

Peaceful Kingdom
475QX2106 • $15

1644.

PEANUTS®
475QX2233 • $28

1645.
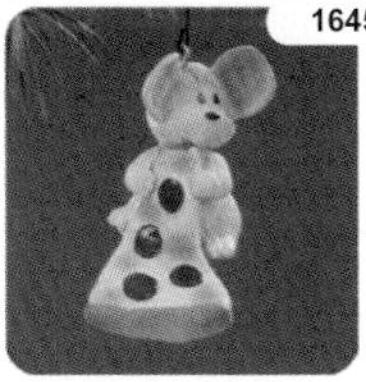
Pepperoni Mouse
675QX4973 • $20

1646.

Perfect Catch
775QX4693 • $24

1647.

Polar Jogger
575QX4666 • $18

1648.

Polar Pair
575QX4626 • $22

1649.

Polar Sport
775QX5156 • $24

1650.
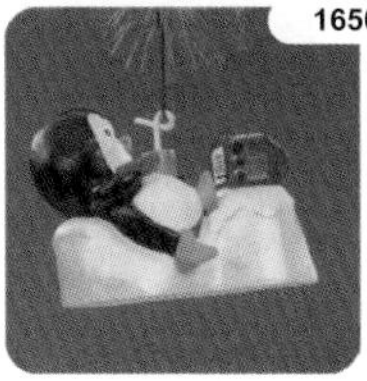
Polar TV
775QX5166 • $18

1651.

Polar V.I.P.
575QX4663 • $16

1652.

Polar Video
575QX4633 • $16

1653.

Poolside Walrus
775QX4986 • $18

1654.

Porcelain Bear 8
875QX4426 • $28

1655.

Reindeer Champs 5: Comet
775QX4433 • $35

1656.

Rocking Horse 10
1075QX4646 • $140

1657.

S. Claus Taxi
1175QX4686 • $28

1658.

Santa Schnoz
675QX4983 • $31

1659.

Santa's Ho-Ho-Hoedown
2500QLX7256 • $108
MAGIC.

1660.

Sister
475QX2273 • $26

1661.

Snoopy® and Woodstock™
675QX4723 • $49

1662.

Son
575QX4516 • $42

1663.

Song and Dance
2000QLX7253 • $88
MAGIC.

1664.

Spencer® Sparrow, Esq.
675QX4312 • $26
Re-issued from 1989.

1665.

Spoon Rider
975QX5496 • $17

1666.

Starlight Angel
1400QLX7306 • $36
MAGIC.

1667.

Starship Christmas
1800QLX7336 • $50
MAGIC.

1668.

Stitches of Joy
775QX5186 • $23

1669.

Stocking Kitten
675QX4565 • $17
Re-issued from 1989.

1670.

Stocking Pals
1075QX5493 • $22

1671.

Sugar Plum Fairy
2775QXC4473 • $58
Limited Edition - 25400.

1672.

Sweetheart
1175QX4893 • $19

1673.

Teacher
775QX4483 • $11

1674.

Ten Years Together
475QX2153 • $14

1675.

Three Little Piggies
775QX4996 • $16

1676.
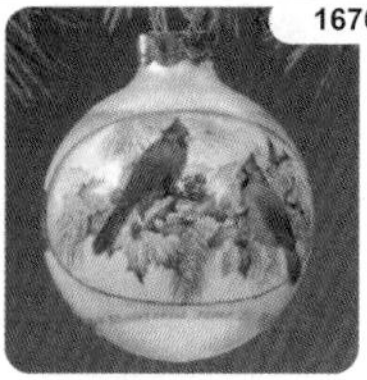
Time for Love
475QX2133 • $24

1677.
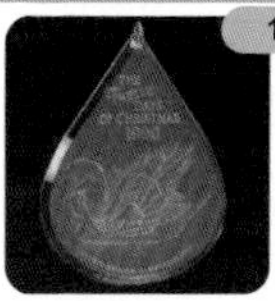
Twelve Days of Christmas 7: Seven Swans A-Swimming
675QX3033 • $28

1678.
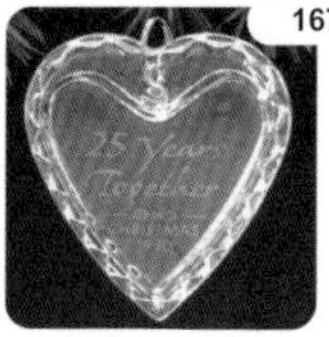
Twenty-Five Years Together
975QX4896 • $20

1679.

Two Peas in a Pod
475QX4926 • $42

1680.

Welcome, Santa
1175QX4773 • $24

1681.

Windows of the World 6: Nollaig Shona
1075QX4636 • $26

1682.
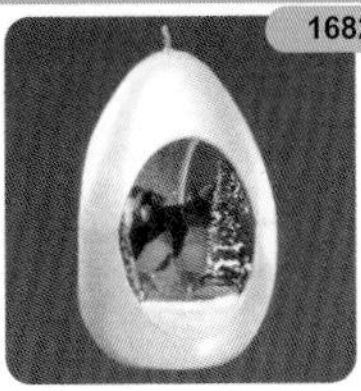
Winter Surprise 2
1075QX4443 • $22

1991

1683.

Across the Miles
675QX3157 • $13

1684.

All-Star
675QX5329 • $19

1685.

Arctic Dome
2500QLX7117 • $45
MAGIC.

1686.

Baby Celebrations: Baby's Christening
1000BBY1317 • $17

1687.

Baby Celebrations: Baby's First Christmas (Boy)
1000BBY1416 • $30

1688.

Baby Celebrations: Baby's First Christmas (Girl)
1000BBY1514 • $30

1689.

Baby's First Christmas
3000QLX7247 • $124
MAGIC.

1690.

Baby's First Christmas
775QX4869 • $28

1691.
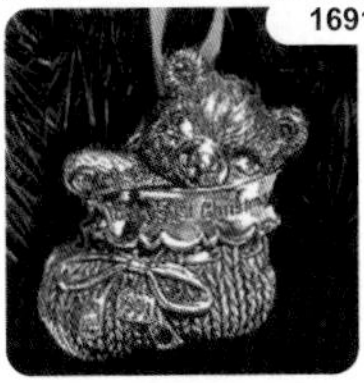
Baby's First Christmas
1775QX5107 • $47

1692.
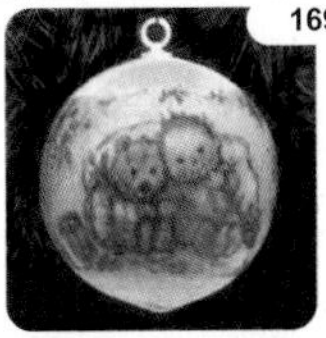
Baby's First Christmas (Boy)
475QX2217 • $24

1693.
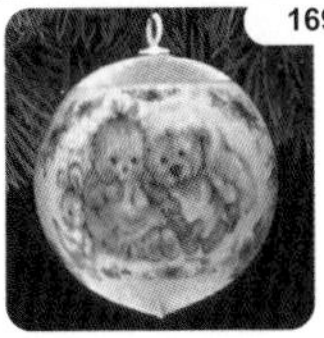
Baby's First Christmas (Girl)
475QX2227 • $28

1694.

Basket Bell Players
775QX5377 • $26

1695.

Beary Artistic
1000QXC7259 • $29
MAGIC.

1696.

Betsey Clark: Home for Christmas 6
500QX2109 • $22

1697.

The Big Cheese
675QX5327 • $14

1698.

Bringing Home The Tree
2800QLX7249 • $64
MAGIC.

1699.

Brother
675QX5479 • $22

1700.

Child's Age: Baby's First Christmas
775QX4889 • $65

1701.

Child's Age: Baby's Second Christmas
675QX4897 • $36

1702.

Child's Age: Child's Third Christmas
675QX4899 • $25

1703.

Child's Age: Child's Fourth Christmas
675QX4907 • $20

1704.
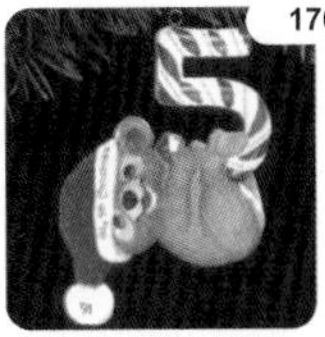
Child's Age: Child's Fifth Christmas
675QX4909 • $19

1705.

A Child's Christmas
975QX4887 • $14

1706.

Chilly Chap
675QX5339 • $22

1707.
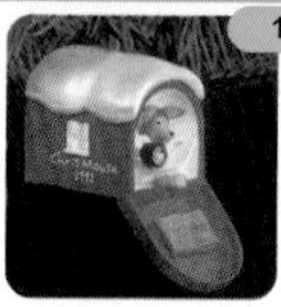
Chris Mouse 7:
Chris Mouse Mail
1000QLX7207 • $42
MAGIC.

1708.

Christmas Carol:
Bob Cratchit
1375QX4997 • $31

1709.

Christmas Carol:
Ebenezer Scrooge
1375QX4989 • $48

1710.

Christmas Carol:
Merry Carolers
2975QX4799 • $89

1711.

Christmas Carol:
Mrs. Cratchitt
1375QX4999 • $36

1712.

Christmas Carol:
Tiny Tim
1075QX5037 • $34

1713.

Christmas Kitty 3
1475QX4377 • $29

1714.
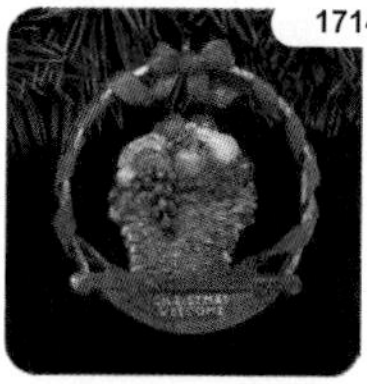
Christmas Welcome
975QX5299 • $28

1715.

Classic American Cars 1:
1957 Corvette®
1275QX4319 • $185

1716.

Claus & Co. RR:
Caboose
395XPR9733 • $13

1717.

Claus & Co. RR:
Gift Car
395XPR9731 • $11

1718.

Claus & Co. RR:
Locomotive
395XPR9730 • $29

1719.

Claus & Co. RR:
Passenger Car
395XPR9732 • $13

1720.
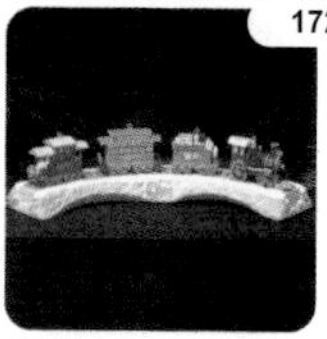
Claus & Co. RR:
Trestle Display Stand
295XPR9734 • $12

1721.

Collector's Plate 5:
Let It Snow!
875QX4369 • $27

1722.

Crayola® Crayon 3:
Bright Vibrant Carols
975QX4219 • $41

1723.

Cuddly Lamb
675QX5199 • $17

1724.

Dad
775QX5127 • $19

1725.

Dad-to-Be
575QX4879 • $11

1726.
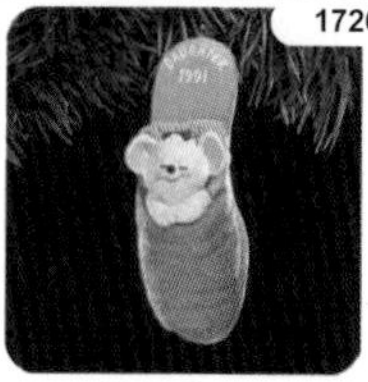
Daughter
575QX5477 • $41

1727.

Dickens Caroler Bell:
Mrs. Beaumont
2175QX5039 • $37

1728.

Dinoclaus
775QX5277 • $16

1729.

Elfin Engineer
1000QLX7209 • $24
MAGIC.

1730.

Extra-Special Friends
475QX2279 • $14

1731.

Fabulous Decade 2
775QX4119 • $40

1732.

Father Christmas
1400QLX7147 • $37
MAGIC.

1733.
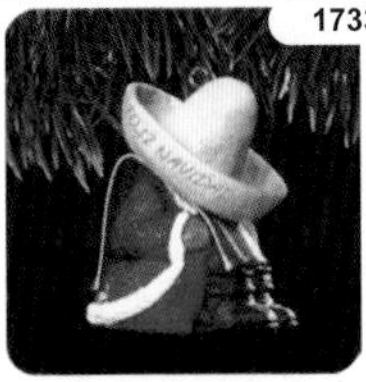
Feliz Navidad
675QX5279 • $32

1734.

Festive Brass Church
1400QLX7179 • $34
MAGIC.

1735.

Fiddlin' Around
775QX4387 • $12

1736.

Fifty Years Together
875QX4947 • $17

1737.
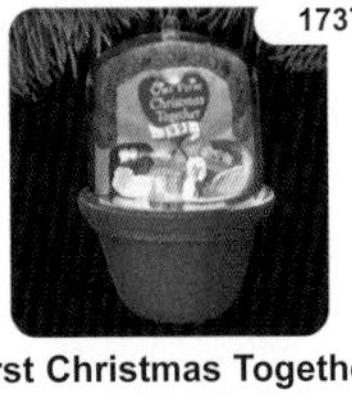
First Christmas Together
2500QLX7137 • $41
MAGIC.

1738.

First Christmas Together
475QX2229 • $30

1739.

First Christmas Together
675QX3139 • $30

1740.

First Christmas Together
875QX4917 • $22

1741.
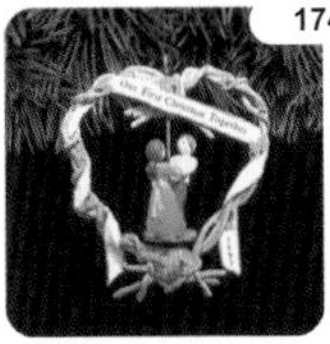
First Christmas Together
875QX4919 • $26
Twirl-About

1742.

Five Years Together
775QX4927 • $14

1743.

Five Years Together
($N/A)QXC3159 • $41

1744.

Flag Of Liberty
675QX5249 • $14

1745.

Folk Art Reindeer
875QX5359 • $13

1746.

Forest Frolics 3
2500QLX7219 • $65
MAGIC.

1747.

Forty Years Together
775QX4939 • $20

1748.

Friends Are Fun
975QX5289 • $22

1749.

Friendship Tree
1000QLX7169 • $28
MAGIC.

1750.

From Our Home to Yours
475QX2287 • $19

1751.

Frosty Friends 12
975QX4327 • $75

1752.

Galloping Into Christmas
1975QXC4779 • $95
Limited Edition - 28400.

1753.
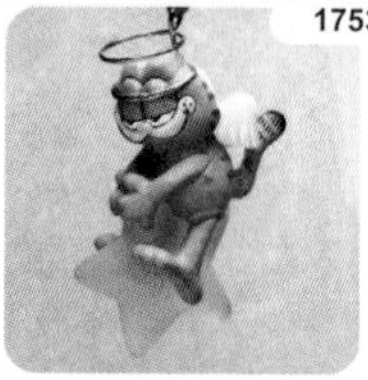
Garfield®
775QX5177 • $32

1754.

Gift Bringers 3: Christkindl
500QX2117 • $20

1755.

Gift of Joy
875QX5319 • $23

1756.

Godchild
675QX5489 • $24

1757.

Granddaughter
475QX2299 • $30

1758.

Granddaughter's First Christmas
675QX5119 • $18

1759.

Grandmother
475QX2307 • $8

1760.

Grandparents
475QX2309 • $10

1761.

Grandson
475QX2297 • $30

1762.

Grandson's First Christmas
675QX5117 • $17

1763.

Greatest Story 2
1275QX4129 • $20

1764.

Hark! It's Herald 3
675QX4379 • $20

1765.

Heart of Christmas 2
1375QX4357 • $25

1766.

Heavenly Angels 1
775QX4367 • $20

1767.

Here Comes Santa 13: Santa's Antique Car
1475QX4349 • $53

1768.

Hidden Treasure and Li'l Keeper
1500QXC4769 • $38 • Set/2

1769.

Holiday Glow
1400QLX7177 • $34
MAGIC.

1770.
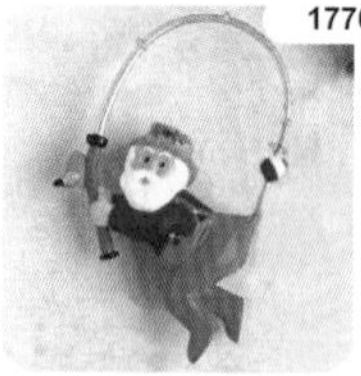
Hooked on Santa
775QX4109 • $35

1771.

It's A Wonderful Life
2000QLX7237 • $71
MAGIC.

1772.

Jesus Loves Me
775QX3147 • $14

1773.

Jingle Bears
2500QLX7323 • $45
MAGIC.

1774.

Jolly Wolly Santa
775QX5419 • $29

1775.

Jolly Wolly Snowman
775QX5427 • $30

1776.

Jolly Wolly Soldier
775QX5429 • $23

1777.

Joyous Memories
675QX5369 • $19

1778.

Kansas City Santa
($N/E)(N/A) • $655
Edition Size - 700.

1779.

Kringle's Bumper Cars
2500QLX7119 • $45
MAGIC.

1780.
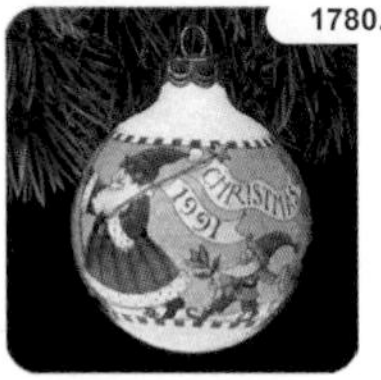

Mary Engelbreit
475QX2237 • $34

1781.

Mary's Angels 4: Iris
675QX4279 • $75

1782.

Matchbox Memories: Evergreen Inn
875QX5389 • $13

1783.

Matchbox Memories: Holiday Café
875QX5399 • $13

1784.

Matchbox Memories: Santa's Studio
875QX5397 • $20

1785.

Merry Olde Santa 2
1475QX4359 • $89

1786.

Mole Family Home
2000QLX7149 • $37
MAGIC.

1787.
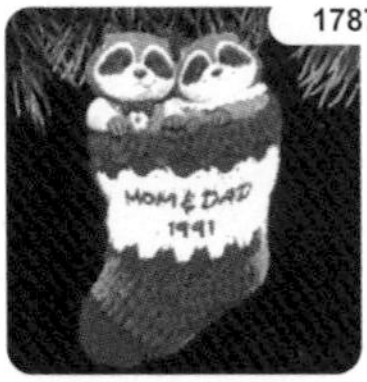

Mom and Dad
975QX5467 • $22

1788.

Mom-to-Be
575QX4877 • $15

1789.

Mother
975QX5457 • $35

1790.

Mr. and Mrs. Claus 6: Checking His List
1375QX4339 • $35

1791.

New Home
675QX5449 • $24

1792.

Night Before Christmas
975QX5307 • $24

1793.
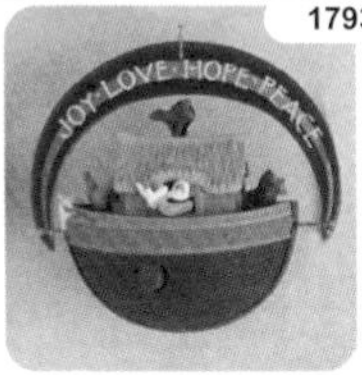

Noah's Ark
1375QX4867 • $39

1794.

Norman Rockwell Art
500QX2259 • $24

1795.

Nostalgic Houses & Shops 8: Fire Station
1475QX4139 • $74

1796.

Notes of Cheer
575QX5357 • $12

1797.
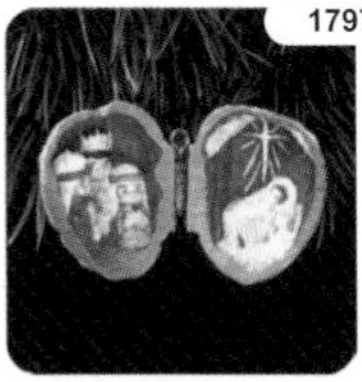

Nutshell Nativity
675QX5176 • $28

1798.

Nutty Squirrel
575QX4833 • $14

1799.

Old-Fashioned Sled
875QX4317 • $19

1800.
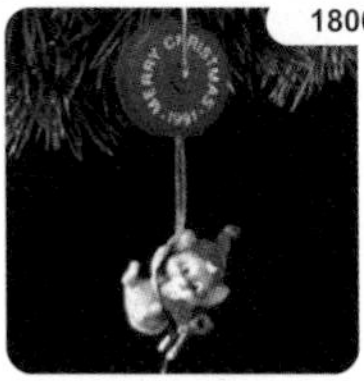

On a Roll
675QX5347 • $18

1801.

Partridge in a Pear Tree
975QX5297 • $19

1802.

Peace on Earth 1: Italy
1175QX5129 • $20

1803.

PEANUTS®
500QX2257 • $32

1804.

PEANUTS® 1
1800QLX7229 • $86
MAGIC.

1805.

Polar Circus Wagon
1375QX4399 • $19

1806.

Polar Classic
675QX5287 • $23

1807.

Puppy Love 1
775QX5379 • $115

1808.

Reindeer Champs 6: Cupid
775QX4347 • $22

1809.

Rocking Horse 11
1075QX4147 • $48

1810.

Salvation Army Band
3000QLX7273 • $90
MAGIC.

1811.

Santa Sailor
975QX4389 • $25

1812.

Santa Special
4000QLX7167 • $74
MAGIC. Re-issued in 1992.

1813.

Santa's Hot Line
1800QLX7159 • $46
MAGIC.

1814.

Santa's Premiere
1075QX5237 • $25

1815.

Secrets For Santa
2375QXC4797 • $46
Limited Edition - 28700.

1816.

Sister
675QX5487 • $19

1817.

Ski Lift Bunny
675QX5447 • $16

1818.
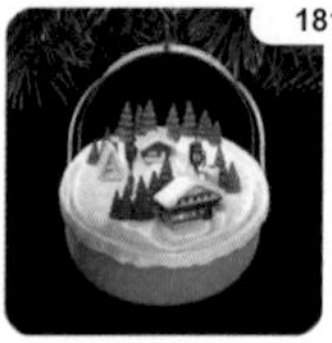
Ski Trip
2800QLX7266 • $38
MAGIC.

1819.

Snoopy® and Woodstock™
675QX5197 • $37

1820.

Snowy Owl
775QX5269 • $22

1821.
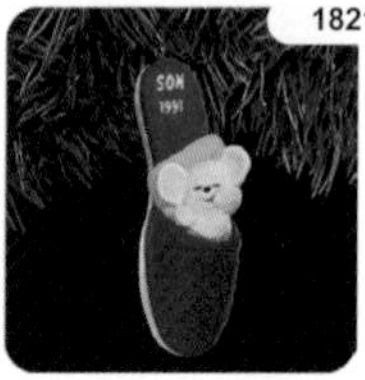
Son
575QX5469 • $30

1822.

Sparkling Angel
1800QLX7157 • $34
MAGIC.

1823.

Starship Enterprise™
2000QLX7199 • $309
MAGIC.

1824.
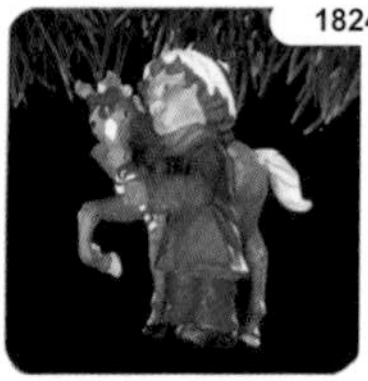
Sweet Talk
875QX5367 • $26

1825.

Sweetheart
975QX4957 • $23

1826.

Teacher
475QX2289 • $10

1827.

Ten Years Together
775QX4929 • $14

1828.

Tender Touches: Fanfare Bear
875QX5337 • $17

1829.

Tender Touches: Glee Club Bears
875QX4969 • $19

1830.

Tender Touches: Look Out Below
875QX4959 • $18

1831.

Tender Touches: Loving Stitches
875QX4987 • $26

1832.

Tender Touches: Plum Delightful
875QX4977 • $17

1833.

Tender Touches: Snow Twins
875QX4979 • $20

1834.

Tender Touches: Yule Logger
875QX4967 • $19

1835.

Terrific Teacher
675QX5309 • $10

1836.

Toyland Tower
2000QLX7129 • $48
MAGIC.

1837.

Tramp and Laddie
775QX4397 • $40

1838.

Twelve Days of Christmas 8: Eight Maids A-Milking
675QX3089 • $20

1839.

Twenty-Five Years Together
875QX4937 • $12

1840.

Under the Mistletoe
875QX4949 • $19

1841.

Up 'N' Down Journey
975QX5047 • $25

1842.

Winnie the Pooh: Christopher Robin
975QX5579 • $41

1843.

Winnie the Pooh: Kanga and Roo
975QX5617 • $49

1844.

Winnie the Pooh: Piglet and Eeyore
975QX5577 • $60

1845.

Winnie the Pooh: Rabbit
975QX5607 • $35

1846.

Winnie the Pooh: Tigger
975QX5609 • $95

1847.

Winnie the Pooh: Winnie the Pooh
975QX5569 • $61

1848.

Winter Surprise 3
1075QX4277 • $36

1992

1849.
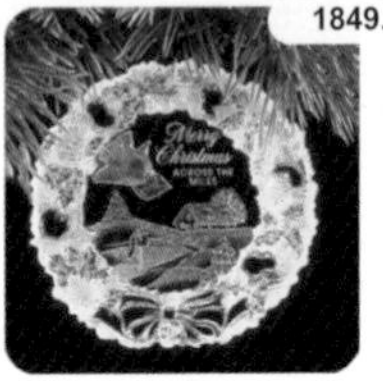
Across The Miles
675QX3044 • $10

1850.

Anniversary Year
975QX4851 • $20

1851.
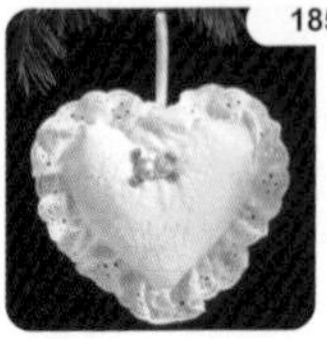
Baby Celebrations: Baby's Christening
850BBY1331 • $19

1852.

Baby Celebrations: Baby's First Christmas (Boy)
850BBY1456 • $28

1853.

Baby Celebrations: Baby's First Christmas (Girl)
850BBY1557 • $19

1854.

Baby's First Christmas
2200QLX7281 • $115
MAGIC.

1855.

Baby's First Christmas
1875QX4581 • $49

1856.

Baby's First Christmas
775QX4641 • $36

1857.

Baby's First Christmas (Boy)
475QX2191 • $25

1858.

Baby's First Christmas (Girl)
475QX2204 • $25

1859.

Bear Bell Champ
775QX5071 • $19

1860.

Betsey's Country Christmas 1
500QX2104 • $22

1861.

Brother
675QX4684 • $12

1862.

Cheerful Santa
975QX5154 • $22

1863.

Child's Age: Baby's First Christmas
775QX4644 • $42

1864.

Child's Age: Baby's Second Christmas
675QX4651 • $35

1865.

Child's Age: Child's Third Christmas
675QX4654 • $28

1866.

Child's Age: Child's Fourth Christmas
675QX4661 • $24

1867.

Child's Age: Child's Fifth Christmas
675QX4664 • $24

1868.

A Child's Christmas
975QX4574 • $17

1869.

Chris Mouse 8: Chris Mouse Tales
1200QLX7074 • $29
MAGIC.

1870.

Christmas Parade
3000QLX7271 • $77
MAGIC.

1871.

Classic American Cars 2: 1966 Mustang
1275QX4284 • $52

1872.

Coca-Cola® - Please Pause Here
1475QX5291 • $32

1873.

Collector's Plate 6: Sweet Holiday Harmony
875QX4461 • $18

1874.

Continental Express
3200QLX7264 • $86
MAGIC.

1875.

Cool Fliers
1075QX5474 • $18 • Set/2

1876.
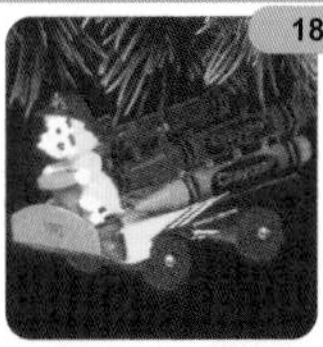
Crayola® Crayon 4: Bright Blazing Colors
975QX4264 • $44

1877.

Dad
775QX4674 • $22

1878.

Dad-To-Be
675QX4611 • $12

1879.

The Dancing Nutcracker
3000QLX7261 • $62
MAGIC.

1880.

Daughter
675QX5031 • $28

1881.

Deck The Hogs
875QX5204 • $25

1882.

Dickens Caroler Bell: Lord Chadwick
2175QX4554 • $29

1883.

Down-Under Holiday
775QX5144 • $16

1884.

Egg Nog Nest
775QX5121 • $21

1885.
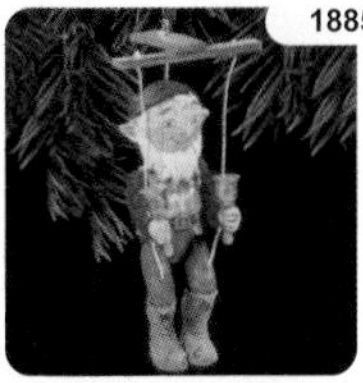
Elfin Marionette
1175QX5931 • $20

1886.

Elvis
1475QX5624 • $34

1887.

Enchanted Clock
3000QLX7274 • $55
MAGIC.

1888.

Fabulous Decade 3
775QX4244 • $65

1889.

Feathered Friends
1400QLX7091 • $35
MAGIC.

1890.

Feliz Navidad
675QX5181 • $35

1891.

For My Grandma
775QX5184 • $17

1892.

For The One I Love
975QX4844 • $23

1893.

Forest Frolics 4
2800QLX7254 • $59
MAGIC.

1894.

Friendly Greetings
775QX5041 • $12

1895.

Friendship Line
975QX5034 • $25

1896.

From Our Home To Yours
475QX2131 • $12

1897.

Frosty Friends 13
975QX4291 • $49

1898.

Fun On A Big Scale
1075QX5134 • $19

1899.

Garfield®
775QX5374 • $26

1900.

Genius At Work
1075QX5371 • $18

1901.

Gift Bringers 4: Kolyada
500QX2124 • $17

1902.

Godchild
675QX5941 • $20

1903.

Golf's A Ball
675QX5984 • $28

1904.

Gone Wishin'
875QX5171 • $35

1905.

Good Sledding Ahead
2800QLX7244 • $54
MAGIC.

1906.
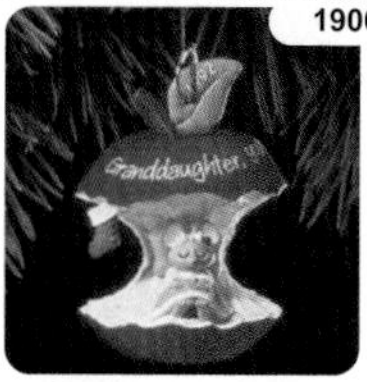
Granddaughter
675QX5604 • $25

1907.

Granddaughter's First Christmas
675QX4634 • $18

1908.

Grandmother
475QX2011 • $16

1909.

Grandparents
475QX2004 • $18

1910.
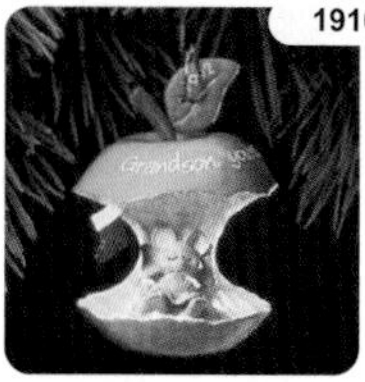
Grandson
675QX5611 • $22

1911.

Grandson's First Christmas
675QX4621 • $17

1912.

Greatest Story 3
1275QX4251 • $20

1913.

Green Thumb Santa
775QX5101 • $17

1914.

Hark! It's Herald 4
775QX4464 • $15

1915.
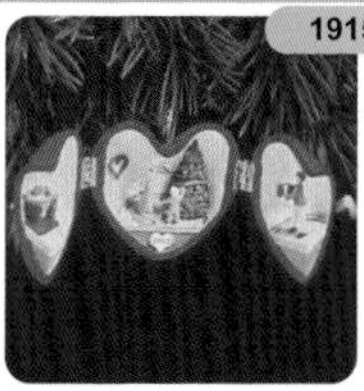
Heart of Christmas 3
1375QX4411 • $23

1916.

Heavenly Angels 2
775QX4454 • $24

1917.

Hello-Ho-Ho
975QX5141 • $21

1918.

Here Comes Santa 14: Kringle Tours
1475QX4341 • $44

1919.

Holiday Memo
775QX5044 • $14

1920.

Holiday Teatime
1475QX5431 • $25 • Set/2

1921.
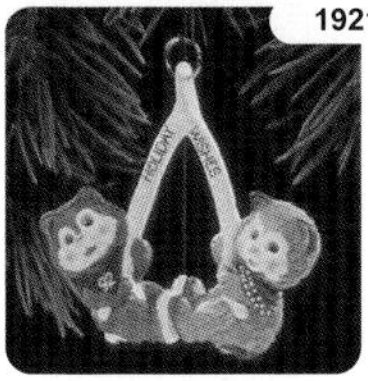
Holiday Wishes
775QX5131 • $19

1922.

Honest George
775QX5064 • $14

1923.

Jesus Loves Me
775QX3024 • $15

1924.

Lighting The Way
1800QLX7231 • $41
MAGIC.

1925.

Look! It's Santa
1400QLX7094 • $42
MAGIC.

1926.

Love To Skate
875QX4841 • $22

1927.

Loving Shepherd
775QX5151 • $18

1928.

Mary's Angels 5: Lily
675QX4274 • $130

1929.

Memories To Cherish
1075QX5161 • $24

1930.

Merry Olde Santa 3
1475QX4414 • $36

1931.

Merry Swiss Mouse
775QX5114 • $16

1932.

Mom
775QX5164 • $26

1933.

Mom and Dad
975QX4671 • $41

1934.

Mom-to-Be
675QX4614 • $12

1935.

Mother Goose
1375QX4984 • $28

1936.

Mr. and Mrs. Claus 7: Gift Exchange
1475QX4294 • $35

1937.

New Home
875QX5191 • $18

1938.

Norman Rockwell Art
500QX2224 • $18

1939.

North Pole Fire Fighter
975QX5104 • $26

1940.

North Pole Nutcrackers: Eric The Baker
875QX5244 • $18

1941.
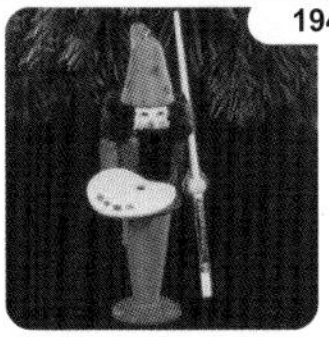
North Pole Nutcrackers: Franz The Artist
875QX5261 • $41

1942.

North Pole Nutcrackers: Frieda The Animals' Friend
875QX5264 • $26

1943.
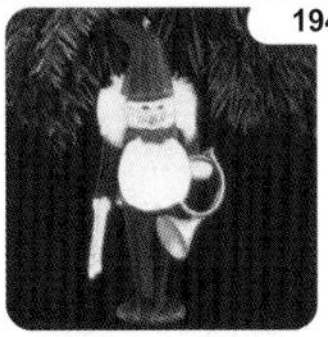
North Pole Nutcrackers: Ludwig The Musician
875QX5281 • $26

1944.

North Pole Nutcrackers: Max The Tailor
875QX5251 • $20

1945.

North Pole Nutcrackers: Otto The Carpenter
875QX5254 • $22

1946.

Nostalgic Houses & Shops 9: Five and Ten Cent Store
1475QX4254 • $52

1947.

Nut Sweet Nut
1000QLX7081 • $24
MAGIC.

1948.

O Christmas Tree
1075QX5411 • $24

1949.

Our First Christmas Together
2000QLX7221 • $48
MAGIC.

1950.

Our First Christmas Together
675QX3011 • $18

1951.

Our First Christmas Together
875QX4694 • $14

1952.

Our First Christmas Together
975QX5061 • $32

1953.

Owl
975QX5614 • $28

1954.

Owliver 1
775QX4544 • $16

1955.
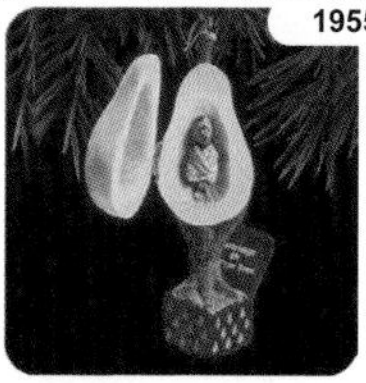
Partridge in a Pear Tree
875QX5234 • $20

1956.

Peace on Earth 2: Spain
1175QX5174 • $24

1957.

PEANUTS®
500QX2244 • $49

1958.

PEANUTS® 2
1800QLX7214 • $55
MAGIC.

1959.

Polar Post
875QX4914 • $24

1960.

Puppy Love 2
775QX4484 • $80

1961.

Rapid Delivery
875QX5094 • $14

1962.
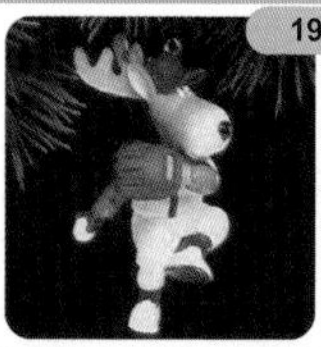
Reindeer Champs 7: Donder
875QX5284 • $30

1963.

Rocking Horse 12
1075QX4261 • $38

1964.

Rodney Takes Flight
($N/E)QXC5081 • $24

1965.

Santa and His Reindeer: Comet and Cupid
495XPR9737 • $26

1966.

Santa and His Reindeer: Dasher and Dancer
495XPR9735 • $36

1967.

Santa and His Reindeer: Donder and Blitzen
495XPR9738 • $32

1968.

Santa and His Reindeer: Prancer and Vixen
495XPR9736 • $28

1969.

Santa and His Reindeer: Santa Claus and Sleigh
495XPR9739 • $22

1970.

Santa Maria
1275QX5074 • $18

1971.

Santa Special
4000QLX7167 • $74
MAGIC. Re-issued from 1991.

1972.

Santa Sub
1800QLX7321 • $42
MAGIC.

1973.

A Santa-Full!
975QX5991 • $41

1974.

Santa's Answering Machine
2200QLX7241 • $36
MAGIC.

1975.

Santa's Club List
1500QXC7291 • $32
MAGIC.

1976.

Santa's Hook Shot
1275QX5434 • $26 • Set/2

1977.

Santa's Roundup
875QX5084 • $20

1978.

Secret Pal
775QX5424 • $10

1979.

Shuttlecraft Galileo™ from the Starship Enterprise™
2400QLX7331 • $42
MAGIC.

1980.

Silver Star Train Set
2800QX5324 • $50 • Set/3

1981.

Sister
675QX4681 • $18

1982.

Skiing 'Round
875QX5214 • $18

1983.

Skyline: Caboose
975QX5321 • $22

1984.

Skyline: Coal Car
975QX5401 • $18

1985.

Skyline: Locomotive
975QX5311 • $38

1986.
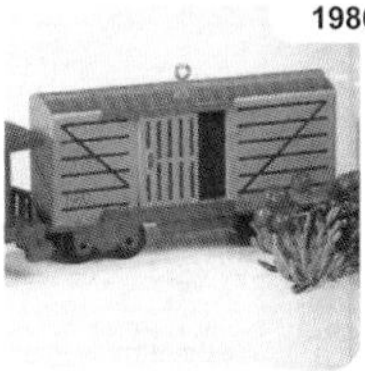
Skyline: Stock Car
975QX5314 • $19

1987.

Snoopy® and Woodstock™
875QX5954 • $42

1988.

Son
675QX5024 • $32

1989.

Special Cat
775QX5414 • $19

1990.

Special Dog
775QX5421 • $23

1991.

Spirit Of Christmas Stress
875QX5231 • $18

1992.

Stocked With Joy
775QX5934 • $21

1993.

Tasty Christmas
975QX5994 • $29

1994.
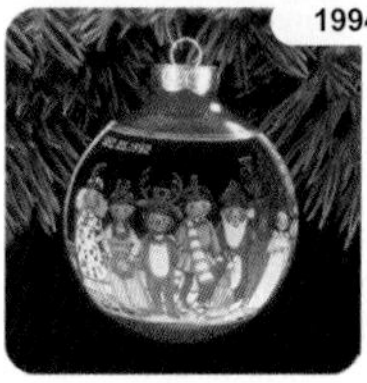
Teacher
475QX2264 • $26

1995.

Tobin Fraley Carousel 1
2800QX4891 • $39

1996.

Toboggan Tail
775QX5459 • $13

1997.
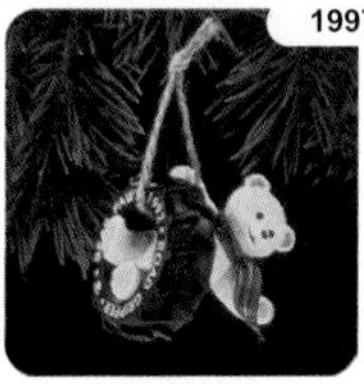
Tread Bear
875QX5091 • $32

1998.

Turtle Dreams
875QX4991 • $26

1999.

Twelve Days of Christmas 9: Nine Ladies Dancing
675QX3031 • $24

2000.

Uncle Art's Ice Cream
875QX5001 • $21

2001.

Under Construction
1800QLX7324 • $40
MAGIC.

2002.

V.P. of Important Stuff
675QX5051 • $18

2003.

Victorian Skater
2500QXC4067 • $53
Limited Edition - 14700.

2004.

Watch Owls
1200QLX7084 • $24
MAGIC.

2005.

Winter Surprise 4
1175QX4271 • $24

2006.

World-Class Teacher
775QX5054 • $13

2007.

Yuletide Rider
2800QLX7314 • $55
MAGIC.

1993

2008.

Across the Miles
875QX5912 • $20

2009.
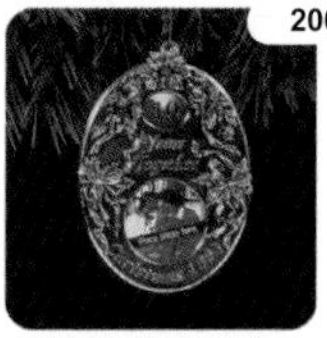
Anniversary Year Photo Holder
975QX5972 • $18

2010.

Apple for Teacher
775QX5902 • $17

2011.

Baby Block Photo Holder
1475QP6035 • $29
Re-issued in 1994.

2012.
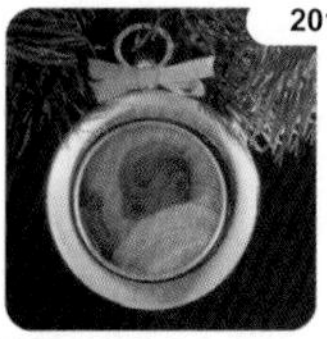
Baby Celebrations: Baby's Christening
1000BBY1335 • $29

2013.

Baby Celebrations: Baby's First Christmas
1000BBY1470 • $32

2014.
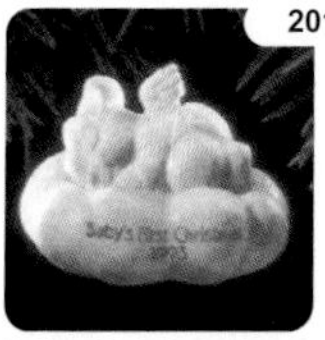
Baby Celebrations: Baby's First Christmas
1200BBY2918 • $23

2015.

Baby Celebrations: Baby's First Christmas
1400BBY2919 • $30

2016.
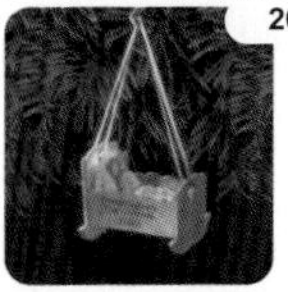
Baby Celebrations: Granddaughter's First Christmas
1400BBY2802 • $30

2017.

Baby Celebrations: Grandson's First Christmas
1400BBY2801 • $30

2018.

Baby's First Christmas
2200QLX7365 • $39
MAGIC.

2019.

Baby's First Christmas
1875QX5512 • $38

2020.
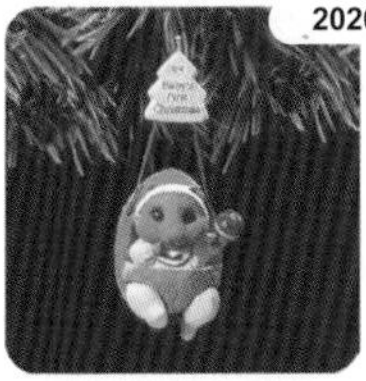
Baby's First Christmas
1075QX5515 • $24

2021.

Baby's First Christmas
775QX5522 • $37

2022.

Baby's First Christmas (Boy)
475QX2105 • $20

2023.

Baby's First Christmas (Girl)
475QX2092 • $20

2024.

Bearingers of Victoria Circle: Abearnathy Bearinger
495XPR9747 • $10

2025.

Bearingers of Victoria Circle: Bearnadette Bearinger
495XPR9748 • $10

2026.

Bearingers of Victoria Circle: Fireplace Base
495XPR9749 • $10

2027.

Bearingers of Victoria Circle: Mama Bearinger
495XPR9745 • $10

2028.

Bearingers of Victoria Circle: Papa Bearinger
495XPR9746 • $10

2029.

Beary Gifted
775QX5762 • $19

2030.

Bells are Ringing
2800QLX7402 • $54
MAGIC.

2031.
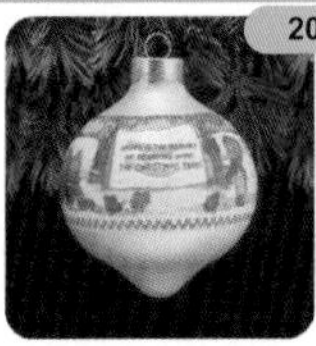
Betsey's Country Christmas 2
500QX2062 • $19

2032.
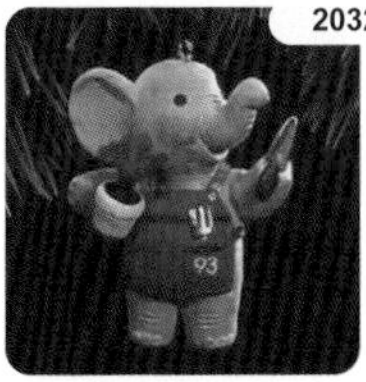
Big On Gardening
975QX5842 • $15

2033.

Big Roller
875QX5352 • $17

2034.

Bird-Watcher
975QX5252 • $13

2035.

Bowling for ZZZs
775QX5565 • $12

2036.

Brother
675QX5542 • $10

2037.

Bugs Bunny™
875QX5412 • $23

2038.

Caring Nurse
675QX5785 • $18

2039.

Child's Age: Baby's First Christmas
775QX5525 • $40

2040.

Child's Age: Baby's Second Christmas
675QX5992 • $30

2041.
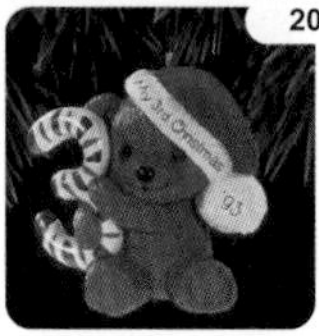
Child's Age: Child's Third Christmas
675QX5995 • $24

2042.

Child's Age: Child's Fourth Christmas
675QX5215 • $22

2043.
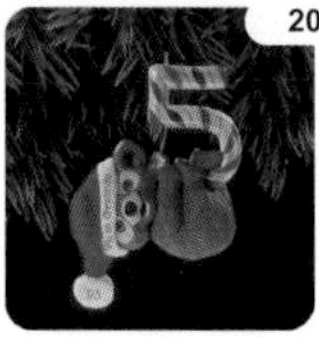
Child's Age: Child's Fifth Christmas
675QX5222 • $19

2044.

A Child's Christmas
975QX5882 • $24

2045.

Chris Mouse 9: Chris Mouse Flight
1200QLX7152 • $29
MAGIC.

2046.

Christmas Break
775QX5825 • $18

2047.

Circle of Friendship
($N/A)QXC2112 • $183

2048.

Classic American Cars 3: 1956 Ford® Thunderbird™
1275QX5275 • $45

2049.

Clever Cookie
775QX5662 • $24

2050.
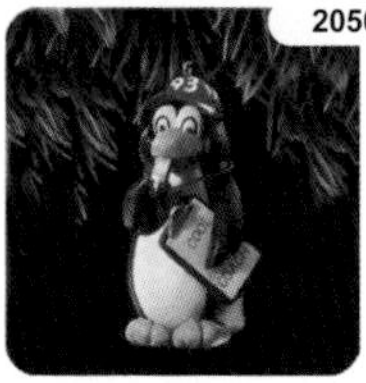
Coach
675QX5935 • $18

2051.

Coca-Cola® - Playful Pals
1475QX5742 • $26

2052.

Cool Snowman
875QP6052 • $30

2053.

Crayola® Crayon 5: Bright Shining Castle
1075QX4422 • $30

2054.
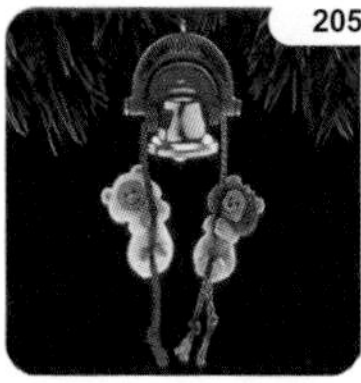
Curly 'n' Kingly
1075QX5285 • $18

2055.

Dad
775QX5855 • $16

2056.

Dad-to-Be
675QX5532 • $10

2057.

Daughter
675QX5872 • $16

2058.

Dickens Caroler Bell: Lady Daphne
2175QX5505 • $31

2059.

Dog's Best Friend
1200QLX7172 • $23
MAGIC.

2060.

Dollhouse Dreams
2200QLX7372 • $44
MAGIC.

2061.

Dunkin' Roo®
775QX5575 • $17

2062.

Elmer Fudd™
875QX5495 • $18

2063.

Fabulous Decade 4
775QX4475 • $19

2064.

Faithful Fire Fighter
775QX5782 • $17

2065.

Feliz Navidad
875QX5365 • $21

2066.

Festive Album Photo Holder
1275QP6025 • $18
Re-issued in 1994.

2067.

Filled with Cookies
1275QP6042 • $18

2068.

Fills the Bill
875QX5572 • $19

2069.

Folk Art Americana: Angel in Flight
1575QK1052 • $44

2070.

Folk Art Americana: Polar Bear Adventure
1500QK1055 • $85

2071.

Folk Art Americana: Riding in the Woods
1575QK1065 • $65

2072.
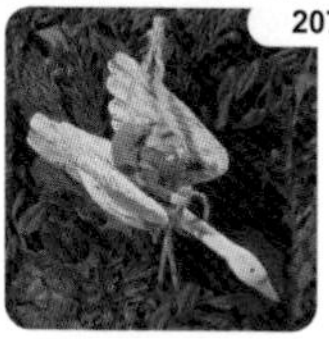
Folk Art Americana: Riding the Wind
1575QK1045 • $50

2073.

Folk Art Americana: Santa Claus
1675QK1072 • $157

2074.

Forest Frolics 5
2500QLX7165 • $53
MAGIC.

2075.

Frosty Friends 14
975QX4142 • $38

2076.

Frosty Friends 20th Anniversary
2000QX5682 • $50

2077.

Gentle Tidings
2500QXC5442 • $43
Limited Edition - 17500.

2078.

Gift Bringers 5: The Magi
500QX2065 • $26

2079.

Glowing Pewter Wreath
1875QX5302 • $32

2080.

Godchild
875QX5875 • $13

2081.

Goin' Golfin'
1275QP6012 • $30
Re-issued in 1994.

2082.

Grandchild's First Christmas
675QX5552 • $13

2083.

Granddaughter
675QX5635 • $20

2084.

Grandmother
675QX5665 • $10

2085.

Grandparents
475QX2085 • $12

2086.

Grandson
675QX5632 • $20

2087.

Great Connections
1075QX5402 • $24 • Set/2

2088.

He Is Born
975QX5362 • $30

2089.
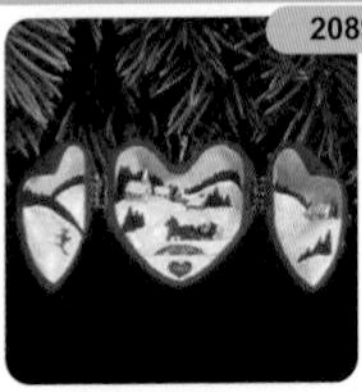
Heart of Christmas 4
1475QX4482 • $19

2090.

Heavenly Angels 3
775QX4945 • $19

2091.

Here Comes Santa 15: Happy Haul-idays
1475QX4102 • $34

2092.

Here's Your Fortune
1075QP6002 • $18

2093.

High Top-purr
875QX5332 • $22

2094.

Holiday BARBIE™ 1
1475QX5725 • $95

2095.

Holiday Enchantment: Angelic Messengers
1375QK1032 • $24

2096.

Holiday Enchantment: Bringing Home the Tree
1375QK1042 • $19

2097.

Holiday Enchantment: Journey to the Forest
1375QK1012 • $19

2098.
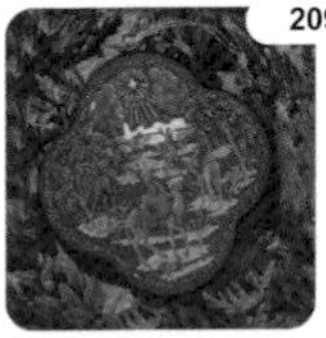
Holiday Enchantment: The Magi
1375QK1025 • $24

2099.
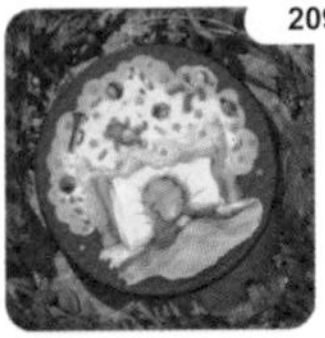
Holiday Enchantment: Visions of Sugarplums
1375QK1005 • $19

2100.

Home for Christmas
775QX5562 • $13

2101.

Home on the Range
3200QLX7395 • $58
MAGIC.

2102.

Howling Good Time
975QX5255 • $19

2103.

Icicle Bicycle
975QX5835 • $19

2104.

It's In the Mail
($N/E)QXC5272 • $19

2105.

Julianne and Teddy
2175QX5295 • $34

2106.

K.C. Angel
($N/E)QXC5445 • $295

2107.

K.C. Angel
($N/E)QXC5445C • $1000
VERY RARE. Edition Size - 1400.

2108.

The Lamplighter
1800QLX7192 • $41
MAGIC.

2109.

Last-Minute Shopping
2800QLX7385 • $62
MAGIC.

2110.

Little Drummer Boy
875QX5372 • $20

2111.

Look for the Wonder
1275QX5685 • $20

2112.

Lou Rankin Polar Bear
975QX5745 • $24

2113.

Mailbox Delivery
1475QP6015 • $30
Re-issued in 1994 & 1995.

2114.

Makin' Music
975QX5325 • $19

2115.

Making Waves
975QX5775 • $28

2116.

Mary Engelbreit
500QX2075 • $22

2117.

Mary's Angels 6: Ivy
675QX4282 • $35

2118.

Maxine
875QX5385 • $30

2119.

Merry Olde Santa 4
1475QX4842 • $36

2120.

Messages of Christmas
3500QLX7476 • $35
MAGIC.

2121.

Mom
775QX5852 • $14

2122.

Mom and Dad
975QX5845 • $24

2123.

Mom-to-Be
675QX5535 • $12

2124.

Mother Goose 1: Humpty Dumpty
1375QX5282 • $29

2125.

Mr. and Mrs. Claus 8: A Fitting Moment
1475QX4202 • $31

2126.

Nephew
675QX5735 • $9

2127.

New Home
775QX5905 • $29

2128.

Niece
675QX5732 • $9

2129.

North Pole Merrython
2500QLX7392 • $65
MAGIC.

2130.

Nostalgic Houses & Shops 10: Cozy Home
1475QX4175 • $46

2131.
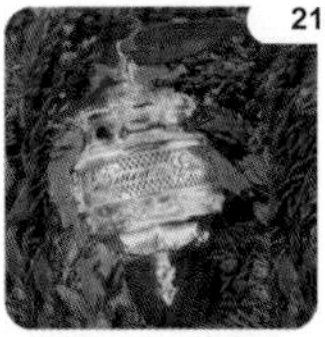
Old-World Silver: Dove of Peace
2475QK1075 • $32

2132.

Old-World Silver: Santa
2475QK1092 • $44

2133.
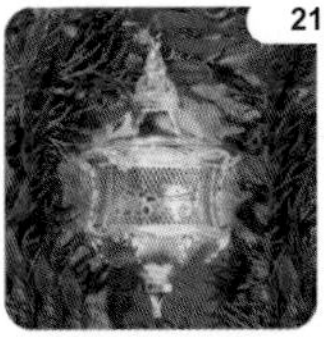
Old-World Silver: Sleigh
2475QK1082 • $27

2134.
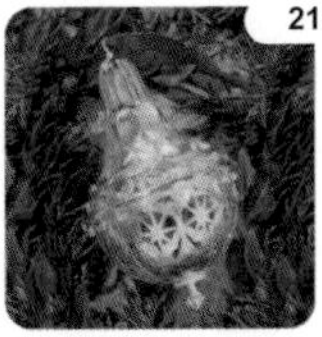
Old-World Silver: Stars & Holly
2475QK1085 • $27

2135.

On Her Toes
875QX5265 • $18

2136.

On the Billboard
1275QP6022 • $30
Re-issued in 1994 & 1995.

2137.
Have You Seen Me?
On the Billboard
($N/E)QP6022C • $50

2138.

One-Elf Marching Band
1275QX5342 • $25

2139.

Our Christmas Together
1075QX5942 • $24

2140.

Our Family
775QX5892 • $18

2141.

Our First Christmas Together
2000QLX7355 • $53
MAGIC.

2142.

Our First Christmas Together
675QX3015 • $20

2143.

Our First Christmas Together
975QX5642 • $20

2144.
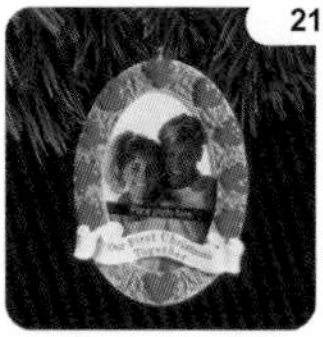
Our First Christmas Together
875QX5952 • $16

2145.

Our First Christmas Together
1875QX5955 • $40
Twirl-About

2146.

Owliver 2
775QX5425 • $14

2147.

Peace on Earth 3: Poland
1175QX5242 • $18

2148.

PEANUTS®
900QP6045 • $20

2149.

PEANUTS®
500QX2072 • $24

2150.

PEANUTS® 3
1800QLX7155 • $48
MAGIC.

2151.

PEANUTS® Gang 1
975QX5315 • $48

2152.

Peek-A-Boo Tree
1075QX5245 • $24

2153.

Peep Inside
1375QX5322 • $24

2154.

People Friendly
875QX5932 • $16

2155.

Perfect Match
875QX5772 • $17

2156.

The Pink Panther™
1275QX5755 • $19

2157.
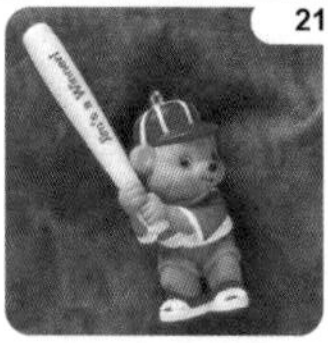
Playing Ball
1275QP6032 • $25
Re-issued in 1994 & 1995.

2158.

Popping Good Times
1475QX5392 • $22 • Set/2

2159.

Porky Pig™
875QX5652 • $18

2160.

Portraits in Bisque: Christmas Feast
1375QK1152 • $23

2161.

Portraits in Bisque: Joy of Sharing
1375QK1142 • $23

2162.

Portraits in Bisque: Mistletoe Kiss
1375QK1145 • $16

2163.

Portraits in Bisque: Norman Rockwell - Filling the Stocking
1375QK1155 • $20

2164.

Portraits in Bisque: Norman Rockwell - Jolly Postman
1375QK1162 • $24

2165.

Puppy Love 3
775QX5045 • $40

2166.

Putt-Putt Penguin
975QX5795 • $17

2167.

Quick as a Fox
875QX5792 • $17

2168.

Radio News Flash
2200QLX7362 • $37
MAGIC.

2169.

Raiding the Fridge
1600QLX7185 • $41
MAGIC.

2170.

Ready for Fun
775QX5124 • $16

2171.

Reindeer Champs 8: Blitzen
875QX4331 • $18

2172.

Reindeer in the Sky
875QP6055 • $30

2173.

Road Runner™ & Wile E. Coyote™
3000QLX7415 • $63
MAGIC.

2174.

Rocking Horse 13
1075QX4162 • $36

2175.

Room for One More
875QX5382 • $38

2176.

Santa Says
1475QP6005 • $30
Re-issued in 1994.

2177.

Santa's Favorite Stop
5500QXC4125 • $317

2178.

Santa's Snow-Getter
1800QLX7352 • $38
MAGIC.

2179.

Santa's Workshop
2800QLX7375 • $60
MAGIC.

2180.

Sharing Christmas
2000QXC5435 • $37
Limited Edition - 16500.

2181.

Shopping With Santa
2400QX5675 • $40

2182.

Silvery Noel
1275QX5305 • $25

2183.

Sister
675QX5545 • $10

2184.

Sister to Sister
975QX5885 • $42

2185.

Smile! It's Christmas
975QX5335 • $25

2186.

Snow Bear Angel
775QX5355 • $17

2187.

Snowbird
775QX5765 • $12

2188.
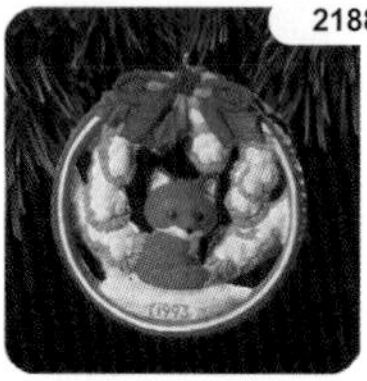
Snowy Hideaway
975QX5312 • $18

2189.

Son
675QX5865 • $20

2190.
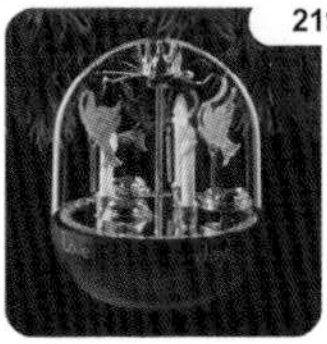
Song of the Chimes
2500QLX7405 • $45
MAGIC.

2191.

Special Cat
775QX5235 • $13

2192.

Special Dog
775QX5962 • $20

2193.

Star Of Wonder
675QX5982 • $31

2194.

Star Teacher
575QX5645 • $10

2195.

Strange and Wonderful Love
875QX5965 • $13

2196.

Superman™
1275QX5752 • $42

2197.

The Swat Team
1275QX5395 • $26 • Set/2

2198.

Sylvester™ and Tweety™
975QX5405 • $30

2199.

Tannenbaum's Dept Store
2600QX5612 • $58

2200.

Tender Touches: You're Always Welcome
975QX5692 • $58

2201.

That's Entertainment
875QX5345 • $16

2202.

Tin Airplane
775QX5622 • $25

2203.

Tin Blimp
775QX5625 • $16

2204.

Tin Hot Air Balloon
775QX5615 • $19

2205.

To My Grandma
775QX5555 • $13

2206.

Tobin Fraley Carousel 2
2800QX5502 • $38

2207.

Top Banana
775QX5925 • $13

2208.

Trimmed with Memories
1200QXC5432 • $34

2209.

Twelve Days of Christmas 10: Ten Lords A-Leaping
675QX3012 • $13

2210.

U.S. Christmas Stamps 1
1075QX5292 • $26

2211.

U.S.S. Enterprise™ - The Next Generation™
2400QLX7412 • $48
MAGIC.

2212.

Wake-Up Call
875QX5262 • $16

2213.

Warm and Special Friends
1075QX5895 • $23

2214.

Water Bed Snooze
975QX5375 • $16

2215.

Winnie the Pooh
2400QLX7422 • $44
MAGIC.

2216.

Winnie the Pooh: Eeyore
975QX5712 • $25

2217.

Winnie the Pooh: Kanga and Roo
975QX5672 • $20

2218.

Winnie the Pooh: Owl
975QX5695 • $19

2219.

Winnie the Pooh: Rabbit
975QX5702 • $19

2220.

Winnie the Pooh: Tigger and Piglet
975QX5705 • $43

2221.

Winnie the Pooh: Winnie the Pooh
975QX5715 • $36

1994

2222.

Across the Miles
895QX5656 • $18

2223.

All Pumped Up
895QX5923 • $17

2224.

Angel Hare
895QX5896 • $18

2225.

Anniversary Year Photo Holder
1095QX5683 • $19

2226.

Away in a Manger
1600QLX7383 • $37
MAGIC.

2227.

Baby Block Photo Holder
1495QP6035 • $29
Re-issued from 1993.

2228.

Baby's First Christmas
2000QLX7466 • $38
MAGIC.

2229.
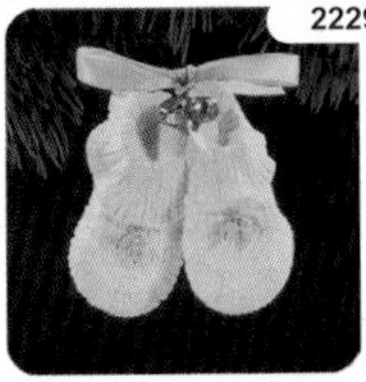
Baby's First Christmas
1895QX5633 • $32

2230.

Baby's First Christmas
795QX5636 • $32

2231.

Baby's First Christmas
1295QX5743 • $32

2232.

Baby's First Christmas (Boy)
500QX2436 • $27

2233.

Baby's First Christmas (Girl)
500QX2433 • $27

2234.

BARBIE™ 1: 1959 BARBIE™
1495QX5006 • $30

2235.

Barney™
2400QLX7506 • $46
MAGIC.

2236.

Barney™
995QX5966 • $21

2237.

Baseball Heroes 1: Babe Ruth
1295QX5323 • $42

2238.

Batman™
1295QX5853 • $42

2239.

The Beatles Gift Set
4800QX5373 • $124 • Set/5

2240.

Betsey's Country Christmas 3
500QX2403 • $20

2241.
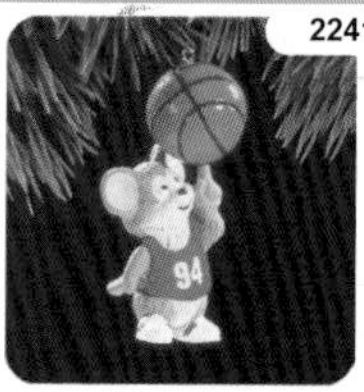

Big Shot
795QX5873 • $28

2242.

Brother
695QX5516 • $13

2243.

Busy Batter
795QX5876 • $20

2244.

Candy Cane Lookout
1800QLX7376 • $88
MAGIC.

2245.

Candy Caper
895QX5776 • $22

2246.

Caring Doctor
895QX5823 • $15

2247.

Cat Naps 1
795QX5313 • $36

2248.
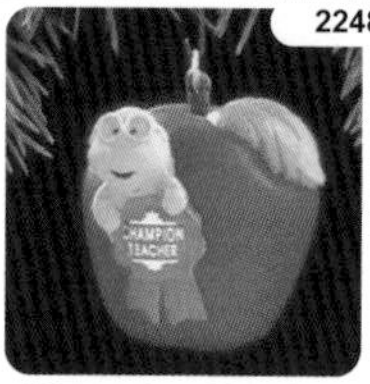

Champion Teacher
695QX5836 • $13

2249.

Cheers to You!
1095QX5796 • $24

2250.

Cheery Cyclists
1295QX5786 • $28

2251.

Child Care Giver
795QX5906 • $14

2252.

Child's Age: Baby's First Christmas
795QX5713 • $38

2253.

Child's Age: Baby's Second Christmas
795QX5716 • $29

2254.

Child's Age: Child's Third Christmas
695QX5723 • $24

2255.

Child's Age: Child's Fourth Christmas
695QX5726 • $24

2256.

Child's Age: Child's Fifth Christmas
695QX5733 • $24

2257.

Chris Mouse 10: Chris Mouse Jelly
1200QLX7393 • $26
MAGIC.

2258.

Christmas Lights: Home for the Holidays
1575QK1123 • $32

2259.

Christmas Lights: Moonbeams
1575QK1116 • $32

2260.

Christmas Lights: Mother and Child
1575QK1126 • $32

2261.

Christmas Lights: Peaceful Village
1575QK1106 • $32

2262.

Classic American Cars 4: 1957 Chevrolet® Bel Air
1295QX5422 • $35

2263.

Classic American Cars 4: 1957 Chevrolet® Bel Air
($N/A)QX5422C • $975
Edition Size - 40.

2264.

Coach
795QX5933 • $17

2265.

Coca-Cola® - Relaxing Moment
1495QX5356 • $28

2266.

Cock-a-Doodle Christmas
895QX5396 • $24

2267.

Collector's Survival Kit
($N/E)(N/A) • $29

2268.

Colors of Joy
795QX5893 • $34

2269.

Computer Cat 'n' Mouse
1295QP6046 • $20
Re-issued in 1995.

2270.

Conversations with Santa
2800QLX7426 • $43
MAGIC.

2271.

Cookie Time
1295QP6073 • $21
Re-issued in 1995.

2272.

Country Showtime
2200QLX7416 • $48
MAGIC.

2273.

Crayola® Crayon 6: Bright Playful Colors
1095QX5273 • $34

2274.

Dad
795QX5463 • $14

2275.

Dad-to-Be
795QX5473 • $18

2276.

Daffy Duck™
895QX5415 • $36

2277.

Daughter
695QX5623 • $18

2278.

Dear Santa Mouse
1495QX5806 • $22 • Set/2

2279.

The Eagle Has Landed
2400QLX7486 • $46
MAGIC.

2280.

Etch-a-Sketch®
1295QP6006 • $60
Re-issued in 1995.

2281.

Extra-Special Delivery
795QX5833 • $18

2282.

Fabulous Decade 5
795QX5263 • $36

2283.

Feelin' Groovy
795QX5953 • $24

2284.

A Feline of Christmas
895QX5816 • $28

2285.

Feliz Navidad
2800QLX7433 • $84
MAGIC.

2286.

Feliz Navidad
895QX5793 • $35

2287.

Festive Album Photo Holder
1295QP6025 • $18
Re-issued from 1993.

2288.

Folk Art Americana: Catching 40 Winks
1675QK1183 • $28

2289.
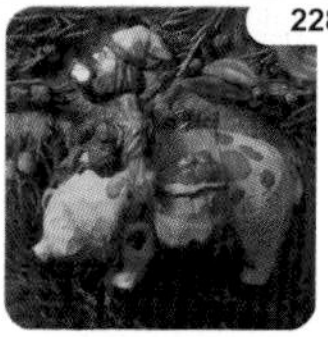
Folk Art Americana: Going to Town
1575QK1166 • $42

2290.

Folk Art Americana: Racing Through the Snow
1575QK1173 • $42

2291.

Folk Art Americana: Rarin' To Go
1575QK1193 • $34

2292.

Folk Art Americana: Roundup Time
1675QK1176 • $34

2293.

Follow the Sun
895QX5846 • $16

2294.

For My Grandma
695QX5613 • $14

2295.

Forest Frolics 6
2800QLX7436 • $53
MAGIC.

2296.

Fred and Barney - The Flintstones™
1495QX5003 • $28

2297.

Friendly Push
895QX5686 • $26

2298.

Friendship Sundae
1095QX4766 • $28

2299.

From the Heart
1495QP6036 • $20
Re-issued in 1995.

2300.

Frosty Friends 15
995QX5293 • $40

2301.

Garden Elves: Daisy Days
995QX5986 • $12

2302.

Garden Elves: Harvest Joy
995QX5993 • $12

2303.

Garden Elves: Tulip Time
995QX5983 • $15

2304.

Garden Elves: Yuletide Cheer
995QX5976 • $15

2305.

Garfield®
1295QX5753 • $26

2306.

Gentle Nurse
695QX5973 • $23

2307.

Gingerbread Fantasy
4400QLX7382 • $92
MAGIC.

2308.

Godchild
895QX4453 • $22

2309.

Godparent
500QX2423 • $17

2310.

Goin' Fishin'
1495QP6023 • $32

2311.

Goin' Golfin'
1295QP6012 • $30
Re-issued from 1993.

2312.

Golden Bow
1000(N/A) • $76
RARER

2313.

Golden Dove of Peace
1000(N/A) • $38

2314.

Golden Poinsettia
1000(N/A) • $93
RARER

2315.
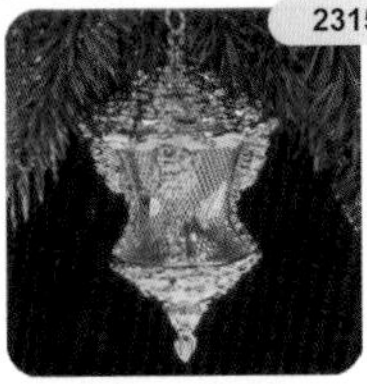
Golden Santa
1000(N/A) • $64

2316.

Golden Sleigh
1000(N/A) • $45

2317.

Golden Stars and Holly
1000(N/A) • $45

2318.

Grandchild's First Christmas
795QX5676 • $18

2319.

Granddaughter
695QX5523 • $18

2320.

Grandmother
795QX5673 • $14

2321.

Grandpa
795QX5616 • $14

2322.

Grandparents
500QX2426 • $16

2323.
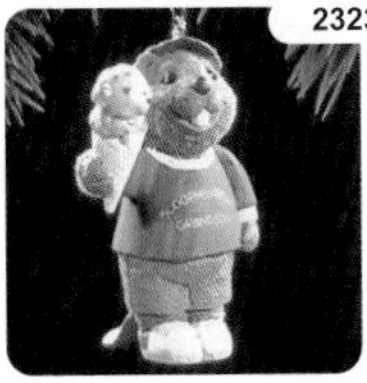
Grandson
695QX5526 • $18

2324.

Happy Birthday, Jesus
1295QX5423 • $23

2325.
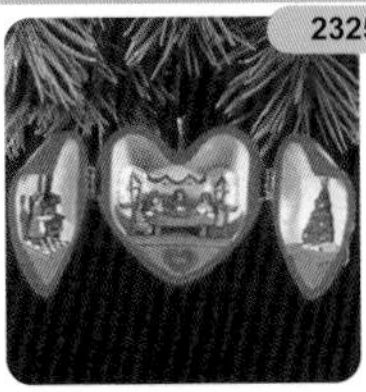
Heart of Christmas 5
1495QX5266 • $22

2326.
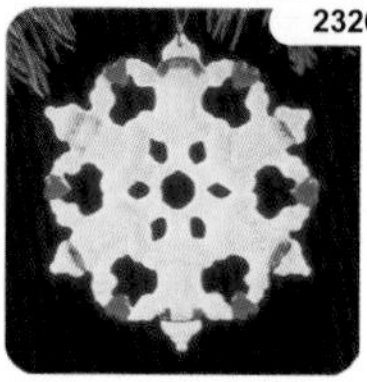
Hearts in Harmony
1095QX4406 • $20

2327.

Helpful Shepherd
895QX5536 • $22

2328.

Here Comes Santa 16: Makin' Tractor Tracks
1495QX5296 • $56

2329.

Here's Your Fortune
($N/A)QP6002C • $40
2 versions.

2330.

Holiday BARBIE™ 2
1495QX5216 • $44

2331.

Holiday Favorites: Dapper Snowman
1375QK1053 • $22

2332.

Holiday Favorites: Graceful Fawn
1175QK1033 • $18

2333.

Holiday Favorites: Jolly Santa
1375QK1046 • $24

2334.

Holiday Favorites: Joyful Lamb
1175QK1036 • $24

2335.
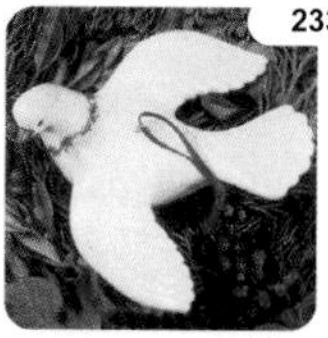
Holiday Favorites: Peaceful Dove
1175QK1043 • $24

2336.

Holiday Hello
2495QXR6116 • $42

2337.

Holiday Patrol
895QX5826 • $14

2338.

Holiday Pursuit
($N/E)QXC4823 • $22

2339.

Ice Show
795QX5946 • $17

2340.

In the Pink
995QX5763 • $23

2341.

It's a Strike
895QX5856 • $16

2342.

Jingle Bell Band
1095QX5783 • $23

2343.

Jolly Holly Santa
2200QXC4833 • $43

2344.

Joyous Song
895QX4473 • $28

2345.

Jump-along Jackalope
895QX5756 • $18

2346.

Keep on Mowin'
895QX5413 • $13

2347.

Kickin' Roo
795QX5916 • $16

2348.

Kiddie Car Classics 1: Murray® Champion
1395QX5426 • $50

2349.
Have You Seen Me?
Kiddie Car Classics 1: Murray® Champion
($N/E)QX5426C • $1000
Red. Edition Size - 40.

2350.

Kitty's Catamaran
1095QX5416 • $20

2351.

Klingon Bird of Prey™
2400QLX7386 • $40
MAGIC.

2352.

Kringle Trolley
2000QLX7413 • $43
MAGIC.

2353.

Kringle's Kayak
795QX5886 • $26

2354.

Lou Rankin Seal
995QX5456 • $20

2355.

Lucinda and Teddy
2175QX4813 • $28

2356.

Magic Carpet Ride
795QX5883 • $22

2357.

Mailbox Delivery
1495QP6015 • $30
Re-issued from 1993.

2358.

Majestic Deer
2500QXC4836 • $69

2359.

Making It Bright
895QX5403 • $28

2360.

Mary Engelbreit
500QX2416 • $31

2361.

Mary's Angels 7: Jasmine
695QX5276 • $42

2362.

Maxine
2000QLX7503 • $71
MAGIC.

2363.

Merry Fishmas
895QX5913 • $27

2364.

Merry Olde Santa 5
1495QX5256 • $32

2365.

Mistletoe Surprise
1295QX5996 • $26 • Set/2

2366.

Mom
795QX5466 • $14

2367.

Mom and Dad
995QX5666 • $40

2368.

Mom-to-Be
795QX5506 • $18

2369.

Mother Goose 2: Hey Diddle, Diddle
1395QX5213 • $36

2370.

Mr. and Mrs. Claus 9: A Hand Warming Present
1495QX5283 • $34

2371.

Mrs. Claus' Cupboard
5500QXC4843 • $181 • Set/11
Edition Size - 12000.

2372.

Mufasa and Simba - The Lion King
1495QX5406 • $28

2373.

Nephew
795QX5546 • $10

2374.

New Home
895QX5663 • $14

2375.

Niece
795QX5543 • $12

2376.
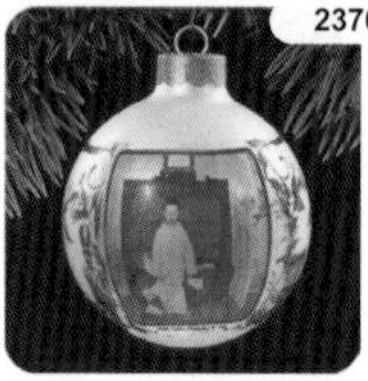
Norman Rockwell Art
500QX2413 • $18

2377.

Nostalgic Houses & Shops 11: Neighborhood Drugstore
1495QX5286 • $40

2378.

Novel Idea
1295QP6066 • $20
Re-issued in 1995.

2379.

Old-World Silver: Bells
2475QK1026 • $25

2380.
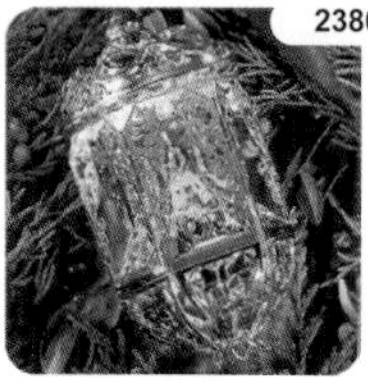
Old-World Silver: Bows
2475QK1023 • $29

2381.

Old-World Silver: Poinsettia
2475QK1006 • $26

2382.
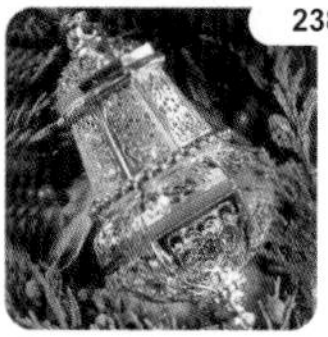
Old-World Silver: Snowflakes
2475QK1016 • $29

2383.

On Cloud Nine
1200QXC4853 • $25

2384.

On the Billboard
1295QP6022 • $30
Also issued in 1993 & 1995.

2385.

Open-and-Shut Holiday
995QX5696 • $20

2386.

Our Christmas Together
995QX4816 • $19

2387.

Our Family
795QX5576 • $26

2388.

Our First Christmas Together
695QX3186 • $26

2389.

Our First Christmas Together
995QX5643 • $28

2390.

Our First Christmas Together
895QX5653 • $18

2391.

Our First Christmas Together
1895QX5706 • $28

2392.

Out of This World Teacher
795QX5766 • $16

2393.

Owliver 3
795QX5226 • $18

2394.

PEANUTS® 4
2000QLX7406 • $54
MAGIC.

2395.

PEANUTS® Gang 2
995QX5203 • $18

2396.

Peekaboo Pup
2000QLX7423 • $38
MAGIC.

2397.

Playing Ball
1295QP6032 • $25
Also issued in 1993 & 1995.

2398.

Practice Makes Perfect
895QX5863 • $12

2399.

Puppy Love 4
795QX5253 • $28

2400.

Red Hot Holiday
795QX5843 • $25

2401.

Reindeer Pro
795QX5926 • $18

2402.

Reindeer Rooters
1295QP6056 • $34
Re-issued in 1995.

2403.

Road Runner™ and Wile E. Coyote™
1295QX5602 • $28

2404.

Rock Candy Miner
2000QLX7403 • $32
MAGIC.

2405.

Rocking Horse 14
1095QX5016 • $32

2406.

Santa Says
1495QP6005 • $30
Re-issued from 1993.

2407.

Santa's Lego® Sleigh
1095QX5453 • $34

2408.

Santa's Sing-Along
2400QLX7473 • $68
MAGIC.

2409.

Sarah Plain and Tall: Country Church
795XPR9450 • $22

2410.

Sarah Plain and Tall: Hays Train Station
795XPR9452 • $22

2411.

Sarah Plain and Tall: Mrs. Parkley's General Store
795XPR9451 • $17

2412.

Sarah Plain and Tall: Sarah's Maine Home
795XPR9454 • $24

2413.

Sarah Plain and Tall: Sarah's Prairie Home
795XPR9453 • $26

2414.

Secret Santa
795QX5736 • $18

2415.

A Sharp Flat
1095QX5773 • $18

2416.

Simba and Nala - The Lion King
1295QX5303 • $26 • Set/2

2417.

Simba, Sarabi, and Mufasa - The Lion King
3200QLX7513 • $65 • Recalled
MAGIC.

2418.
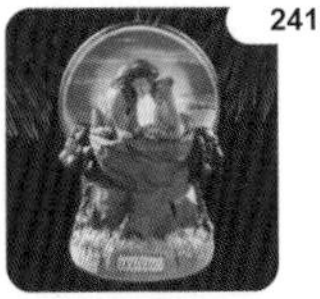
Simba, Sarabi, and Mufasa - The Lion King
3200QLX7516 • $48
MAGIC.

2419.

Sister
695QX5513 • $16

2420.

Sister to Sister
995QX5533 • $16

2421.

Son
695QX5626 • $26

2422.

Special Cat
795QX5606 • $16

2423.

Special Dog
795QX5603 • $13

2424.

Speedy Gonzales™
895QX5343 • $26

2425.

Stamp of Approval
795QX5703 • $13

2426.

Sweet Greeting
1095QX5803 • $26 • Set/2

2427.

The Tale of Peter Rabbit - Beatrix Potter™
500QX2443 • $26

2428.

Tasmanian Devil
895QX5605 • $48

2429.

Tender Touches: Eager For Christmas
1500QX5336 • $20

2430.

Thick 'n' Thin
1095QX5693 • $29

2431.

Thrill a Minute
895QX5866 • $22

2432.

Time of Peace
795QX5813 • $14

2433.

Timon and Pumbaa - The Lion King
895QX5366 • $20

2434.

Tobin Fraley Carousel 3
2800QX5223 • $50

2435.

Tobin Fraley Holiday Carousel 1
3200QLX7496 • $66
MAGIC.

2436.

Tou Can Love
895QX5646 • $17

2437.

Twelve Days of Christmas 11: Eleven Pipers Piping
695QX3183 • $15

2438.

U.S. Christmas Stamps 2
1095QX5206 • $26

2439.

Very Merry Minutes
2400QLX7443 • $72
MAGIC.

2440.

White Christmas
2800QLX7463 • $65
MAGIC.

2441.

Winnie the Pooh and Tigger
1295QX5746 • $42

2442.

Winnie the Pooh Parade
3200QLX7493 • $76
MAGIC.

2443.

Wizard of Oz™: Dorothy and Toto™
1095QX5433 • $95

2444.

Wizard of Oz™: The Cowardly Lion™
995QX5446 • $72

2445.

Wizard of Oz™: The Scarecrow™
995QX5436 • $71

2446.

Wizard of Oz™: The Tin Man™
995QX5443 • $71

2447.

Yosemite Sam™
895QX5346 • $26

2448.

Yuletide Central 1: Locomotive
1895QX5316 • $35

1995

2449.

1958 Ford® Edsel™ Citation Convertible
1295QXC4167 • $70

2450.

Accessories for Nostalgic Houses & Shops
895QX5089 • $20 • Set/3

2451.

Acorn 500
1095QX5929 • $18

2452.

Across the Miles
895QX5847 • $12

2453.

Air Express
795QX5977 • $12

2454.
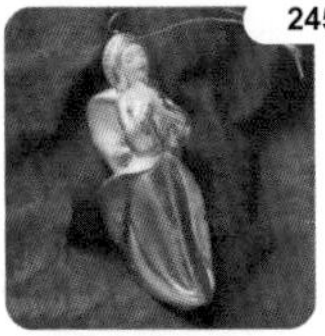
All Is Bright: Angel of Light
1195QK1159 • $16

2455.
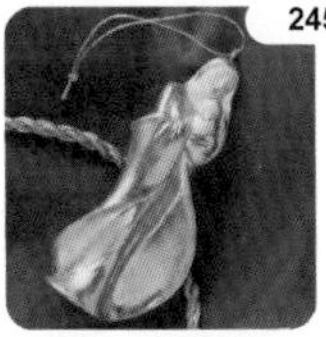
All Is Bright: Gentle Lullaby
1195QK1157 • $16

2456.

All-American Trucks 1: 1956 Ford® Truck
1395QX5527 • $31

2457.

All-American Trucks 1: 1956 Ford® Truck
($N/A)QX5527C • $675
Edition Size - 64.

2458.

Angel Bells: Carole
1295QK1147 • $28

2459.

Angel Bells: Joy
1295QK1137 • $29

2460.

Angel Bells: Noelle
1295QK1139 • $23

2461.

Anniversary Year Photo Holder
895QX5819 • $13

2462.

Artists' Caricature Ball
795(N/A) • $29

2463.

Baby Bear
1295QP6157 • $30

2464.

Baby's First Christmas
2200QLX7317 • $34
MAGIC.

2465.
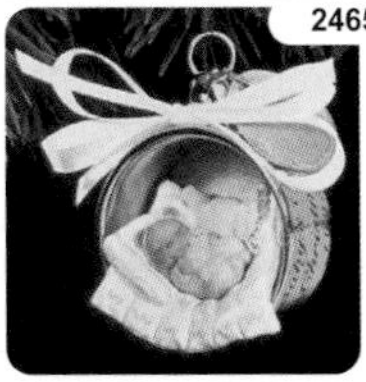
Baby's First Christmas
1895QX5547 • $45

2466.

Baby's First Christmas
795QX5549 • $24

2467.

Baby's First Christmas
995QX5557 • $17

2468.

Baby's First Christmas (Boy)
500QX2319 • $19

2469.

Baby's First Christmas (Girl)
500QX2317 • $19

2470.

BARBIE™ 2: Solo in the Spotlight
1495QXI5049 • $22

2471.

Barrel-Back Rider
995QX5189 • $18

2472.

Baseball Heroes 2: Lou Gehrig
1295QX5029 • $19

2473.

Batmobile™
1495QX5739 • $24

2474.

Betty and Wilma - The Flintstones™
1495QX5417 • $24

2475.

Beverly and Teddy
2175QX5259 • $25

2476.

Bingo Bear
795QX5919 • $13

2477.

Bobbin' Along
895QX5879 • $25

2478.

Brother
695QX5679 • $12

2479.
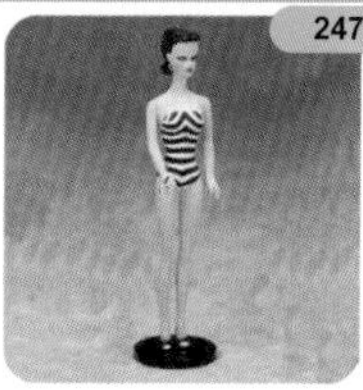
Brunette Debut - 1959
1495QXC5397 • $56

2480.

Bugs Bunny™
895QX5019 • $16

2481.

Captain James T. Kirk
1395QXI5539 • $30

2482.

Captain Jean-Luc Picard
1395QXI5737 • $30

2483.

Captain John Smith and Meeko - Pochahontas
1295QXI6169 • $13

2484.

Cat Naps 2
795QX5097 • $20

2485.

Catch the Spirit
795QX5899 • $16

2486.

A Celebration of Angels 1
1295QX5077 • $19

2487.
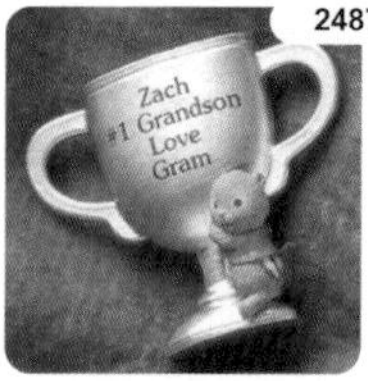

The Champ
1295QP6127 • $18

2488.

A Charlie Brown® Christmas: Charlie Brown™
395QRP4207 • $26

2489.

A Charlie Brown® Christmas: Linus
395QRP4217 • $16

2490.

A Charlie Brown® Christmas: Lucy
395QRP4209 • $18

2491.

A Charlie Brown® Christmas: Snoopy™
395QRP4219 • $30

2492.

A Charlie Brown® Christmas: Snow Scene
395QRP4227 • $14

2493.

Child's Age: Baby's First Christmas
795QX5559 • $29

2494.

Child's Age: Baby's Second Christmas
795QX5567 • $20

2495.

Child's Age: Child's Third Christmas
795QX5627 • $20

2496.

Child's Age: Child's Fourth Christmas
695QX5629 • $20

2497.

Child's Age: Child's Fifth Christmas
695QX5637 • $24

2498.

Chris Mouse 11: Chris Mouse Tree
1250QLX7307 • $25
MAGIC.

2499.
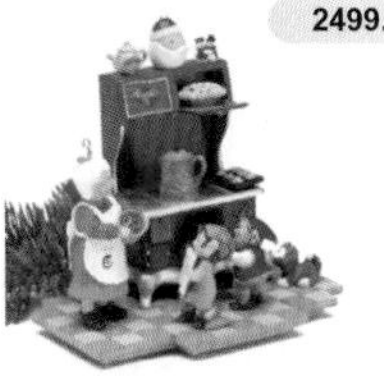
Christmas Eve Bake-Off
6000QXC4049 • $84

2500.

Christmas Fever
795QX5967 • $13

2501.

Christmas Morning
1095QX5997 • $15

2502.

Christmas Patrol
795QX5959 • $16

2503.

Christmas Visitors 1: St. Nicholas
1495QX5087 • $22

2504.

Classic American Cars 5: 1969 Chevrolet® Camaro
1295QX5239 • $23

2505.

Coca-Cola® - Refreshing Gift
1495QX4067 • $26

2506.

Collecting Memories
($N/E)QXC4117 • $16

2507.

Colorful World
1095QX5519 • $22

2508.

Coming to See Santa
3200QLX7369 • $65
MAGIC.

2509.

Computer Cat 'n' Mouse
1295QP6046 • $20
Re-issued from 1994.

2510.

Cookie Time
1295QP6073 • $21
Re-issued from 1994.

2511.
Have You Seen Me?
Cookie Time
1295QP6073C • $30

2512.

Cows of Bali
895QX5999 • $14

2513.

Crayola® Crayon 7: Bright 'n' Sunny Tepee
1095QX5247 • $22

2514.

Dad
795QX5649 • $16

2515.

Dad-to-Be
795QX5667 • $10

2516.

Daughter
695QX5677 • $20

2517.
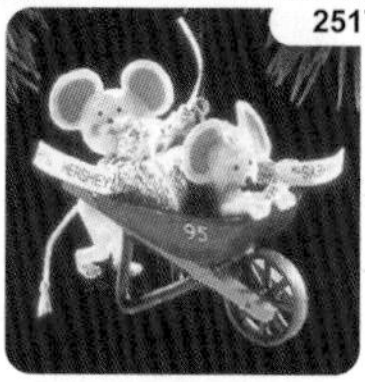
Delivering Kisses
1095QX4107 • $30

2518.

Dream On
1095QX6007 • $18

2519.

Dudley the Dragon
1095QX6209 • $16

2520.

Etch-A-Sketch®
1295QP6006 • $60
Re-issued from 1994.

2521.

Fabulous Decade 6
795QX5147 • $18

2522.

Faithful Fan
895QX5897 • $16

2523.

Feliz Navidad
795QX5869 • $20

2524.

Fishing for Fun
($N/E)QXC5207 • $20

2525.

Folk Art Americana: Fetching the Firewood
1595QK1057 • $29

2526.
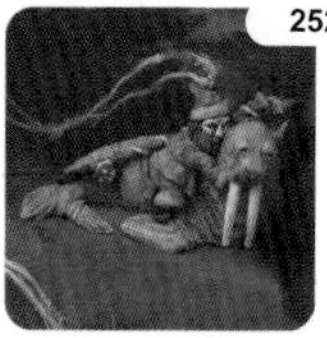
Folk Art Americana: Fishing Party
1595QK1039 • $29

2527.

Folk Art Americana: Guiding Santa
1895QK1037 • $37

2528.

Folk Art Americana: Home from the Woods
1595QXC1059 • $40

2529.

Folk Art Americana: Learning to Skate
1495QK1047 • $29

2530.

Football Legends 1: Joe Montana
1495QXI5759 • $30

2531.

For My Grandma
695QX5729 • $13

2532.

Forest Frolics 7
2800QLX7299 • $47
MAGIC.

2533.

Forever Friends Bear
895QX5258 • $19

2534.

Fred and Dino - The Flintstones™
2800QLX7289 • $53
MAGIC.

2535.

Friendly Boost
895QX5827 • $22

2536.

Friends Share Fun
1650QLX7349 • $29
MAGIC.

2537.

From the Heart
1495QP6036 • $20
Re-issued from 1994.

2538.

Frosty Friends 16
1095QX5169 • $31

2539.

Garfield®
1095QX5007 • $18

2540.
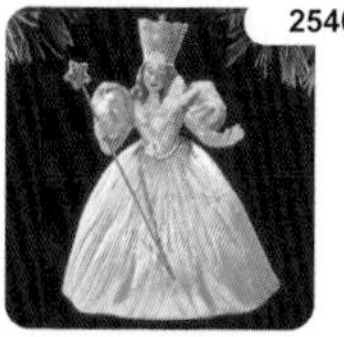
Glinda, Witch of the North™
1395QX5749 • $40

2541.

Godchild
795QX5707 • $28

2542.

Godparent
500QX2417 • $13

2543.
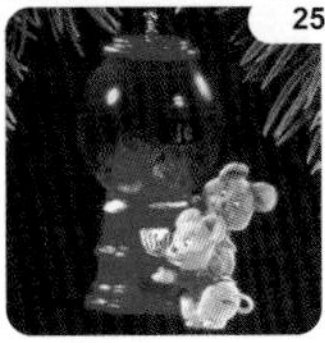

Goody Gumballs!
1250QLX7367 • $28
MAGIC.

2544.

Gopher Fun
995QX5887 • $19

2545.

Grandchild's First Christmas
795QX5777 • $20

2546.

Granddaughter
695QX5779 • $19

2547.

Grandmother
795QX5767 • $12

2548.

Grandpa
895QX5769 • $12

2549.

Grandparents
500QX2419 • $12

2550.

Grandson
695QX5787 • $20

2551.

Happy Holidays
295QX6307 • $8

2552.

Happy Wrappers
1095QX6037 • $17 • Set/2

2553.

Headin' Home
2200QLX7327 • $49
MAGIC.

2554.

Heaven's Gift
2000QX6057 • $46 • Set/2

2555.

Here Comes Santa 17: Santa's Roadster
1495QX5179 • $26

2556.

Hockey Pup
995QX5917 • $22

2557.

Holiday BARBIE™ 3
1495QXI5057 • $31

2558.

Holiday Enchantment: Away in a Manger
1395QK1097 • $18

2559.
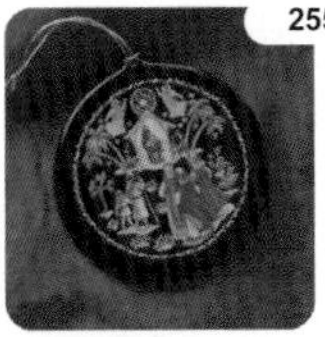

Holiday Enchantment: Following the Star
1395QK1099 • $19

2560.

Holiday Swim
1850QLX7319 • $29
MAGIC.

2561.

Hoop Stars 1: Shaqille O' Neal
1495QXI5517 • $29

2562.

Important Memo
895QX5947 • $12

2563.

In a Heartbeat
895QX5817 • $16

2564.

In Time With Christmas
1295QX6049 • $19

2565.

Invitation to Tea: Cozy Cottage Teapot
1595QK1127 • $22

2566.

Invitation to Tea: European Castle Teapot
1595QK1129 • $29

2567.

Invitation to Tea: Victorian Home Teapot
1595QK1119 • $22

2568.

Joe Montana - Kansas City
1495QXI6207 • $55

2569.

Joy to the World
895QX5867 • $14

2570.

Jumping for Joy
2800QLX7347 • $53
MAGIC.

2571.

Key Note
1295QP6149 • $30

2572.

Kiddie Car Classics 2: 1955 Murray® Fire Truck
1395QX5027 • $25

2573.

Kiddie Car Classics 2: 1955 Murray® Fire Truck
($N/A)QX5027C • $1000
Edition Size - 64.

2574.

Lego® Fireplace with Santa
1095QX4769 • $19

2575.

Lou Rankin Bear
995QX4069 • $18

2576.

The Magic School Bus
1095QX5849 • $22

2577.

Mailbox Delivery
1495QP6015 • $30
Re-issued from 1993 & 1994.

2578.

Mary Engelbreit
500QX2409 • $22

2579.

Mary's Angels 8: Camellia
695QX5149 • $35

2580.

Merry Olde Santa 6
1495QX5139 • $23

2581.

Merry RV
1295QX6027 • $18

2582.

Mom
795QX5647 • $15

2583.

Mom and Dad
995QX5657 • $28

2584.

Mom-to-Be
795QX5659 • $14

2585.

Mother Goose 3: Jack and Jill
1395QX5099 • $22

2586.

Mr. and Mrs. Claus 10: Christmas Eve Kiss
1495QX5157 • $23

2587.

Muletide Greetings
795QX6009 • $20

2588.

My First Hot Wheels™
2800QLX7279 • $48
MAGIC.

2589.
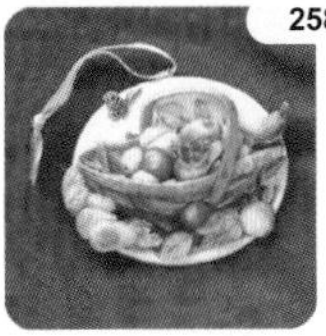
Nature's Sketchbook: Backyard Orchard
1895QK1069 • $30

2590.

Nature's Sketchbook: Christmas Cardinal
1895QK1077 • $38

2591.

Nature's Sketchbook: Raising a Family
1895QK1067 • $26

2592.

Nature's Sketchbook: Violets and Butterflies
1695QK1079 • $37

2593.

New Home
895QX5839 • $14

2594.

NFL®: Carolina Panthers™
595PNA2035 • $16
Re-issued in 1996.

2595.

NFL®: Carolina Panthers™
995QSR6227 • $30

2596.

NFL®: Chicago Bears™
595BRS2035 • $16
Re-issued in 1996.

2597.

NFL®: Chicago Bears™
995QSR6237 • $30

2598.

NFL®: Dallas Cowboys™
595COW2035 • $16
Re-issued in 1996.

2599.

NFL®: Dallas Cowboys™
995QSR6217 • $30

2600.

NFL®: Kansas City Chiefs™
595CHF2035 • $16
Re-issued in 1996.

2601.

NFL®: Kansas City Chiefs™
995QSR6257 • $30

2602.

NFL®: Los Angeles Raiders™
995QSR6249 • $30

2603.

NFL®: Los Angeles Raiders™
595RDR2035 • $16
Re-issued in 1996.

2604.
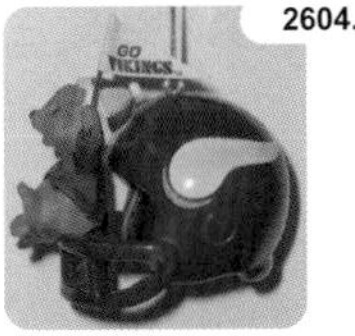
NFL®: Minnesota Vikings™
995QSR6267 • $30

2605.

NFL®: Minnesota Vikings™
595VIK2035 • $16
Re-issued in 1996.

2606.

NFL®: New England Patriots™
595NEP2035 • $16
Re-issued in 1996.

2607.

NFL®: New England Patriots™
995QSR6228 • $30

2608.

NFL®: Philadelphia Eagles™
595EAG2035 • $16
Re-issued in 1996.

2609.

NFL®: Philadelphia Eagles™
995QSR6259 • $30

2610.

NFL®: San Francisco 49ers™
595FOR2035 • $16
Re-issued in 1996.

2611.
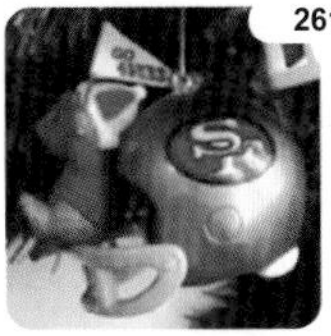
NFL®: San Francisco 49ers™
995QSR6239 • $30

2612.

NFL®: Washington Redskins™
995QSR6247 • $30

2613.

NFL®: Washington Redskins™
595RSK2035 • $16
Re-issued in 1996.

2614.

Norman Rockwell Art
500QX2407 • $29

2615.

North Pole 911
1095QX5957 • $19

2616.

Nostalgic Houses & Shops 12: Town Church
1495QX5159 • $29

2617.

Novel Idea
1295QP6066 • $20
Re-issued from 1994.

2618.

Number One Teacher
795QX5949 • $12

2619.

The Olympic Spirit
795QX3169 • $10

2620.

On the Billboard
1295QP6022 • $30
Re-issued from 1993 & 1994.

2621.

On the Ice
795QX6047 • $16

2622.

Our Christmas Together
995QX5809 • $24

2623.

Our Family
795QX5709 • $14

2624.

Our First Christmas Together
695QX3177 • $24

2625.

Our First Christmas Together
1695QX5797 • $29

2626.

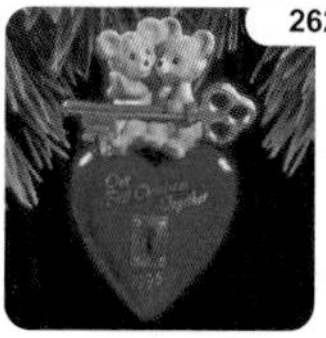

Our First Christmas Together
895QX5799 • $24

2627.

Our First Christmas Together
895QX5807 • $18

2628.

Our Little Blessings
1295QX5209 • $20

2629.

Packed with Memories
795QX5639 • $17

2630.

PEANUTS® 5
2450QLX7277 • $59
MAGIC.

2631.

PEANUTS® Gang 3
995QX5059 • $24

2632.

Percy, Flit and Meeko - Pochahontas
995QXI6179 • $19

2633.

Perfect Balance
795QX5927 • $12

2634.

Pewter Rocking Horse
2000QX6167 • $41

2635.

Pez® Santa
795QX5267 • $18

2636.

Playing Ball
1295QP6032 • $25
Re-issued from 1993 & 1994.

2637.

Pocahontas
1295QXI6177 • $17

2638.

Pocahontas and Capt John Smith
1495QXI6197 • $20

2639.

Polar Coaster
895QX6117 • $18

2640.

Popeye
1095QX5257 • $18

2641.

Puppy Love 5
795QX5137 • $45

2642.

Reindeer Rooters
1295QP6056 • $34
Re-issued from 1994.

2643.

Rejoice!
1095QX5987 • $17

2644.

Rocking Horse 15
1095QX5167 • $23

2645.

Roller Whiz
795QX5937 • $13

2646.

Romulan Warbird™
2400QXI7267 • $39
MAGIC.

2647.

Santa In Paris
895QX5877 • $29

2648.

Santa's Diner
2450QLX7337 • $34
MAGIC.

2649.

Santa's Serenade
895QX6017 • $13

2650.

Simba, Pumbaa and Timon - The Lion King
1295QX6159 • $20

2651.

Sister
695QX5687 • $20

2652.

Sister to Sister
895QX5689 • $16

2653.

Ski Hound
895QX5909 • $19

2654.

Son
695QX5669 • $20

2655.

Space Shuttle
2450QLX7396 • $55
MAGIC.

2656.

Special Cat
795QX5717 • $19

2657.

Special Dog
795QX5719 • $18

2658.

Superman™
2800QLX7309 • $38
MAGIC.

2659.

Surfin' Santa
995QX6019 • $24

2660.

Sylvester™ and Tweety™
1395QX5017 • $23 • Set/2

2661.

Symbols of Christmas: Jolly Santa
1595QK1087 • $19

2662.

Symbols of Christmas: Sweet Song
1595QK1089 • $16

2663.

Takin' a Hike
795QX6029 • $17

2664.

Tender Touches: Wish List
1500QX5859 • $19

2665.

Tennis, Anyone?
795QX5907 • $13

2666.

Thomas the Tank® Engine - No. 1
995QX5857 • $36

2667.

Three Wishes
795QX5979 • $18

2668.

Tobin Fraley Carousel 4
2800QX5069 • $43

2669.

Tobin Fraley Holiday Carousel 2
3200QLX7269 • $60
MAGIC.

2670.

Too Much Hunny
2450QLX7297 • $62
MAGIC.

2671.

Turn of the Century Parade 1: The Fireman
1695QK1027 • $32

2672.

Twelve Days of Christmas 12: Twelve Drummers Drumming
695QX3009 • $14

2673.

Two for Tea
995QX5829 • $22

2674.

U.S. Christmas Stamps 3
1095QX5067 • $19

2675.

Vera the Mouse
895QX5537 • $13

2676.

Victorian Toy Box
4200QLX7357 • $56
MAGIC.

2677.

Waiting up for Santa
895QX6106 • $14

2678.

Water Sports
1495QX6039 • $41 • Set/2

2679.

Wee Little Christmas
2200QLX7329 • $40
MAGIC.

2680.

Wheel of Fortune®
1295QX6187 • $19

2681.

Winnie the Pooh and Tigger
1295QX5009 • $30

2682.

The Winning Play
795QX5889 • $16

2683.

Yuletide Central 2: Coal Car
1895QX5079 • $19

1996

2684.

101 Dalmatians
1295QXI6544 • $16

2685.

1937 Steelcraft Auburn by Murray®
1595QXC4174 • $58

2686.

Airmail for Santa
($N/E)QXC4194 • $26

2687.

All God's Children 1: Christy
1295QX5564 • $23

2688.

All-American Trucks 2: 1955 Chevrolet® Cameo
1395QX5241 • $24

2689.

All-American Trucks 2: 1955 Chevrolet® Cameo
($N/A)QX5241C • $782
Edition Size - 256.

2690.

Antlers Aweigh!
995QX5901 • $26

2691.

Apple for Teacher
795QX6121 • $10

2692.

At the Ballpark 1: Nolan Ryan
1495QXI5711 • $29

2693.

Baby's First Christmas
2200QLX7404 • $42
MAGIC.

2694.

Baby's First Christmas
1895QX5744 • $25

2695.

Baby's First Christmas
1095QX5751 • $26

2696.

Baby's First Christmas
995QX5754 • $32

2697.
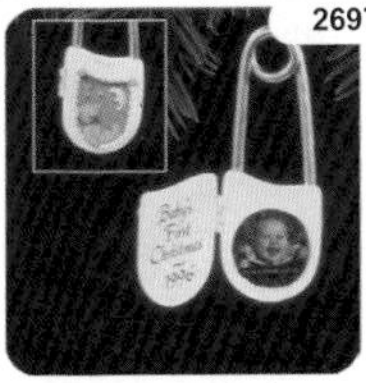
Baby's First Christmas
795QX5761 • $20

2698.

BARBIE™ 3: Enchanting Evening BARBIE™
1495QXI6541 • $22

2699.

Baseball Heroes 3: Satchel Paige
1295QX5304 • $18

2700.

Bounce Pass
795QX6031 • $13

2701.

Bowl 'em Over
795QX6014 • $14

2702.

Cat Naps 3
795QX5641 • $20

2703.

A Celebration of Angels 2
1295QX5634 • $16

2704.

Chicken Coop Chorus
2450QLX7491 • $42
MAGIC.

2705.

Child Care Giver
895QX6071 • $10

2706.

Child's Age: Baby's First Christmas
795QX5764 • $38

2707.

Child's Age: Baby's Second Christmas
795QX5771 • $32

2708.

Child's Age: Child's Third Christmas
795QX5774 • $24

2709.

Child's Age: Child's Fourth Christmas
795QX5781 • $24

2710.

Child's Age: Child's Fifth Christmas
695QX5784 • $24

2711.

Chris Mouse 12: Chris Mouse Inn
1450QLX7371 • $40
MAGIC.

2712.

Christmas Joy
1495QX6241 • $23

2713.

Christmas Snowman
995QX6214 • $28

2714.

Christmas Visitors 2: Christkindl
1495QX5631 • $15

2715.

Classic American Cars 6: 1959 Cadillac® De Ville
1295QX5384 • $23

2716.

Close-Knit Friends
995QX5874 • $23

2717.

Coca-Cola® - Welcome Guest
1495QX5394 • $20

2718.

Come All Ye Faithful
1295QX6244 • $20

2719.

Commander William T. Riker
1495QXI5551 • $28

2720.

Cookie Jar Friends: Carmen
1595QK1164 • $22

2721.

Cookie Jar Friends: Clyde
1595QK1161 • $20

2722.

Crayola® Crayon 8: Bright Flying Colors
1095QX5391 • $32

2723.
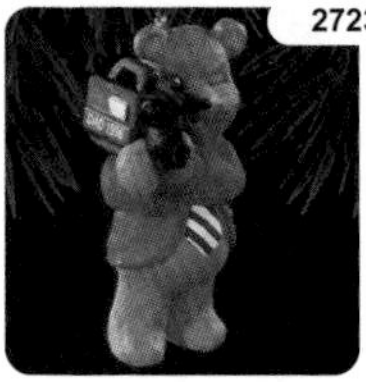
Dad
795QX5831 • $20

2724.

Daughter
895QX6077 • $26

2725.

Dolls of the World 1: Native American BARBIE™
1495QX5561 • $20

2726.

Emerald City™
3200QLX7454 • $95
MAGIC.

2727.

Esmeralda and Djali - Hunchback of Notre Dame
1495QXI6351 • $15

2728.

Evergreen Santa
2200QX5714 • $25

2729.

Fabulous Decade 7
795QX5661 • $28

2730.

Fan-tastic Season
995QX5924 • $14

2731.

Father Time
2450QLX7391 • $38
MAGIC.

2732.

Feliz Navidad
995QX6304 • $17

2733.

Foghorn Leghorn™ & Henery Hawk™
1395QX5444 • $28 • Set/2

2734.

Folk Art Americana: Caroling Angel
1695QK1134 • $26

2735.

Folk Art Americana: Mrs. Claus
1895QK1204 • $29

2736.

Folk Art Americana: Santa's Gifts
1895QK1124 • $35

2737.

Football Legends 2: Troy Aikman
1495QXI5021 • $20

2738.

Frosty Friends 17
1095QX5681 • $24

2739.

Get Hooked on Collecting Starter Set
799XPR837 • $12

2740.

Glad Tidings
1495QX6231 • $24

2741.

Goal Line Glory
1295QX6001 • $20 • Set/2

2742.

Godchild
895QX5841 • $14

2743.

Granddaughter
795QX5697 • $13

2744.

Grandma
895QX5844 • $25

2745.

Grandpa
895QX5851 • $12

2746.

Grandson
795QX5699 • $12

2747.

Growth of a Leader - Boy Scouts®
995QX5541 • $23

2748.

Happy Holidays® BARBIE™ 1
1495QXC4181 • $56

2749.

Happy Holi-doze
995QX5904 • $12

2750.

Hearts Full of Love
995QX5814 • $28

2751.

Here Comes Santa 18: Santa's 4 X 4
1495QX5684 • $29

2752.

High Style
895QX6064 • $13

2753.

Hillside Express
1295QX6134 • $26

2754.

Holiday BARBIE™ 4
1495QXI5371 • $25

2755.

Holiday Haul
1495QX6201 • $28

2756.

Hoop Stars 2: Larry Bird
1495QXI5014 • $24

2757.

Hurrying Downstairs
895QX6074 • $28

2758.

I Dig Golf
1095QX5891 • $13

2759.

Invitation to the Games
1495QXE5511 • $15 • Set/2

2760.

It's a Wonderful Life™
1495QXI6531 • $32

2761.

Izzy™ - The Mascot
995QXE5724 • $10

2762.
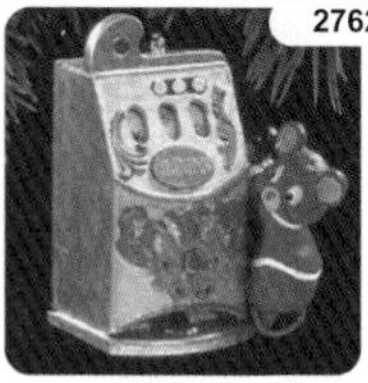
Jackpot Jingle
995QX5911 • $20

2763.

The Jetsons™
2800QLX7411 • $71
MAGIC.

2764.

Jolly Wolly Ark
1295QX6221 • $22

2765.

Journeys Into Space 1: Freedom 7
2400QLX7524 • $69
MAGIC.

2766.

Jukebox Party
2450QLX7339 • $49
MAGIC.

2767.

Kiddie Car Classics 3: Murray® Spitfire
1395QX5364 • $23

2768.

Kiddie Car Classics 3: Murray® Spitfire
($N/A)QX5364C • $775
Edition Size - 256.

2769.

Kindly Shepherd
1295QX6274 • $40

2770.

Language of Flowers 1: Pansy
1595QK1171 • $50

2771.

Laverne, Victor and Hugo - Hunchback of Notre Dame
1295QXI6354 • $13

2772.

Let Us Adore Him
1650QLX7381 • $32
MAGIC.

2773.

Lighting the Flame
2800QXE7444 • $28
MAGIC.

2774.

Lighting the Way
1295QX6124 • $20

2775.

LIONEL® Trains 1: Hudson Steam Locomotive
1895QX5531 • $62

2776.

A Little Song and Dance
995QX6211 • $17

2777.

Little Spooners
1295QX5504 • $18

2778.

Madame Alexander® 1: Cinderella
1495QX6311 • $29

2779.

Madonna and Child
1295QX6324 • $13

2780.

Magi Bells: Balthasar - Frankincense
1395QK1174 • $18

2781.

Magi Bells: Caspar - Myrrh
1395QK1184 • $18

2782.

Magi Bells: Melchior - Gold
1395QK1181 • $16

2783.

Making His Rounds
1495QX6271 • $33

2784.

Marvin the Martian™
1095QX5451 • $24

2785.

Mary's Angels 9: Violet
695QX5664 • $33

2786.

Matchless Memories
995QX6061 • $17

2787.

Maxine
995QX6224 • $28

2788.
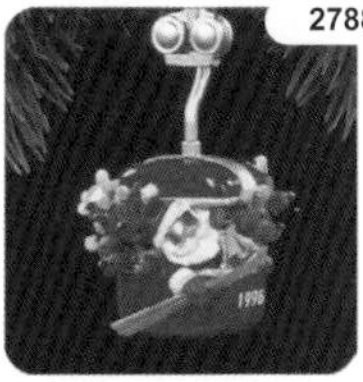
Merry Carpoolers
1495QX5884 • $25

2789.

Merry Olde Santa 7
1495QX5654 • $29

2790.
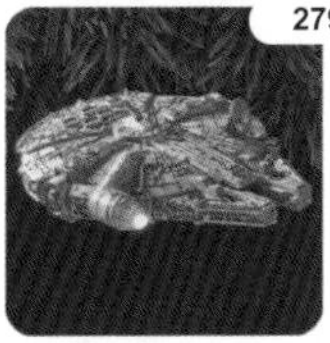
Millennium Falcon™
2400QLX7474 • $56
MAGIC.

2791.

Mom
795QX5824 • $19

2792.

Mom and Dad
995QX5821 • $26

2793.

Mom-to-Be
795QX5791 • $16

2794.

Mother Goose 4: Mary Had a Little Lamb
1395QX5644 • $20

2795.

Mr. Spock
1495QXI5544 • $28

2796.

Nature's Sketchbook: Birds' Christmas Tree
1895QK1114 • $28

2797.

Nature's Sketchbook: Christmas Bunny
1895QK1104 • $42

2798.

Nature's Sketchbook: Holly Basket
1895QK1094 • $23

2799.

New Home
895QX5881 • $28

2800.

NFL®: Arizona Cardinals™
995QSR6484 • $14

2801.

NFL®: Atlanta Falcons™
995QSR6364 • $14

2802.

NFL®: Buffalo Bills™
595BIL2035 • $16

2803.

NFL®: Buffalo Bills™
995QSR6371 • $14

2804.

NFL®:
Carolina Panthers™
595PNA2035 • $16
Re-issued from 1995.

2805.

NFL®:
Carolina Panthers™
995QSR6374 • $14

2806.

NFL®: Chicago Bears™
595BRS2035 • $16
Re-issued from 1995.

2807.

NFL®: Chicago Bears™
995QSR6381 • $14

2808.

NFL®:
Cincinnati Bengals™
995QSR6384 • $14

2809.

NFL®:
Cleveland Browns™
995QSR6391 • $14

2810.

NFL®: Dallas Cowboys™
595COW2035 • $16
Re-issued from 1995.

2811.

NFL®: Dallas Cowboys™
995QSR6394 • $14

2812.

NFL®:
Denver Broncos™
995QSR6411 • $14

2813.

NFL®: Detroit Lions™
995QSR6414 • $14

2814.

NFL®:
Green Bay Packers™
595PKR2035 • $16

2815.

NFL®:
Green Bay Packers™
995QSR6421 • $14

2816.

NFL®: Houston Oilers™
995QSR6424 • $14

2817.

NFL®:
Indianapolis Colts™
995QSR6431 • $14

2818.

NFL®:
Jacksonville Jaguars™
995QSR6434 • $14

2819.

NFL®:
Kansas City Chiefs™
595CHF2035 • $16
Re-issued from 1995.

2820.

NFL®:
Kansas City Chiefs™
995QSR6361 • $14

2821.

NFL®:
Los Angeles Raiders™
595RDR2035 • $16
Re-issued from 1995.

2822.

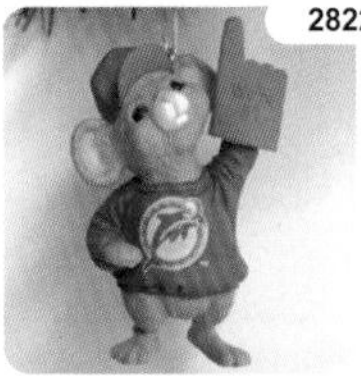

NFL®: Miami Dolphins™
995QSR6451 • $14

2823.

NFL®:
Minnesota Vikings™
995QSR6454 • $14

2824.

NFL®:
Minnesota Vikings™
595VIK2035 • $16
Re-issued from 1995.

2825.

NFL®:
New England Patriots™
595NEP2035 • $16
Re-issued from 1995.

2826.

NFL®:
New England Patriots™
995QSR6461 • $14

2827.

NFL®:
New Orleans Saints™
995QSR6464 • $14

2828.

NFL®: New York Giants™
995QSR6471 • $14

2829.

NFL®: New York Jets™
995QSR6474 • $14

2830.

NFL®: Oakland Raiders™
995QSR6441 • $14

2831.

NFL®: Philadelphia Eagles™
595EAG2035 • $16
Re-issued from 1995.

2832.

NFL®: Philadelphia Eagles™
995QSR6481 • $14

2833.

NFL®: Pittsburgh Steelers™
595PIT2035 • $16

2834.

NFL®: Pittsburgh Steelers™
995QSR6491 • $14

2835.

NFL®: San Diego Chargers™
995QSR6494 • $14

2836.

NFL®: San Francisco 49ers™
595FOR2035 • $16
Re-issued from 1995.

2837.

NFL®: San Francisco 49ers™
995QSR6501 • $14

2838.

NFL®: Seattle Seahawks™
995QSR6504 • $14

2839.

NFL®: St. Louis Rams™
995QSR6444 • $14

2840.

NFL®: St. Louis Rams™
595RAM2035 • $16

2841.

NFL®: Tampa Bay Buccaneers™
995QSR6511 • $14

2842.

NFL®: Washington Redskins™
995QSR6514 • $14

2843.

NFL®: Washington Redskins™
595RSK2035 • $16
Re-issued from 1995.

2844.

North Pole Volunteers
4200QLX7471 • $91
MAGIC.

2845.

Nostalgic Houses & Shops 13: Victorian Painted Lady
1495QX5671 • $26

2846.

Olive Oyl and Swee' Pea
1095QX5481 • $19

2847.

Olympic Triumph
1095QXE5731 • $16

2848.

On My Way
795QX5861 • $14

2849.

Our Christmas Together
1895QX5794 • $40

2850.

Our Christmas Together
895QX5804 • $15

2851.

Our First Christmas Together
695QX3051 • $28

2852.

Our First Christmas Together
1095QX5801 • $24

2853.

Our First Christmas Together
995QX5811 • $28

2854.

Over the Rooftops
1450QLX7374 • $35
MAGIC.

2855.

Parade of Nations
1095QXE5741 • $12

2856.

PEANUTS® - Schroeder and Lucy
1850QLX7394 • $52
MAGIC.

2857.

PEANUTS® Gang 4
995QX5381 • $17

2858.

Peppermint Surprise
795QX6234 • $21

2859.

Percy the Small Engine - No. 6
995QX6314 • $24

2860.

Pez® Snowman
795QX6534 • $18

2861.

Pinball Wonder
2800QLX7451 • $55
MAGIC.

2862.

Polar Cycle
1295QX6034 • $23

2863.

Prayer for Peace
795QX6261 • $13

2864.

Precious Child
895QX6251 • $13

2865.
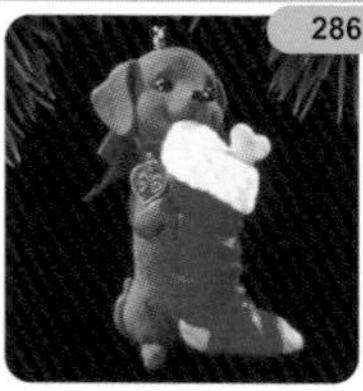
Puppy Love 6
795QX5651 • $26

2866.
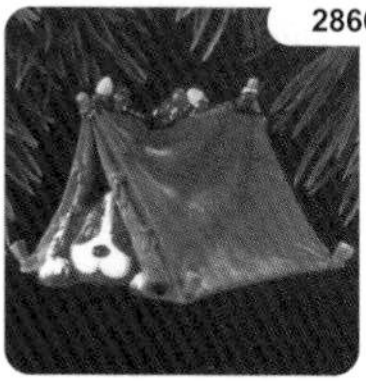
Pup-Tenting
795QX6011 • $24

2867.

Quasimodo - Hunchback of Notre Dame
995QXI6341 • $10

2868.

Regal Cardinal
995QX6204 • $40

2869.

Rocking Horse 16
1095QX5674 • $20

2870.

Rudolph the Red-Nosed Reindeer®
($N/E)QXC7341 • $28
MAGIC.

2871.

Sacred Masterworks: Madonna and Child
1595QK1144 • $23

2872.

Sacred Masterworks: Praying Madonna
1595QK1154 • $23

2873.

Santa
($N/E)QXC4164 • $14

2874.

Santa's Toy Shop
6000QXC4201 • $130

2875.
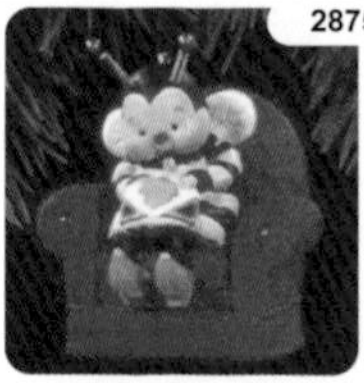
Sew Sweet
895QX5921 • $26

2876.

Sharing a Soda
2450QLX7424 • $34
MAGIC.

2877.

Sister to Sister
995QX5834 • $16

2878.

Slippery Day
2450QLX7414 • $49
MAGIC.

2879.

Son
895QX6079 • $32

2880.
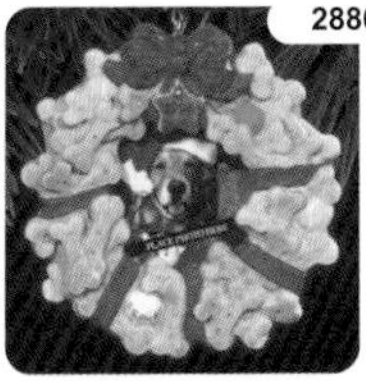
Special Dog
795QX5864 • $29

2881.

Spider-Man™
1295QX5757 • $42

2882.
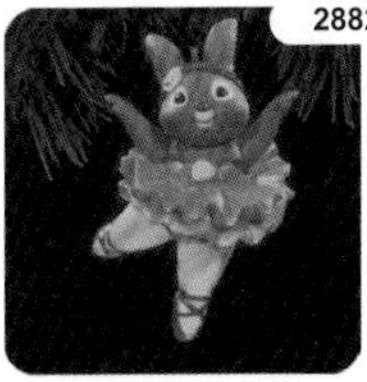
Star of the Show
895QX6004 • $17

2883.
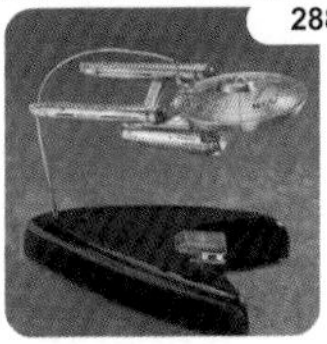
Star Trek™ - 30 Years
4500QXI7534 • $89 • Set/2
MAGIC.

2884.

The Statue of Liberty
2450QLX7421 • $60
MAGIC.

2885.

Tamika
795QX6301 • $12

2886.

Tender Lovin' Care
795QX6114 • $18

2887.

Tender Touches: Welcome Sign
1500QX6331 • $20

2888.

Thank You, Santa
795QX5854 • $17

2889.

This Big!
995QX5914 • $25

2890.
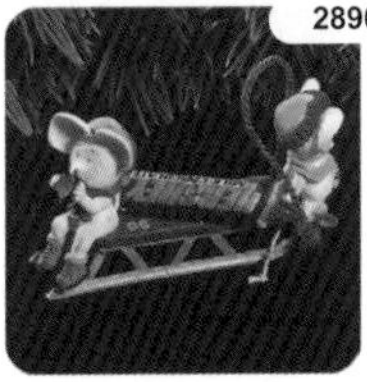
Time for a Treat
1195QX5464 • $23

2891.

Tobin Fraley Holiday Carousel 3
3200QLX7461 • $46
MAGIC.

2892.

Tonka® Mighty Dump Truck
1395QX6321 • $42

2893.

Toy Shop Santa
1495(N/A) • $38

2894.

Treasured Memories
1850QLX7384 • $32
MAGIC.

2895.

A Tree for Snoopy®
895QX5507 • $18

2896.

Turn of the Century Parade 2: Uncle Sam
1695QK1084 • $26

2897.

U.S.S. Voyager™
2400QXI7544 • $48
MAGIC.

2898.

Video Party
2800QLX7431 • $40
MAGIC.

2899.

Welcome Him
895QX6264 • $17

2900.

Winnie the Pooh and Piglet
1295QX5454 • $28

2901.

Witch of the West™
1395QX5554 • $32

2902.

The Wizard of Oz™
1295QXC4161 • $85

2903.

Wonder Woman™
1295QX5941 • $26

2904.

Woodland Santa
1295QX6131 • $22

2905.

Yogi Bear™ and Boo Boo™
1295QX5521 • $28

2906.

Yuletide Central 3: Mail Car
1895QX5011 • $34

2907.

Yuletide Cheer
795QX6054 • $10

2908.

Ziggy®
995QX6524 • $17

1997

2909.

1937 Steelcraft Airflow by Murray®
1595QXC5185 • $46

2910.
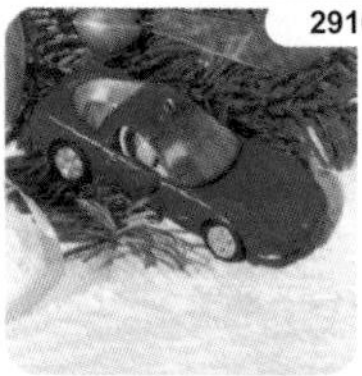
1997 Corvette®
1395QXI6455 • $18

2911.

All God's Children 2: Nikki
1295QX6142 • $22 • Set/2

2912.

All-American Trucks 3: 1953 GMC
1395QX6105 • $31

2913.

All-American Trucks 3: 1953 GMC
($N/A)QX6105C • $375
Edition Size - 320.

2914.

All-Round Sports Fan
895QX6392 • $29

2915.

All-Weather Walker
895QX6415 • $13

2916.

Angel Friend
1495QX6762 • $24

2917.

Ariel - The Little Mermaid
1295QXI4072 • $25

2918.

Artists On Tour Volunteer Thank You
($N/A)(N/A) • $75
RARE

2919.

At the Ballpark 2: Hank Aaron
1495QXI6152 • $21

2920.

Away to the Window
($N/E)QXC5135 • $10

2921.

Baby's First Christmas
795QX6482 • $30

2922.

Baby's First Christmas
995QX6485 • $24

2923.

Baby's First Christmas
995QX6492 • $17

2924.

Baby's First Christmas
1495QX6535 • $24

2925.

BARBIE™ 4: Wedding Day 1959 - 1962
1595QXI6812 • $20

2926.

BARBIE™ and KEN™ Wedding Day
3500QXI6815 • $48 • Set/2

2927.

Baseball Heroes 4: Jackie Robinson
1295QX6202 • $18

2928.

Biking Buddies
1295QX6682 • $13

2929.

Book of the Year
795QX6645 • $24

2930.
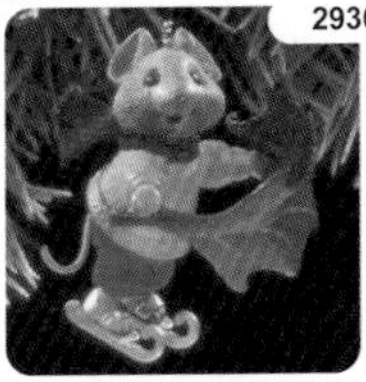
Breezin' Along
895QX6722 • $17

2931.

Bucket Brigade
895QX6382 • $18

2932.

Cat Naps 4
895QX6205 • $19

2933.

Catch of the Day
995QX6712 • $18

2934.

A Celebration of Angels 3
1395QX6175 • $25

2935.
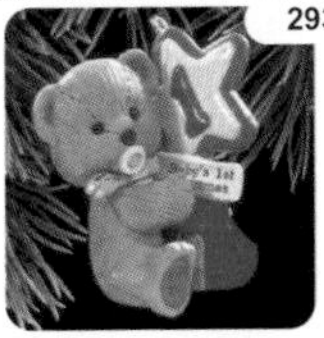
Child's Age: Baby's First Christmas
795QX6495 • $24

2936.

Child's Age: Baby's Second Christmas
795QX6502 • $24

2937.

Child's Age: Child's Third Christmas
795QX6505 • $18

2938.

Child's Age: Child's Fourth Christmas
795QX6512 • $18

2939.

Child's Age: Child's Fifth Christmas
795QX6515 • $18

2940.

Chris Mouse 13: Chris Mouse Luminara
1495QLX7525 • $30
MAGIC.

2941.

Christmas Checkup
795QX6385 • $14

2942.

Christmas Visitors 3: Kolyada
1495QX6172 • $19

2943.

Classic American Cars 7: 1969 Hurst Oldsmobile 442
1395QX6102 • $34

2944.
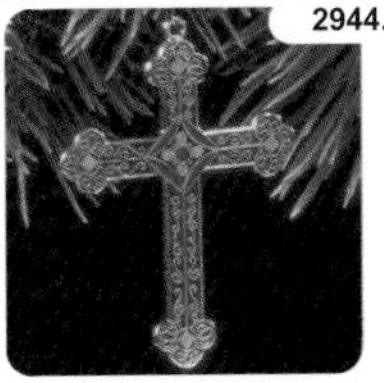
Classic Cross
1395QX6805 • $24

2945.

The Clauses on Vacation 1
1495QX6112 • $22

2946.

Clever Camper
795QX6445 • $14

2947.

Coca-Cola® - Taking a Break
1495QX6305 • $25

2948.

Commander Data
1495QXI6345 • $30

2949.

Crayola® Crayon 9: Bright Rocking Colors
1295QX6235 • $23

2950.

Cycling Santa
1495QX6425 • $25

2951.

Dad
895QX6532 • $20

2952.

Darth Vader™
2400QXI7531 • $36
MAGIC.

2953.

Daughter
795QX6612 • $15

2954.

Decorator Taz™
3000QLX7502 • $42
MAGIC.

2955.

Dolls of the World 2: Chinese BARBIE™
1495QX6162 • $20

2956.
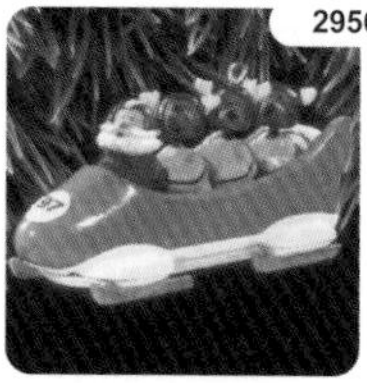
Downhill Run
995QX6705 • $20

2957.

Dr. Leonard H. McCoy
1495QXI6352 • $35

2958.

Elegance on Ice
995QX6432 • $16

2959.

Enchanted Memories 1: Cinderella
1495QXD4045 • $28

2960.

Expressly for Teacher
795QX6375 • $14

2961.

Fabulous Decade 8
795QX6232 • $18

2962.

Feliz Navidad
895QX6665 • $40

2963.

First Class Thank You
($N/E)(N/A) • $16

2964.

Football Legends 3: Joe Namath
1495QXI6182 • $19

2965.

Friendship Blend
995QX6655 • $18

2966.

Frosty Friends 18
1095QX6255 • $23

2967.

Gift of Friendship - Winnie the Pooh® Plate
1295QXE6835 • $19

2968.

Glowing Angel
1895QLX7435 • $28
MAGIC.

2969.

Godchild
795QX6662 • $14

2970.

God's Gift of Love
1695QX6792 • $50

2971.

Goofy®'s Ski Adventure
1295QXD4042 • $17

2972.

Granddaughter
795QX6622 • $30

2973.

Grandma
895QX6625 • $14

2974.

Grandson
795QX6615 • $30

2975.

Gus & Jaq - Cinderella
1295QXD4052 • $28

2976.

Hallmark Archives 1: Donald's Surprising Gift
1295QXD4025 • $19

2977.

Happy Christmas to All!
($N/E)QXC5132 • $10

2978.

Happy Holidays® BARBIE™ 2
1595QXC5162 • $53

2979.

Heavenly Song
1295QX6795 • $22

2980.

Hercules®
1295QXI4005 • $24

2981.

Here Comes Santa 19: The Claus-Mobile
1495QX6262 • $25

2982.

Hockey Greats 1: Wayne Gretsky
1595QXI6275 • $25

2983.

Holiday BARBIE™ 5
1595QXI6212 • $20

2984.

Holiday Serenade
2400QLX7485 • $34
MAGIC.

2985.

Holiday Traditions BARBIE™ Ornament
1495QHB6002 • $20

2986.

Hoop Stars 3: Magic Johnson
1495QXI6832 • $20

2987.

Howdy Doody™
1295QX6272 • $18

2988.

The Incredible Hulk™
1295QX5471 • $30

2989.

Jasmine & Aladdin - Aladdin and the King of Thieves
1495QXD4062 • $22

2990.

Jingle Bell Jester
995QX6695 • $19

2991.
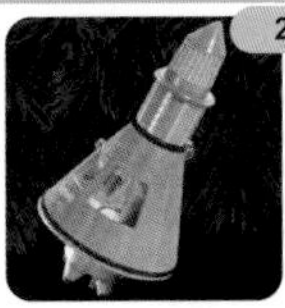
Journeys Into Space 2: Friendship 7
2400QLX7532 • $64
MAGIC.

2992.
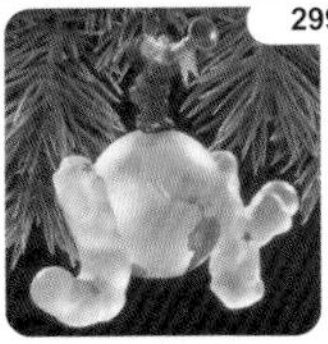
Joy to the World
1495QLX7512 • $24
MAGIC.

2993.

Juggling Stars
995QX6595 • $17

2994.

Kiddie Car Classics 4: Murray® Dump Truck
1395QX6195 • $23

2995.

Kiddie Car Classics 4: Murray® Dump Truck
($N/A)QX6195C • $600
Edition Size - 320.

2996.

Language of Flowers 2: Snowdrop Angel
1595QX1095 • $20

2997.

Leading the Way
1695QX6782 • $34

2998.

Legend of the Three Kings 1: King Noor - First King
1295QX6552 • $34

2999.

Lighthouse Greetings 1
2400QLX7442 • $118
MAGIC.

3000.

Lincoln Memorial
2400QLX7522 • $40
MAGIC.

3001.

Lion and Lamb
795QX6602 • $16

3002.

LIONEL® Trains 2: 1950 Santa Fe F3 Deisel Locomotive
1895QX6145 • $37

3003.

The Lone Ranger™
1295QX6265 • $22

3004.

Love to Sew
795QX6435 • $16

3005.

Madame Alexander® 2: Little Red Riding Hood
1495QX6155 • $22

3006.

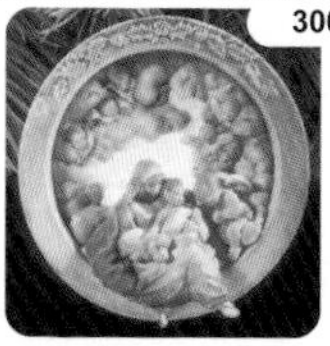

Madonna and Child
1995QLX7425 • $31
MAGIC.

3007.

Madonna del Rosario
1295QX6545 • $28

3008.

Majestic Wilderness 1: Snowshoe Rabbits in Winter
1295QX5694 • $29

3009.

Marbles Champion
1095QX6342 • $17

3010.

Marilyn Monroe 1
1495QX5704 • $28

3011.

Mary's Angels 10: Daisy
795QX6242 • $30

3012.

Meadow Snowman
1295QX6715 • $28

3013.

Megara and Pegasus - Hercules
1695QXI4012 • $23

3014.

Merry Olde Santa 8
1495QX6225 • $25

3015.

Michigan J. Frog™
995QX6332 • $20

3016.

Mickey's Holiday Parade 1: Bandleader Mickey
1395QXD4022 • $22

3017.

Mickey's Long Shot
1095QXD6412 • $18

3018.

Mickey's Snow Angel
995QXD4035 • $16

3019.

Miss Gulch™
1395QX6372 • $48

3020.

Mom
895QX6525 • $19

3021.

Mom and Dad
995QX6522 • $13

3022.

Mother Goose 5: Little Boy Blue
1395QX6215 • $20

3023.
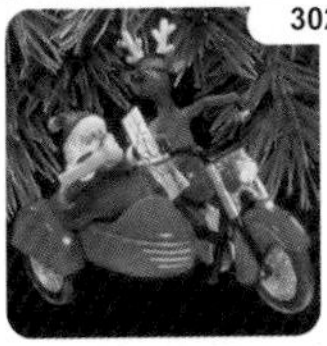
Motorcycle Chums
2400QLX7495 • $42
MAGIC.

3024.

Mr. Potato Head®
1095QX6335 • $24

3025.

Mrs. Claus's Story
1495(N/A) • $34

3026.
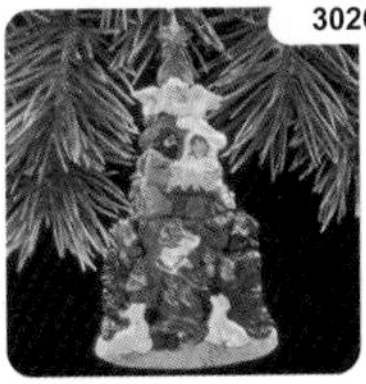
Nativity Tree
1495QX6575 • $26

3027.

Nature's Sketchbook: Garden Bouquet
1495QX6752 • $23

3028.

Nature's Sketchbook: Honored Guests
1495QX6745 • $29

3029.

NBA®: Charlotte Hornets™
995QSR1222 • $11

3030.

NBA®: Chicago Bulls™
995QSR1232 • $11

3031.

NBA®: Detroit Pistons™
995QSR1242 • $11

3032.

NBA®: Houston Rockets™
995QSR1245 • $11

3033.

NBA®: Indiana Pacers™
995QSR1252 • $11

3034.

NBA®: Los Angeles Lakers™
995QSR1262 • $11

3035.

NBA®: New York Knickerbockers™
995QSR1272 • $11

3036.

NBA®: Orlando Magic™
995QSR1282 • $11

3037.

NBA®: Phoenix Suns™
995QSR1292 • $11

3038.

NBA®: Seattle Supersonics™
995QSR1295 • $11

3039.

New Home
895QX6652 • $18

3040.

New Pair of Skates
1395QXD4032 • $19

3041.
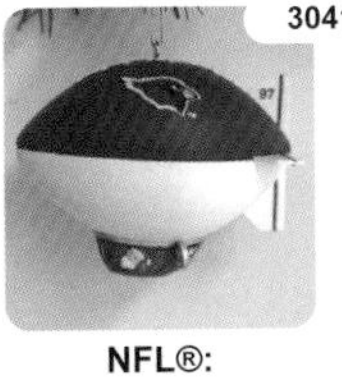
NFL®: Arizona Cardinals™
995QSR5505 • $13

3042.

NFL®: Atlanta Falcons™
995QSR5305 • $13

3043.
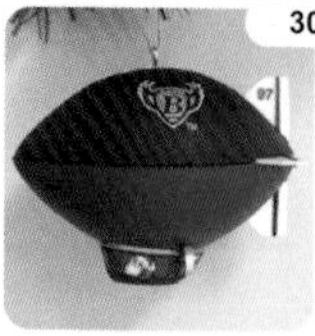
NFL®:
Baltimore Ravens™
995QSR5352 • $13

3044.

NFL®: Buffalo Bills™
995QSR5312 • $13

3045.

NFL®:
Carolina Panthers™
995QSR5315 • $13

3046.

NFL®: Chicago Bears™
995QSR5322 • $13

3047.

NFL®:
Cincinnati Bengals™
995QSR5325 • $13

3048.

NFL®: Dallas Cowboys™
995QSR5355 • $13

3049.

NFL®:
Denver Broncos™
995QSR5362 • $13

3050.

NFL®: Detroit Lions™
995QSR5365 • $13

3051.

NFL®:
Green Bay Packers™
995QSR5372 • $13

3052.
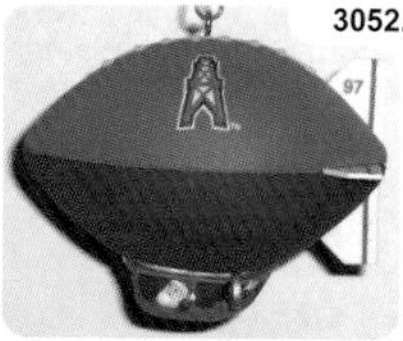
NFL®: Houston Oilers™
995QSR5375 • $13

3053.

NFL®:
Indianapolis Colts™
995QSR5411 • $13

3054.
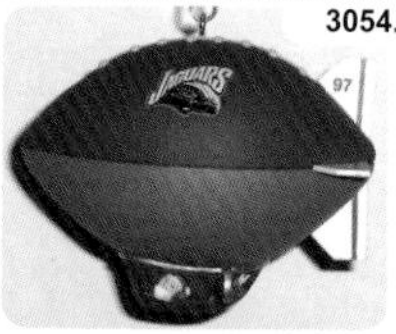
NFL®:
Jacksonville Jaguars™
995QSR5415 • $13

3055.

NFL®:
Kansas City Chiefs™
995QSR5302 • $13

3056.
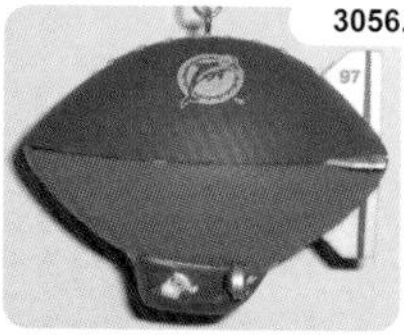
NFL®: Miami Dolphins™
995QSR5472 • $13

3057.

NFL®:
Minnesota Vikings™
995QSR5475 • $13

3058.
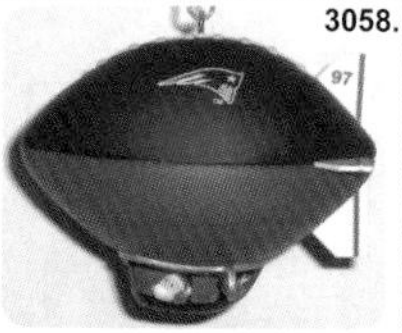
NFL®:
New England Patriots™
995QSR5482 • $13

3059.
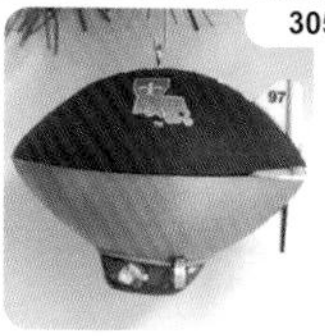
NFL®:
New Orleans Saints™
995QSR5485 • $13

3060.

NFL®:
New York Giants™
995QSR5492 • $13

3061.

NFL®: New York Jets™
995QSR5495 • $13

3062.

NFL®:
Oakland Raiders™
995QSR5422 • $13

3063.

NFL®:
Philadelphia Eagles™
995QSR5502 • $13

3064.

NFL®:
Pittsburgh Steelers™
995QSR5512 • $13

3065.

NFL®:
San Diego Chargers™
995QSR5515 • $13

3066.
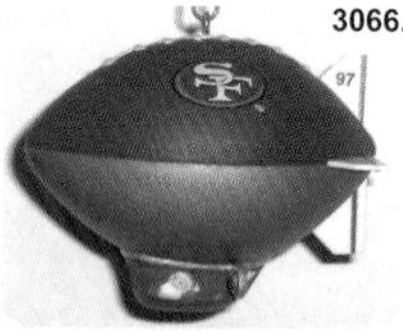
NFL®:
San Francisco 49ers™
995QSR5522 • $13

3067.

NFL®: Seattle Seahawks™
995QSR5525 • $13

3068.
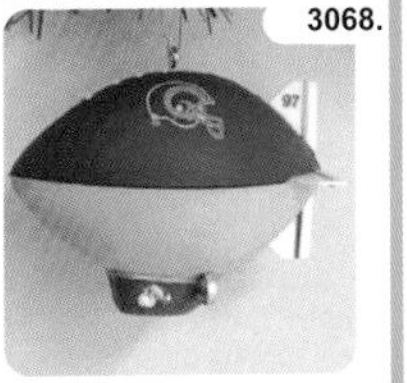
NFL®: St. Louis Rams™
995QSR5425 • $13

3069.

NFL®: Tampa Bay Buccaneers™
995QSR5532 • $13

3070.
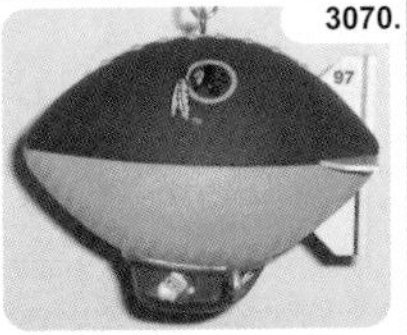
NFL®: Washington Redskins™
995QSR5535 • $13

3071.

The Night Before Christmas
2400QX5721 • $42

3072.

Nostalgic Houses & Shops 14: Café
1695QX6245 • $24

3073.

Our Christmas Together
1695QX6475 • $19

3074.

Our First Christmas Together
795QX3182 • $14

3075.
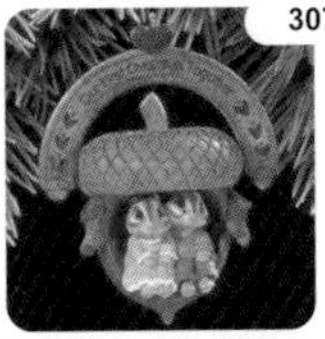
Our First Christmas Together
1095QX6465 • $22

3076.

Our First Christmas Together
895QX6472 • $14

3077.
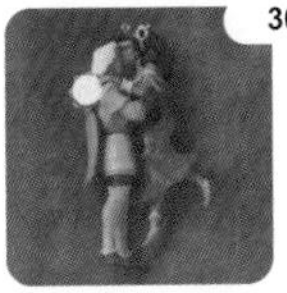
Phoebus & Esmeralda - Hunchback of Notre Dame
1495QXD6344 • $20

3078.

Playful Shepherd
995QX6592 • $19

3079.
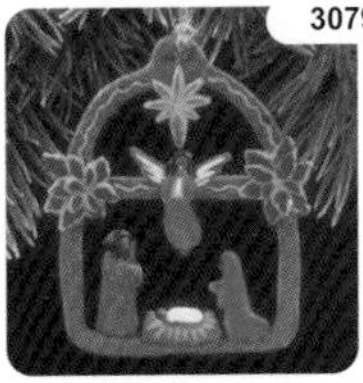
Praise Him
895QX6542 • $30

3080.

Prize Topiary
1495QX6675 • $22

3081.

Puppy Love 7
795QX6222 • $40

3082.
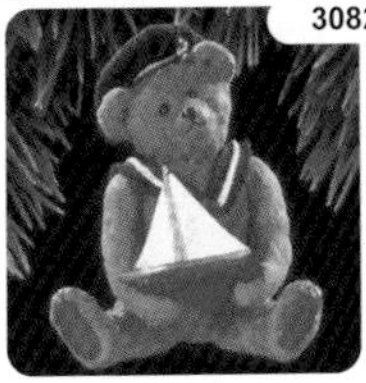
Sailor Bear
1495QX6765 • $19

3083.

Santa Mail
1095QX6702 • $28

3084.

Santa's Friend
1295QX6685 • $19

3085.

Santa's Magical Sleigh
2400QX6672 • $37

3086.

Santa's Magical Sleigh
($N/A)QX6672C • $500

3087.
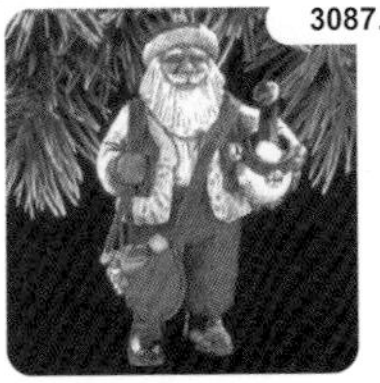
Santa's Merry Path
1695QX6785 • $29

3088.
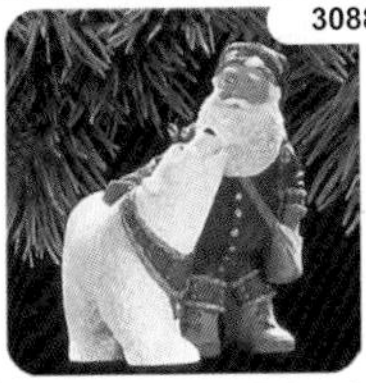
Santa's Polar Friend
1695QX6755 • $32

3089.

Santa's Secret Gift
2400QLX7455 • $38
MAGIC.

3090.

Santa's Showboat
4200QLX7465 • $80
MAGIC.

3091.

Santa's Ski Adventure
1295QX6422 • $25

3092.

Scarlett O'Hara™ 1
1495QX6125 • $26

3093.

Sister to Sister
995QX6635 • $24

3094.
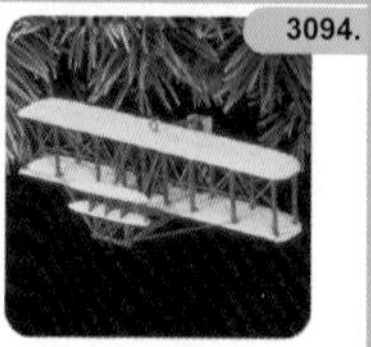
Sky's the Limit 1: The Flight at Kitty Hawk
1495QX5574 • $28

3095.

Snoopy® Plays Santa
2200QLX7475 • $55
MAGIC.

3096.

Snow Bowling
695QX6395 • $13

3097.

Snow White Anniversary Edition
1695QXD4055 • $25 • Set/2

3098.
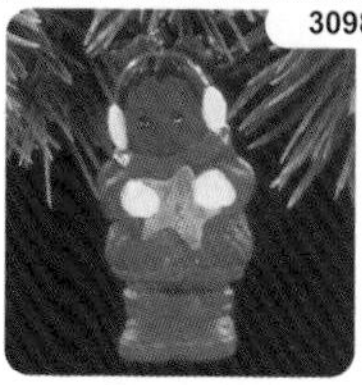
Snowgirl
795QX6562 • $20

3099.

Snowman Hinged Box
1495QX6772 • $25

3100.

Son
795QX6605 • $20

3101.
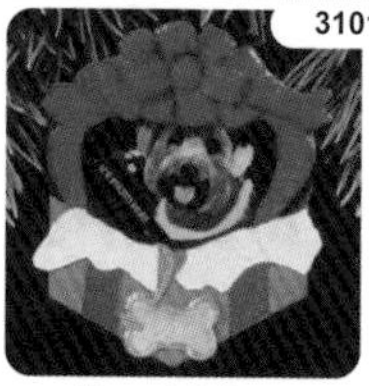
Special Dog
795QX6632 • $14

3102.

The Spirit of Christmas
995QX6585 • $34

3103.

Star Wars™ 1: Luke Skywalker™
1395QXI5484 • $24

3104.

Stealing a Kiss
1495QX6555 • $20

3105.

Stock Car Champions 1: Jeff Gordon
1595QXI6165 • $30

3106.

Sweet Discovery
1195QX6325 • $24

3107.

Sweet Dreamer
695QX6732 • $30

3108.

Swinging in the Snow
1295QX6775 • $30

3109.

Teapot Party
1895QLX7482 • $29
MAGIC.

3110.

Tender Touches: The Perfect Tree
1500QX6572 • $22

3111.

Thomas Kinkade, Painter of Light 1: Victorian Christmas
1095QXI6135 • $26

3112.
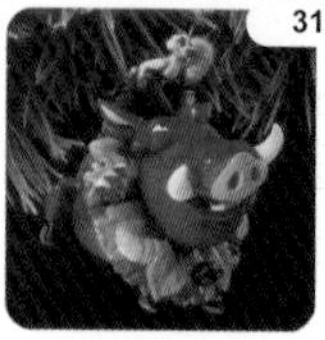
Timon & Pumbaa - The Lion King
1295QXD4065 • $18

3113.

Tomorrow's Leader - Boy Scouts®
995QX6452 • $18

3114.

Tonka® Mighty Front Loader
1395QX6362 • $31

3115.

Trimming Santa's Tree
6000QXC5175 • $95

3116.

Turn of the Century Parade 3: Santa Claus
1695QX1215 • $23

3117.

Two-Tone - 101 Dalmatians®
995QXD4015 • $24

3118.

U.S.S. Defiant™
2400QXI7481 • $37
MAGIC.

3119.

Victorian Elegance BARBIE™ Ornament
1495QHB6004 • $24

3120.

Waitin' on Santa
1295QXD6365 • $24

3121.

The Warmth of the Home
1895QXI7545 • $19
MAGIC.

3122.

What a Deal!
895QX6442 • $14

3123.

Yoda™
995QXI6355 • $38

3124.

Yuletide Central 4: Cargo Car
1895QX5812 • $28

1998

3125.

#1 Student
795QX6646 • $11

3126.

1935 Steelcraft by Murray®
1595QXC4496 • $49

3127.

1955 Murray® Fire Truck
3500QBG6909 • $46

3128.

1998 Corvette®
2400QLX7605 • $33
MAGIC.

3129.

1998 Corvette® Convertible
1395QX6416 • $30

3130.
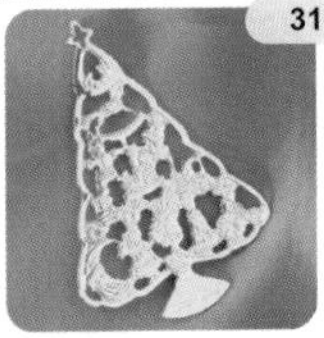
25th Anniversary Silver Tree
($N/A)(N/A) • $32

3131.

African-American Holiday BARBIE™ 1
1595QX6936 • $28

3132.

All God's Children 3: Martha Root
1295QX6363 • $28

3133.

All-American Trucks 4: 1937 Ford® V-8
1395QX6263 • $34

3134.

Angelic Flight
8500QXI4146 • $85
Limited Edition - 25000.

3135.

Angelic Flight
($N/E)QXI4146C • $1000
VERY RARE

3136.

At the Ballpark 3: Cal Ripken Jr.
1495QXI4033 • $30

3137.

Baby's First Christmas
995QX6233 • $14

3138.

Baby's First Christmas
995QX6586 • $20

3139.

Baby's First Christmas
895QX6596 • $26

3140.

BARBIE™ 5: Silken Flame BARBIE™
1595QXI4043 • $23

3141.

Blessed Nativity: The Holy Family
2500QX6523 • $45 • Set/3
Re-issued in 1999 & 2000.

3142.

Boba Fett™
1495QXI4053 • $40

3143.

Bouncy Baby-sitter
1295QXD4096 • $22

3144.

Bugs Bunny™
1395QX6443 • $17

3145.

Building a Snowman
1495QXD4133 • $24

3146.

Buzz Lightyear - Toy Story
1495QXD4066 • $40

3147.

Candlelight Services 1: The Stone Church
1895QLX7636 • $52
MAGIC.

3148.

Captain Kathryn Janeway
1495QXI4046 • $40

3149.

Cat Naps 5
895QX6383 • $20

3150.

Catch of the Season
1495QX6786 • $26

3151.

A Celebration of Angels 4
1395QX6366 • $35

3152.

Chatty Chipmunk
995QX6716 • $20

3153.

Checking Santa's Files
895QX6806 • $15

3154.

A Child is Born
1295QX6176 • $32

3155.

Child's Age: Baby's First Christmas
795QX6603 • $45

3156.

Child's Age: Baby's Second Christmas
795QX6606 • $28

3157.

Child's Age: Child's Third Christmas
795QX6613 • $22

3158.

Child's Age: Child's Fourth Christmas
795QX6616 • $22

3159.

Child's Age: Child's Fifth Christmas
795QX6623 • $22

3160.
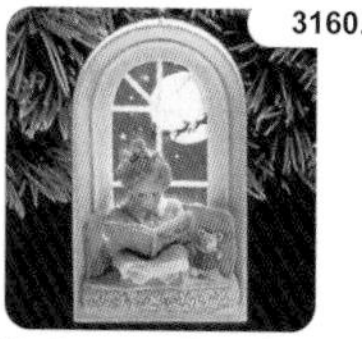
A Christmas Eve Story - Becky Kelly
1395QX6873 • $23

3161.

Christmas Eve's Preparations
8500QXC4506 • $345
Edition Size - 3900

3162.

Christmas Request
1495QX6193 • $28

3163.

Christmas Sleigh Ride
1295QX6556 • $22

3164.

Cinderella at the Ball
2400QXD7576 • $85
MAGIC.

3165.

Cinderella's Coach
1495QXD4083 • $32

3166.

Classic American Cars 8: 1970 Plymouth® Hemi 'Cuda
1395QX6256 • $40

3167.

The Clauses on Vacation 2
1495QX6276 • $18

3168.

Collegiate: Florida State Seminoles™
995QSR2316 • $14

3169.
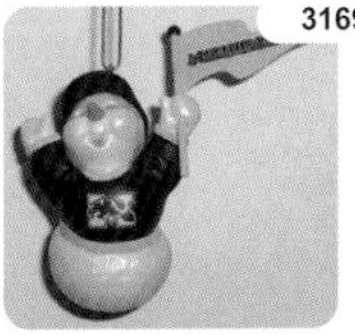
Collegiate: Michigan Wolverines™
995QSR2323 • $14

3170.

Collegiate: North Carolina Tar Heels™
995QSR2333 • $14

3171.

Collegiate: Notre Dame Fighting Irish™
995QSR2313 • $14

3172.

Collegiate: Penn State Nittany Lions™
995QSR2326 • $14

3173.

Compact Skater
995QX6766 • $14

3174.

Crayola® Crayon 10: Bright Sledding Colors
1295QX6166 • $26

3175.

Cross of Peace
995QX6856 • $22

3176.

Crown Reflections 1: Red Poinsettias
3500QBG6906 • $50

3177.

Cruising into Christmas
1695QX6196 • $25

3178.

Dad
895QX6663 • $13

3179.

Daughter
895QX6673 • $19

3180.

Daydreams - The Little Mermaid
1395QXD4136 • $32

3181.

Decorating Maxine Style
1095QXE6883 • $16

3182.

Dolls of the World 3: Mexican BARBIE™
1495QX6356 • $30

3183.

Downhill Dash
1395QX6776 • $40

3184.

Enchanted Memories 2: Snow White
1495QXD4056 • $28

3185.

Fabulous Decade 9
795QX6393 • $40

3186.

Fancy Footwork
895QX6536 • $28

3187.

Feliz Navidad
895QX6173 • $17

3188.

Festive Locomotive
3500QBG6903 • $46

3189.

Flik - A Bug's Life
1295QXD4153 • $32

3190.

Follow the Leader
1695QXC4503 • $35 • Set/2

3191.

Football Legends 4: Emmitt Smith
1495QXI4036 • $50

3192.

Forever Friends Bear
895QX6303 • $14

3193.

Frankincense
2200QBG6896 • $38
Re-issued in 1999.

3194.
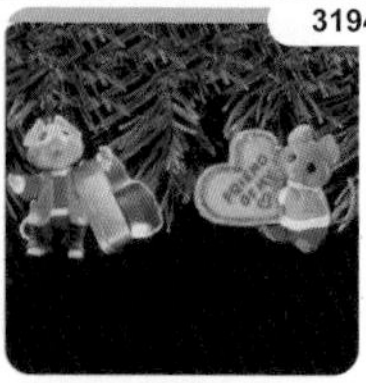
Friend of My Heart
1495QX6723 • $20 • Set/2

3195.

Frosty Friends
4800QBG6907 • $63 • Set/2

3196.

Frosty Friends 19
1095QX6226 • $48

3197.

Future Ballerina
795QX6756 • $17

3198.

Gifted Gardener
795QX6736 • $12

3199.

Godchild
795QX6703 • $25

3200.

Gold
2200QBG6836 • $43
Re-issued in 1999.

3201.

Good Luck Dice
995QX6813 • $12

3202.

Goofy® Soccer Star
1095QXD4123 • $20

3203.

Granddaughter
795QX6683 • $12

3204.

Grandma's Memories
895QX6686 • $17

3205.

Grandson
795QX6676 • $12

3206.

The Grinch™
1395QXI6466 • $75

3207.

Guardian Friend
895QX6543 • $20

3208.

Hallmark Archives 2: Ready For Christmas
1295QXD4006 • $32

3209.

Halls Station
2500QX6833 • $40

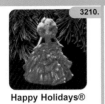

3210.

Happy Holidays® BARBIE™ 3
1595QXC4493 • $56

3211.

Heavenly Melody
1895QX6576 • $28

3212.

Here Comes Santa 20: Santa's Bumper Car
1495QX6283 • $22

3213.

Hockey Greats 2: Mario Lemieux
1595QXI6476 • $22

3214.

Holiday BARBIE™ 6
1595QXI4023 • $28

3215.

Holiday Camper
1295QX6783 • $22

3216.

Holiday Decorator
1395QX6566 • $20

3217.

Holiday Memories BARBIE™ Ornament
1495QHB6020 • $26

3218.

Holiday Voyage BARBIE™ Ornament
1495QHB6016 • $26

3219.

Hoop Stars 4: Grant Hill
1495QXI6846 • $19

3220.

Hot Wheels™
1395QX6436 • $23

3221.

Iago, Abu and the Genie - Aladdin and the King of Thieves
1295QXD4076 • $24

3222.

Joe Montana - Notre Dame
1495QXI6843 • $17

3223.

Journey to Bethlehem
1695QX6223 • $24

3224.
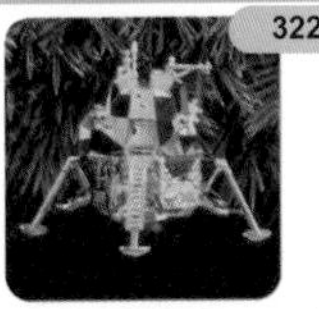
Journeys Into Space 3: Apollo Lunar Module
2400QLX7543 • $62
MAGIC.

3225.

Joyful Messenger
1895QXI6733 • $24

3226.

K.C. Drummer Boy
($N/A)QXC4533 • $180
Edition Size - 3380

3227.

Kiddie Car Classics 5: 1955 Murray® Tractor and Trailer
1695QX6376 • $23

3228.

Kiddie Car Classics 5: 1955 Murray® Tractor and Trailer
($N/A)QX6376C • $750
Edition Size - 339.

3229.

Language of Flowers 3: Iris Angel
1595QX6156 • $19

3230.
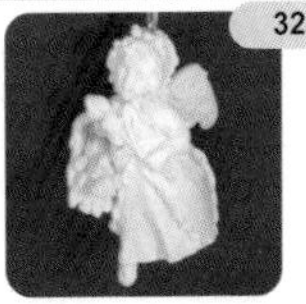
Language of Flowers 3: Iris Angel
($N/A)QX6156C • $45
Unpainted.

3231.

Larry, Moe, and Curly
2700QX6503 • $49 • Set/3

3232.

A Late Night Snack
1995QXC4536 • $225
Edition Size - 3900.

3233.

Legend of the Three Kings 2: King Kharoof - Second King
1295QX6186 • $26

3234.

Lighthouse Greetings 2
2400QLX7536 • $48
MAGIC.

3235.

LIONEL® Trains 3: Pennsylvania GG-1 Locomotive
1895QX6346 • $30

3236.

Madame Alexander® 3: Moptop Wendy
1495QX6353 • $32

3237.

Madame Alexander® Holiday Angels 1: Glorious Angel
1495QX6493 • $24

3238.

Madonna and Child
1295QX6516 • $20

3239.

Majestic Wilderness 2: Timber Wolves at Play
1295QX6273 • $20

3240.

Make-Believe Boat
1295QXD4113 • $22

3241.

Making His Way
($N/E)QXC4523 • $19

3242.

Marilyn Monroe 2
1495QX6333 • $30

3243.

Mary's Angels 11: Daphne
795QX6153 • $34

3244.

Maxine
995QX6446 • $14

3245.

Memories of Christmas
595QX2406 • $23

3246.

Merry Chime
995QX6692 • $30

3247.

Merry Olde Santa 9
1595QX6386 • $28

3248.

Mickey and Minnie Handcar
1495QXD4116 • $22

3249.

Mickey's Comet
2400QXD7586 • $40
MAGIC.

3250.

Mickey's Favorite Reindeer
1395QXD4013 • $29

3251.

Mickey's Holiday Parade 2: Minnie Plays the Flute
1395QXD4106 • $20

3252.

Miracle in Bethlehem
1295QX6513 • $45

3253.

Mistletoe Fairy
1295QX6216 • $42

3254.

Mom
895QX6656 • $14

3255.

Mom and Dad
995QX6653 • $14

3256.

Mother and Daughter
895QX6696 • $20

3257.

Mrs. Potato Head®
1095QX6886 • $19

3258.

Mulan, Mushu and Cri-Kee
1495QXD4156 • $48 • Set/2

3259.

Munchkinland™ Mayor and Coroner
1395QX6463 • $24 • Set/2

3260.

Myrrh
2200QBG6893 • $38
Re-issued in 1999.

3261.
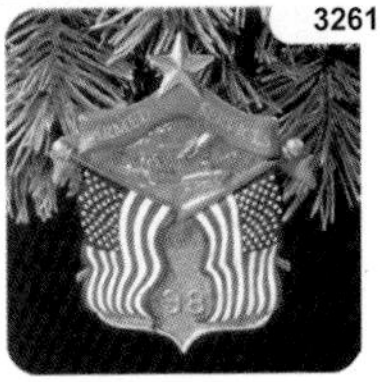
National Salute
895QX6293 • $30

3262.

Nature's Sketchbook: Country Home
1095QX5172 • $25

3263.

NBA®: Charlotte Hornets™
995QSR1033 • $11

3264.

NBA®: Chicago Bulls™
995QSR1036 • $11

3265.

NBA®: Detroit Pistons™
995QSR1043 • $11

3266.

NBA®: Houston Rockets™
995QSR1046 • $11

3267.

NBA®: Indiana Pacers™
995QSR1053 • $11

3268.

NBA®: Los Angeles Lakers™
995QSR1056 • $11

3269.

NBA®: New York Knickerbockers™
995QSR1063 • $11

3270.

NBA®: Orlando Magic™
995QSR1066 • $11

3271.

NBA®: Seattle Supersonics™
995QSR1076 • $11

3272.

NBA®: Utah Jazz™
995QSR1083 • $11

3273.

New Arrival
1895QX6306 • $19

3274.

New Christmas Friend
($N/E)QXC4516 • $19

3275.

New Home
995QX6713 • $40

3276.
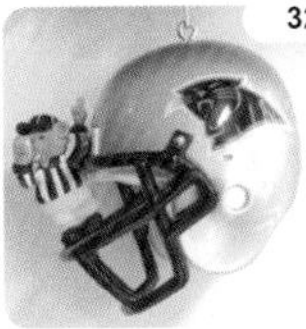
NFL®: Carolina Panthers™
995QSR5026 • $14

3277.

NFL®: Chicago Bears™
995QSR5033 • $14

3278.

NFL®: Dallas Cowboys™
995QSR5046 • $14

3279.

NFL®: Denver Broncos™
995QSR5053 • $14

3280.

NFL®: Green Bay Packers™
995QSR5063 • $14

3281.

NFL®: Kansas City Chiefs™
995QSR5013 • $14

3282.
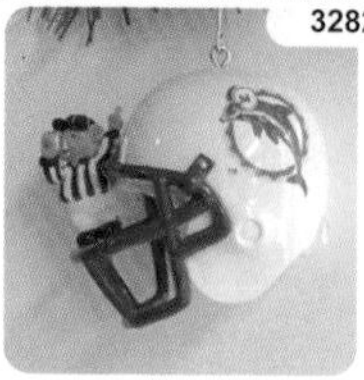
NFL®: Miami Dolphins™
995QSR5096 • $14

3283.

NFL®:
Minnesota Vikings™
995QSR5126 • $14

3284.

NFL®:
New York Giants™
995QSR5143 • $14

3285.

NFL®:
Oakland Raiders™
995QSR5086 • $14

3286.

NFL®:
Philadelphia Eagles™
995QSR5153 • $14

3287.

NFL®:
Pittsburgh Steelers™
995QSR5163 • $14

3288.

NFL®:
San Francisco 49ers™
995QSR5173 • $14

3289.

NFL®: St. Louis Rams™
995QSR5093 • $14

3290.

NFL®:
Washington Redskins™
995QSR5186 • $14

3291.

Nick's Wish List
895QX6863 • $28

3292.

Night Watch
995QX6725 • $28

3293.

North Pole Reserve
1095QX6803 • $20

3294.

Nostalgic Houses &
Shops 15: Grocery Store
1695QX6266 • $28

3295.

Old West 1:
Pony Express Rider
1395QX6323 • $25

3296.
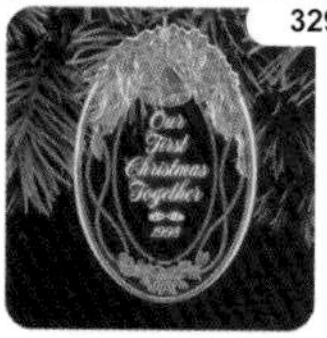
Our First Christmas
Together
795QX3193 • $19

3297.

Our First Christmas
Together
895QX6636 • $19

3298.

Our First Christmas
Together
1895QX6643 • $19

3299.

Our Song
995QX6183 • $17

3300.

Peekaboo Bears
1295QX6563 • $32

3301.

A Perfect Match
1095QX6633 • $24

3302.

Pink Poinsettias
2500QBG6926 • $41

3303.

Polar Bowler
795QX6746 • $17

3304.

A Pony for Christmas 1
1095QX6316 • $35

3305.

A Pony for Christmas 1
($N/A)QX6316C • $513
Edition Size - 508.

3306.

Princess Aurora - Sleeping Beauty
1295QXD4126 • $36 • Set/2

3307.

Puppy Love 8
795QX6163 • $28

3308.

Purr-fect Little Deer
795QX6526 • $40

3309.

Puttin' Around
895QX6763 • $14

3310.

Rocket to Success
895QX6793 • $11

3311.

Romantic Vacations 1: Donald and Daisy in Venice
1495QXD4103 • $28

3312.

Runaway Toboggan
1695QXD4003 • $26 • Set/2

3313.

Santa's Deer Friend
2400QX6583 • $46

3314.

Santa's Deer Friend
($N/A)QX6583C • $300
Edition Size - 750.

3315.

Santa's Flying Machine
1695QX6573 • $26

3316.

Santa's Hidden Surprise
1495QX6913 • $20

3317.

Santa's Merry Workshop
3200QX6816 • $59

3318.

Santa's Show 'n' Tell
1895QLX7566 • $26
MAGIC.

3319.

Santa's Spin Top
2200QLX7573 • $42
MAGIC.

3320.

Scarlett O'Hara™ 2
1495QX6336 • $42

3321.

Sew Gifted
795QX6743 • $17

3322.

Simba & Nala - The Lion King
1395QXD4073 • $34

3323.

Sister to Sister
895QX6693 • $13

3324.

Sky's the Limit 2: 1917 Curtiss JN-4D "Jenny"
1495QX6286 • $48

3325.
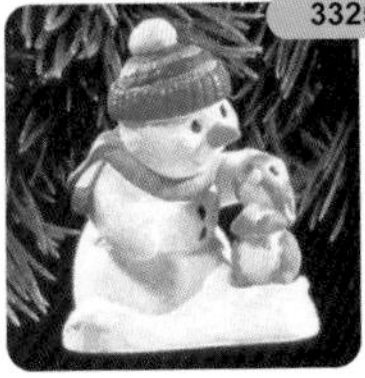
Snow Buddies 1
795QX6853 • $53

3326.

Snow Buddies 1
($N/A)QX6853C • $414
Edition Size - 800.

3327.

Soaring with Angels
1695QX6213 • $29

3328.

Son
895QX6666 • $12

3329.

Special Dog
795QX6706 • $20

3330.

Spoonful of Love
895QX6796 • $25

3331.

Spotlight on Snoopy® 1: Joe Cool
995QX6453 • $33

3332.

Spotlight on Snoopy® 1: Joe Cool
($N/A)QX6453C • $773
Edition Size - 84.

3333.

St. Nicholas Circle
1895QXI7556 • $28
MAGIC.

3334.

Star Wars™ 2: Princess Leia™
1395QXI4026 • $24

3335.

Stock Car Champions 2: Richard Petty
1595QXI4143 • $26

3336.

Sugarplum Cottage
3500QBG6917 • $52

3337.

Superman™
1295QX6423 • $16

3338.

Surprise Catch
795QX6753 • $18

3339.
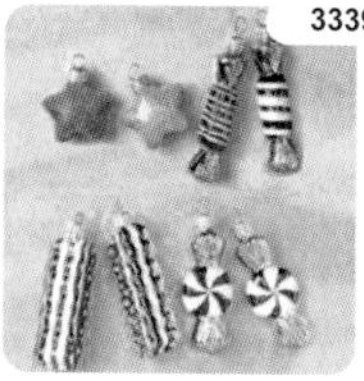
Sweet Memories
4500QBG6933 • $65 • Set/8

3340.

Sweet Rememberings
895QX6876 • $15

3341.
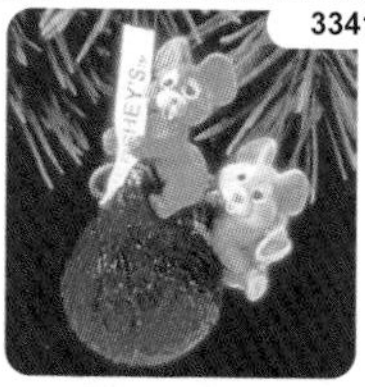
Sweet Treat
1095QX6433 • $28

3342.

Thomas Kinkade, Painter of Light 2: Victorian Christmas II
1095QX6343 • $32

3343.

Tin Locomotive
2500QX6826 • $37

3344.

Tonka® Road Grader
1395QX6483 • $32

3345.

Treetop Choir
995QX6506 • $28

3346.
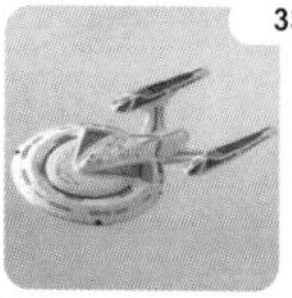
U.S.S. Enterprise NCC-1701-E™
2400QXI7633 • $70
MAGIC.

3347.

Unforgettable Villains 1: Cruella de Vil - 101 Dalmatians
1495QXD4063 • $28

3348.

Warm and Cozy
895QX6866 • $26

3349.

The Washington Monument
2400QLX7553 • $40
MAGIC.

3350.

Watchful Shepherd
895QX6496 • $26

3351.

White Poinsettias
2500QBG6923 • $69

3352.

Winnie the Pooh 1: A Visit From Piglet
1395QXD4086 • $24

3353.

Winter Wonderland
($N/A)QXC4543 • $132

3354.

Woody the Sheriff - Toy Story
1495QXD4163 • $38

3355.

Writing to Santa
795QX6533 • $22

3356.

X-Wing Starfighter™
2400QXI7596 • $48
MAGIC.

3357.

Yuletide Central 5: Caboose
1895QX6373 • $40

1999

3358.

1939 Garton® Ford® Station Wagon
1595QXC4509 • $37

3359.

1949 Cadillac® Coupe deVille
1495QX6429 • $28

3360.

1950 LIONEL® Santa Fe F3 Diesel Locomotive
3500QBG6119 • $60

3361.

1955 Murray® Ranch Wagon
3500QBG6077 • $56

3362.

40th Anniversary BARBIE™ Ornament
1595QXI8049 • $29

3363.

Adding the Best Part
795QX6569 • $16

3364.

African-American Millennium Princess BARBIE™
1595QXI6449 • $34

3365.

All Sooted Up
995QX6837 • $14

3366.

All-American Trucks 5: 1957 Dodge® Sweptside D100
1395QX6269 • $28

3367.

Angel in Disguise
895QX6629 • $18

3368.

Angel of Hope
1495QXI6339 • $32

3369.

Angel Song
1895QX6939 • $29

3370.

Arctic Artist
($N/E)QXC4527 • $10

3371.

At the Ballpark 4: Ken Griffey Jr.
1495QXI4037 • $34

3372.

Baby Mickey's Sweet Dreams
1095QXD4087 • $19

3373.

Baby's First Christmas
1895QX6647 • $34

3374.

Baby's First Christmas
795QX6649 • $24

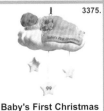

3375.

Baby's First Christmas
895QX6657 • $22

3376.

Baby's First Christmas
795QX6659 • $22

3377.

BARBIE™ 6: Gay Parisienne BARBIE™
1595QXI5301 • $28

3378.

BARBIE™ Doll Dreamhouse™ Playhouse Ornament
1495QXI8047 • $25

3379.
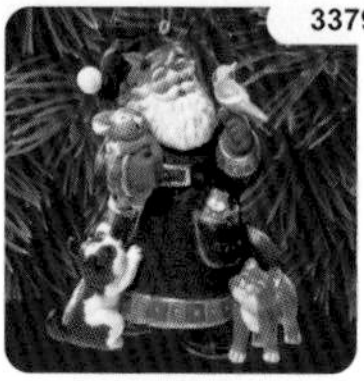
Best Pals
1895QX6879 • $53

3380.

Blessed Nativity: Balthasar - The Magi
1295QX8037 • $22
Re-issued in 2000.

3381.

Blessed Nativity: Caspar - The Magi
1295QX8039 • $26
Re-issued in 2000.

3382.

Blessed Nativity: Melchior - The Magi
1295QX6819 • $26
Re-issued in 2000.

3383.

Blessed Nativity: The Holy Family
2500QX6523 • $45 • Set/3
Also issued in 1998 & 2000.

3384.

Bowling's a Ball
795QX6577 • $16

3385.

Candlelight Services 2: Colonial Church
1895QLX7387 • $29
MAGIC.

3386.

Century Stamp: I Love Lucy
995QXI8567 • $29

3387.

Century Stamp: Silken Flame BARBIE™
995QXI8559 • $19

3388.

Century Stamp: Superman™
995QXI8569 • $18

3389.

Century Stamp: The Cat in the Hat™ - Dr. Seuss® Books
995QXI8579 • $15

3390.

Century Stamp: U.S.S Enterprise NCC-1701™
995QXI8557 • $29

3391.

Century Stamp: Yellow Submarine™ - The Beatles
995QXI8577 • $22

3392.

Chewbacca™
1495QXI4009 • $32

3393.

Child of Wonder
1495QX6817 • $25

3394.

Child's Age: Baby's First Christmas
795QX6667 • $20

3395.

Child's Age: Baby's Second Christmas
795QX6669 • $22

3396.

Child's Age: Child's Third Christmas
795QX6677 • $18

3397.

Child's Age: Child's Fourth Christmas
795QX6687 • $18

3398.

Child's Age: Child's Fifth Christmas
795QX6679 • $18

3399.

Childhood Treasures
3000QBG4237 • $50 • Set/3

3400.

The Christmas Story
2200QX6897 • $36

3401.

Classic American Cars 9: 1955 Chevrolet® Nomad Wagon
1395QX6367 • $34

3402.

The Clauses on Vacation 3
1495QX6399 • $20

3403.

Clownin' Around
1095QX6487 • $20

3404.

Cocoa Break
1095QX8009 • $23

3405.

Cocoa Break
($N/A)QX8009C • $47

3406.

Collecting Friends
($N/E)QXC4679 • $59

3407.

Collegiate: Arizona Wildcats™
995QSR2429 • $12

3408.

Collegiate: Duke Blue Devils™
995QSR2437 • $12

3409.

Collegiate: Florida State Seminoles™
995QSR2439 • $12

3410.

Collegiate: Georgetown Hoyas™
995QSR2447 • $12

3411.

Collegiate: Kentucky Wildcats™
995QSR2449 • $12

3412.

Collegiate: Michigan Wolverines™
995QSR2457 • $12

3413.

Collegiate: Nebraska Cornhuskers™
995QSR2459 • $12

3414.

Collegiate: North Carolina Tar Heels™
995QSR2467 • $12

3415.

Collegiate: Notre Dame Fighting Irish™
995QSR2427 • $12

3416.

Collegiate: Penn State Nittany Lions™
995QSR2469 • $12

3417.

Counting on Success
795QX6707 • $12

3418.

Cross of Hope
995QX6557 • $23

3419.

Crown Reflections 2: Festival of Fruit
3500QBG6069 • $45

3420.

Dad
895QX6719 • $14

3421.

Dance for the Season
995QX6587 • $24

3422.

Darth Vader's TIE Fighter™
2400QXI7399 • $35
MAGIC.

3423.

Daughter
895QX6729 • $28

3424.

Dolls of the World 4: Russian BARBIE™
1495QX6369 • $21

3425.

Dorothy and Glinda, the Good Witch™
2400QX6509 • $47

3426.

Dr. Seuss® Books 1: The Cat in the Hat™
1495QXI6457 • $28 • Set/2

3427.

Dumbo's First Flight
1395QXD4117 • $26

3428.
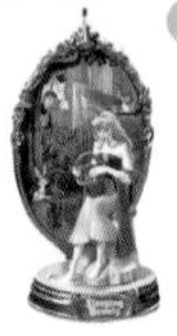
Enchanted Memories 3: Sleeping Beauty
1495QXD4097 • $32

3429.

Fabulous Decade 10
795QX6357 • $32

3430.

The Family Portrait - Lady and the Tramp
1495QXD4149 • $35

3431.

Favorite Bible Stories 1: David and Goliath
1395QX6447 • $22

3432.

Feliz Navidad
895QX6999 • $18

3433.

Flame-Fighting Friends
1495QX6619 • $19

3434.

The Flash™
1295QX6469 • $20

3435.

Football Legends 5: Dan Marino
1495QXI4029 • $38

3436.

For My Grandma
795QX6747 • $17

3437.

Forecast for Fun
1495QX6869 • $24

3438.

Frankincense
2200QBG6896 • $38
Re-issued from 1998.

3439.

Frosty Friends
3500QBG6067 • $67

3440.

Frosty Friends 20
1295QX6297 • $30

3441.

G.I. Joe® - Action Soldier
1395QX6537 • $19

3442.

Gift Bearers 1
1295QX6437 • $28

3443.

Godchild
795QX6759 • $17

3444.

Gold
2200QBG6836 • $43
Re-issued from 1998.

3445.

Goofy® as Santa's Helper
1295QXD4079 • $25

3446.

Granddaughter
895QX6739 • $26

3447.

Grandson
895QX6737 • $26

3448.

Hallmark Archives 3: Minnie Trims the Tree
1295QXD4059 • $23

3449.

Handled with Care
895QX6769 • $13

3450.

Happy Holidays® BARBIE™ 4
1595QXC4507 • $59

3451.

Harley-Davidson® Motorcycle Milestones 1: Heritage Springer
1495QXI8007 • $44

3452.

Harvest of Grapes
2500QBG6047 • $54

3453.

Hello, Hello
1495QX6777 • $21 • Set/2

3454.

Here Comes Santa 21: Santa's Golf Cart
1495QX6337 • $23

3455.

Hockey Greats 3: Gordie Howe
1595QXI4047 • $29

3456.

Hollow Log Cafe
1495QXC4667 • $44

3457.

The Holy Family
3000QBG6127 • $59

3458.

Hoop Stars 5: Scottie Pippen
1495QXI4177 • $24

3459.

Howdy Doody™ Lunchbox Set
1495QX6519 • $24 • Set/2

3460.

In The Workshop
995QX6979 • $12

3461.

Jazzy Jalopy
2400QX6549 • $39

3462.

Jet Threat Car With Case
1295QX6527 • $19 • Set/2

3463.

Jolly Locomotive
1495QX6859 • $26

3464.

Jolly Locomotive
($N/A)QX6859C • $95
Edition Size - 5000.

3465.

Jolly Snowman
2000QBG6059 • $37

3466.

Journeys Into Space 4: Lunar Rover Vehicle
2400QLX7377 • $38
MAGIC.

3467.

Joyful Santa 1
1495QX6949 • $25

3468.

Joyous Angel
895QX6787 • $28

3469.

A Joyous Christmas
595QX6827 • $24

3470.

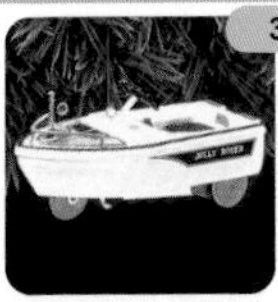

Kiddie Car Classics 6: 1968 Murray® Jolly Roger Flagship
1395QX6279 • $20

3471.

Kiddie Car Classics 6: 1968 Murray® Jolly Roger Flagship
($N/A)QX6279C • $523
Edition Size - 192.

3472.

Kringle's Whirligig
1295QX6847 • $24

3473.

Language of Flowers 4: Rose Angel
1595QX6289 • $23

3474.

Larry, Moe, and Curly
3000QX6499 • $48 • Set/3

3475.
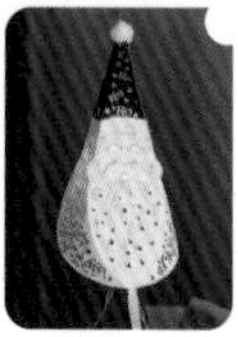
Laser Creations: A Visit from St. Nicholas
595QLZ4229 • $19

3476.

Laser Creations: A Wish for Peace
695QLZ4249 • $12

3477.

Laser Creations: Angelic Messenger
795QLZ4287 • $14

3478.

Laser Creations: Christmas in Bloom
895QLZ4257 • $12

3479.

Laser Creations: Don't Open Till 2000
895QLZ4289 • $17

3480.

Laser Creations: Inside Santa's Workshop
895QLZ4239 • $14

3481.

Laser Creations: Ringing in Christmas
695QLZ4277 • $10

3482.

Laser Creations: Yuletide Charm
795QLZ4269 • $14

3483.

Legend of the Three Kings 3: King Malh - Third King
1395QX6797 • $26

3484.

Let it Snow
1895QLX7427 • $25
MAGIC.

3485.

Lieutenant Commander Worf
1495QXI4139 • $26

3486.

Lighthouse Greetings 3
2400QLX7379 • $165
MAGIC.

3487.

LIONEL® 746 Norfolk and Western Tender
1495QX6497 • $38

3488.
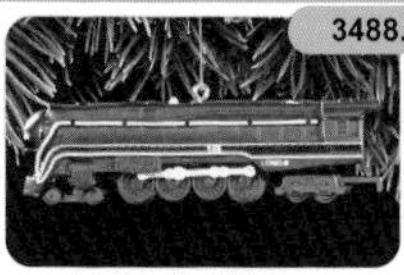
LIONEL® Trains 4: 746 Norfolk and Western Steam Locomotive
1895QX6377 • $34

3489.

Little Cloud Keeper
1695QX6877 • $28

3490.

The Lollipop Guild™
1995QX8029 • $46 • Set/3

3491.

Lucy Gets in Pictures
1395QX6547 • $25

3492.

Madame Alexander® 4: Red Queen - Alice in Wonderland®
1495QX6379 • $22

3493.

Madame Alexander® Holiday Angels 2: Angel of the Nativity
1495QX6419 • $34

3494.

Majestic Wilderness 3: Curious Raccoons
1295QX6287 • $20

3495.

Marilyn Monroe 3
1495QX6389 • $28

3496.

Mary's Angels 12: Heather
795QX6329 • $28

3497.

Mary's Bears
1295QX5569 • $18

3498.

Merry Motorcycle
895QX6637 • $17

3499.

Merry Olde Santa 10
1595QX6359 • $26

3500.

Mickey's Holiday Parade 3: Donald Plays the Cymbals
1395QXD4057 • $36

3501.

Military on Parade
1095QX6639 • $30

3502.

Milk 'n' Cookies Express
895QX6839 • $16

3503.

Millennium Princess BARBIE™
1595QXI4019 • $38

3504.

Millennium Snowman
895QX8059 • $38

3505.

Mischievous Kittens 1
995QX6427 • $96

3506.

Mischievous Kittens 1
($N/A)QX6427C • $225
Edition Size - 5000.

3507.

Mom
895QX6717 • $14

3508.

Mom and Dad
995QX6709 • $19

3509.

Mother and Daughter
895QX6757 • $34

3510.

Muhammad Ali
1495QXI4147 • $19

3511.

A Musician of Note
795QX6567 • $17

3512.

My Sister, My Friend
995QX6749 • $17

3513.

Myrrh
2200QBG6893 • $38
Re-issued from 1998.

3514.

Naboo Starfighter™
1895QXI7613 • $32

3515.

NBA®: Charlotte Hornets™
1095QSR1057 • $12

3516.

NBA®: Chicago Bulls™
1095QSR1019 • $12

3517.

NBA®: Detroit Pistons™
1095QSR1027 • $12

3518.

NBA®: Houston Rockets™
1095QSR1029 • $12

3519.

NBA®: Indiana Pacers™
1095QSR1037 • $12

3520.

NBA®: Los Angelas Lakers™
1095QSR1039 • $12

3521.

NBA®: New York Knicks™
1095QSR1047 • $12

3522.

NBA®: Orlando Magic™
1095QSR1059 • $12

3523.

NBA®: Seattle SuperSonics™
1095QSR1067 • $12

3524.

NBA®: Utah Jazz™
1095QSR1069 • $12

3525.

New Home
995QX6347 • $19

3526.

NFL®: Carolina Panthers™
1095QSR5217 • $14

3527.

NFL®: Chicago Bears™
1095QSR5219 • $14

3528.

NFL®: Dallas Cowboys™
1095QSR5227 • $14

3529.

NFL®: Denver Broncos™
1095QSR5229 • $14

3530.

NFL®: Green Bay Packers™
1095QSR5237 • $14

3531.

NFL®: Kansas City Chiefs™
1095QSR5197 • $14

3532.

NFL®: Miami Dolphins™
1095QSR5239 • $14

3533.

NFL®: Minnesota Vikings™
1095QSR5247 • $14

3534.

NFL®: New England Patriots™
1095QSR5279 • $14

3535.

NFL®: New York Giants™
1095QSR5249 • $14

3536.

NFL®: Oakland Raiders™
1095QSR5257 • $14

3537.

NFL®: Philadelphia Eagles™
1095QSR5259 • $14

3538.

NFL®: Pittsburgh Steelers™
1095QSR5267 • $14

3539.

NFL®: San Francisco 49ers™
1095QSR5269 • $14

3540.

NFL®: Washington Redskins™
1095QSR5277 • $14

3541.

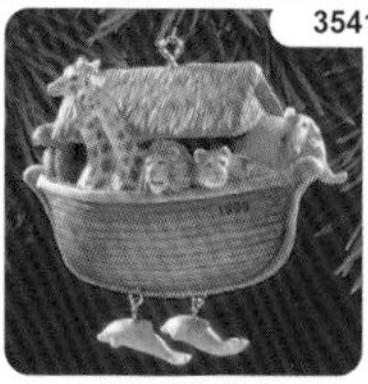

Noah's Ark
1295QX6809 • $23

3542.

North Pole Mr. Potato Head®
1095QX8027 • $23

3543.

North Pole Pond
4000QXC4677 • $94

3544.

North Pole Star
895QX6589 • $14

3545.

Nostalgic Houses & Shops 16: House on Holly Lane
1695QX6349 • $26

3546.

Old West 2: Prospector
1395QX6317 • $19

3547.

On Thin Ice
1095QX6489 • $17

3548.

Our Christmas Together
995QX6689 • $18

3549.

Our First Christmas Together
795QX3207 • $17

3550.

Our First Christmas Together
895QX6697 • $20

3551.

Our First Christmas Together
2200QX6699 • $32

3552.

Outstanding Teacher
895QX6627 • $11

3553.

Pepe LePew™ and Penelope™
1295QX6507 • $25

3554.

Piano Player Mickey
2400QXD7389 • $68
MAGIC.

3555.

Pinocchio and Geppetto
1695QXD4107 • $24

3556.

Playful Snowman
1295QX6867 • $23

3557.

The Poky Little Puppy
1195QX6479 • $20

3558.

A Pony for Christmas 2
1095QX6299 • $28

3559.

A Pony for Christmas 2
($N/A)QX6299C • $195

3560.

Praise the Day
1495QX6799 • $19

3561.

Presents From Pooh
1495QXD4093 • $25

3562.

Puppy Love 9
795QX6327 • $24

3563.
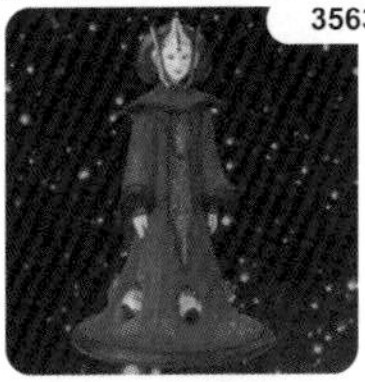
Queen Amidala™
1495QXI4187 • $19

3564.

Red Barn
1595QX6947 • $23

3565.

Reel Fun
1095QX6609 • $25

3566.

Rhett Butler™
1295QX6467 • $24

3567.

Romantic Vacations 2: Mickey and Minnie in Paradise
1495QXD4049 • $30

3568.
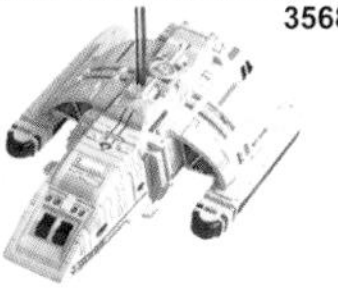
Runabout - U.S.S. Rio Grande™
2400QXI7593 • $38
MAGIC.

3569.

Scarlett O'Hara™ 3
1495QX6397 • $25

3570.

Scooby-Doo™ Lunchbox Set
1495QX6997 • $24 • Set/2

3571.

Sew Handy
895QX6597 • $24

3572.

Sky's the Limit 3: Curtiss R3C-2 Seaplane
1495QX6387 • $38

3573.

Sleddin' Buddies
995QX6849 • $22

3574.

Snow Buddies 2
795QX6319 • $25

3575.

Snow Day
1895QXC4517 • $48 • Set/2

3576.

The Snowmen of Mitford
1595QXI8587 • $47 • Set/3

3577.

Snowy Plaza
3500QXC4669 • $101

3578.

Son
895QX6727 • $28

3579.

Special Dog
795QX6767 • $20

3580.

Spellin' Santa
995QX6857 • $16

3581.

Spotlight on Snoopy® 2: Famous Flying Ace
995QX6409 • $34

3582.

Sprinkling Stars
995QX6599 • $18

3583.

Star Wars™ 3: Han Solo™
1395QXI4007 • $28

3584.

Stock Car Champions 3: Bill Elliott
1595QXI4039 • $31

3585.

Sundae Golfer
1295QX6617 • $18

3586.

Surfin' the Net
995QX6607 • $24

3587.

Sweet Friendship
995QX6779 • $17

3588.

Sweet Skater
795QX6579 • $13

3589.

Thomas Kinkade, Painter of Light 3: Victorian Christmas III
1095QX6407 • $23

3590.

Tigger Plays Soccer
1095QXD4119 • $22

3591.

A Time of Peace
895QX6807 • $16

3592.

Tonka® 1956 Suburban Pumper No. 5
1395QX6459 • $32

3593.

Town and Country 1: Farm House
1595QX6439 • $23

3594.

The Toymaker's Gift
($N/E)QXC4519 • $16

3595.

U.S.S Enterprise NCC-1701™
2500QBG6117 • $109

3596.

Unforgettable Villains 2: Snow White's Jealous Queen
1495QXD4089 • $24

3597.

Village Church
3000QBG6057 • $48

3598.

Waiting for a Hug
($N/A)QXC4537 • $29

3599.

Warm Welcome
1695QLX7417 • $26
MAGIC.

3600.

Welcome to 2000
1095QX6829 • $36

3601.

Winnie the Pooh 2: Honey Time
1395QXD4129 • $25

3602.

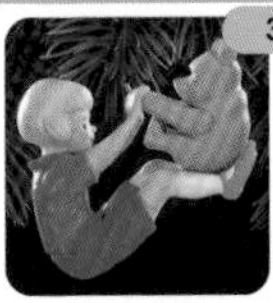

Winnie the Pooh and Christopher Robin®, Too 1
1395QXD4197 • $24

3603.

Wintertime Treat
1295QX6989 • $23

3604.

Woody's Roundup - Toy Story
1395QXI4207 • $28

3605.

Yummy Memories
4500QBG6049 • $83 • Set/8

3606.

Yummy Memories
($N/A)QBG6049C • $323
Set/8 • Edition Size - 192.

3607.

Zebra Fantasy
1495QX6559 • $23

2000

3608.

102 Dalmations
1295QXI5231 • $40

3609.

1938 Garton® Lincoln Zephyr
1595QXC4501 • $50

3610.

1955 Murray® Dump Truck
3500QBG4081 • $38

3611.

1962 BARBIE™ Hatbox Doll Case
1295QX6791 • $19

3612.

Alice Meets the Chesire Cat
1495QXD4011 • $23

3613.

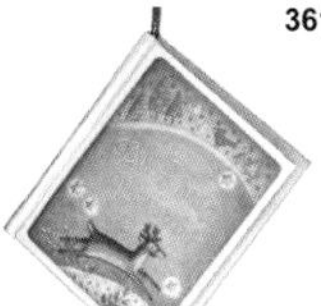

All Things Beautiful
1395QX8351 • $16

3614.

All-American Trucks 6: 1978 Dodge® Li'l Red Express Truck
1395QX6581 • $28

3615.

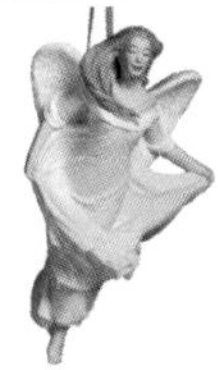

Angel of Promise
1495QXI4144 • $22

3616.

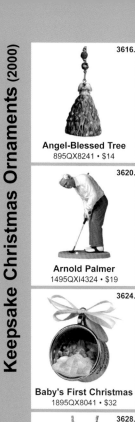

Angel-Blessed Tree
895QX8241 • $14

3617.

Angelic Bell
1695QXC4504 • $28

3618.

Angelic Trio
1095QX8234 • $28

3619.

Angels Over Bethlehem
1895QLX7563 • $35
MAGIC.

3620.

Arnold Palmer
1495QXI4324 • $19

3621.

At the Ballpark 5: Mark McGwire
1495QXI5361 • $23

3622.

Baby's First Christmas
895QX8031 • $14

3623.

Baby's First Christmas
1095QX8034 • $14

3624.

Baby's First Christmas
1895QX8041 • $32

3625.

Backpack Bear
3000QBG4071 • $39

3626.

BARBIE™ 7: BARBIE™ Commuter Set
1595QX6814 • $26 • Set/2

3627.

BARBIE™ 2000
1995QXC4602 • $120

3628.

BARBIE™ Angel of Joy™
1495QXI6861 • $20

3629.

Bell-Bearing Elf
($N/A)QXC4514 • $17

3630.

Big Twin Evolution® Engine - Harley-Davidson®
2400QXI7571 • $30
MAGIC.

3631.

The Blessed Family
1895QLX7564 • $28
MAGIC.

3632.

Blessed Nativity: Balthasar - The Magi
1295QX8037 • $22
Re-issued from 1999.

3633.

Blessed Nativity: Caspar - The Magi
1295QX8039 • $26
Re-issued from 1999.

3634.

Blessed Nativity: Melchior - The Magi
1295QX6819 • $26
Re-issued from 1999.

3635.

Blessed Nativity: The Holy Family
2500QX6523 • $45 • Set/3
Re-issued from 1998 & 1999.

3636.

Blessed Nativity: The Shepherds
2500QX8361 • $113 • Set/2

3637.

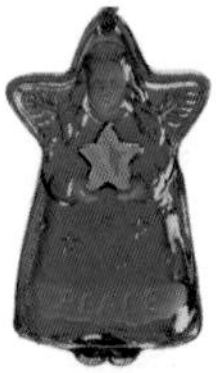

Blue Glass Angel
1095QX8381 • $17

3638.

Borg™ Cube
2400QLX7354 • $40
MAGIC.

3639.

Bringing Her Gift
1095QX8334 • $16

3640.

Bugs Bunny™ and Gossamer™
1295QX6574 • $23

3641.

Busy Bee Shopper
795QX6964 • $13

3642.

Busy Bee Shopper
($N/A)QX6964C • $48
Edition Size - 5000.

3643.

Buzz Lightyear - Toy Story
1495QXI5234 • $26

3644.

Candlelight Services 3: Adobe Church
1895QLX7334 • $28
MAGIC.

3645.

Caroler's Best Friend
1295QX8354 • $18

3646.

Celebrate His Birth!
695QX2464 • $14

3647.

Celebration BARBIE™ 1
1595QXI6821 • $28

3648.

Child's Age: Baby's First Christmas
795QX6914 • $26

3649.

Child's Age: Baby's Second Christmas
795QX6921 • $23

3650.

Child's Age: Child's Third Christmas
795QX6924 • $20

3651.

Child's Age: Child's Fourth Christmas
795QX6931 • $20

3652.

Child's Age: Child's Fifth Christmas
795QX6934 • $20

3653.

The Christmas Belle
1095QX8311 • $17

3654.

Christmas Tree Surprise
1695QX8321 • $24

3655.

A Class Act
795QX8074 • $23

3656.

Classic American Cars 10: 1969 Pontiac® GTO™ - The Judge
1395QX6584 • $28

3657.

Close-Knit Friends
1495QX8204 • $26 • Set/2

3658.

Collegiate: Alabama Crimson Tide™
995QSR2344 • $12

3659.
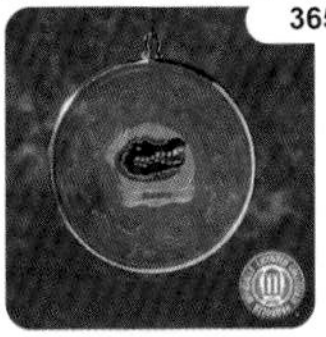
Collegiate: Florida Gators™
995QSR2324 • $12

3660.
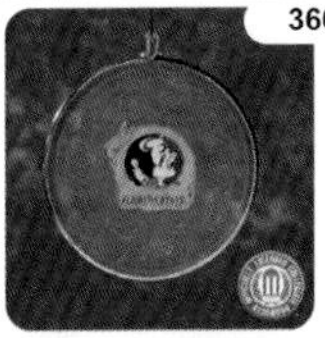
Collegiate: Florida State Seminoles™
995QSR2341 • $12

3661.

Collegiate: Kentucky Wildcats™
995QSR2291 • $12

3662.

Collegiate: Michigan Wolverines™
995QSR2271 • $12

3663.

Collegiate: Nebraska Cornhuskers™
995QSR2321 • $12

3664.
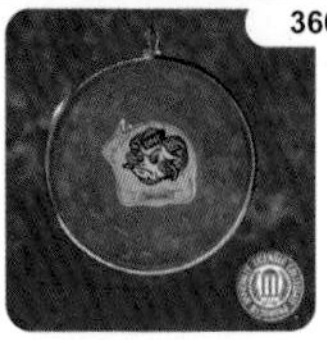
Collegiate: North Carolina Tar Heels™
995QSR2304 • $12

3665.

Collegiate: Notre Dame Fighting Irish™
995QSR2284 • $12

3666.
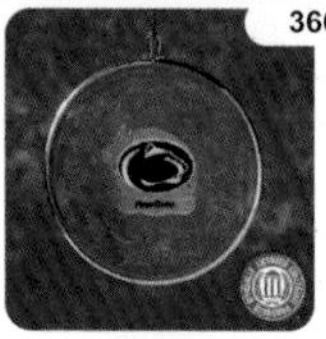
Collegiate: Penn State Nittany Lions™
995QSR2311 • $12

3667.

Collegiate: Tennessee Volunteers™
995QSR2334 • $12

3668.

Cool Character
1295QX8271 • $19

3669.

Cool Decade 1
795QX6764 • $19

3670.

Cool Decade 1
($N/A)QX6764C • $80

3671.

Crown Reflections 3: Christmas Rose
3500QBG4054 • $59

3672.

Dad
895QX8071 • $13

3673.

Dale Earnhardt
1495QXI6754 • $60

3674.

Dancin' In Christmas
795QX6971 • $13

3675.

Darth Maul™
1495QXI6885 • $29

3676.

Daughter
895QX8081 • $26

3677.

Dog Dish Delimma
1295QXD4044 • $24

3678.

Dousin' Dalmation
995QX8024 • $25

3679.

Dr. Seuss® Books 2: One Fish Two Fish Red Fish Blue Fish™
1495QX6781 • $40

3680.

Dressing Cinderella
1295QXD4109 • $27

3681.

Fashion Afoot 1
1495QX8341 • $22

3682.
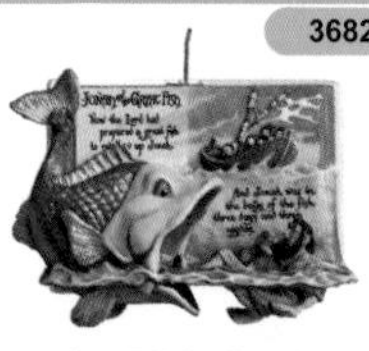
Favorite Bible Stories 2: Jonah and the Great Fish
1395QX6701 • $26

3683.

Feliz Navidad
895QX8214 • $26

3684.

The Fishing Hole
1295QX6984 • $15

3685.

Football Legends 6: John Elway
1495QXI6811 • $22

3686.

Friendly Greeting
995QX8174 • $23

3687.

Friends in Harmony
995QX8001 • $16

3688.

Frosty Friends
4000QBG4094 • $62 • Set/2

3689.

Frosty Friends
1895QX8524 • $25 • Set/3

3690.

Frosty Friends 21
1095QX6601 • $19

3691.

Frosty Friends 21
($N/A)QX6601C • $150
Edition Size - 5000.

3692.

G.I. Joe® - Action Pilot
1395QX6734 • $26

3693.

Gift Bearers 2
1295QX6651 • $30

3694.

Gifts for the Grinch™
1295QXI5344 • $31

3695.

Gingerbread Church
995QX8244 • $20

3696.

Godchild
795QX8161 • $18

3697.

Gold-Star Teacher
795QX6951 • $12

3698.

Gold-Star Teacher
($N/A)QX6951C • $28

3699.

Golfer Supreme
1095QX6991 • $19

3700.

The Good Book
1395QX8254 • $26

3701.

Graceful Glory
1895QX8304 • $28

3702.

Granddaughter
895QX8091 • $23

3703.

Grandma's House
1095QX8141 • $16

3704.

Grandson
895QX8094 • $23

3705.

The Great Oz™
3200QLX7361 • $59
MAGIC.

3706.
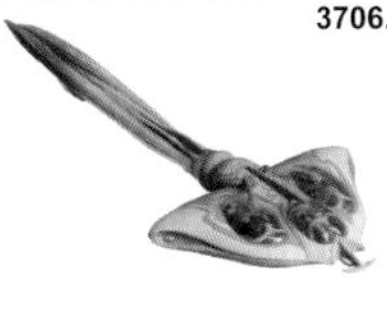
Gungan™ Submarine
2400QXI7351 • $40
MAGIC.

3707.

Happy Holidays® BARBIE™ 5
1595QXC4494 • $60

3708.

Harley-Davidson® BARBIE™
1495QXI8554 • $19

3709.

Harley-Davidson® Motorcycle Milestones 2: Fat Boy
1495QXI6774 • $27

3710.

Harry Potter™: Harry Potter™
1295QXE4381 • $28

3711.

Harry Potter™: Hedwig the Owl™
795QXE4394 • $28

3712.

Harry Potter™: Hermione Granger™
1295QXE4391 • $28

3713.

Harry Potter™: Hogwarts™ Charms
1295QXE4404 • $35 • Set/6

3714.

Harry Potter™: Hogwarts™ Crest
1495QXE4411 • $30

3715.

Harry Potter™: Professor Dumbledore™
1295QXE4384 • $28

3716.

Here Comes Santa 22: Sleigh X-2000
1495QX6824 • $23

3717.

Hockey Greats 4: Eric Lindros
1595QXI6801 • $28

3718.

A Holiday Gathering
1095QX8561 • $19

3719.

Holly Berry Bell
1495QX8291 • $19

3720.

Hoop Stars 6: Karl Malone
1495QXI6901 • $28

3721.

Hooray for the U.S.A.
995QX8281 • $17

3722.

Hopalong Cassidy™ Lunchbox Set
1495QX6714 • $24 • Set/2

3723.

Hot Wheels™ 1968 Deora Car
1495QXI6891 • $23

3724.

Imperial Stormtrooper™
1495QXI6711 • $28

3725.

Jeannie - I Dream of Jeannie™
1495QXI8564 • $24 • Set/2

3726.

Jingle Bell Kringle
($N/E)QXC4481 • $20

3727.

Joyful Santa 2
1495QX6784 • $28

3728.

Ken Griffey, Jr.
1495QXI5251 • $22

3729.

Kiddie Car Classics 7: 1924 Toledo Fire Engine #6
1395QX6691 • $35

3730.

King of the Ring
1095QX6864 • $19

3731.

Kris Cross-Country Kringle
1295QX6954 • $20

3732.

Kristi Yamaguchi
1395QXI6854 • $19

3733.

Larry, Moe, and Curly
3000QX6851 • $47 • Set/3

3734.

Laser Creations: A Visit from Santa
895QLZ4281 • $12

3735.

Laser Creations: Angel Light
795QLZ4311 • $17

3736.

Laser Creations: Fun-Stuffed Stocking
595QLZ4291 • $10

3737.

Laser Creations: Heavenly Peace
695QLZ4314 • $11

3738.

Laser Creations: Jack-in-the-Box
895QLZ4321 • $10

3739.
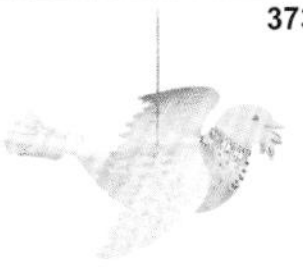
Laser Creations: Lovely Dove
795QLZ4294 • $10

3740.

Laser Creations: The Nativity
895QLZ4301 • $17

3741.

Laser Creations: The Nutcracker
595QLZ4284 • $10

3742.

Lieutenant Commander Worf
3000QBG4064 • $48

3743.

Lighthouse Greetings 4
2400QLX7344 • $42
MAGIC.

3744.

Li'l Apple
795QBG4261 • $13

3745.

Li'l Cascade (Red)
795QBG4241 • $13

3746.

Li'l Cascade (White)
795QBG4244 • $13

3747.

Li'l Christmas Tree
795QBG4361 • $13

3748.
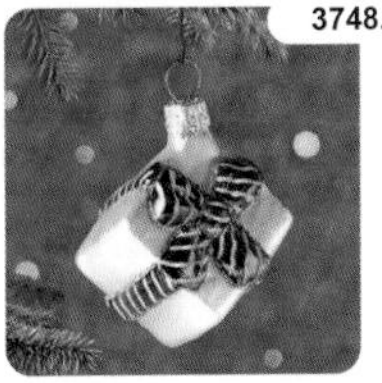
Li'l Gift (Green Bow)
795QBG4344 • $12

3749.

Li'l Gift (Red Bow)
795QBG4341 • $12

3750.

Li'l Grapes
795QBG4141 • $12

3751.

Li'l Hearts
($N/A)(N/A) • $26

3752.

Li'l Jack-In-The-Box
795QBG4274 • $12

3753.

Li'l Mr. Claus
795QBG4364 • $13

3754.

Li'l Mrs. Claus
795QBG4371 • $10

3755.

Li'l Partridge
795QBG4374 • $12

3756.
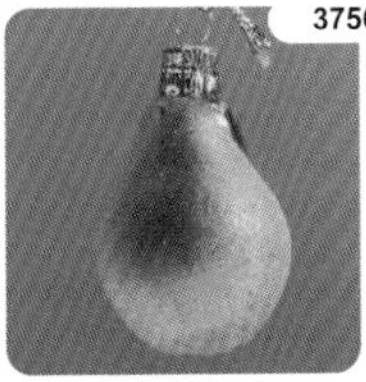
Li'l Pear
795QBG4254 • $12

3757.
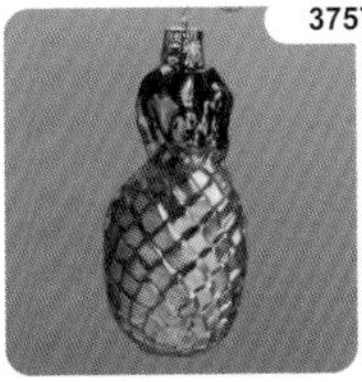
Li'l Pineapple
795QBG4251 • $12

3758.
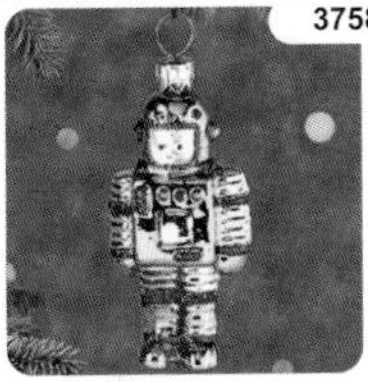
Li'l Robot
795QBG4271 • $12

3759.

Li'l Roly-Poly Penguin
795QBG4281 • $12

3760.

Li'l Roly-Poly Santa
795QBG4161 • $12

3761.

Li'l Roly-Poly Snowman
795QBG4284 • $13

3762.

Li'l Santa (Traditional)
795QBG4354 • $13

3763.

Li'l Snowman (Traditional)
795QBG4351 • $12

3764.

Li'l Stars (Metallic Look)
($N/E)QBG4221 • $28

3765.

Li'l Stars (Patriotic)
995QBG4214 • $35

3766.

Li'l Stars (Traditional)
995QBG4224 • $28

3767.

Li'l Swirl (Green)
795QBG4234 • $12

3768.

Li'l Swirl (Red)
795QBG4231 • $12

3769.

Li'l Teddy Bear
795QBG4264 • $12

3770.

LIONEL® 4501 Southern Mikado Steam Locomotive
3500QBG4074 • $68

3771.

LIONEL® 700E J-1E Hudson Steam Locomotive
2200QXI5261 • $43

3772.

LIONEL® General Steam Locomotive Tender
1595QX6834 • $25

3773.

LIONEL® Trains 5: LIONEL® General Steam Locomotive
1895QX6684 • $31

3774.

Loggin' On To Santa
1295QX8224 • $14

3775.

The Lone Ranger™
1595QX6941 • $40

3776.

Lucy Is Enciente
1595QX6884 • $50

3777.

The Lullabye League™
1995QX6604 • $32 • Set/3

3778.

Madame Alexander® 5: Christmas Holly
1495QX6611 • $32

3779.

Madame Alexander® Holiday Angels 3: Twilight Angel
1495QX6614 • $54

3780.

Majestic Wilderness 4: Foxes in the Forest
1295QX6794 • $28

3781.

Mary's Angels
1895QLX7561 • $46
MAGIC.

3782.

Mary's Angels 13: Marguerite
795QX6571 • $25

3783.

Max
795QX8584 • $26

3784.
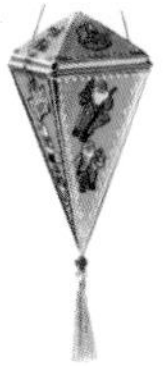
Memories of Christmas
1295QX8264 • $19

3785.

Merry Ballooning
1695QX8384 • $24

3786.

Mickey's Bedtime Reading
1095QXD4077 • $28

3787.

Mickey's Holiday Parade 4: Baton Twirler Daisy
1395QXD4034 • $26

3788.

Mickey's Sky Rider
1895QXD4159 • $32

3789.

Millennium Express
4200QLX7364 • $105
MAGIC.

3790.

Millennium Snowma'am
895QXI5241 • $14

3791.

Millennium Snowman
895QX8059C1 • $303

3792.

Millennium Time Capsule
1895QX8044 • $26

3793.

Mischievous Kittens 2
995QX6641 • $19

3794.

Mom
895QX8064 • $13

3795.

Mom and Dad
995QX8061 • $19

3796.

Mother and Daughter
995QX8154 • $28

3797.

Mr. Monopoly™
1095QX8101 • $17

3798.

Mrs. Claus's Holiday
995QX8011 • $14

3799.

Nature's Sketchbook: Snowy Garden
1395QX8284 • $26

3800.

New Home
895QX8171 • $28

3801.
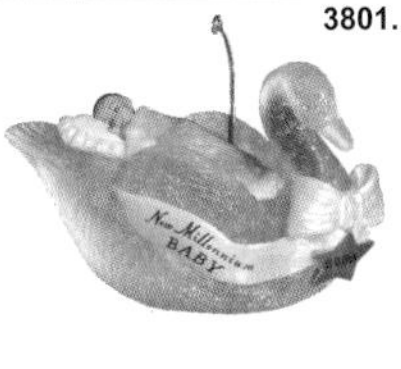

New Millennium Baby
1095QX8581 • $17

3802.

The Newborn Prince - Bambi
1395QXD4194 • $20

3803.

NFL®: Cleveland Browns™
995QSR5161 • $14

3804.

NFL®: Dallas Cowboys™
995QSR5121 • $14

3805.

NFL®: Denver Broncos™
995QSR5111 • $14

3806.

NFL®: Green Bay Packers™
995QSR5114 • $14

3807.

NFL®: Kansas City Chiefs™
995QSR5131 • $14

3808.

NFL®: Miami Dolphins™
995QSR5144 • $14

3809.

NFL®: Minnesota Vikings™
995QSR5164 • $14

3810.

NFL®: Pittsburgh Steelers™
995QSR5124 • $14

3811.

NFL®: San Francisco 49ers™
995QSR5134 • $14

3812.

NFL®: Washington Redskins™
995QSR5151 • $14

3813.

North Pole Network
1095QX6994 • $18

3814.

Northern Art Bear
895QX8294 • $26

3815.

Nostalgic Houses & Shops 17: Schoolhouse
1495QX6591 • $32

3816.

Off to Neverland! - Peter Pan
1295QXD4004 • $31

3817.

Old West 3: Mountain Man
1595QX6594 • $40

3818.

Our Christmas Together
995QX8054 • $14

3819.

Our Family
795QX8211 • $24

3820.

Our First Christmas Together
795QX3104 • $13

3821.

Our First Christmas Together
895QX8051 • $13

3822.

Our First Christmas Together
1095QX8701 • $19

3823.

Our Lady of Guadalupe
1295QX8231 • $23

3824.

A Pony for Christmas 3
1295QX6624 • $22

3825.

A Pony for Christmas 3
($N/A)QX6624C • $86

3826.

The Proud Collector
($N/E)QXC4511 • $28

3827.

Puppy Love 10
795QX6554 • $15

3828.

Qui-Gon Jinn™
1495QXI6741 • $26

3829.

A Reader to the Core
995QX6974 • $26

3830.

Rhett Butler™
1295QX6674 • $28

3831.

Ringing Reindeer
($N/E)QXC4484 • $22

3832.

Robot Parade 1
1695QX6771 • $19

3833.

Romantic Vacations 3: Donald and Daisy at Lovers' Lodge
1495QXD4031 • $28

3834.

Safe in Noah's Ark
1095QX8514 • $20

3835.

Santa Mail
($N/E)QX6702C • $30

3836.

Santa's Chair
1295QX8314 • $25

3837.

Scarlett O'Hara™ 4
1495QX6671 • $42

3838.

Scooby-Doo™
1295QXI8394 • $29

3839.

Scuffy the Tugboat™
1195QX6871 • $18

3840.

Self-Portrait
1095QX6644 • $22

3841.

Seven of Nine
1495QX6844 • $28

3842.

Signature Snowman
995QXC4524 • $17

3843.

Sister to Sister
1295QX8144 • $19

3844.

Sky's the Limit 4: Spirit of St. Louis
1495QX6634 • $45

3845.

A Snoopy® Christmas: Charlie Brown™
495QRP4191 • $14

3846.

A Snoopy® Christmas: Linus
495QRP4204 • $9

3847.

A Snoopy® Christmas: Lucy
495QRP4174 • $9

3848.

A Snoopy® Christmas: Snoopy™
495QRP4184 • $14

3849.

A Snoopy® Christmas: Woodstock™ on Doghouse
495QRP4211 • $10

3850.

Snow Buddies 3
795QX6654 • $26

3851.

Snow Girl
995QX8274 • $23

3852.

The Snowmen of Mitford
1995QXI5244 • $26 • Set/4

3853.

Son
895QX8084 • $14

3854.

Spotlight on Snoopy® 3: The Detective
995QX6564 • $22

3855.

Star Wars™ 4: Obi-Wan Kenobi™
1495QXI6704 • $32

3856.

Stroll Round the Pole
1095QX8164 • $14

3857.

Super Friends™ Lunchbox Set
1495QX6724 • $19 • Set/2

3858.

Surprise Package - Blue's Clues™
1095QXI8391 • $23

3859.

Tending Her Topiary
995QX8004 • $13

3860.

Thimble Soldier
2200QBG4061 • $38

3861.

Time for Joy
2400QX6904 • $48

3862.

Together We Serve
995QX8021 • $16

3863.

Tonka® Dump Truck
1395QX6681 • $26

3864.

Town and Country 2: Bait Shop with Boat
1595QX6631 • $23

3865.

Toy Shop Serenade
1695QX8301 • $23

3866.

Toymaker Santa 1
1495QX6751 • $23

3867.

Treasure Tree
6500QXC4521 • $140 • Set/19
Limited Edition - 25000.

3868.

Tree Guy
895QX6961 • $13

3869.

Unforgettable Villains 3: Sleeping Beauty's Maleficent
1495QXD4001 • $35

3870.

VeggieTales® - Bob the Tomato™ and Larry the Cucumber™
995QXI4334 • $20

3871.

A Visit from St. Nicholas
1095QX8344 • $17

3872.

Warm Kindness
895QX8014 • $32

3873.

Warmed by Candleglow
695QX2471 • $17

3874.

Winnie the Pooh: Piglet's Jack-in-the-Box
1495QXD4187 • $20

3875.

Winnie the Pooh: Pooh Chooses the Tree
1295QXD4157 • $32

3876.

Winnie the Pooh 3: A Blustery Day
1395QXD4021 • $23

3877.

Winnie the Pooh and Christopher Robin®, Too 2
1395QXD4024 • $20

3878.

Winter Fun with BARBIE™ and Kelly™
1595QXI6561 • $22

3879.

Winterberry Santa
1495QXI4331 • $19

3880.
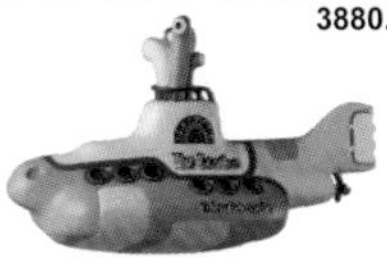

The Yellow Submarine™ - The Beatles
1395QXI6841 • $28

3881.

Yule Tide Runner
995QX6981 • $32

2001

3882.

1950s BARBIE™ Ornament
1495QXI8882 • $32

3883.

1958 Custom Corvette®
1795QXC4505 • $42

3884.

1961 BARBIE™ Hatbox Case
995QX6922 • $17

3885.

1968 Silhouette™ and Case
1495QX6605 • $19 • Set/2

3886.

2000 Oscar Mayer Wienermobile™
1295QX6935 • $25

3887.

2001 Jeep™ Sport Wrangler
1495QXI6362 • $34

3888.

2001 Time Capsule
995QX2802 • $22

3889.

2001 Vacation
995QX2822 • $16

3890.

All-American Trucks 7: 1959 Chevrolet® El Camino™
1395QX6072 • $32

3891.

All-Sport Santa
995QX8332 • $16

3892.

All-Star Kid Memory Keeper
995QX2805 • $18

3893.

America for Me!
995QX2882 • $31

3894.

Anakin Skywalker™
1495QX6942 • $25

3895.

Angel of Faith
1495QXI5375 • $30

3896.

Angel's Whisper
995QX8852 • $18

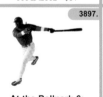

3897.

At the Ballpark 6: Sammy Sosa
1495QXI6375 • $25

3898.

Baby's First Christmas
895QX8355 • $32

3899.

Baby's First Christmas
895QX8362 • $16

3900.

Baby's First Christmas
995QX8482 • $17

3901.

Baby's First Christmas (Boy)
895QX8365 • $19

3902.

Baby's First Christmas (Girl)
895QX8372 • $18

3903.

Bambi Discovers Winter
2400QXD7541 • $38
MAGIC.

3904.

BARBIE™ 8: BARBIE™ in Busy Gal™ Fashion
1595QX6965 • $23 • Set/2

3905.

BARBIE™ 2001
1995QXC4531 • $89

3906.

BARBIE™ and Kelly™ on the Ice
1595QXI6915 • $20

3907.
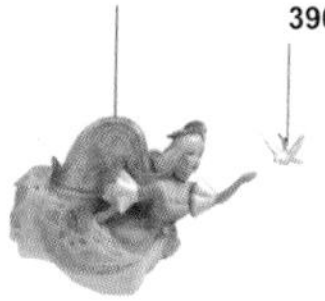
BARBIE™ Angel Ornament
1595QXI6925 • $23 • Set/2

3908.

BARBIE™ as the Sugar Plum Princess
1595QXI6132 • $36 • Set/2

3909.

Beautiful Cross
995QX8825 • $19

3910.

Beginning Ballet
1295QX2875 • $16

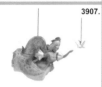

3911.

Bell-Ringing Santa - Mickey Mouse
995QXD4125 • $19

3912.

Blue and Periwinkle - Blue's Clues™
995QXI6142 • $18

3913.

Candlelight Services 4: Brick Church
1895QLX7552 • $34
MAGIC.

3914.

Captain Benjamin Sisko
1495QX6865 • $24

3915.

Carving Santa
1295QX8265 • $18

3916.

Carving Santa
($N/A)QX8265C • $698
Edition Size - 54.

3917.

Celebration BARBIE™ 2
1595QXI5202 • $26

3918.

Child's Age: Baby's First Christmas
795QX8375 • $24

3919.

Child's Age: Baby's Second Christmas
795QX8382 • $20

3920.

Child's Age: Child's Third Christmas
795QX8385 • $15

3921.

Child's Age: Child's Fourth Christmas
795QX8392 • $15

3922.

Child's Age: Child's Fifth Christmas
795QX8395 • $15

3923.

Christmas Brings Us Together
995QX8285 • $29

3924.

The Christmas Cone
895QX8875 • $16

3925.

Christmas Parrot
895QX8175 • $20

3926.

Cinderella's Castle
1800QXD4172 • $31

3927.

Classic American Cars 11: 1953 Buick® Roadmaster Skylark
1395QX6872 • $24

3928.

Coca-Cola® - Cool Sport
1495QHB9002 • $15

3929.

Collegiate: Alabama Crimson Tide™
995QSR2132 • $12

3930.

Collegiate: Florida Gators™
995QSR2165 • $12

3931.

Collegiate: Florida State Seminoles™
995QSR2162 • $12

3932.

Collegiate: Kentucky Wildcats™
995QSR2152 • $12

3933.

Collegiate: Michigan Wolverines™
995QSR2142 • $12

3934.

Collegiate: Nebraska Cornhuskers™
995QSR2135 • $12

3935.

Collegiate: North Carolina Tar Heels™
995QSR2155 • $12

3936.

Collegiate: Notre Dame Fighting Irish™
995QSR2145 • $12

3937.

Collegiate: Penn State Nittany Lions™
995QSR2122 • $12

3938.

Collegiate: Tennessee Volunteers™
995QSR2125 • $12

3939.

Color Crew Chief
1095QX6185 • $20

3940.

Cooking for Christmas: Creative Cutter
995QX8865 • $16

3941.

Cooking for Christmas: Creative Cutter
($N/A)QX8865C • $60
Edition Size - 5000.

3942.

Cooking for Christmas: Santa Sneaks a Sweet
1595QX8862 • $25

3943.

Cooking for Christmas: Sharing Santa's Snacks
895QX8212 • $23

3944.

Cooking for Christmas: Sharing Santa's Snacks
($N/A)QX8212C • $62

3945.

Cool Decade 2
795QX6992 • $14

3946.

Cool Decade 2
($N/A)QX6992C • $65
Edition Size - 15000.

3947.

Cool Patriot
995QX8059C2 • $28

3948.

Cozy Home
995QX8965 • $17

3949.

A Cup of Friendship
895QX8472 • $17

3950.

Dad
895QX8422 • $20

3951.

Dale Jarrett
1495QXI5205 • $23

3952.

Daughter
895QX8425 • $22

3953.

Disney's School Bus Lunchbox Set
1495QXD4115 • $35 • Set/2

3954.

Donald Goes Motoring
1295QXD4122 • $20

3955.

Dr. Seuss® Books 3: Horton™ Hatches the Egg
1495QX6282 • $30 • Set/2

3956.

Farewell Scene - Gone With The Wind™
2400QLX7562 • $40
MAGIC.

3957.

Fashion Afoot 2
1495QX8105 • $22

3958.

Favorite Bible Stories 3: Daniel in the Lions' Den
1395QX8122 • $26

3959.

Feliz Navidad
995QX8185 • $13

3960.

The First Walgreen's Drugstore
995QGO3082 • $22

3961.

Flying School Airplane Hanger
1595QX8172 • $34

3962.

Football Legends 7: Brett Favre
1495QXI5232 • $30

3963.

Four-Alarm Friends
995QX8325 • $18

3964.

Friendly Elves
1495QX8805 • $15 • Set/2

3965.

Frostlight Faeries: Beaded Snowflakes (Blue)
995QP1712 • $17 • Set/3
Re-issued in 2002.

3966.

Frostlight Faeries: Beaded Snowflakes (Periwinkle)
995QP1725 • $28 • Set/3
Re-issued in 2002.

3967.

Frostlight Faeries: Beaded Snowflakes (Violet)
995QP1732 • $28 • Set/3
Re-issued in 2002.

3968.

Frostlight Faeries: Faerie Brilliana
1495QP1672 • $34

3969.

Frostlight Faeries: Faerie Candessa
1495QP1665 • $25

3970.

Frostlight Faeries: Faerie Delandra
1495QP1685 • $34

3971.

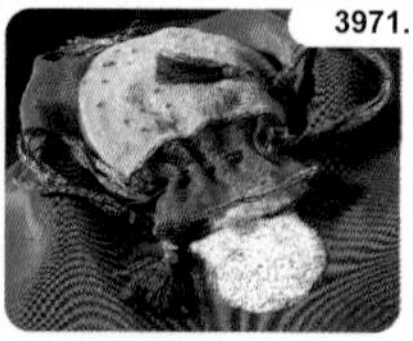

Frostlight Faeries: Faerie Dust
595QP1752 • $18

3972.

Frostlight Faeries: Faerie Estrella
1495QP1695 • $22

3973.

Frostlight Faeries: Faerie Floriella
1495QP1692 • $29

3974.

Frostlight Faeries: Frostlight Fir Tree
4500QP1762 • $69

3975.

Frostlight Faeries: Frostlight Flowers
1595QP1705 • $20

3976.
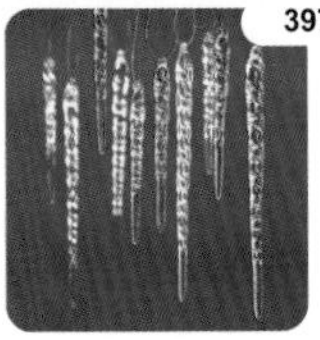
Frostlight Faeries: Glistening Icicles
1295QP1742 • $34 • Set/12

3977.
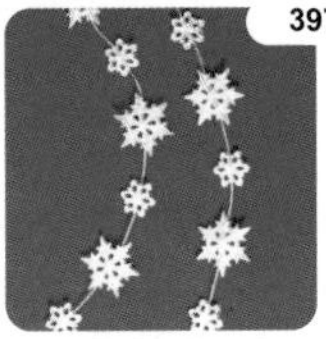
Frostlight Faeries: Snowflake Garland
1295QP1745 • $17

3978.

Frosty Friends 22
1095QX8012 • $24

3979.

Frosty Friends 22
1095QX8012C • $48

3980.

G.I. Joe® - Fighter Pilot
1395QX6045 • $29

3981.

Gift Bearers 3
1295QX8115 • $21

3982.

Godchild
795QX8452 • $17

3983.

Gouda Reading
995QX2855 • $24

3984.

Graceful Angel Bell
1295QX8182 • $17

3985.

Graceful Reindeer
2095QX8912 • $25 • Set/3

3986.
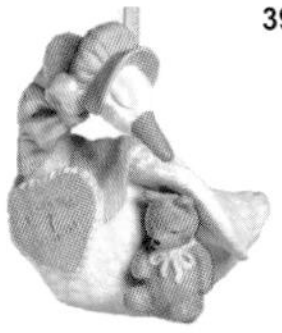
Grandchild's First Christmas
895QX8485 • $14

3987.

Granddaughter
895QX8435 • $14

3988.

Grandmother
995QX8445 • $17

3989.

Grandson
895QX8442 • $13

3990.

Guiding Star
995QX8962 • $12

3991.

Happy Snowman
895QX8942 • $19

3992.

Harley-Davidson® BARBIE™
1595QXI8885 • $30

3993.

Harley-Davidson® Motorcycle Milestones 3: 1957 XL Sportster®
1495QXI8125 • $32

3994.

Harry Potter™: Fluffy™ on Guard
1295QXE4415 • $32

3995.

Harry Potter™: Hagrid™ and Norbert the Dragon™
1595QXE4412 • $29

3996.

Harry Potter™: Harry Potter™
1295QXE4402 • $25

3997.

Harry Potter™: Hermione Granger™'s Trunk
1495QXE4422 • $31 • Set/6

3998.
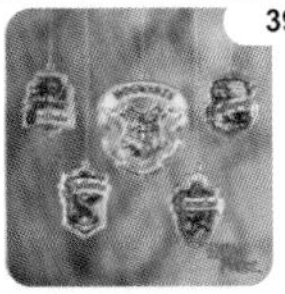
Harry Potter™: Hogwarts™ School Crests
1295QXE4452 • $35 • Set/5

3999.

Harry Potter™: Ron Weasley and Scabbers™
1295QXE4405 • $26

4000.

Hello Dumbo
1295QXD4162 • $23

4001.

Here Comes Santa 23: Santa's Snowplow
1495QX8065 • $25

4002.

Hockey Greats 5: Jaromir Jagr
1595QXI6852 • $25

4003.

Holiday Spa Tweety™
995QX6945 • $20

4004.

Hoop Stars 7: Tim Duncan
1495QXI5235 • $29

4005.

I Love My Dog
795QX8802 • $17

4006.

It Had to be You
995QX2815 • $20

4007.

Jar Jar Binks™
1495QX6882 • $24

4008.

The Jetsons™ Lunchbox Set
1495QX6312 • $18 • Set/2

4009.

Jolly Santa Bells
1995QX8915 • $32 • Set/3

4010.

Jolly Visitor
695QX2235 • $11

4011.

Journey to Bethlehem Bell
1495QX8386 • $25

4012.

Joyful Santa 3
1495QX8152 • $23

4013.

Kiddie Car Classics 8: 1930 Custom Biplane
1395QX6975 • $38

4014.

Kiss the Cook
995QX2852 • $17

4015.

Kris and the Kringles 1
2400QX8112 • $34

4016.

The Land of Christmastime
1295QX8282 • $17

4017.

Laptop Santa
795QX8972 • $18

4018.
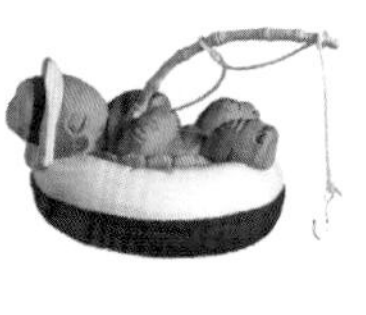
Lazy Afternoon
995QX8335 • $16

4019.

Legend Of Santa Claus
4000QXC4585 • $75 • Set/5

4020.

Lighthouse Greetings 5
2400QLX7572 • $42
MAGIC.

4021.

Lionel Plays with Words
1495QXI6902 • $15

4022.

LIONEL® I-400E Blue Comet Locomotive
3500QBG4355 • $60

4023.

LIONEL® Trains 6: LIONEL® Chessie Steam Special Locomotive
1895QX6092 • $32

4024.

Local Clubs Pop
($N/E)QXC4512 • $24

4025.

Lucy Does a TV Commercial
1595QX6862 • $32

4026.

Madame Alexander® 6: Victorian Christmas
1495QX6855 • $23

4027.

Madame Alexander® Little Women 1: Margaret "Meg" March
1595QX6315 • $23

4028.

A Magical Dress for Briar Rose - Sleeping Beauty
1495QXD4202 • $24

4029.

Mario Lemieux
1595QXI6155 • $23

4030.

Mary and Joseph
1895QX8195 • $28

4031.

Mary Hamilton Angel Chorus
695QX2232 • $14

4032.

Mary's Angels 14: Chrysantha
795QX6985 • $28

4033.

Mary's Angels 14: Chrysantha
($N/A)QX6985C • $89
Edition Size - 15000.

4034.

Merry Carolers
2400QXD7585 • $37

4035.

Mickey Mantle - New York Yankees™
1495QXI6804 • $38

4036.

Mickey's Holiday Parade 5: Pluto Plays Triangle
1395QXD4112 • $29

4037.

Mickey's Sweetheart Minnie Mouse
995QXD4192 • $17

4038.

Minnie's Sweetheart Mickey Mouse
995QXD4195 • $17

4039.

The Mirror of Erised™ - Harry Potter™
1595QXI8645 • $24

4040.

Mischievous Kittens 3
995QX8025 • $30

4041.

Miss Rose - Snowman of Mitford
($N/E)(N/A) • $35
Edition Size - 15000.

4042.

Mistletoe Miss 1
1495QX8092 • $22

4043.

Mitford Snowman Jubilee
1995QX2825 • $56 • Set/4

4044.

Mom
895QX8415 • $23

4045.

Mom and Dad
995QX8462 • $17

4046.

Monsters, Inc.
1295QXI6145 • $34

4047.

Moose's Merry Christmas
1295QX8835 • $25

4048.

Mother and Daughter
995QX6962 • $18

4049.

Mrs. Claus's Chair
1295QX6955 • $20

4050.

Mrs. Potts and Chip - Beauty and the Beast
1295QXD4165 • $23 • Set/2

4051.

The Mystery Machine™
1395QX6295 • $26

4052.
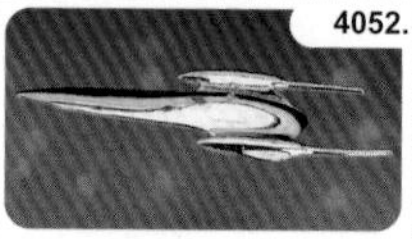
Naboo Royal Starship™
1895QX8475 • $31

4053.

Nature's Sketchbook: My First Snowman
995QX4442 • $19

4054.

Nesting Nativity
2000QXC4502 • $39 • Set/5

4055.

NFL®: Cleveland Browns™
995QSR5572 • $14

4056.

NFL®: Dallas Cowboys™
995QSR5622 • $14

4057.

NFL®: Denver Broncos™
995QSR5545 • $14

4058.

NFL®: Green Bay Packers™
995QSR5625 • $14

4059.
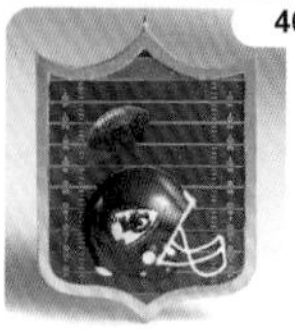
NFL®: Kansas City Chiefs™
995QSR5542 • $14

4060.

NFL®: Miami Dolphins™
995QSR5555 • $14

4061.

NFL®: Minnesota Vikings™
995QSR5575 • $14

4062.

NFL®: Pittsburgh Steelers™
995QSR5565 • $14

4063.

NFL®: San Francisco 49ers™
995QSR5562 • $14

4064.

NFL®: Washington Redskins™
995QSR5552 • $14

4065.

Night Before Christmas: Hung With Care
495QRP4485 • $7

4066.

Night Before Christmas: Not Even a Mouse
495QRP4482 • $6

4067.

Night Before Christmas: Santa
495QRP4495 • $8

4068.

Night Before Christmas: Tiny Reindeer
495QRP4492 • $10

4069.

No. 1 Teacher
995QX2865 • $16

4070.

Noah's Ark
1295QX2835 • $21

4071.

Noche de Paz
1295QX8192 • $19

4072.

Nostalgic Houses & Shops 18: Service Station
1495QX8045 • $34

4073.

Nostalgic Houses & Shops 18: Service Station
($N/A)QX8045C • $925
Edition Size - 54.

4074.

Old-World Santa
995QX8975 • $18

4075.

One Little Angel
895QX8935 • $18

4076.

Our Christmas Together
1995QX8412 • $30 • Set/4

4077.

Our Family
895QX8995 • $30

4078.

Our Family
($N/A)QX8995C • $35
Edition Size - 15000.

4079.

Our First Christmas Together
795QX3162 • $19

4080.

Our First Christmas Together
895QX6012 • $16

4081.

Our First Christmas Together
995QX8405 • $17

4082.

A Partridge in a Pear Tree
1295QX8215 • $22

4083.

Pat the Bunny
995QX8582 • $14

4084.

PEANUTS® Pageant
1495QX2832 • $25 • Set/2

4085.

Peek-a-Boo Present
995QX8302 • $14

4086.

Peggy Fleming
1495QXI6845 • $20

4087.

Penguins at Play
995QX8982 • $27

4088.

A Perfect Blend
995QX8985 • $19

4089.

A Perfect Christmas!
1295QXI6895 • $18

4090.

A Pony for Christmas 4
1295QX6995 • $20

4091.
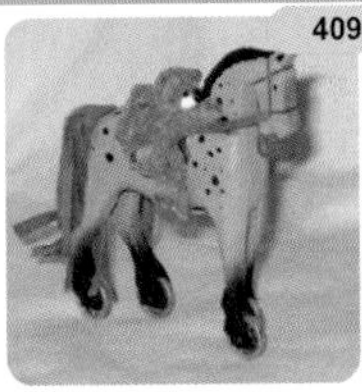
A Pony for Christmas 4
($N/A)QX6995C • $53

4092.

Poppy Field - The Wizard of Oz™
2400QLX7565 • $42
MAGIC.

4093.

Portrait of Scarlett
1595QX2885 • $34

4094.

The Potions Master - Harry Potter™
1495QXI8652 • $24

4095.

Puppy Love 11
795QX6982 • $14

4096.

Q
2400QBG4345 • $48

4097.

Raggedy Andy®
1095QX8574 • $19

4098.

Raggedy Ann®
1095QX8571 • $23

4099.

Ready Teddy
995QX8842 • $18

4100.

Robot Parade 2
1495QX8162 • $20

4101.

Rocking Reindeer
1295QX8261 • $19

4102.

Safe and Snug 1
1295QX8342 • $17

4103.

Safe and Snug 1
($N/A)QX8342C • $748
Edition Size - 54.

4104.

Samantha "Sam" Stephens - Bewitched™
1495QXI6892 • $24

4105.

Santa Marionette
1395QXC4525 • $26

4106.

Santa's Day Off
995QX2872 • $16

4107.

Santa's Sweet Surprise
1495QX8275 • $25

4108.

Santa's Workshop
995QX2812 • $19

4109.

Sew Sweet Angel
995QX2862 • $19

4110.

Sisters
895QX8455 • $18

4111.

Skating Sugar Bear Bell
995QX6005 • $17

4112.

Sky's the Limit 5: Gee Bee R-1 Super Sportster®
1495QX8005 • $74

4113.

Snoozing Santa
1895QX8165 • $23

4114.

Snow Blossom
995QX8494 • $18

4115.

Snow Buddies 4
795QX6972 • $16

4116.
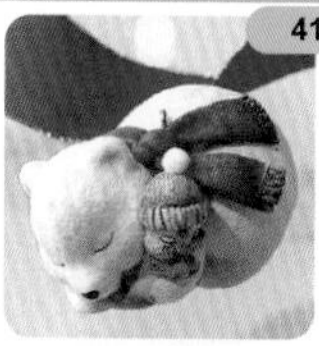
Snowball and Tuxedo 1: A Little Nap
795QX8072 • $19

4117.

Snuggly Sugar Bear Bell
995QX8922 • $16

4118.

Son
895QX8432 • $44

4119.

Space Station Deep Space 9™
3200QX6065 • $47
MAGIC.

4120.

Spotlight on Snoopy® 4: Beaglescout
995QX6085 • $18

4121.

Spotlight on Snoopy® 4: Beaglescout
($N/A)QX6085C • $823
Edition Size - 54.

4122.

Springing Santa
795QX8085 • $13

4123.

Star Wars™ 5: R2-D2™
1495QX6875 • $58

4124.

Stars & Stripes Forever
($N/E)QHB2892 • $20

4125.

Steve Young - San Francisco 49ers™
1495QXI6305 • $32

4126.

Sylvester™'s Bang-Up Gift
1295QX6912 • $19

4127.

Tender - LIONEL® Chessie Steam Special
1395QX6285 • $78

4128.

Thomas O'Malley and Duchess - The Aristocats®
1495QXD4175 • $25

4129.

Tonka® 1955 Steam Shovel
1395QX6292 • $32

4130.

Tootle the Train
1195QX6052 • $23

4131.

Town and Country 3: Fire Station No. 1
1595QX8052 • $28

4132.

Toymaker Santa 2
1495QX8032 • $32

4133.

Twas the Night Before...: Curius
($N/A)PR2318 • $13

4134.

Twas the Night Before...: Gift for a Friend
($N/E)QXC4545 • $95 • Set/2

4135.

Twas the Night Before...: Lettera, Mrs. Claus, & Globus
($N/E)QXC2001 • $29 • Set/3

4136.

Twas the Night Before...: Ready for Delivery
($N/A)QXC4552 • $44

4137.

Twas the Night Before...: Ready Reindeer
1395QX8295 • $24

4138.

Twas the Night Before...: Ready Reindeer
($N/A)QX8295C • $698
Edition Size - 54.

4139.

Twas the Night Before...: Santa Claus With Mini Panda Bear
1895QXI5395 • $24 • Set/2

4140.

Twas the Night Before...: Santa's Desk
7500QXC4562 • $95

4141.

Twas the Night Before...: Santa's Sleigh With Sack and Miniature Ornament
1895QX8872 • $25 • Set/3

4142.

Twas the Night Before...: Santa's Toy Box With 3 Miniature Ornaments
1295QXI5392 • $17 • Set/4

4143.

'Twas the Night Before...: With Help From Pup
995QXC4565 • $96 • Set/2

4144.

Up on the Housetop
4200QLX7575 • $42
MAGIC.

4145.

VeggieTales® - Waiting for Santa
1295QXI6932 • $19

4146.

Victorian BARBIE™ with Cedric Bear Ornament
1595QXI6952 • $22

4147.

Victorian Christmas Memories
1455QX8292 • $29 • Set/3

4148.

Victorian Sleigh
1295QX8855 • $20

4149.

Waddles
895QX8952 • $12

4150.

Waggles
895QX8945 • $18

4151.

What a Grinchy Trick!
1495QXI6405 • $23

4152.

Wiggles
895QX8955 • $14

4153.

Winnie the Pooh: A Familiar Face
1295QXD4152 • $26

4154.

Winnie the Pooh: Eeyore Helps Out
1295QXD4145 • $35

4155.

Winnie the Pooh: Just What They Wanted!
1295QXD4142 • $24

4156.

Winnie the Pooh 4: Tracking the Jagular®
1395QXD4132 • $24

4157.

Winnie the Pooh and Christopher Robin®, Too 3
1395QXD4135 • $23

4158.

Winter Friends
695QX2242 • $11

4159.

A Wise Follower
895QX8202 • $16

4160.
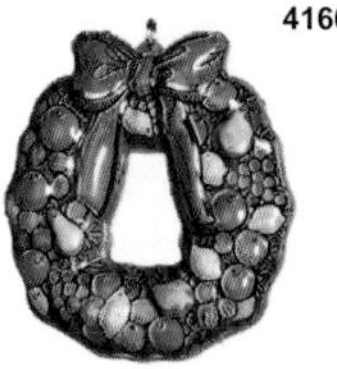
Wreath of Evergreens
895QX8832 • $16

2002

4161.

1961 BARBIE™ Travel Pal Case and Accessories
1495QX8293 • $20 • Set/5

4162.

29-C Fire Pumper
1495QXI8846 • $22 • Set/2

4163.

All-American Trucks 8: 1957 Ford® Ranchero™
1495QX8066 • $28

4164.

American Girls: Addy
1500QAC6406 • $28

4165.

American Girls: Felicity
1500QAC6404 • $28

4166.

American Girls: Josefina
1500QAC6405 • $28

4167.

American Girls: Kaya
1500QAC6407 • $28

4168.

American Girls: Kirsten
1500QAC6403 • $28

4169.

American Girls: Kit
1500QAC6411 • $28

4170.

American Girls: Kit's Treasures Miniature Ornament Set
1500QAC6408 • $28 • Set/4

4171.

American Girls: Molly
1500QAC6409 • $28

4172.

American Girls: Samantha
1500QAC6410 • $28

4173.

Angel In Disguise
995QX8983 • $24

4174.

Angel of Comfort
1495QXI6363 • $42

4175.

Angelic Visitation
1495QX2853 • $22

4176.

Arthur® and D.W®. - A Perfect Christmas!
1295QX8843 • $20

4177.

At the Ballpark 7: Derek Jeter
1495QXI5242 • $24

4178.

Baby's First Christmas
1695QX8616 • $26

4179.

Baby's First Christmas
995QX8913 • $19

4180.

Baby's First Christmas (Boy)
995QX8596 • $16

4181.

Baby's First Christmas (Girl)
995QX8806 • $16

4182.

Back to School
995QX8696 • $17

4183.

Baking Memories
1295QX6956 • $26

4184.

Ballet Photo Holder
995QX2873 • $17

4185.

BARBIE™ 9: Sophisticated Lady BARBIE™
1595QX8203 • $32

4186.

BARBIE™ 2002
2390QXC4653 • $61

4187.

BARBIE™ as Rapunzel
1495QXI5326 • $28 • Set/2

4188.

BARBIE™ as Snowflake
1495QXI8303 • $25

4189.

The Beatles - Yellow Submarine™ Lunchbox Set
1495QXI5313 • $23 • Set/2

4190.

Belle - Beauty and the Beast
1295QXD4946 • $26

4191.

Between Us: A Heartful of Grateful
995QP1523 • $23

4192.

Between Us: Always Near
995QP1503 • $23

4193.
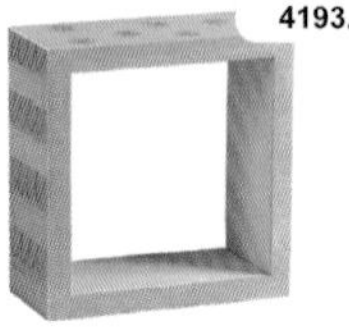
Between Us: Display Base
995QP1553 • $17

4194.

Between Us: Dreams Have Wings
995QP1536 • $23

4195.

Between Us: Kindred Spirits
995QP1546 • $36

4196.
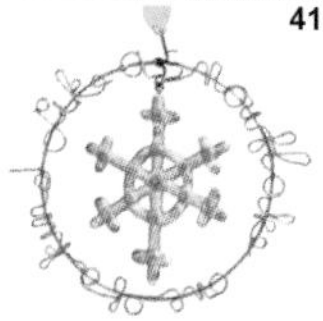
Between Us: Like a Snowflake
995QP1533 • $23

4197.
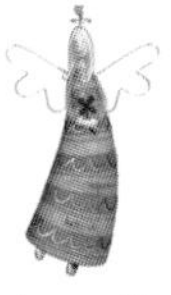
Between Us: Lucky Sisters... Lucky Us
995QP1516 • $22

4198.

Between Us: Make a Wish
995QP1526 • $23

4199.

Between Us: Mom
995QP1543 • $20

4200.

Between Us: You Inspire Me
995QP1513 • $25

4201.

The Biggest Fan
995QX8733 • $20

4202.

Blue Comet 400T Oil Tender
1295QX8243 • $32

4203.

Blue Comet Passenger Car
1295QX8833 • $72

4204.

Blushing Bride BARBIE™
1995QXI5323 • $28
Auburn hair.

4205.

Blushing Bride BARBIE™
1995QXI5323 • $22
Blonde hair.

4206.

Blushing Bride BARBIE™
1995QXI5323 • $22
Brunette hair.

4207.

Buzz Lightyear - Toy Story
1495QXD4606 • $32

4208.

Calling All Firefighters
995QX8746 • $20

4209.

Calling the Caped Crusader - Batman™
1495QXI8856 • $28

4210.

Candlelight Services 5: Country Church
1895QLX7653 • $29
MAGIC.

4211.

Castle in the Forest - Beauty and the Beast
1800QXD4953 • $40

4212.

Celebration BARBIE™ 3
1595QXI8163 • $23

4213.

Change of Heart - How The Grinch Stole Christmas™
1495QXI5273 • $19

4214.

Checking the List
1495QX8493 • $28

4215.

Cheer for Fun! BARBIE™
1495QXI8306 • $23

4216.

Child's Age: Baby's First Christmas
795QX8326 • $20

4217.

Child's Age: Baby's Second Christmas
795QX8333 • $19

4218.

Child's Age: Child's Third Christmas
795QX8336 • $14

4219.

Child's Age: Child's Fourth Christmas
795QX8343 • $14

4220.

Child's Age: Child's Fifth Christmas
795QX8346 • $14

4221.

Christmas Around The World
695QX8436 • $26

4222.

Christmas Fairy
1495QX8396 • $22

4223.

Christmas Floral
695QX2963 • $13

4224.

Christmas Growth Chart
1295QX8896 • $23

4225.

Christmas Habitat - Tweety™
995QX2913 • $22

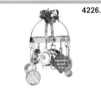

4226.

Christmas In The Kitchen
1295QX8956 • $32

4227.

Christmas Tree Gift Clip
995QX2896 • $17

4228.

Cinderella
995QXD4956 • $22

4229.

Circus Mountain Railroad
4200QLX7686 • $56
MAGIC.

4230.

Clara's Hallmark Shop
1995QXC4583 • $85

4231.

Classic American Cars 12: 1970 Ford® Mach 1 Mustang™
1495QX8073 • $60

4232.

Club Star Ornaments
($N/E)QXC4693 • $N/E • Set/3

4233.

Cool Decade 3
795QX8016 • $32

4234.

Cool Friends
995QX8706 • $20

4235.

Dad
995QX8936 • $16

4236.

Daughter
995QX8946 • $20

4237.

Death Star™
2400QLX7656 • $35
MAGIC.

4238.

Decorating Scooby-Doo™ Style
1295QX8256 • $20

4239.

Deer Creek Cottage
1495QXI5276 • $20

4240.

Delta Flyer™
2400QLX7663 • $42
MAGIC.

4241.

Doctor
1495QX8226 • $28

4242.

Don't Get Into Mischief, Beatrix Potter™
995QX2906 • $19

4243.

Dorothy & Scarecrow™
1595QX8246 • $20

4244.

Dr. Seuss® Books 4: Green Eggs and Ham™
1495QX8083 • $28

4245.

E.T. The Extraterrestrial™ 20th Anniversary
1495QXI5333 • $23

4246.

Enterprise NX-01™
2400QXI2943 • $44 • Set/2

4247.

Faerie Gabriella and Faerie Castle Ornament Stand
3500QXC4656 • $100 • Set/2

4248.

Family Photo Holder
1295QX8693 • $26

4249.

Fashion Afoot 3
1495QX8116 • $28

4250.

Fill 'Er Up! Daffy Duck™
995QX8266 • $20

4251.

First Snow
1295QX8403 • $23

4252.

First Snow
($N/A)QX8403C • $42

4253.

The First Snow - Blue's Clues™
995QXI5266 • $20

4254.

Fishin' Mission
995QX8736 • $26

4255.

Football Legends 8: Kurt Warner
1495QXI8143 • $28

4256.
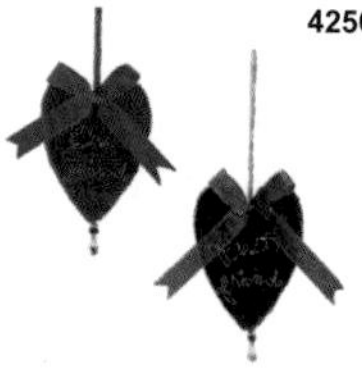
Friendship Hearts
1495QX8713 • $28 • Set/2

4257.

Frostlight Faeries, Too: Baby Brilliana
1495QP1683 • $20

4258.
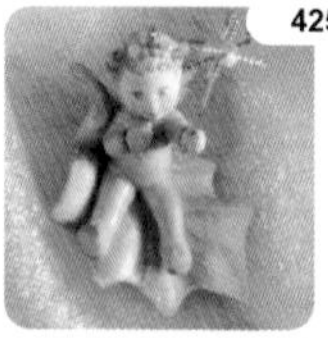
Frostlight Faeries, Too: Baby Candessa
1495QP1676 • $20

4259.

Frostlight Faeries, Too: Baby Delandra
1495QP1666 • $20

4260.

Frostlight Faeries, Too: Baby Estrella
1495QP1663 • $20

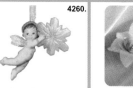

4261.
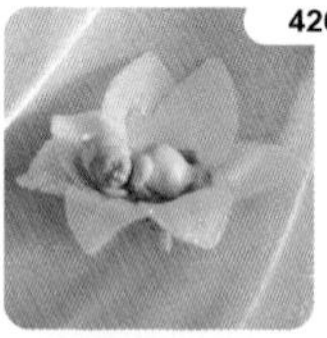
Frostlight Faeries, Too: Baby Floriella
1495QP1673 • $20

4262.

Frostlight Faeries, Too: Beaded Snowflakes (Blue)
995QP1712 • $17 • Set/3
Re-issued from 2001.

4263.

Frostlight Faeries, Too: Beaded Snowflakes (Periwinkle)
995QP1725 • $28 • Set/3
Re-issued from 2001.

4264.

Frostlight Faeries, Too: Beaded Snowflakes (Violet)
995QP1732 • $28 • Set/3
Re-issued from 2001.

4265.

Frosty Friends 23
1095QX8053 • $29

4266.

Frosty Friends Porcelain Box
1895QXC4573 • $55

4267.

G.I. Joe® Lunchbox Set
1495QX8286 • $20 • Set/2

4268.

Gardener's Christmas Corner
995QX2866 • $26

4269.

George Brett
1495QXI5296 • $22

4270.

Gift Bearers 4
1295QX8883 • $23

4271.

Gingerbread Cottage
1995QLX7683 • $38
MAGIC.

4272.

God With Us
695QX8893 • $13

4273.

Godchild
1295QX8953 • $20

4274.

Goofy® Clockworks
1495QXD4923 • $23

4275.

Granddaughter
995QX8663 • $13

4276.

Grandma
695QX8676 • $12

4277.

Grandson
995QX8666 • $13

4278.

The Great Ski Challenge
1295QXD4926 • $23

4279.

Harley-Davidson® Motorcycle Milestones 4: FX-1200 Super Glide®
1495QXI8123 • $25

4280.

Having Fun With Friends
($N/E)QXC4553 • $25

4281.

Heavenly Carols
1695QXI7713 • $28

4282.

Here Comes Santa 24: North Pole Towing Service
1495QX8106 • $29

4283.

Holiday Treat Taz™
995QX8263 • $20

4284.

Hoop Stars 8: Kevin Garnett
1495QXI8146 • $23

4285.

Hope Cross
995QX8886 • $23

4286.

Hope, Joy, and Love
1595QX8433 • $28 • Set/3

4287.

Horse of a Different Color™
3600QLX7673 • $43
MAGIC.

4288.

I Don't Do Jolly!
1995QX2806 • $40

4289.

The Invisibility Cloak - Harry Potter™
1295QXI8663 • $34

4290.

Jango Fett™
1495QXI4386 • $36

4291.

Jesus and Friends
1495QX2843 • $26

4292.

Job Switching - I Love Lucy® 50th Anniversary
1695QXI5316 • $26

4293.

A Joyful Noise
1495QX2816 • $32

4294.

Juice Machine and Revvin' Heaven
1495QX8236 • $23 • Set/2

4295.

Kiddie Car Classics 9: 1928 Jingle Bell Express
1395QX8076 • $22

4296.

Kris and the Kringles 2
2400QX8173 • $38

4297.

The Light Within
1295QX2846 • $23

4298.

Lighthouse Greetings 6
2400QLX7646 • $44
MAGIC.

4299.

LIONEL® Trains 7: Blue Comet 400E Steam Locomotive
1895QX8166 • $29

4300.

Look Out Below! Sylvester™ & Tweety™
995QX8273 • $20

4301.

Loving Angel
995QX8366 • $23

4302.

Luke Skywalker™
1495QX8206 • $32

4303.

Madame Alexander® 7: Winter Wonderland
1495QX8086 • $29

4304.

Madame Alexander® Little Women 2: Josephine "Jo" March
1595QX8126 • $52

4305.

Madeline and Genevieve
1295QXI5286 • $26 • Set/2

4306.

Malibu BARBIE™ Lunchbox
1995QXC4686 • $60 • Set/6

4307.

Mary's Angels 15: Willow
795QX8013 • $13

4308.

Mary's Angels 15: Willow
($N/A)QX8013C • $79

4309.

Medal For America
995QX2936 • $20

4310.

Memories of Christmas: Christmas Joy
1295QP1413 • $26

4311.

Memories of Christmas: Flicker Flame Lights
1495QP1443 • $23 • Set/7

4312.

Memories of Christmas: Gentle Angel
1495QP1426 • $28

4313.

Memories of Christmas: Joyous Angel
1495QP1433 • $20

4314.

Memories of Christmas: Snowflakes
1295QP1436 • $23 • Set/3

4315.

Memories of Christmas: Snowy Friend
995QP1406 • $32

4316.

Memories of Christmas: Winter Angel
995QP1423 • $28

4317.

Memories of Christmas: Winter's Ride
1295QP1416 • $26

4318.

Memories of Christmas: Yuletide Santa
995QP1403 • $33

4319.

Merry Music Makers
2400QX8523 • $35

4320.

Mickey's Holiday Parade 6: Goofy Toots the Tuba
1395QXD4903 • $32

4321.

Mickey's Skating Party
995QXD4913 • $25

4322.

Mischievous Kittens 4
995QX8046 • $19

4323.

Mistletoe Miss 2
1495QX8113 • $26

4324.

Mom
995QX8933 • $23

4325.

Mother and Daughter Ornaments
1495QX2926 • $28 • Set/2

4326.

Mother-Daughter Photo Holder
1295QX8683 • $26

4327.

My First Christmas Memory Book
1295QX8613 • $23

4328.

Naughty or Nice? Elf
995QX2823 • $23

4329.

New Home
1295QX8636 • $23

4330.

Nostalgic Houses & Shops 19: Victorian Inn
1495QX8103 • $55

4331.

Obi Wan Kenobi™
1495QXI8216 • $40

4332.

Oddball, Domino and Little Dipper - 102 Dalmatians
1295QXD4936 • $23

4333.

One Cool Snowboarder
995QX2876 • $28

4334.

Our Christmas Together
995QX8623 • $20

4335.

Our Christmas Together
1495QX8926 • $24

4336.

Our First Christmas
1895QX8816 • $32

4337.

Our First Christmas Together
795QX3233 • $13

4338.

Our First Christmas Together
995QX8626 • $20

4339.

Peace on Earth Harmony Bell
995QX8393 • $24

4340.

Perfect Harmony: Display Stand
1000QP1236 • $14

4341.

Perfect Harmony: Hope
995QP1206 • $17

4342.

Perfect Harmony: Joy
995QP1233 • $17

4343.

Perfect Harmony: Kind World
995QP1203 • $17

4344.

Perfect Harmony: Love
995QP1226 • $17

4345.

Perfect Harmony: New Hope
995QP1213 • $17

4346.

Perfect Harmony: Peace
995QP1216 • $17

4347.

Perfect Harmony: Peace & Goodwill
995QP1223 • $17

4348.

Playful Minnie
995QXD4906 • $17

4349.

A Pony for Christmas 5
1295QX8056 • $25

4350.

Puppy Love 12
795QX8006 • $14

4351.

Quidditch™ Season - Harry Potter™
2400QXI8656 • $40

4352.

Rainbow Snowman
995QX8283 • $28

4353.

Robot Parade 3
1495QX8133 • $23

4354.

Safe and Snug 2
1295QX8036 • $23

4355.

Santa and His Sweetest Friends
1995QX2923 • $26 • Set/4

4356.

Santa's Big Night: Christmas Morning Treasures
1895QXI5346 • $28 • Set/3

4357.

Santa's Big Night: Christmas Tree With Decorations
1895QX4476 • $29

4358.

Santa's Big Night: Curius the Elf
($N/A)QXC4623 • $26

4359.

Santa's Big Night: Family Room
7500QXC4566 • $150

4360.

Santa's Big Night: Santa's Big Night
($N/E)QXC2002 • $28 • Set/4

4361.

Santa's Big Night: Snowman
($N/A)QXC4613 • $21

4362.

Santa's Mailbox
1295QX6943 • $23

4363.

Santa's Racin' Sleigh - NASCAR®
1495QXI5306 • $28

4364.

Santa's Workshop Lunchbox
1895QXC4586 • $49

4365.

Scarlett O'Hara™
1595QX8253 • $25

4366.

Scooby-Doo™ and Shaggy
1695QXI5283 • $24

4367.

Sisters
1295QX8686 • $36

4368.

Sky's the Limit 6: Staggerwing
1495QX8093 • $38

4369.

Slave I Starship™
1895QXI8223 • $36

4370.

Snow Belles
1595QX8446 • $35 • Set/3

4371.

Snow Buddies 5
795QX8003 • $22

4372.

Snow Buddies 5
($N/E)QX8003C • $75

4373.

Snow Cub Club: Calvin Carver
495QRP4646 • $8

4374.

Snow Cub Club: Dexter Next
495QRP4633 • $8

4375.

Snow Cub Club: Gracie Skates
495QRP4643 • $11

4376.

Snow Cub Club: Hollyday Hill Display Base
495QRP4683 • $8

4377.

Snow Cub Club: Wendy Whoosh
495QRP4626 • $8

4378.

Snowball and Tuxedo 2: The Wishing Star
795QX8033 • $23

4379.

Snuggle Time - Mickey and Minnie
1495QXD4916 • $28

4380.

Son
995QX8943 • $20

4381.

A Song For The Lamb Of God
1495QX8376 • $28

4382.

Sooo Fast™ Custom Car Set
1695QX8876 • $26 • Set/2

4383.

Special Cat
995QX2863 • $14

4384.

Special Dog
995QX8716 • $17

4385.

Spotlight on Snoopy® 5: Literary Ace
995QX8043 • $19

4386.

Star Gazer Shepherd
995QX2836 • $20

4387.

Star Wars™ 6: Darth Vader™
1495QX8136 • $22

4388.

Sulley and Mike - Monsters, Inc.
1495QXD4613 • $31

4389.

Sunday Evening Sleigh Ride
1495QX2903 • $23

4390.

Sweet Tooth Treats 1
1495QX8193 • $28 • Set/4

4391.

Teacher
995QX8973 • $16

4392.

Tee's the Season
1295QX8726 • $23

4393.

Teetering Toddler
1495QX8916 • $23

4394.

"Thank You" Ball
695QX8986 • $8

4395.

Thank You Hug
995QX2893 • $14

4396.

Thanks, Coach!
995QX8976 • $14

4397.

Thanks, Mom!
995QX8963 • $14

4398.

Threadbear
995QX2916 • $28

4399.

Three Kings Lantern
1295QX8853 • $23

4400.

Tickle Tickle Santa
1995QX2826 • $36

4401.

A Time to Believe
1895QX8506 • $26

4402.

Tinker Bell - Peter Pan
1495QXD4943 • $33

4403.

Toddler Photo Holder
1295QX2856 • $20

4404.

Tonka® 1961 Cement Truck
1495QX8233 • $24

4405.

Topping the Tree
1495QX6953 • $24

4406.

Town and Country 4: Grandmother's House and Covered Bridge
1695QX8156 • $43 • Set/2

4407.

Toymaker Santa 3
1295QX8096 • $43

4408.

Treasures and Dreams 1: Jewelry Box Ballet
1995QX8183 • $40

4409.

True Love is Our Love
1495QX8923 • $31

4410.

Tucked In Tenderly
995QX2886 • $17

4411.

Up Up and Away
995QX8466 • $23

4412.

VeggieTales®
1295QXI5293 • $22

4413.

A Very Carrot Christmas - Bugs Bunny™
995QX8276 • $20

4414.

Village Toy Shop
2400QLX7676 • $33
MAGIC.

4415.

We Call Him Santa
1295QX2883 • $26

4416.

Welcoming the Savior
1295QX8356 • $20

4417.

White Poinsettia
695QX2953 • $13

4418.

The Wild Thornberrys™
1295QXI5263 • $19

4419.

Winnie the Pooh: Piglet's First Ride
1295QXD4963 • $20

4420.

Winnie the Pooh: Skating in Circles
2400QXD7526 • $42
MAGIC.

4421.

Winnie the Pooh: Tigger's Springy Tree
995QXD4966 • $23

4422.

Winnie the Pooh 5: School Days
1395QXD4983 • $23

4423.

Winter Wonderland 1: Bringing Home the Tree
1295QX8186 • $32

4424.

Woodland Friends
1495QX8536 • $23

4425.

Woodland Frolic
1495QX8543 • $23 • Set/3

4426.

Woody and Bullseye - Toy Story
1495QXD4933 • $25

4427.

Worldwide Celebration
1295QX2833 • $23

4428.

A Year To Remember - 2002
2400QX2813 • $35

4429.

You're A Star
995QX8966 • $20

2003

4430.

100 Years of Fun
1995QXI8769 • $38

4431.

The 1990s Batmobile™
1495QXI8297 • $25

4432.
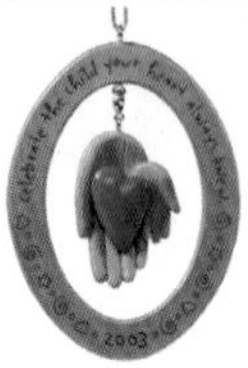
Adoption 2003
1295QXG2497 • $19

4433.

Adventures of a Book Lover
995QXG8589 • $18

4434.

All-American Trucks 9: 1972 Chevrolet® Cheyenne Super
1495QX8117 • $24

4435.

The Amazing Little Tree
2400QXI7517 • $46

4436.

American Girls: Addy
1500QAC6412 • $19

4437.

American Girls: Felicity
1500QAC6413 • $17

4438.

American Girls: Josefina
1500QAC6415 • $19

4439.

American Girls: Kaya
1500QAC6414 • $16

4440.

American Girls: Kirsten
1500QAC6416 • $16

4441.

American Girls: Kit
1500QAC6417 • $16

4442.

American Girls: Molly
1500QAC6418 • $16

4443.

American Girls: Samantha
1500QAC6419 • $22

4444.

American Patriot Santa
1495QXG2549 • $23

4445.

Amiga Por Siempre
1495QXG2529 • $20

4446.

Angel at My Side
995QXG8659 • $26

4447.
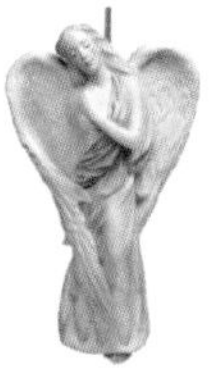
Angel of Serenity
1495QXG8999 • $28

4448.

Angels of Virtue
1595QXG8839 • $19 • Set/3

4449.

Angels We Have Heard
2400QLX7527 • $32
MAGIC.

4450.

Angels We Have Heard
($N/A)QLX7527C • $623
MAGIC. Edition Size - 75.

4451.

Around the World - Harley-Davidson® Motorcycles
4400QXI7489 • $55

4452.

Arthur® and Pal - A Perfect Christmas!
995QXI8359 • $13

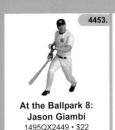

4453.

At the Ballpark 8: Jason Giambi
1495QX2449 • $22

4454.

Away to the Manger
995QXG8669 • $28

4455.

Baby's First Christmas
1295QXG8719 • $22

4456.

Baby's First Christmas
1495QXG8729 • $22

4457.

Baby's First Christmas
995QXG8737 • $18

4458.

BARBIE™ 10: Mailbu BARBIE™
1595QX8107 • $22

4459.

BARBIE™ 2003
1995QXC4589 • $68

4460.

BARBIE™ Fashion Model: BARBIE™ In The Pink
2500QXI8439 • $32

4461.

BARBIE™ Ornament Photo Holder
1495QXI4269 • $19

4462.

BARBIE™ Swan Lake
1495QXI8447 • $32 • Set/2

4463.

Based on Celebration BARBIE™ #4
1595QXI4357 • $34

4464.

Basket of Joy
995QXG8599 • $14

4465.

Bearing the Colors
995QXG2499 • $14

4466.

Bubble Bath - Sylvester™ and Tweety™
1495QXI8277 • $19

4467.

Bugs Bunny™ and Daffy Duck™ - Back In Action
1495QXI4329 • $23

4468.

Bugs the Barnstormer - Bugs Bunny™
1695QXI8279 • $23

4469.

Burrton, Coldwell and Windfield
1495QXG2557 • $20 • Set/3

4470.

Candlelight Services 6: Fieldstone Church
1895QX7429 • $29
MAGIC.

4471.

Captain Jonathan Archer
1495QXI8349 • $22

4472.

Caroling at the Door
1495QXG8819 • $19

4473.

The Cat Arrives! - The Cat in the Hat™
995QXI8379 • $26

4474.

Celebrate, Decorate, Enjoy!
695QXG8779 • $10

4475.

Celebration BARBIE™ 4
1595QX2459 • $34

4476.

Child's Age: My First Christmas (Boy)
995QXG8697 • $24

4477.

Child's Age: My First Christmas (Girl)
995QXG2487 • $24

4478.

Child's Age: Baby's Second Christmas
895QXG8699 • $15

4479.

Child's Age: Child's Third Christmas
895QXG8707 • $15

4480.

Child's Age: Child's Fourth Christmas
895QXG8709 • $15

4481.

Child's Age: Child's Fifth Christmas
895QXG8717 • $15

4482.

Christmas Tree Dreams
2400QLX7477 • $35
MAGIC.

4483.

Christmas Tree Gift Clip
995QXG8637 • $14

4484.

Christmas Window 1: Christmas Window 2003
1995QXC3003 • $37

4485.

Christmastime in the City
1295QXG8817 • $20

4486.

The Church Choir
1695QXG2429 • $24

4487.

Cinderella and Prince Charming - Cinderella
1695QXD5139 • $24

4488.

Classic American Cars 13: 1963 Corvette® Sting Ray Coupe
1495QX8129 • $36

4489.

Click Your Heels
3200QXI7487 • $39

4490.

Coach of the Year
995QXG8639 • $12

4491.

Commemorative Bells
4000QXC4617 • $70 • Set/3

4492.

Cool Decade 4
795QX8079 • $18

4493.

Cool Decade 4
($N/E)QX8079C • $55

4494.

Countdown to Christmas
1995QLX7529 • $25
MAGIC.

4495.

Cross of Glory
995QXG8977 • $16

4496.

Dad
995QXG8889 • $13

4497.

Dancer in Flight
1295QXG8619 • $23

4498.

Daughter
995QXG8899 • $14

4499.

Daylight Observation Car
1295QXI8327 • $22

4500.

The Decision
995QXG8569 • $16

4501.

The Decision
($N/E)QXG8569C • $34

4502.

Defending the Flag
1295QXG8577 • $19

4503.

Delicious Christmas
1495QXG8657 • $19

4504.

Disney's It's A Small World After All
8500QXC4689 • $150 • Set/3

4505.

Dorothy and Tin Man™
1595QXI8299 • $20

4506.

Dr. Seuss® Books 5: Hop on Pop
1495QX8179 • $24

4507.

Feliz Navidad
1295QXG8689 • $22

4508.

Fire Brigade 1: 1929 Chevrolet® Fire Engine
1895QX8449 • $46

4509.

Fire Brigade 1: 1929 Chevrolet® Fire Engine
1895QX8449C • $70

4510.

First Christmas Together
895QXG3257 • $19

4511.

Flying Over London - Peter Pan
1495QXD5137 • $20

4512.

Football Legends 9: Jerry Rice - San Francisco 49ers™
1495QX2457 • $28

4513.

Forever Friend
1495QXG8967 • $25

4514.

Friendship
695QXG8879 • $14

4515.

Frostlight Faeries: Frostlight Faerie Sisters
2495QXG2479 • $44 • Set/3

4516.

Frosty Friends 24
1295QX8089 • $23

4517.

Gift Bearers 5
1295QX8239 • $38

4518.

A Gift for Raggedy Ann®
1295QXI8417 • $17

4519.

Glad Tidings Angel
1895QRP4249 • $19

4520.

Glory Shining Down
1095QXG8667 • $16

4521.

Godchild
1295QXG8939 • $28

4522.

Goofy® Helps Out
1295QXD5037 • $23

4523.

Gopher Par
995QXG8587 • $17

4524.

Grandchild's First Christmas
995QXG2437 • $17

4525.

Granddaughter
995QXG8907 • $17

4526.

Grandson
995QXG8909 • $19

4527.

The Grinch™ and Cindy-Lou Who™ - How the Grinch Stole Christmas™
1495QXI8377 • $22 • Set/2

4528.

Harley-Davidson® Motorcycle Milestones 5: 100th Anniversary Ultra Classic Electra Glide®
1495QX8169 • $25

4529.

Here Comes Santa 25: Santa's Big Rig
1495QX8167 • $23

4530.

Here Comes Santa 25: Santa's Big Rig
($N/A)QX8167C1 • $100

4531.

Here Comes Santa 25: Santa's Big Rig
($N/A)QX8167C2 • $850

4532.

Holiday Adventure
1495QXI8289 • $19

4533.

Holiday Advice Booth - Lucy
1495QXI4257 • $24

4534.

Home Bright Home - Mickey and Pluto
1495QXD2509 • $23

4535.

Home for the Holidays
1695QXG8837 • $25

4536.

Hoop Stars 9: Kobe Bryant
1495QX8237 • $24

4537.
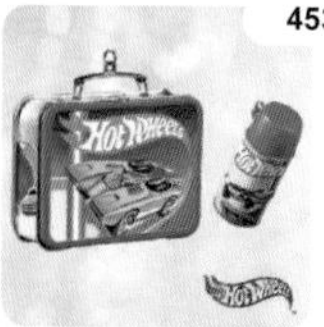
Hot Wheels™ Lunchbox Set
1495QXI8427 • $19 • Set/2

4538.

I'll Be Home for Christmas
1995QLX7519 • $28
MAGIC.

4539.

I'll Be Home for Christmas
($N/A)QLX7519C • $40
MAGIC.

4540.
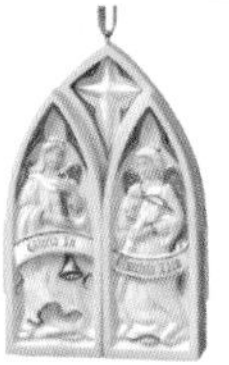
In Excelsis Deo
1495QXG2427 • $23

4541.

Jack-in-the-Box Memories 1: Pop! Goes the Snowman
1495QX8457 • $45

4542.

Jerry Rice – Oakland Raiders™
1495QXI4267 • $24

4543.

Jimmie Johnson
1495QXI8389 • $20

4544.

Jingle All the Way! - Tweety™
1495QXI8267 • $19

4545.

Jingle Bells
695QXG8777 • $14

4546.
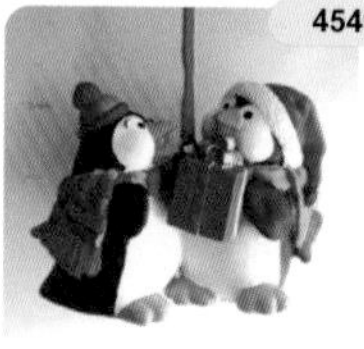
Just for You
($N/E)QXC4567 • $24

4547.

Kiddie Car Classics 10: 1949 Gillham™ Sport
1395QX8139 • $24 • Set/2

4548.

Kris and the Kringles 3
2400QX7439 • $50
MAGIC.

4549.

Lighthouse Greetings 7
2400QX7409 • $50
MAGIC.

4550.

LIONEL® Daylight Oil Tender
1295QXI8249 • $22

4551.

LIONEL® Holiday Special Train Set
7500QXC4587 • $125 • Set/3

4552.

LIONEL® Trains 8: 4449 Daylight Steam Locomotive
1895QX8087 • $23

4553.

The List
1295QXG8829 • $22

4554.

Little Christmas Helper
1295QXG8747 • $22

4555.

Love Ya, Grandma!
995QXG8917 • $14

4556.

Love Ya, Grandma!
($N/E)QXG8917C • $25

4557.

Love Ya, Grandpa!
995QXG8919 • $14

4558.

Lucy's Italian Movie - I Love Lucy®
1695QXI8387 • $25

4559.

Madame Alexander® 8: Holiday Snowflake Skater
1495QX8137 • $24

4560.

Madame Alexander® Little Women 3: Elizabeth "Beth" March
1595QX8187 • $30

4561.

Madeline
1295QXI8409 • $19

4562.

Marlin and Nemo - Finding Nemo
1295QXD5147 • $50

4563.

Mary's Angels 16: Sweet William
795QX8119 • $23

4564.

Mary's Angels 16: Sweet William
($N/A)QX8119C • $79

4565.
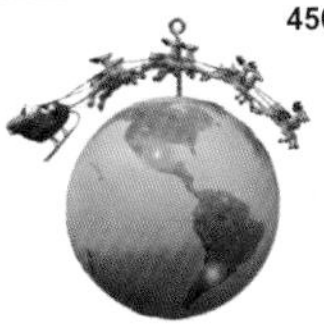
Merry Christmas World!
1995QLX7449 • $28
MAGIC.

4566.

Merry Glitzmas!
1495QLX7537 • $19
MAGIC.

4567.

Mighty Tonka® Crane
1495QXI8367 • $30

4568.

Mischievous Kittens 5
995QX8109 • $16

4569.

Have You Seen Me?
Mischievous Kittens 5
($N/A)QX8109C • $67

4570.

Mistletoe Miss 3
1495QX8219 • $20 • Set/2

4571.

Mistletoe Time - Mickey and Minnie
1495QXD5057 • $24

4572.

The Mistletot Faeries
1995QXC3001 • $38

4573.

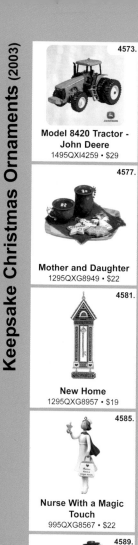

Model 8420 Tractor - John Deere
1495QXI4259 • $29

4574.

Mom
995QXG8887 • $14

4575.

Moose on the Loose
995QXG8579 • $18

4576.

Moose on the Loose
($N/A)QXG8579C • $648

4577.

Mother and Daughter
1295QXG8949 • $22

4578.

Mr. Potato Head®
1295QXI4277 • $20

4579.

Mufasa and Simba - The Lion King
1295QXD5087 • $18 • Set/2

4580.

Nature's Sketchbook: Nature's Sketchbook 1
995QX8679 • $19

4581.

New Home
1295QXG8957 • $19

4582.

Noah's Ark
1695QXG8997 • $25

4583.

Nostalgic Houses & Shops 20: The Grand Theater
1495QX8149 • $22

4584.

Nuestra Familia
1295QXG2537 • $18

4585.

Nurse With a Magic Touch
995QXG8567 • $22

4586.

Nutcracker Soldier
1695QXC4599 • $39

4587.

On Frozen Pond: Kermit™ and Miss Piggy™
1495QXI4289 • $19

4588.

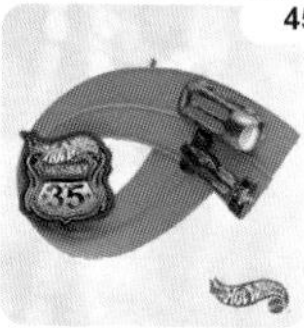

On Track: Deora II and Sweet Sixteen II
1695QXI8429 • $19

4589.

Our Best Buddy - Buzz Lightyear and Woody - Toy Story
1495QXD5129 • $17

4590.

Our Family
1295QXG8947 • $22

4591.

Our First Christmas
1895QXG8877 • $29

4592.

Our Love Story Photo Holder
1295QXG8859 • $18

4593.

Padme Amidala™
1495QXI8339 • $19

4594.

Pals at the Pole
1495QXG8827 • $18

4595.

Pals at the Pole
($N/A)QXG8827C • $50

4596.

Parents-to-Be
1295QXG2469 • $19

4597.

Platform Nine 3/4™ - Harry Potter™
1295QXI4279 • $20

4598.

Play It Again, Santa!
2400QLX7469 • $32
MAGIC.

4599.

Polar Coaster
4200QLX7459 • $50
MAGIC.

4600.

A Pony for Christmas 5
($N/A)QX8056C • $54

4601.

A Pony for Christmas 6
1295QX8229 • $26

4602.

A Pony for Christmas 6
($N/A)QX8229C • $60

4603.

Pretty As a Princess
1295QXD5079 • $28

4604.

Primera Navidad de Bebé
1295QXG2517 • $16

4605.

Puppy Love 13
795QX8127 • $22

4606.

Red Power Ranger™ - Power Rangers: Ninja Storm™
1295QXD2439 • $18

4607.

Rock 'n' Roll Stitch - Lilo & Stitch
995QXD2447 • $29

4608.

Rockin' & Rollin'!
3200QLX7457 • $41
MAGIC.

4609.

Ruff and Tuff Hero
995QXG8557 • $16

4610.

Safe and Snug 3
1295QX8217 • $18

4611.
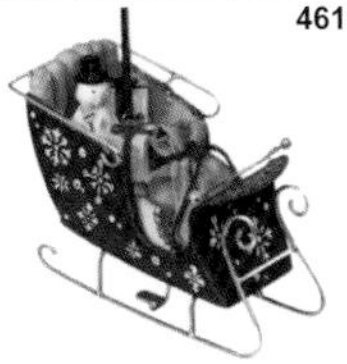
Santa's Magical Sleigh
1895QRP4247 • $30

4612.

Santa's on His Way
1495QXG8809 • $23

4613.

Santa's on His Way
($N/E)QXG8809C • $44

4614.

Scarlett O'Hara™
1595QXI8307 • $32

4615.

Scarlett O'Hara™ and Rhett Butler™
1895QXI4287 • $58

4616.

School Photo Holder
995QXG8929 • $16

4617.

Scooby-Doo™ Takes Aim
995QXI8287 • $17

4618.

The Scorpion™
3200QXI7509 • $43
MAGIC.

4619.

Serial Number One & 2003 Harley-Davidson® Ultra Classic Electra Glide®
2800QXI8317 • $42 • Set/2

4620.

Shrek® and Donkey
1495QXI8759 • $29 • Set/2

4621.

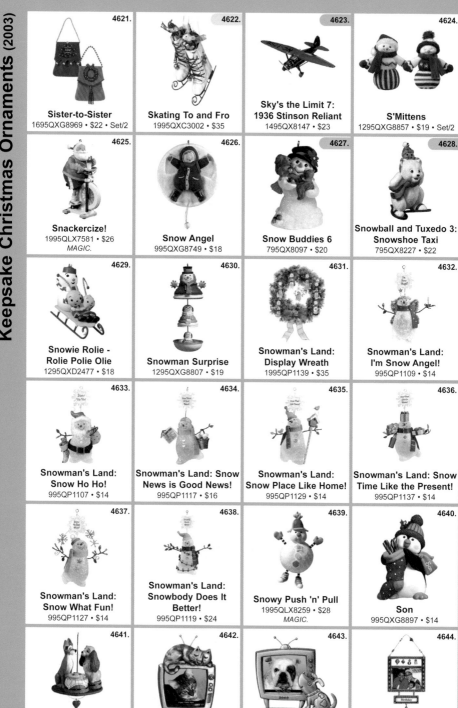

Sister-to-Sister
1695QXG8969 • $22 • Set/2

4622.

Skating To and Fro
1995QXC3002 • $35

4623.

Sky's the Limit 7: 1936 Stinson Reliant
1495QX8147 • $23

4624.

S'Mittens
1295QXG8857 • $19 • Set/2

4625.

Snackercize!
1995QLX7581 • $26
MAGIC.

4626.

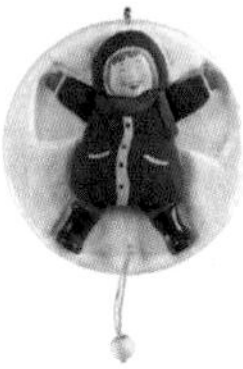

Snow Angel
995QXG8749 • $18

4627.

Snow Buddies 6
795QX8097 • $20

4628.

Snowball and Tuxedo 3: Snowshoe Taxi
795QX8227 • $22

4629.

Snowie Rolie - Rolie Polie Olie
1295QXD2477 • $18

4630.

Snowman Surprise
1295QXG8807 • $19

4631.

Snowman's Land: Display Wreath
1995QP1139 • $35

4632.

Snowman's Land: I'm Snow Angel!
995QP1109 • $14

4633.

Snowman's Land: Snow Ho Ho!
995QP1107 • $14

4634.

Snowman's Land: Snow News is Good News!
995QP1117 • $16

4635.

Snowman's Land: Snow Place Like Home!
995QP1129 • $14

4636.

Snowman's Land: Snow Time Like the Present!
995QP1137 • $14

4637.

Snowman's Land: Snow What Fun!
995QP1127 • $14

4638.

Snowman's Land: Snowbody Does It Better!
995QP1119 • $24

4639.

Snowy Push 'n' Pull
1995QLX8259 • $28
MAGIC.

4640.

Son
995QXG8897 • $14

4641.

Spaghetti Supper - Lady and the Tramp
1495QXD5099 • $22

4642.

Special Cat
995QXG8609 • $13

4643.

Special Dog
995QXG8607 • $13

4644.

Special Event Photo Holder
1295QXG8959 • $20

4645.
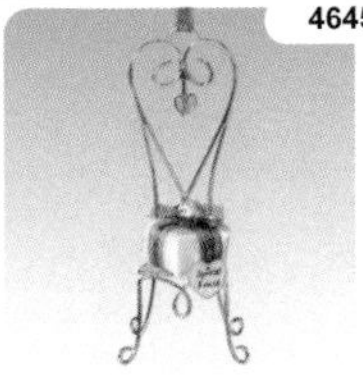
Special Friend
995QXG8927 • $17

4646.

Spotlight on Snoopy® 6: Joe Cool
995QX8099 • $16

4647.

Star of Belief
1495QXC4619 • $28

4648.

Star Wars™ 7: C-3PO™
1495QX8177 • $23

4649.

Steamboat Willie - Mickey Mouse
2400QXD5047 • $31
MAGIC.

4650.

Stuck on You
995QXG8867 • $16

4651.

Sub-Commander T'Pol
1495QXI8757 • $23

4652.

Sweet Tooth Treats 2
1495QX8199 • $23 • Set/4

4653.

Sweetest Little Angel
1695QLX7574 • $26
MAGIC.

4654.

Taz™ as the Nutcracker
995QXI8269 • $14

4655.

Teachers Rule
995QXG8629 • $14

4656.

Ted Williams - Boston Red Sox™
1495QXI8397 • $28

4657.

This is the Life
995QXG8597 • $22

4658.

TIE Fighter™
2400QXI7507 • $31

4659.

Toddler Photo Holder
995QXG8739 • $24

4660.

Town and Country 5: Schoolhouse and Flagpole
1695QX8247 • $22 • Set/2

4661.

Town Hall and Mayor's Christmas Tree
1995QX2467 • $36

4662.

Town Hall and Mayor's Christmas Tree: Special Anniversary Edition
($N/A)QX2467C • $748
Edition Size - 75.

4663.

Toymaker Santa 4
1295QX8159 • $34

4664.

Treasures and Dreams 2: Jewelry Box Carousel
1995QX8197 • $38

4665.

Uncle Sam Nutcracker
995QXG2489 • $13

4666.

VeggieTales®
1295QXI4337 • $19

4667.

A Visit From Santa: A Christmas Story
995QP1429 • $13

4668.

A Visit From Santa: A Very Good Girl
1295QP1477 • $18

4669.

A Visit From Santa: A Very Merry Snowman
1495QP1417 • $18

4670.

A Visit From Santa: Giddy-Up, Christmas!
1295QP1437 • $18

4671.

A Visit From Santa: Gifts for Everyone
1695QP1409 • $25

4672.

A Visit From Santa: Oh, What Fun!
1295QP1427 • $18

4673.

A Visit From Santa: Sweet Little Lad
995QP1469 • $14

4674.

A Visit From Santa: Sweet Shopper
995QP1447 • $16

4675.

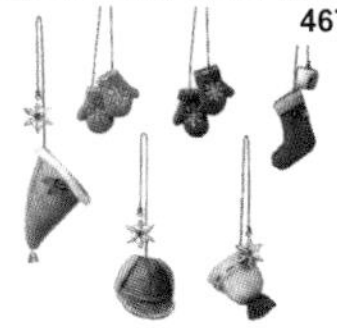

A Visit From Santa: Winter Trimmers
995QP1497 • $14 • Set/6

4676.

Waiting For Santa
1995QRP4327 • $24

4677.

What Child Is This
1295QXG8989 • $32

4678.

What Child Is This
($N/A)QXG8989C • $435
Edition Size - 75.

4679.

Winnie the Pooh: A Boost for Piglet
1495QXD5069 • $24

4680.

Winnie the Pooh: Our Friendship
1295QXD5067 • $25

4681.

Winnie the Pooh: Soccer Tigger-Style
995QXD5119 • $13

4682.

Winnie the Pooh: Twinkle, Twinkle
1295QXD8767 • $22

4683.

Winnie the Pooh 6: Little Rain Cloud
1395QXD5117 • $20

4684.

Winter Wonderland 2: Sleigh Ride
1295QX8207 • $28

4685.

Words of Love
1495QXG8869 • $25 • Set/7

4686.

World-Famous Christmas Decorator Snoopy®
1995QXC3004 • $48

4687.

Wreath of Peace
995QXG8687 • $18

4688.

Yoda™
1495QXI8337 • $36

4689.

You've Got Games
995QXG8627 • $19

2004

4690.

Adoption 2004
1295QXG5641 • $19

4691.

Affection for Confections
1895QRP4291 • $28 • Set/2

4692.

¡Al Mundo Paz!
1495QXG5471 • $23

4693.

All-American Trucks 10: 2000 Ford® F-150
1495QX8154 • $20

4694.

Amazing Number 53 - Herbie, The Love Bug
1495QXD5071 • $23

4695.

American Girls: Addy With Coin
1500QAC6421 • $22

4696.

American Girls: Felicity With Horse Brush
1500QAC6431 • $22

4697.

American Girls: Josefina With Memory Box
1500QAC6434 • $18

4698.

American Girls: Kaya With Moccasins
1500QAC6461 • $22

4699.

American Girls: Kirsten With Swedish Tine
1500QAC6424 • $22

4700.

American Girls: Kit With Notebook
1500QAC6441 • $22

4701.

American Girls: Molly With Envelope
1500QAC6444 • $22

4702.

American Girls: Samantha With Sampler
1500QAC6451 • $26

4703.

An Angel's Touch
1295QXG5634 • $18

4704.

Anakin Skywalker™
1495QXI4071 • $30

4705.

Angel of Compassion
1495QXG5381 • $23

4706.

Anything For A Friend
1495QXG5511 • $24

4707.

Ariel - The Little Mermaid
1295QXD5061 • $20

4708.

At the Ballpark 9: Barry Bonds - San Francisco Giants™
1495QX8551 • $18

4709.
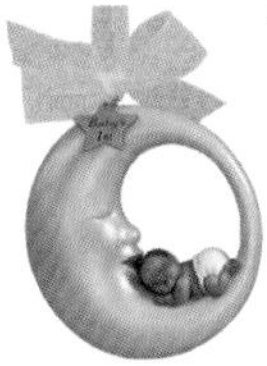
Baby's First Christmas
995QXG5711 • $17

4710.

Baby's First Christmas
1295QXG5714 • $20

4711.

Baby's First Christmas
1295QXG5724 • $20

4712.

Baby's First Christmas
1895QXG5731 • $30

4713.

"The Ballet"
1695QXI5311 • $26

4714.

Bambi and Friends
1695QXD5044 • $26

4715.

BARBIE™ 11: Smasheroo BARBIE™ Ornament
1595QX8591 • $25

4716.

BARBIE™ as The Princess and The Pauper Ornament
1895QXI8614 • $30

4717.

BARBIE™ Fashion Model: Lisette BARBIE™ Ornament
2500QXI8541 • $40

4718.

BARBIE™s 45th Anniversary Ornament
2500QHB6601 • $34
MAGIC.

4719.

BARBIE™s 45th Shoe Tree Ornament
1995QHB6604 • $38

4720.

Beak To Beak
995QXG5331 • $16

4721.

Billions of Dreams BARBIE™ Ornament
1995QXC4009 • $51

4722.

Born To Shop
995QXG5414 • $26

4723.

Buzz Lightyear and The Claw - Toy Story
1495QXD8671 • $23

4724.

Candlelight Services 7: Colonial Church
1895QX8451 • $28
MAGIC.

4725.

The Caped Crusader - Batman™
1495QXI4041 • $24
MAGIC.

4726.

Carousel Ride 1: Majestic Lion
1295QX8464 • $23

4727.

Carousel Ride Display
4500QX8481 • $51
Re-issued in 2005.

4728.

Catch of the Day
995QXG5541 • $14

4729.

Celebration BARBIE™ 5
1595QX8604 • $20

4730.

Celebration BARBIE™ Ornament
1595QXI8664 • $25

4731.

Child's Age: My First Christmas (Boy)
995QXG5661 • $18
Re-issued in 2005 as QXG4542.

4732.

Child's Age: My First Christmas (Girl)
995QXG5671 • $18
Re-issued in 2005 as QXG4565.

4733.

Child's Age: My Second Christmas (Boy)
995QXG5664 • $15
Re-issued in 2005 as QXG4545.

4734.

Child's Age: My Second Christmas (Girl)
995QXG5674 • $15
Re-issued in 2005 as QXG4572.

4735.

Child's Age: My Third Christmas (Boy)
995QXG5681 • $15
Re-issued in 2005 as QXG4552.

4736.

Child's Age: My Third Christmas (Girl)
995QXG5691 • $15
Re-issued in 2005 as QXG4575.

4737.

Child's Age: Child's Third Christmas
895QXG5764 • $14

4738.

Child's Age: My Fourth Christmas (Boy)
995QXG5684 • $15
Re-issued in 2005 as QXG4555.

4739.

Child's Age: My Fourth Christmas (Girl)
995QXG5694 • $15
Re-issued in 2005 as QXG4582.

4740.

Child's Age: Child's Fourth Christmas
895QXG5771 • $14

4741.

Child's Age: My Fifth Christmas (Boy)
995QXG5701 • $15
Re-issued in 2005 as QXG4562.

4742.

Child's Age: My Fifth Christmas (Girl)
995QXG5704 • $15
Re-issued in 2005 as QXG4585.

4743.

Child's Age: Child's Fifth Christmas
895QXG5774 • $14

4744.

Christmas Cookies!
2500QLX7611 • $41
MAGIC.

4745.

Christmas Crossing - Thomas The Tank®
1295QXI8661 • $35

4746.

Christmas Eve Snack - Tweety™
1295QXI4001 • $20

4747.

Christmas Window 2: Christmas Window 2004
1995QXC4003 • $32

4748.

"City on the Edge of Forever"
2800QXI4094 • $44
MAGIC.

4749.

Classic American Cars 14: 1966 Oldsmobile Toronado Coupe
1495QX8151 • $23

4750.

Commander Trip Tucker
1495QXI4091 • $20

4751.

Cookie Doe
995QXG5441 • $29

4752.

Cool Decade 5
795QX8134 • $17

4753.

Cool Decade 5
($N/E)QX8134C • $84

4754.

A Cool Holiday!
3200QLX7621 • $42
MAGIC.

4755.

Cuando Él Nació
1295QXG5361 • $20

4756.

Dad
995QXG5551 • $15

4757.

Dancer En Pointe
1295QXG5394 • $23

4758.

Daughter
995QXG5561 • $15

4759.

Deck the Hall Dog
1995QLX7584 • $N/E
MAGIC.

4760.

Deck The Halls! - Tweety™
1495QXI4004 • $20
MAGIC.

4761.

Dorothy and the Cowardly Lion™
1595QXI4021 • $24

4762.

Dr. Seuss® Books 6: Yertle The Turtle™
1495QX8421 • $24

4763.

Electrical Spectacle!
4200QLX7624 • $60
MAGIC.

4764.

Father Christmas 1
1895QX8471 • $20

4765.

Feliz Navidad
1295QXG5504 • $35

4766.

Fire Brigade 2: American LaFrance 700 Series Pumper
1895QX8424 • $29
MAGIC.

4767.

Fire Brigade 2: American LaFrance 700 Series Pumper
($N/E)QX8424C • $45
Edition Size - 6400.

4768.

First Christmas Together
1295QXG5334 • $34

4769.
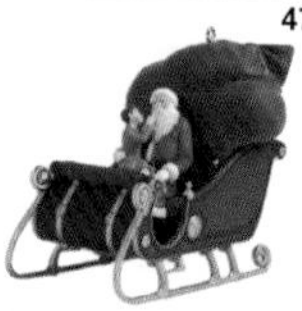
First Gift of Christmas! - The Polar Express™
1495QSR5811 • $20

4770.

Football Legends 10: Peyton Manning - Indianapolis Colts™
1495QX8521 • $38

4771.

For A Friend
995QXG5604 • $16

4772.

For Grandma
995QXG5574 • $16

4773.

For Grandpa
995QXG5581 • $16

4774.

Frodo Baggins - The Lord of the Rings™
1495QXI8624 • $24

4775.

Frostlight Faeries, Too: Collection
1995QXG5531 • $30 • Set/3

4776.

Frosty Friends 25
1295QX8331 • $23

4777.

Frosty Friends 25
($N/E)QX8331C • $105

4778.

Frosty Fun
2495QRP4304 • $36

4779.

G.I. Joe®
1495QXI8601 • $23

4780.

Garage Ramp Race
995QXI8631 • $16

4781.

Gift Bearers 6
1295QX8401 • $17

4782.

Gift of Friendship
1295QXG5611 • $20

4783.

Gingerbread Home
1295QXI5294 • $24

4784.

Go Teams!
995QXG5401 • $16

4785.

Godchild
1295QXG5644 • $20

4786.

Grandchild's First Christmas
995QXG5741 • $16

4787.

Granddaughter
995QXG5571 • $14

4788.

Grandson
995QXG5564 • $14

4789.

The Grinch™ and Max - How The Grinch Stole Christmas™
1495QXI8534 • $23

4790.

Happy Birthday, Jesus
995QXG5354 • $19

4791.

Harley-Davidson® Motorcycle Milestones 6: 2002 VRSCA V-Rod
1495QX8184 • $24

4792.

Harry Potter™ and Hedwig™
1495QXI4044 • $20 • Set/2

4793.

Heads-Up Play
1295QXI4061 • $24

4794.

Hidden Wishes
1995QXC4001 • $31

4795.

Holiday Hug
1495QXI5284 • $24

4796.

Hoop Stars 10: Jason Kidd - New Jersey Nets™
1495QX8531 • $24

4797.

I'm Melting! Melting!
3600QXI4024 • $72
MAGIC.

4798.

Jack Skellington - The Nightmare Before Christmas™
1695QXI8644 • $39

4799.

Jack-in-the-Box Memories 2: Pop! Goes the Santa
1495QX8411 • $28
MAGIC.

4800.

Jolly Old Kris Jingle
1295QXG5501 • $20

4801.

Jolly Old Kris Jingle
($N/E)QXG5501C • $25

4802.

Journey of the Train - The Polar Express™
1695QSR5804 • $26
MAGIC.

4803.

Joyful Christmas Village
3400QXC4007 • $48

4804.

A Joyful Noise
1295QXG5374 • $17

4805.

Joyful Trio
1295QXG5481 • $26

4806.

Kaleidoscope Fairy
995QXG5461 • $16

4807.

Keepsake Kids: "Countdown to Christmas" Tree
3995QKK3001 • $45
Re-issued in 2005.

4808.

Keepsake Kids: From a Stable So Small Storybook Set
2495QKK3014 • $29 • Set/7
Re-issued in 2005.

4809.

Keepsake Kids: Jolly Ol' St. Nicholas Storybook and Ornaments
2495QKK3011 • $30 • Set/6
Re-issued in 2005.

4810.

Keepsake Kids: My Very Own Christmas Tree
1495QKK3004 • $20
Re-issued in 2005.

4811.

Kiddie Car Classics 11: 1935 Timmy Racer
1395QX8444 • $23

4812.

Kindred Spirits
1295QXG5781 • $17

4813.

Kris and the Kringles 4
2400QX8114 • $36
MAGIC.

4814.

Lighthouse Greetings 8
2400QX8104 • $35
MAGIC.

4815.

LIONEL® Hiawatha Observation Car
1295QXI4104 • $20

4816.

LIONEL® Hiawatha Tender
1295QXI4101 • $20

4817.

LIONEL® Trains 9: 1939 Hiawatha Steam Locomotive
1895QX8454 • $30

4818.

LIONEL®ville
4400QXI4111 • $84
MAGIC.

4819.

Little Nurse, Big Heart
995QXG5424 • $16

4820.

Love To Dance! - Snoopy™
2400QXI4114 • $36
MAGIC.

4821.

Lunch Wagon for Porky Pig™
1495QXI4051 • $24 • Set/2

4822.

Madame Alexander® 9: Dancing Clara
1495QX8111 • $25

4823.

Madame Alexander® Little Women 4: Amy March
1595QX8404 • $23

4824.

The Magic Bell - The Polar Express™
2400QSR5801 • $52
MAGIC.

4825.

Mary's Angels 17: Sweet Pea
795QX8324 • $28

4826.

Mary's Angels 17: Sweet Pea
($N/E)QX8324C • $89

4827.

Maxine's Crabby Mall-idays
1995QLX7641 • $30
MAGIC.

4828.

Merry Christmas, Snoopy™!
1495QXI4081 • $33

4829.

Mischievous Kittens 6
995QX8194 • $16

4830.

Model 4010 Tractor - John Deere
1495QXI5291 • $20

4831.

Mom
995QXG5544 • $15

4832.

Monkey See - Curious George™
995QXI8654 • $16

4833.

Mother and Daughter
1295QXG5651 • $19

4834.

Mr. Incredible - The Incredibles
1295QXD5081 • $23

4835.

My Christmas Slippers
1495QLX7554 • $30
MAGIC.

4836.

Nature's Sketchbook: Nature's Sketchbook 2
995QX8554 • $16

4837.

New Home
1295QXG5621 • $19

4838.

Nick and Christopher 1: Downhill Delivery
1295QX2834 • $19

4839.

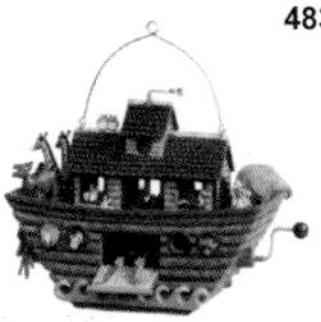

Noah's Ark
1695QXG5371 • $25
MAGIC.

4840.

North Pole Patriot
1295QXG5451 • $20

4841.

North Pole Patriot
($N/A)QXG5451C • $40

4842.

Nostalgic Houses & Shops 21: Barber Shop & Beauty Shop
1495QX8181 • $28

4843.

Nuestra Familia
1295QXG5744 • $24

4844.

Nutcracker King
1695QXC4006 • $30

4845.

Oddball, Little Dipper, and Domino - 102 Dalmatians
1495QXD5074 • $23

4846.

On, Tweety™! On, Daffy™!
1995QXI4011 • $31

4847.

Our Christmas
1295QXG5341 • $26

4848.

Our Christmas
1495QXG5344 • $29

4849.

Our Family
1295QXG5601 • $20

4850.

Our First Christmas
1895QXG5351 • $29

4851.

Our First Christmas Together
895QXG5324 • $14

4852.

Over Par Snowman
995QXG5421 • $16

4853.

Parents-To-Be
1295QXG5734 • $28

4854.

The PEANUTS® Games
1895QXI8691 • $28 • Set/4

4855.

Pedal Power - Kermit The Frog™
1495QXI5304 • $23

4856.

Peppermint Candy Cane BARBIE™ Ornament
1495QXI8544 • $28

4857.

Plotting The Course
1995QXC4002 • $30

4858.

Pocket Watch Ornament - Mickey Mouse
2400QXD5001 • $36

4859.

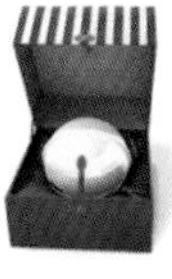

Polar Express™ - First Gift Of Christmas Bell
1295unknown • $75
Re-issued in 2005.

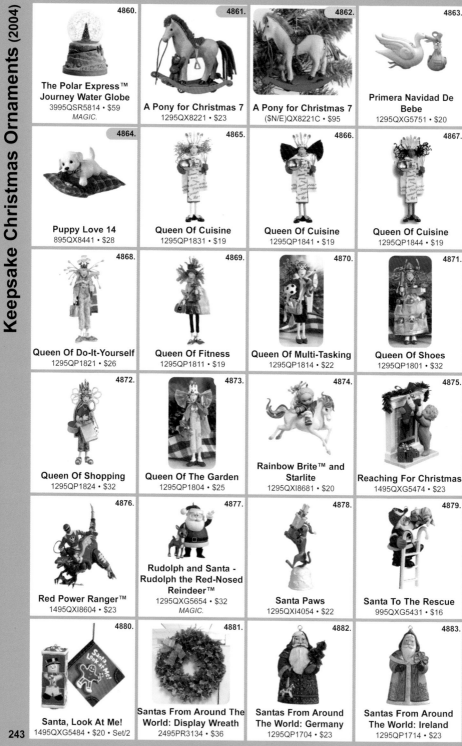

4860.

The Polar Express™ Journey Water Globe
3995QSR5814 • $59
MAGIC.

4861.

A Pony for Christmas 7
1295QX8221 • $23

4862.

A Pony for Christmas 7
($N/E)QX8221C • $95

4863.

Primera Navidad De Bebe
1295QXG5751 • $20

4864.

Puppy Love 14
895QX8441 • $28

4865.

Queen Of Cuisine
1295QP1831 • $19

4866.

Queen Of Cuisine
1295QP1841 • $19

4867.

Queen Of Cuisine
1295QP1844 • $19

4868.

Queen Of Do-It-Yourself
1295QP1821 • $26

4869.

Queen Of Fitness
1295QP1811 • $19

4870.

Queen Of Multi-Tasking
1295QP1814 • $22

4871.

Queen Of Shoes
1295QP1801 • $32

4872.

Queen Of Shopping
1295QP1824 • $32

4873.

Queen Of The Garden
1295QP1804 • $25

4874.

Rainbow Brite™ and Starlite
1295QXI8681 • $20

4875.

Reaching For Christmas
1495QXG5474 • $23

4876.

Red Power Ranger™
1495QXI8604 • $23

4877.

Rudolph and Santa - Rudolph the Red-Nosed Reindeer™
1295QXG5654 • $32
MAGIC.

4878.

Santa Paws
1295QXI4054 • $22

4879.

Santa To The Rescue
995QXG5431 • $16

4880.

Santa, Look At Me!
1495QXG5484 • $20 • Set/2

4881.

Santas From Around The World: Display Wreath
2495PR3134 • $36

4882.

Santas From Around The World: Germany
1295QP1704 • $23

4883.

Santas From Around The World: Ireland
1295QP1714 • $23

4884.

Santas From Around The World: Italy
1295QP1724 • $28

4885.

Santas From Around The World: Mexico
1295QP1721 • $39

4886.

Santas From Around The World: Norway
1295QP1711 • $23

4887.

Santas From Around The World: Russia
1295QP1701 • $23

4888.

Santas From Around The World: USA
1295QP1731 • $23

4889.

Santas From Around The World: USA
1295QP1734 • $33

4890.

Santa's Hula-day!
2800QLX7631 • $45
MAGIC.

4891.

Scarlett O'Hara™
1595QXI4031 • $31

4892.

Scarlett O'Hara™ and Rhett Butler™
1895QXI4034 • $34

4893.

School Days
995QXG5624 • $16

4894.

Season of the Heart
4000QXC4015 • $59

4895.

Sew Merry, Sew Bright
995QXG5434 • $22

4896.
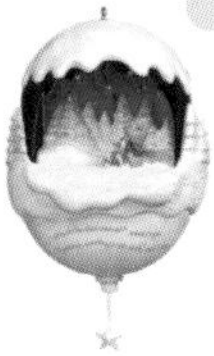
Sharing The Stars
1995QXC4004 • $36

4897.

Shining Promise
1295QXG5364 • $19

4898.

Silent Night
2500QLX7591 • $38
MAGIC.

4899.

Sisters
1295QXG5594 • $20

4900.

Sisters
1295QXG5761 • $20

4901.

Sittin' on Santa's Lap
2500QLX7594 • $31
MAGIC.

4902.

Sky's the Limit 8: Spartan Model 7-W Executive
1495QX8391 • $26

4903.

Small World
3200QXD5021 • $49

4904.

Sneaking a Treat
1895QRP4294 • $28

4905.

Snow Buddies 7
895QX8131 • $30

4906.

Snow Sculpture - Mickey Mouse
995QXD5014 • $25

4907.

Snowball and Tuxedo 4: Fancy Footwork
795QX8414 • $19

4908.
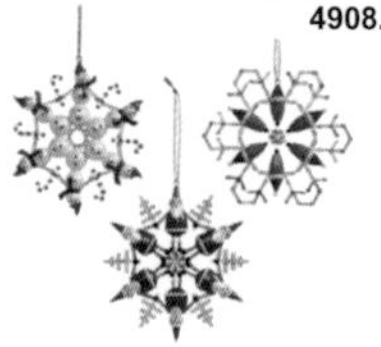
Snowflake Fun
1595QXG5524 • $25 • Set/3

4909.

Snowy Day
695QXG5454 • $11

4910.

So Much To Do!
995PR3035 • $13

4911.

Son
995QXG5554 • $15

4912.

The Sorcerer's Apprentice - Fantasia
1495QXD5011 • $23

4913.

Special Cat
995QXG5591 • $16

4914.

Special Dog
995QXG5584 • $23

4915.

Special Event
1295QXG5614 • $19

4916.

Spider-Man™
1495QXI8611 • $26

4917.

Spotlight on Snoopy® 7: The Winning Ticket
995QX8371 • $15

4918.

Stanley and Dennis - Playhouse Disney
1295QXD8674 • $20 • Set/2

4919.

Star Destroyer™ and Blockade Runner™
2800QXI4064 • $50
MAGIC.

4920.

Star Wars™: A New Hope Theater One-Sheet
1995QXI4074 • $31

4921.

Star Wars™ 8: Chewbacca™ and C-3PO™
1495QX8431 • $24

4922.

Sweet Tooth Treats 3
1495QX8191 • $24 • Set/4

4923.

Sweet Tooth Treats 3
($N/E)QX8191C • $28

4924.

Sweetest Little Shepherd
1695QLX7634 • $28
MAGIC.

4925.

Swinging On A Star
1695QXC4005 • $25

4926.

Teacher
995QXG5631 • $16

4927.

That Holy Night
1695QXG5391 • $40 • Set/3

4928.

Those Who Serve
1295QXG5444 • $20

4929.

Three Beautiful Princesses
1695QXD5054 • $28

4930.

Thrill Drivers Corkscrew Race
1495QXI8634 • $24

4931.

Ticktock Workshop
2800QLX7614 • $44
MAGIC.

4932.
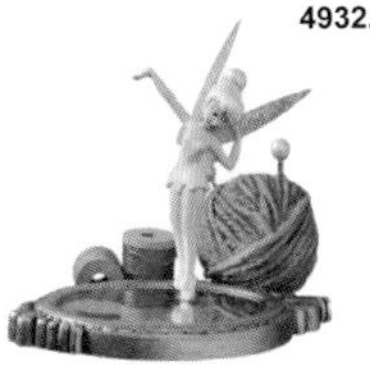
Tinker Bell - Peter Pan
1695QXD4232 • $26

4933.

Tonka® Giant Bulldozer
1495QXI5281 • $24

4934.

Tony Stewart - NASCAR®
1495QXI8651 • $24

4935.

Town and Country 6: Hometown Church
1695QX8201 • $33 • Set/2

4936.

Toymaker Santa 5
1295QX8124 • $20

4937.

Treasures and Dreams 3: Jewelry Box Gazebo
1995QX8121 • $31
MAGIC.

4938.

Triple-Decker Treat
995QXG5491 • $22

4939.

VeggieTales® - Drummer Boy
895QXG4454 • $18

4940.

Victorian Christmas
1695QXG5521 • $26

4941.

Vulcan™ Command Ship
2800QXI4084 • $50
MAGIC.

4942.

Walt Disney's Snow White and The Seven Dwarfs
3600QXD5064 • $65
MAGIC.

4943.

Whirlwind Decorating - Taz™
1495QXI4014 • $24
MAGIC.

4944.

Willie Mays - San Francisco Giants™
1495QXI5314 • $23

4945.

Winnie the Pooh: 100 Acre Express
1995QXD5034 • $31

4946.

Winnie the Pooh: Amigos Por Siempre
1295QXG5754 • $20

4947.

Winnie the Pooh: Baby's First Christmas
1495QXG5721 • $22

4948.

Winnie the Pooh: Friends Forever
1295QXG5024 • $21

4949.

Winnie the Pooh: Stocking Stuffers
1495QXD5041 • $23

4950.

Winnie the Pooh: Wings For Eeyore
1495QXD5031 • $26

4951.

Winnie the Pooh: The Winning Bounce
995QXD8561 • $16

4952.

Winnie the Pooh 7: A Sticky Situation
1495QXD5084 • $22

4953.

Winter Garden
1295QXG5534 • $24

4954.

Winter In Paris - Madeline™
1295QXI5321 • $20

4955.

Winter Wonderland 3: Building a Snowman
1295QX8251 • $23

4956.

Winterfest
1695QX8474 • $41
25 years of Frosty Friends.

4957.

A Wish For Peace
2400QXC4013 • $39

4958.

World-Class Shoppers - Mickey and Minnie
1895QXD5004 • $32

4959.

Yule Express
1995QLX7644 • $31
MAGIC.

2005

4960.

50 Years of Music and Fun - Disney's Mickey Mouse Club®
1995QXD4075
MAGIC.

4961.

Academics
995QXG4795

4962.

All Decked Out
1495QXC5006

4963.

All-American Trucks 11: 2003 Chevrolet® Silverado™ SS
1495QX2032

4964.

Anakin Skywalker™'s Jedi™ Starfighter™
2800QXI6192

4965.

And the Winner is...
1495QXI6195

4966.
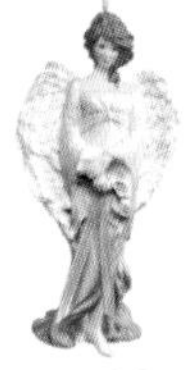
Angel of Grace
1495QXG4375

4967.

Angel on Earth
995QXG4372

4968.

Arctic Adventurers
1295QXG4452

4969.

At the Ballpark 10: Albert Pujols - St. Louis Cardinals™
1495QX2282

4970.
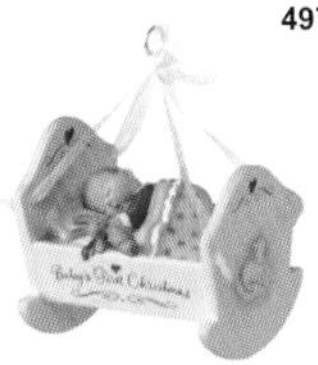
Baby's First Christmas
1295QXG4592

4971.

Baby's First Christmas
995QXG4602

4972.

Baby's First Christmas
1295QXG4622

4973.

Baby's First Christmas
1895QXG4625

4974.

Ballet
995QXG4782

4975.

BARBIE™ 12: Fashion Luncheon™ BARBIE™ Ornament
1595QX2305

4976.

BARBIE™ and the Magic of Pegasus
2500QXI6415

4977.

BARBIE™ as Titania™ Ornament
1495QXI6412

4978.

BARBIE™ Fairytopia™ Ornament
1895QXI6512
MAGIC.

4979.

BARBIE™ Fashion Model: Delphine™ BARBIE™ Ornament
2500QXI6432

4980.

Baseball/Softball
995QXG4762

4981.

Basketball
995QXG4752

4982.

The Batcycle™
1495QXI8902

4983.
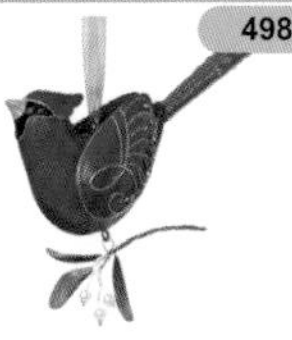

The Beauty of Birds 1: Northern Cardinal
1495QX2135

4984.

Best in Show
995QXG4705

4985.

Best Night of the Week - Wonderful World of Disney
2400QXD4085
MAGIC.

4986.

Buzz Lightyear and RC Racer - Toy Story
1495QXD4225

4987.

Camping
995QXG4775

4988.

Candlelight Services 8: Central Tower Church
1895QX2262

4989.

Carousel Ride 2: Proud Giraffe
1295QX2012

4990.

Carousel Ride Display
4500QX8481
Re-issued from 2004.

4991.

Celebration BARBIE™ 6
1595QX2202

4992.

Have You Seen Me?

Celebration BARBIE™ 6
1595QXI6422

4993.

A Charlie Brown® Christmas
3000QFM6482
MAGIC.

4994.

Cheerleading
995QXG4785

4995.

Chicken Little
1295QXD4815

4996.

Child's Age: My First Christmas (Boy)
995QXG4542
Re-issue of 2004 QXG5661.

4997.

Child's Age: My First Christmas (Girl)
995QXG4565
Re-issue of 2004 QXG5671.

4998.

Child's Age: My Second Christmas (Boy)
995QXG4545
Re-issue of 2004 QXG5664.

4999.

Child's Age: My Second Christmas (Girl)
995QXG4572
Re-issue of 2004 QXG5674.

5000.

Child's Age: My Third Christmas (Boy)
995QXG4552
Re-issue of 2004 QXG5681.

5001.

Child's Age: My Third Christmas (Girl)
995QXG4575
Re-issue of 2004 QXG5691.

5002.

Child's Age: My Fourth Christmas (Boy)
995QXG4555
Re-issue of 2004 QXG5684.

5003.

Child's Age: My Fourth Christmas (Girl)
995QXG4582
Re-issue of 2004 QXG5694.

5004.

Child's Age: Child's Fourth Christmas
895QXG4532

5005.

Child's Age: My Fifth Christmas (Boy)
995QXG4562
Re-issue of 2004 QXG5701.

5006.

Child's Age: My Fifth Christmas (Girl)
995QXG4585
Re-issue of 2004 QXG5704.

5007.

Child's Age: Child's Fifth Christmas
895QXG4535

5008.
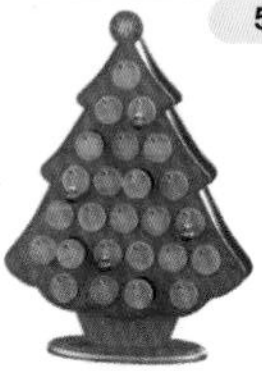
Christmas At Last!
7500QXC5012

5009.

Christmas Countdown
1495QXG4455

5010.

Christmas Window 3: Christmas Window 2005
1995QXC5003

5011.

Christmas With the Family - Lady and the Tramp
1695QXD4235

5012.

City Sidewalks
4400QLX7635
MAGIC.

5013.

Classic American Cars 15: 1968 Pontiac® Firebird™
1495QX2025

5014.

Clone Trooper™ Lieutenant
1495QXI6175

5015.

Color Me Curious - Curious George™
995QXI6222

5016.

Cool Decade 6
795QX2195

5017.

The Crabby Caroler - Maxine
1995QLX7592
MAGIC.

5018.

Crack the Whip! - PEANUTS®
2400QXI6292
MAGIC.

5019.

Cutest Kitty
995QXG4712

5020.

Dad
995QXG4672

5021.

Darth Vader™
1895QXI6185

5022.

Daughter
995QXG4682

5023.

Designer Spotlight™ BARBIE™ Ornament
($N/E)QXC5008

5024.

Dr. Seuss® Books 7: Oh, the Places You'll Go!
1495QX2112

5025.

Dreaming Big
995QXG4325

5026.

Duck Dodgers™ and Marvin The Martian™
1495QXI8765

5027.

Fairy Messengers 1: Poinsettia Fairy
995QX2145

5028.

Family Ties
1295QXG4742

5029.

Father Christmas 2
1895QX2155

5030.

Feliz Navidad
1295QXG4492

5031.

Fire Brigade 3: 1938 Chevrolet® Fire Engine
1895QX2035
MAGIC.

5032.

First Christmas Together
895QXG4392

5033.

First Christmas Together
1295QXG4402

5034.

Football
995QXG4772

5035.

Football Legends 11: Michael Vick - Atlanta Falcons™
1495QX2292

5036.

For Grandma
995QXG4695

5037.

For Grandpa
995QXG4702

5038.

For You, Teacher!
995QXG4315

5039.

Ford® Thunderbird™ 50th Anniversary Set
2400QXI6172 • Set/2

5040.

Friends at Large - Madagascar™
1295QXI6495

5041.
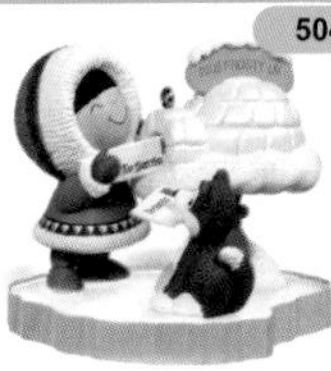
Frosty Friends 26
1295QX2325

5042.

G.I. Joe®
1495QXI6262

5043.

Gandalf the Grey™ - The Lord of the Rings™
1495QXI6232

5044.

Gardener's Paradise
1295QXG4285

5045.

Gift Bearers 7
1295QX2222

5046.

Godchild
995QXG4735

5047.

Grandchild's First Christmas
995QXG4612

5048.

Granddaughter
995QXG4692

5049.

Grandson
995QXG4685

5050.
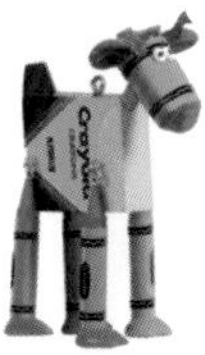

Happy Hues
1295QXI6225

5051.

A Happy Snowman
995PR3570

5052.

Harley-Davidson® Motorcycle Milestones 7: 2000 Softtail® Deuce™
1495QX2042

5053.

The Heart of the Season
695QXG4645

5054.

Here Comes Santa 9: Santa's Woody Special Edition
1495QXE2355

5055.

Holiday Serenade
2400QXG4422

5056.

Holiday Sledding - Raggedy Ann and Andy®
1495QXI6282 • Set/2

5057.

Hoop Stars 11: Carmelo Anthony - Denver Nuggets™
1495QX2345

5058.

I.C. Pete's Frozen Treats
1995QLX7595
MAGIC.

5059.

"It's Christmas Eve!"
($N/E)QXC5007

5060.

Jack-in-the-Box Memories 3: Pop! Goes the Reindeer
1495QX2125
MAGIC.

5061.

Jingle Bell Memories - The Polar Express™
1495QXI6462

5062.

The Journey of the Kings
1895QXG4382

5063.

The Joy of Music
995QXG4322

5064.

The Joy of Nursing
995QXG4305

5065.

Joyful Bells
695QXG4425

5066.

Joyful Jumping Jacks
1695QXG4462 • Set/3

5067.

Joyful Tidings: Arianne
1295QP1822

5068.

Joyful Tidings: Azura
1295QP1825

5069.

Joyful Tidings: Cordelia
1295QP1805

5070.

Joyful Tidings: Cordelia
1295QP1832

5071.

Joyful Tidings: Cordelia
1295QP1835

5072.

Joyful Tidings: Esmeralda
1295QP1812

5073.

Joyful Tidings: Gilda
1295QP1815

5074.

Joyful Tidings: Display Wreath
2495QP1842

5075.

Keepsake Kids: "Countdown to Christmas" Tree
3995QKK3001
Re-issued from 2004.

5076.

Keepsake Kids: From a Stable So Small Storybook Set
2495QKK3014 • Set/7
Re-issued from 2004.

5077.

Keepsake Kids: Jolly Ol' St. Nicholas Storybook and Ornaments
2495QKK3011 • Set/6
Re-issued from 2004.

5078.

Keepsake Kids: My Very Own Christmas Tree
1495QKK3004
Re-issued from 2004.

5079.
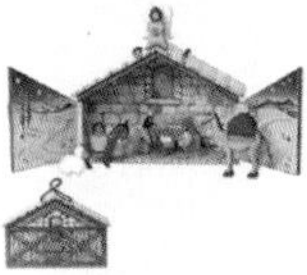
Keepsake Kids: Nativity Play Set
3995QKK3025 • Set/8

5080.
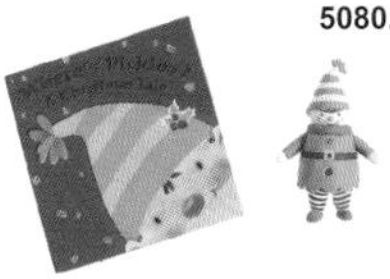
Keepsake Kids: Pickles, The Elf "Find Me, If You Can" Game
995QKK3072

5081.

Keepsake Kids: Santa's Workshop Play Set
3995QKK3032 • Set/8

5082.

Keepsake Kids: Three Kings From Afar
2495QKK3002 • Set/6

5083.

Keepsake Kids: Where's Pickles?
2495QKK3015 • Set/6

5084.

Khan
1495QXI6202

5085.

Kiddie Car Classics 12: 1926 Murray® Steelcraft Speedster
1395QX2295

5086.

The Kiss
1295QXG4412

5087.

Kris and the Kringles 5
2400QX2185

5088.

L.A.at Last! - I Love Lucy®
1695QXI6252

5089.

Leap of Love
995QXG4395

5090.

Leonardo - Teenage Mutant Ninja Turtles™
1295QXI6435

5091.

Light of Liberty
1295QXG4332

5092.

Lighthouse Greetings 9
2400QX2272

5093.

LIONEL® No. 714 Boxcar
1295QXI6125

5094.

LIONEL® No. 717 Caboose
1295QX2122

5095.

LIONEL® Pennsylvania B6 Tender
1295QXI6122

5096.

LIONEL® Trains 10: Pennsylvania B6 Steam Locomotive
1895QX2052

5097.

Little Helpers: Mailing A Letter to Santa
1295QXG4435

5098.

Little Helpers: Baking Cookies
1295QXG4445

5099.

Little Helpers: Hanging the Wreath
1295QXG4442

5100.

Little Shepherd
995QXG4345

5101.

Locutus of Borg™
2800QXI6205

5102.

Madame Alexander® 10: Sweet Irish Dancer
1495QX2055

5103.

Mailbox Melodies
3200QLX7632
MAGIC.

5104.

Make Way! - Taz™
1295QXI8772

5105.

Mary's Angels 18: Forsythia
795QX2315

5106.

Matt Kenseth
1495QXI6272

5107.

Melody of Praise
1295QXG4365

5108.

Merry Mayhem Workshop
($N/E)unknown • $75

5109.

Mighty Simba - The Lion King
1495QXD4222
MAGIC.

5110.

Mighty Tonka® Wrecker
1495QXI6255

5111.

Mischievous Kittens 7
995QX2225

5112.

Model B Tractor - John Deere
1495QXI6245

5113.

Mom
995QXG4665

5114.

Mooster Fix-It
1295QXG4272

5115.
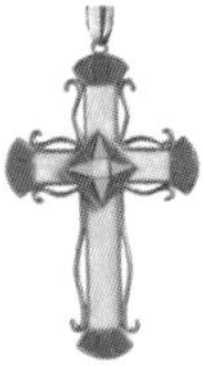
Mosaic of Faith
1295QXG4352

5116.

Mother and Daughter
1295QXG4745

5117.

Muscle Cars
($N/E)QXC5009 • Set/3

5118.

Music
995QXG4792

5119.

Nació el Amor
1295QXG4362

5120.

Nature's Sketchbook: Nature's Sketchbook 3
995QX2115

5121.

New Home
1295QXG4635

5122.

Nick and Christopher 2: Hockey Thrills
1295QX2152

5123.

Have You Seen Me?

Nick and Christopher 2: Hockey Thrills
($N/A)QX2152C • $N/E

5124.

Noah's Ark
1495QXG4355

5125.

Nostalgic Houses & Shops 22: Victorian Home
1495QX2322

5126.

Nuestra Familia
1295QXG4732

5127.

O Kitchen Rack
995QXG4282

5128.

Off to See the Wizard! - The Wizard of Oz™
1995QXI8925

5129.

Once Upon a Starry Night
1295QXG4385

5130.

One Cute Cookie
995QXG4632

5131.

The Opening Game
1995QXC5002

5132.

Order Up!
1895QRP4082 • Set/2

5133.

Ornament Display Stand
595QXG4802

5134.

Our Christmas
1295QXG4405

5135.

Our Family
1295QXG4725

5136.

Our First Christmas
1895QXG4415

5137.

Over the Rainbow - The Wizard of Oz™
2800QXI8932

5138.

Packed With Love
995QXG4642

5139.

Parents-to-Be
1295QXG4605

5140.

PEANUTS® Christmas Pageant
($N/E)QXC5011

5141.

Peek-a-Boo! - Sylvester™ and Tweety™
1495QXI8755

5142.

Pinball Action - Bugs Bunny™ and Daffy Duck™
2400QXI8775

5143.

Polar Express™ - First Gift Of Christmas Bell
1295unknown
Re-issued from 2004.

5144.

A Pony for Christmas 8
1295QX2265

5145.

Primera Navidad de Bebé
1295QXG4595

5146.

Puppy Love 15
895QX2312

5147.

A Putter for Santa
995QXG4312

5148.

Quidditch™ Match - Harry Potter™
1495QXI8915

5149.

Rockin' With Santa
2800QLX7622
MAGIC.

5150.

Ruby Slippers - The Wizard of Oz™
1995QXC5004

5151.

Rudolph® and Bumble™ The Abominable Snowmonster
1495QXG4475

5152.

Santa Beagle and Friends: PEANUTS®
1495QXI6485

5153.

Santa Knows!
2400QLX7612
MAGIC.

5154.

Santa Nutcracker
($N/E)QXC5005

5155.

Santas From Around The World: England
1295QXG4822

5156.

Santa's Helpers - Mickey and Pluto
1495QXD4012

5157.

Santa's Little Shopper
995QXG4302

5158.

Santa's Magic Sack
1295QXG4465

5159.

Santa's Magic Sack
1295QXG4472

5160.

Santa's Midnight Ride: Dash Away All
2995QP1762

5161.

Santa's Midnight Ride: Ready for Flight
1495QP1745 • Set/2

5162.

Santa's Midnight Ride: Two for the Skies
1495QP1755 • Set/2

5163.

Scarlett O'Hara™: Gone With the Wind™
1595QXI6002

5164.

Scarlett O'Hara™ and Rhett Butler™ - Gone With the Wind™
1895QXI6015

5165.

A Season to Sing - Kermit the Frog™
1295QXI6242

5166.

Shake it, Santa!
695WD3533

5167.

Shiver-Me Tim Brrr
1695QLX7582
MAGIC.

5168.

Shrek® and Princess Fiona - Shrek 2®
1495QXI6492

5169.

Silent Night
1495QXG4482

5170.

Sisters
1295QXG4715

5171.

Sisters
1295QXG4722

5172.

Skating Lessons - Bambi
1695QXD4242

5173.

Sky's the Limit 9: 1931 Laird Super Solution
1495QX2045

5174.

Snow Bear Buddies
995QXG4432

5175.

Have You Seen Me?
Snow Bear Buddies
($N/A)QXG4432C

5176.

Snow Buddies 8
895QX2245

5177.

Snow Day Magic
1995QXC5001

5178.

Snowball and Tuxedo 5: Two Sweet!
795QX2192

5179.

Snowtop Lodge 1: Skylar A. Woolscarf
1895QX2405

5180.

Soccer
995QXG4755

5181.

Soda Shop Sweethearts
1695QRP4072

5182.

Son
995QXG4675

5183.

The Sorcerer's Apprentice - Fantasia
3200QXD4082
MAGIC.

5184.

Space Alien Alert! - Power Rangers SPD™
1495QXI6505

5185.

Speak! - Scooby-Doo™
1695QXI8905

5186.

Special Edition Repaint Rocking Horse
1295QXE2352

5187.

Spider-Man™
1495QXI6265

5188.

Spirit of St. Nick
1995QLX7645
MAGIC.

5189.

Spirit of St. Nick
($N/E)QLX7645C
MAGIC.

5190.

Spotlight on Snoopy® 8: Snoopy™ the Magnificent
995QX2132

5191.

Star Wars™ 9: Princess Leia™
1495QX2015

5192.

Sweeeeet Friendship - Finding Nemo
1495QXD4812

5193.

Sweet Tooth Treats 4
1495QX2175 • Set/4

5194.

Thomas the Tank®
1295QXI6235

5195.

Tinker Bell - Peter Pan
1495QXD4265

5196.

To My Gouda Friend
995QXG4662

5197.

Touchdown, Snoopy®!
1495QXI6285

5198.

Toyland Treasures
3200QLX7625
MAGIC.

5199.

Toymaker Santa 6
1295QX2205

5200.

Treasures and Dreams 4: Jewelry Box Carol
1995QX2172
MAGIC.

5201.

Tree-Napper at Work - Dr. Seuss's® How the Grinch Stole Christmas™
1295QXI6162

5202.

Trim A Tiny Tree
995QXG4295

5203.

Triple Dippin'!
695WD3532

5204.

True Patriot - Mickey Mouse®
995QXD4005

5205.

Tweety™ Plays an Angel
1695QXI8762

5206.

U.S.S. Enterprise NCC-1701-A™
2800QXI6215

5207.

Volleyball
995QXG4765

5208.

Wedding Day Dance - Cinderella
2400QXD4245
MAGIC.

5209.

Winnie the Pooh: Amigos de Verdad
1295QXG4655

5210.

Winnie the Pooh: Baby's First Christmas
1495QXG4615

5211.

Winnie the Pooh: Bounce Practice - Tigger
1295QXD4092

5212.

Winnie the Pooh: Getting Ready for Christmas
3200QXD4212

5213.

Winnie the Pooh: Gift Exchange
1495QXD4105

5214.

Winnie the Pooh: True Friends
1295QXG4652

5215.

Winnie the Pooh: Unlikely Friends - Pooh's Heffalump Movie™
1295QXD4215

5216.

Winnie the Pooh 8: Rainy Day Rescue
1495QXD4102

5217.

Winter Wonderland 4: Ice-Skaters' Delight
1295QX2182

5218.

Yankee Doodle Santa
1295QXG4335

5219.

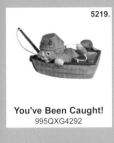

You've Been Caught!
995QXG4292

Miniature Ornaments

Introduced in 1988, Miniature Ornaments are tiny, yet full of personality and amazing detail. A tabletop tree full of these mini ornaments will fill the room with fun.

1988

5220.
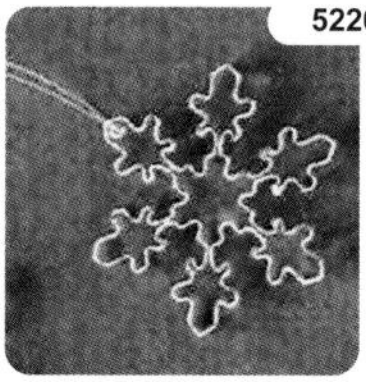
Acrylic Snowflakes
400QXM5781 • $12 • Set/10

5221.

Baby's First Christmas
600QXM5744 • $14

5222.
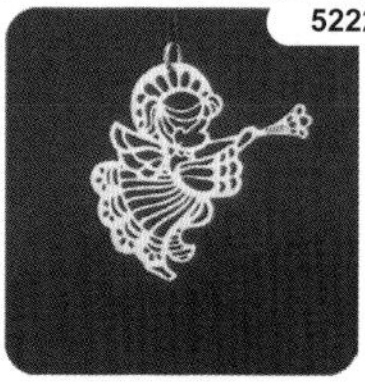
Brass Angel
150QXM5671 • $16

5223.

Brass Star
150QXM5664 • $14

5224.

Brass Tree
150QXM5674 • $10

5225.

Candy Cane Elf
300QXM5701 • $17

5226.

Country Wreath
400QXM5731 • $9
Re-issued in 1989.

5227.

First Christmas Together
400QXM5741 • $12

5228.

Folk Art Lamb
275QXM5681 • $18

5229.

Folk Art Reindeer
300QXM5684 • $12

5230.

Friends Share Joy
200QXM5764 • $14

5231.
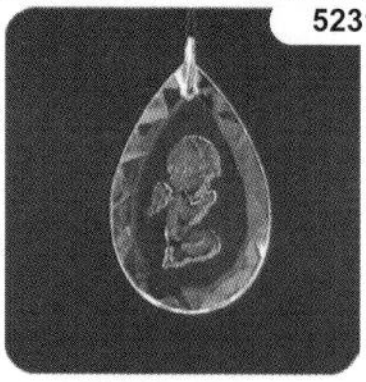
Gentle Angel
200QXM5771 • $16

5232.

Happy Santa
450QXM5614 • $16

5233.

Hold On Tight
($N/A)QXC5704 • $35

5234.

Holy Family
850QXM5611 • $12
Re-issued in 1989.

5235.

Jolly St. Nick
800QXM5721 • $19

5236.

Joyous Heart
350QXM5691 • $19

5237.

Kittens In Toyland 1
500QXM5621 • $19

5238.

Little Drummer Boy
450QXM5784 • $14

5239.

Love Is Forever
200QXM5774 • $14

5240.

Miniature Rocking Horse 1
450QXM5624 • $42

5241.

Mother
300QXM5724 • $13

5242.
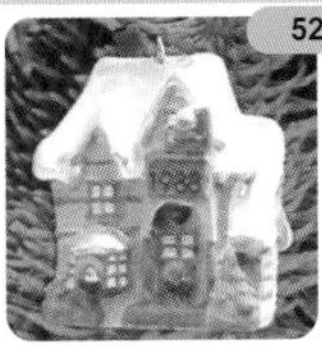
Old English Village 1: Family Home
850QXM5634 • $34

5243.

Penguin Pal 1
375QXM5631 • $19

5244.

Skater's Waltz
700QXM5601 • $17

5245.
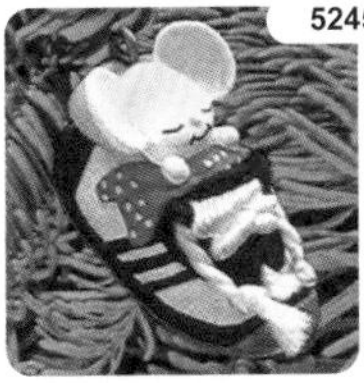
Sneaker Mouse
400QXM5711 • $15

5246.

Snuggly Skater
450QXM5714 • $15

5247.

Sweet Dreams
700QXM5604 • $17

5248.

Three Little Kitties
600QXM5694 • $16
Re-issued in 1989.

5249.

Wooden Ornaments
400QXM5651 • $10 • Set/6

1989

5250.

Acorn Squirrel
450QXM5682 • $14
Re-issued in 1990.

5251.

Baby's First Christmas
600QXM5732 • $17

5252.

Brass Partridge
300QXM5725 • $13

5253.

Brass Snowflake
450QXM5702 • $13

5254.
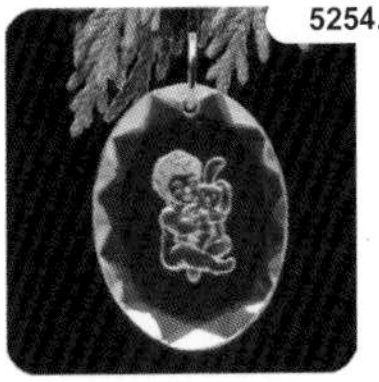
Bunny Hug
300QXM5775 • $10

5255.

Country Wreath
450QXM5731 • $9
Re-issued from 1988.

5256.

Cozy Skater
450QXM5735 • $13
Re-issued in 1990.

5257.

First Christmas Together
850QXM5642 • $10

5258.

Folk Art Bunny
450QXM5692 • $8

5259.

Happy Bluebird
450QXM5662 • $15
Re-issued in 1990.

5260.

Holiday Deer
300QXM5772 • $10

5261.

Holy Family
850QXM5611 • $12
Re-issued from 1988.

5262.

Kittens In Toyland 2
450QXM5612 • $18

5263.
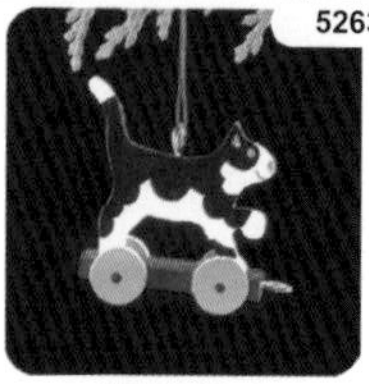
Kitty Cart
300QXM5722 • $8

5264.

The Kringles 1
600QXM5625 • $22

5265.

Little Soldier
450QXM5675 • $13
Re-issued in 1990.

5266.

Little Star Bringer
600QXM5622 • $17

5267.

Load Of Cheer
600QXM5745 • $13

5268.

Lovebirds
600QXM5635 • $11

5269.

Merry Seal
600QXM5755 • $13

5270.

Miniature Rocking Horse 2
450QXM5605 • $31

5271.

Mother
600QXM5645 • $11

5272.

Noel RR 1: Locomotive
850QXM5762 • $41

5273.

Old English Village 2: Sweet Shop
850QXM5615 • $26

5274.

Old-World Santa
300QXM5695 • $13
Re-issued in 1990.

5275.

Penguin Pal 2
450QXM5602 • $17

5276.

Pinecone Basket
450QXM5734 • $8

5277.

Puppy Cart
300QXM5715 • $8

5278.

Rejoice
300QXM5782 • $8

5279.
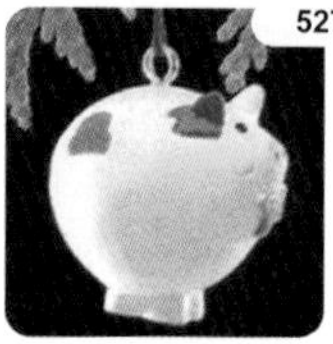
Roly-Poly Pig
300QXM5712 • $15
Re-issued in 1990.

5280.
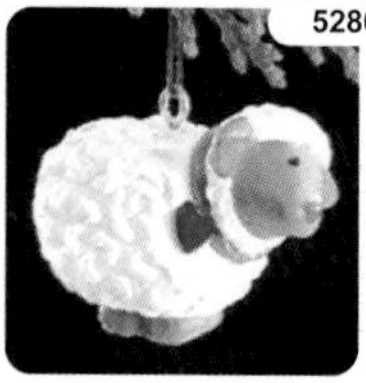
Roly-Poly Ram
300QXM5705 • $10

5281.

Santa's Magic Ride
850QXM5632 • $19

5282.

Santa's Roadster
600QXM5665 • $17

5283.

Scrimshaw Reindeer
450QXM5685 • $11

5284.

Sharing A Ride
850QXM5765 • $17

5285.

Sitting Purrty
($N/E)QXC5812 • $12

5286.
Slow Motion
600QXM5752 • $17

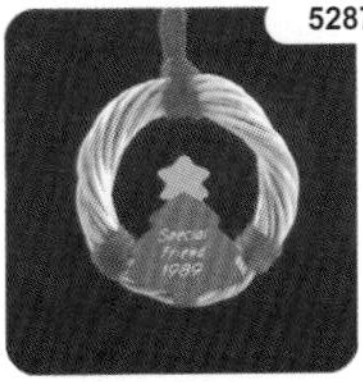
5287.
Special Friend
450QXM5652 • $9

5288.
Starlit Mouse
450QXM5655 • $17

5289.
Stocking Pal
450QXM5672 • $12
Re-issued in 1990.

5290.
Strollin' Snowman
450QXM5742 • $14

5291.
Three Little Kitties
600QXM5694 • $16
Re-issued from 1988.

1990

5292.
Acorn Squirrel
450QXM5682 • $14
Re-issued from 1989.

5293.
Acorn Wreath
600QXM5686 • $13

5294.
Air Santa
450QXM5656 • $17

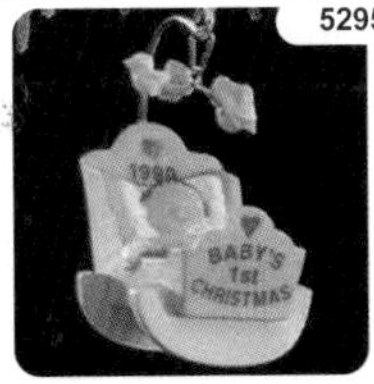

5295.
Baby's First Christmas
850QXM5703 • $13

5296.
Basket Buddy
600QXM5696 • $17

5297.
Bear Hug
600QXM5633 • $12

5298.
Brass Bouquet
600QXM5776 • $10

5299.
Brass Horn
300QXM5793 • $10

5300.
Brass Peace
300QXM5796 • $12

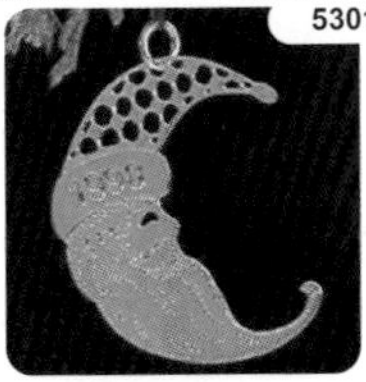
5301.
Brass Santa
300QXM5786 • $12

5302.
Brass Year
300QXM5833 • $10

5303.
Busy Carver
450QXM5673 • $12

5304.
Christmas Dove
450QXM5636 • $17

5305.
Cloisonne Poinsettia
1050QXM5533 • $23

5306.
Country Heart
450QXM5693 • $8

5307.
Cozy Skater
450QXM5735 • $13
Re-issued from 1989.

5308.
Crown Prince
($N/E)QXC5603 • $23

5309.

First Christmas Together
600QXM5536 • $12

5310.

Going Sledding
450QXM5683 • $14

5311.

Grandchild's First Christmas
600QXM5723 • $12

5312.

Happy Bluebird
450QXM5662 • $15
Re-issued from 1989.

5313.
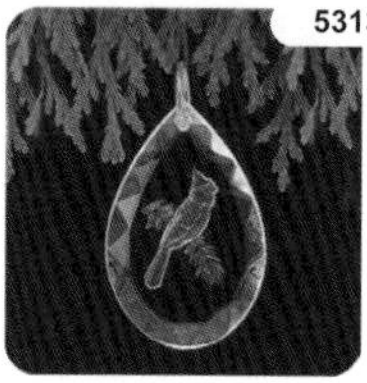
Holiday Cardinal
300QXM5526 • $14

5314.

Kittens In Toyland 3
450QXM5736 • $18

5315.

The Kringles 2
600QXM5753 • $19

5316.

Lion and Lamb
450QXM5676 • $14

5317.

Little Frosty Friends: Little Bear
295XPR9723 • $12

5318.

Little Frosty Friends: Little Frosty
295XPR9720 • $14

5319.

Little Frosty Friends: Little Husky
295XPR9722 • $20

5320.

Little Frosty Friends: Little Seal
295XPR9721 • $12

5321.

Little Frosty Friends: Memory Wreath
295XPR9724 • $14

5322.

Little Frosty Friends: Set
1475XPR9725 • $65 • Set/5

5323.

Little Soldier
450QXM5675 • $13
Re-issued from 1989.

5324.

Loving Hearts
300QXM5523 • $12

5325.

Madonna and Child
600QXM5643 • $12

5326.

Miniature Rocking Horse 3
450QXM5743 • $29

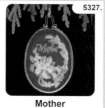

5327.
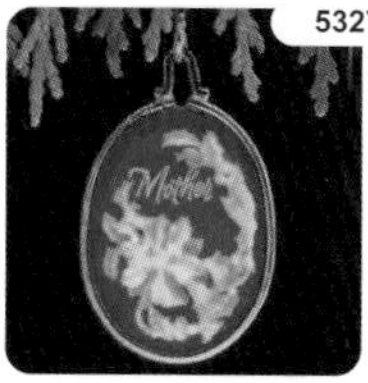

Mother
450QXM5716 • $12

5328.

Nativity
450QXM5706 • $20

5329.

Nature's Angels 1
450QXM5733 • $23

5330.

Noel RR 2: Coal Car
850QXM5756 • $20

5331.

Old English Village 3: School
850QXM5763 • $26

5332.

Old-World Santa
450QXM5695 • $13
Re-issued from 1989.

5333.
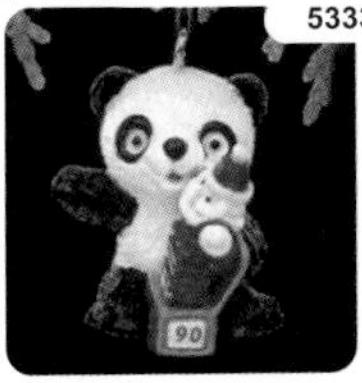
Panda's Surprise
450QXM5616 • $13

5334.

Penguin Pal 3
450QXM5746 • $14

5335.

Perfect Fit
450QXM5516 • $12

5336.

Puppy Love
600QXM5666 • $12

5337.
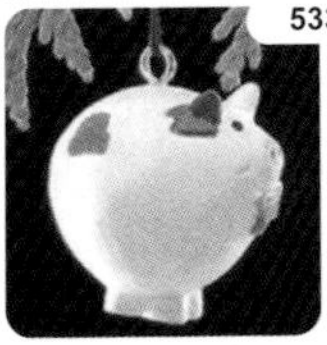
Roly-Poly Pig
300QXM5712 • $15
Re-issued from 1989.

5338.

Ruby Reindeer
600QXM5816 • $12

5339.

Santa's Journey
850QXM5826 • $15

5340.

Santa's Streetcar
850QXM5766 • $13

5341.
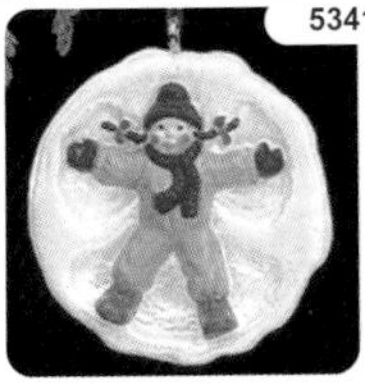
Snow Angel
600QXM5773 • $13

5342.

Special Friends
600QXM5726 • $13

5343.

Stamp Collector
450QXM5623 • $12

5344.

Stocking Pal
450QXM5672 • $12
Re-issued from 1989.

5345.

Stringing Along
850QXM5606 • $14

5346.

Sweet Slumber
450QXM5663 • $13

5347.

Teacher
450QXM5653 • $12

5348.
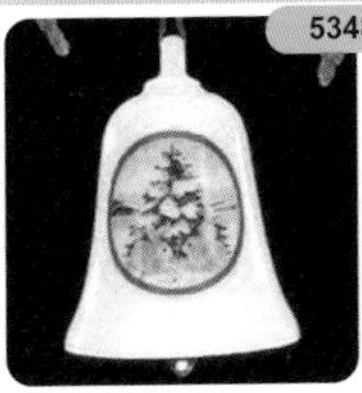
Thimble Bells 1
600QXM5543 • $19

5349.

Type Of Joy
450QXM5646 • $12

5350.

Warm Memories
450QXM5713 • $10

5351.

Wee Nutcracker
850QXM5843 • $13

1991

5352.

All Aboard
450QXM5869 • $13

5353.

Baby's First Christmas
600QXM5799 • $17

5354.

Brass Bells
300QXM5977 • $8

5355.

Brass Church
300QXM5979 • $7

5356.

Brass Soldier
300QXM5987 • $7

5357.

Bright Boxers
450QXM5877 • $12

5358.

Busy Bear
450QXM5939 • $12

5359.

Cardinal Cameo
600QXM5957 • $14

5360.

Caring Shepherd
600QXM5949 • $12

5361.

Cool 'n' Sweet
450QXM5867 • $22

5362.

Country Sleigh
450QXM5999 • $12

5363.
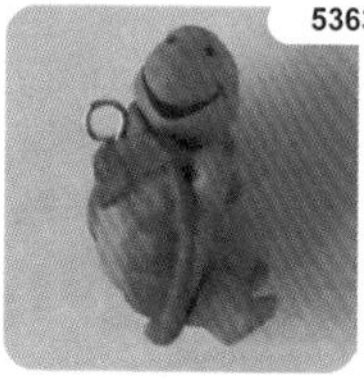
Courier Turtle
450QXM5857 • $12

5364.
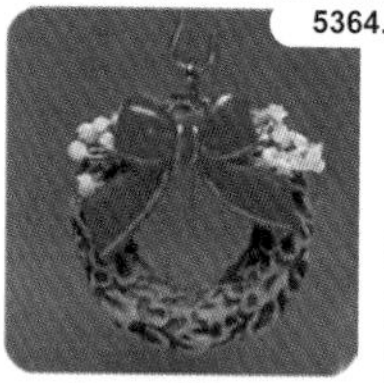
Fancy Wreath
450QXM5917 • $9

5365.

Feliz Navidad
600QXM5887 • $13

5366.

First Christmas Together
600QXM5819 • $12

5367.

Fly By
450QXM5859 • $13

5368.

Friendly Fawn
600QXM5947 • $17

5369.

Grandchild's First Christmas
450QXM5697 • $10

5370.

Heavenly Minstrel
975QXM5687 • $19

5371.
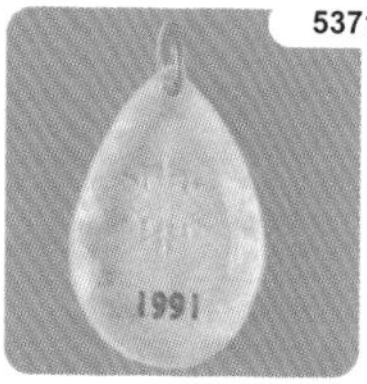
Holiday Snowflake
300QXM5997 • $13

5372.
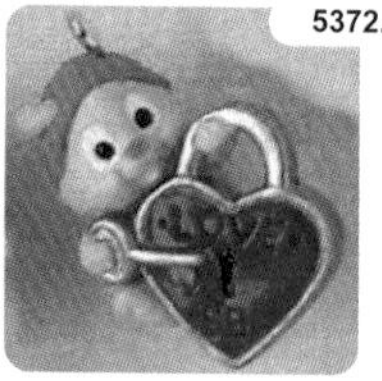
Key To Love
450QXM5689 • $12

5373.

Kittens In Toyland 4
450QXM5639 • $13

5374.

Kitty in a Mitty
450QXM5879 • $12

5375.

The Kringles 3
600QXM5647 • $30

5376.

Li'l Popper
450QXM5897 • $20

5377.
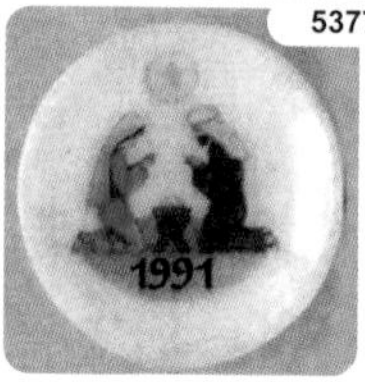
Love Is Born
600QXM5959 • $20

5378.

Lulu & Family
600QXM5677 • $23

5379.
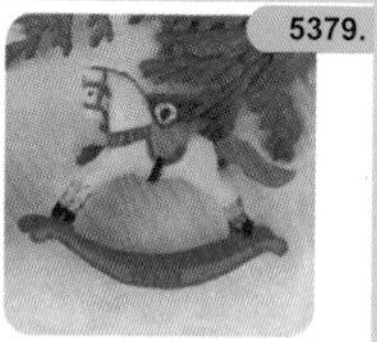
Miniature Rocking Horse 4
450QXM5637 • $24

5380.

Mom
600QXM5699 • $17

5381.

N. Pole Buddy
450QXM5927 • $14

5382.

Nature's Angels 2
450QXM5657 • $18

5383.

Noel
300QXM5989 • $14

5384.

Noel RR 3: Passenger Car
850QXM5649 • $55

5385.

Old English Village 4: Inn
850QXM5627 • $25

5386.

Penguin Pal 4
450QXM5629 • $12

5387.

Ring-A-Ding Elf
850QXM5669 • $14

5388.

Seaside Otter
450QXM5909 • $11

5389.

Silvery Santa
975QXM5679 • $16

5390.

Six Mice: Tiny Tea Party Set
2900QXM5827 • $130 • Set/6

5391.

Special Friends
850QXM5797 • $17

5392.

Thimble Bells 2
600QXM5659 • $15

5393.

Top Hatter
600QXM5889 • $13

5394.

Treeland Trio
850QXM5899 • $12

5395.

Upbeat Bear
600QXM5907 • $14

5396.

Vision Of Santa
450QXM5937 • $11

5397.

Wee Toymaker
850QXM5967 • $13

5398.

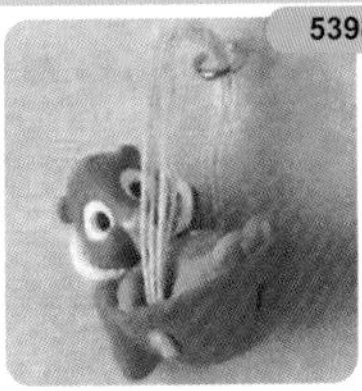

Woodland Babies 1
600QXM5667 • $18

1992

5399.

A+ Teacher
375QXM5511 • $10

5400.

Angelic Harpist
450QXM5524 • $16

5401.

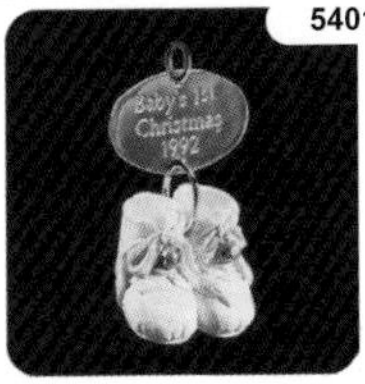

Baby's First Christmas
450QXM5494 • $22

5402.

The Bearymores 1
575QXM5544 • $13

5403.
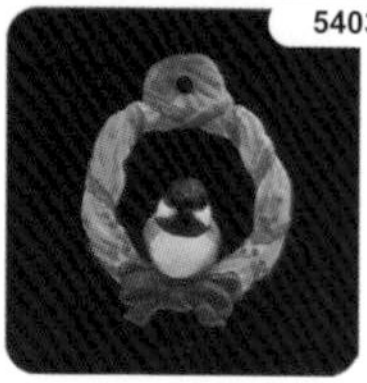
Black-Capped Chickadee
300QXM5484 • $20

5404.
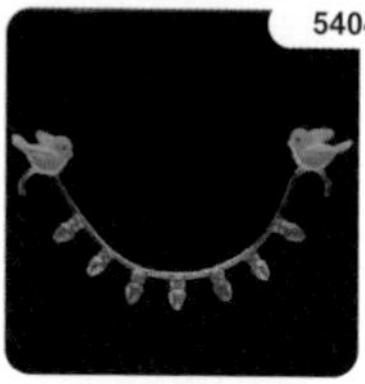
Bright Stringers
375QXM5841 • $23

5405.

Buck-A-Roo
450QXM5814 • $14

5406.

Chipmunk Parcel Service
($N/A)QXC5194 • $25

5407.

Christmas Bonus
300QXM5811 • $13

5408.

Christmas Copter
575QXM5844 • $13

5409.

Christmas Treasures
2200QXC5464 • $145 • Set/4
Limited Edition - 15500.

5410.

Coca-Cola® Santa
575QXM5884 • $15

5411.

Cool Uncle Sam
300QXM5561 • $17

5412.

Cozy Kayak
375QXM5551 • $13

5413.

Fast Finish
375QXM5301 • $13

5414.

Feeding Time
575QXM5481 • $18

5415.

Friendly Tin Soldier
450QXM5874 • $14

5416.

Friends Are Tops
450QXM5521 • $13

5417.

Gerbil, Inc.
375QXM5924 • $10

5418.

Going Places
375QXM5871 • $10

5419.

Grandchild's First Christmas
575QXM5501 • $11

5420.

Grandma
450QXM5514 • $11

5421.

Harmony Trio
1175QXM5471 • $17 • Set/3

5422.

Hickory, Dickory, Dock
375QXM5861 • $12

5423.

Holiday Holly
975QXM5364 • $13

5424.

Holiday Splash
575QXM5834 • $13

5425.

Hoop It Up
450QXM5831 • $10

5426.

Inside Story
725QXM5881 • $14

5427.

Kittens In Toyland 5
450QXM5391 • $14

5428.

The Kringles 4
600QXM5381 • $14

5429.

Little Town of Bethlehem
300QXM5864 • $17

5430.

Miniature Rocking Horse 5
450QXM5454 • $28

5431.

Minted for Santa
375QXM5854 • $10

5432.

Mom
450QXM5504 • $12

5433.

Nature's Angels 3
450QXM5451 • $17

5434.

The Night Before Christmas 1
1375QXM5541 • $25

5435.

Noel RR 4: Box Car
700QXM5441 • $28

5436.

Old English Village 5: Church
700QXM5384 • $31

5437.

Perfect Balance
300QXM5571 • $12

5438.

Polar Polka
450QXM5534 • $12

5439.

Puppet Show
300QXM5574 • $10

5440.

Six Mice: Sew, Sew Tiny
2900QXM5794 • $43 • Set/6

5441.

Ski For Two
450QXM5821 • $12

5442.

Snowshoe Bunny
375QXM5564 • $12

5443.

Snug Kitty
375QXM5554 • $12

5444.

Spunky Monkey
300QXM5921 • $12

5445.

Thimble Bells 3
600QXM5461 • $15

5446.
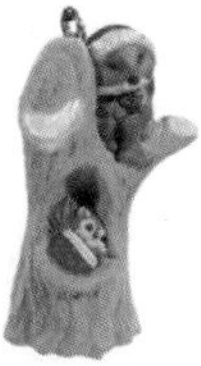
Visions Of Acorns
450QXM5851 • $12

5447.

Wee Three Kings
575QXM5531 • $17

5448.
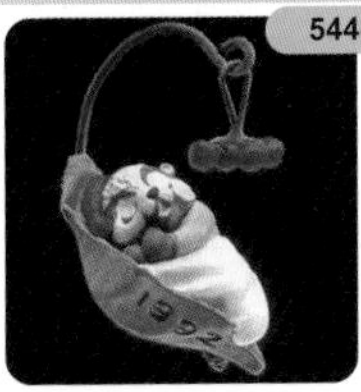
Woodland Babies 2
600QXM5444 • $12

1993

5449.

Baby's First Christmas
575QXM5145 • $12

5450.

The Bearymores 2
575QXM5125 • $14

5451.

Cheese Please
375QXM4072 • $9

5452.

Christmas Castle
575QXM4085 • $11

5453.

Cloisonne Snowflake
975QXM4012 • $16

5454.

Coca-Cola® - Refreshing Flight
575QXM4112 • $12

5455.

Country Fiddling
375QXM4062 • $10

5456.

Crystal Angel
975QXM4015 • $55

5457.

Ears to Pals
375QXM4075 • $8

5458.

Grandma
450QXM5162 • $12

5459.

Holiday Express Train Base
5000QXM5452 • $90
Re-issued in 1994 & 1995.

5460.

I Dream of Santa
375QXM4055 • $9

5461.

Into the Woods
375QXM4045 • $8

5462.

The Kringles 5
575QXM5135 • $14

5463.

Learning to Skate
300QXM4122 • $8

5464.

Lighting a Path
300QXM4115 • $8

5465.

March of the Teddy Bears 1
450QXM4005 • $16

5466.

Merry Mascot
375QXM4042 • $12

5467.

Miniature Rocking Horse 6
450QXM5112 • $19

5468.

Mom
450QXM5155 • $10

5469.

Monkey Melody
575QXM4092 • $12

5470.

Nature's Angels 4
450QXM5122 • $16

5471.

The Night Before Christmas 2
450QXM5115 • $16

5472.

Noel RR 5: Flatbed Car
700QXM5105 • $23

5473.

North Pole Fire Truck
475QXM4105 • $11

5474.

Old English Village 6: Toy Shop
700QXM5132 • $17

5475.

On the Road 1
575QXM4002 • $19

5476.

Pear-Shaped Tones
375QXM4052 • $8

5477.

Pull Out a Plum
575QXM4095 • $12

5478.

Round the Mountain
725QXM4025 • $13

5479.

Santa's Club Soda: Forty Winks
($N/E)QXC5294 • $24

5480.

Secret Pal
375QXM5172 • $8

5481.

Six Mice: Tiny Green Thumbs
2900QXM4032 • $42 • Set/6

5482.

Snuggle Birds
575QXM5182 • $11

5483.

Special Friends
450QXM5165 • $10

5484.
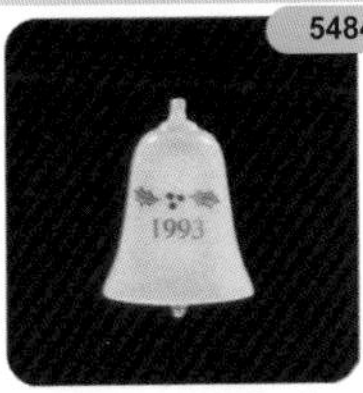

Thimble Bells 4
575QXM5142 • $12

5485.

Visions of Sugarplums
725QXM4022 • $12

5486.

Woodland Babies 3
575QXM5102 • $12

1994

5487.
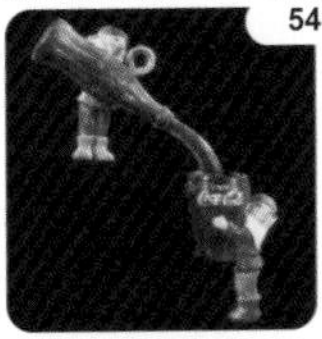
Coca-Cola® - Pour Some More
575QXM5156 • $13

5488.

Babs Bunny
575QXM4116 • $13

5489.

Baby's First Christmas
575QXM4003 • $12

5490.

Beary Perfect Tree
475QXM4076 • $11

5491.

The Bearymores 3
575QXM5133 • $12

5492.

Buster Bunny™
575QXM5163 • $12

5493.

Centuries of Santa 1
600QXM5153 • $28

5494.

Corny Elf
450QXM4063 • $12

5495.
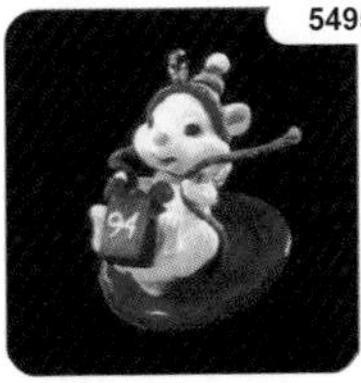
Cute as a Button
375QXM4103 • $13

5496.

Dazzling Reindeer
975QXM4026 • $16

5497.

Dizzy Devil
575QXM4133 • $16

5498.

Friends Need Hugs
450QXM4016 • $13

5499.

Graceful Carousel Horse
775QXM4056 • $16

5500.

Hamton™
575QXM4126 • $12

5501.
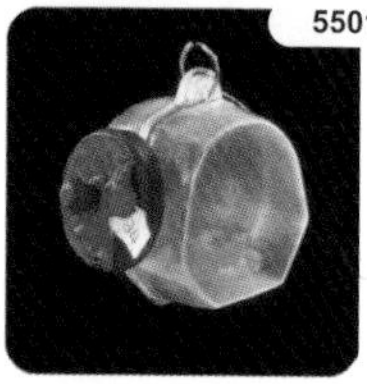
Have a Cookie
575QXM5166 • $17

5502.

Hearts A-Sail
575QXM4006 • $10

5503.

Holiday Express Train Base
5000QXM5452 • $90
Also issued in 1993 & 1995.

5504.

Jolly Visitor
575QXM4053 • $12

5505.

Jolly Wolly Snowman
375QXM4093 • $14

5506.

Journey to Bethlehem
575QXM4036 • $26

5507.

Just My Size
375QXM4086 • $13

5508.
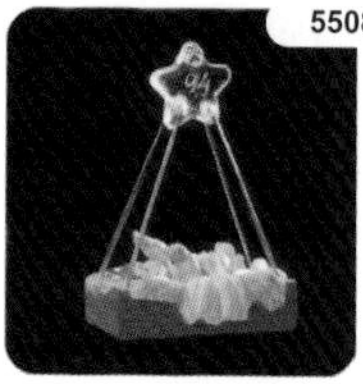
Love Was Born
450QXM4043 • $17

5509.

March of the Teddy Bears 2
450QXM5106 • $16

5510.

Melodic Cherub
375QXM4066 • $17

5511.

A Merry Flight
575QXM4073 • $13

5512.

Miniature Rocking Horse 7
450QXM5116 • $20

5513.

Mom
450QXM4013 • $12

5514.

Nature's Angels 5
450QXM5126 • $12

5515.

The Night Before Christmas 3
450QXM5123 • $10

5516.

Noah's Ark: Noah's Ark
2450QXM4106 • $77 • Set/3

5517.

Noel RR 6: Stock Car
700QXM5113 • $22

5518.

Nutcracker Guild 1
575QXM5146 • $26

5519.

Old English Village 7: Hat Shop
700QXM5143 • $16

5520.

On the Road 2
575QXM5103 • $16

5521.

Plucky Duck
575QXM4123 • $13

5522.

Santa's Club Soda: Sweet Bouquet
($N/E)QXC4806 • $23

5523.

Scooting Along
675QXM5173 • $12

5524.

Six Mice: Baking Tiny Treats
2900QXM4033 • $70 • Set/6

5525.

Sweet Dreams
300QXM4096 • $17

5526.

Tea with Teddy
725QXM4046 • $13

1995

5527.

Alice in Wonderland 1: Alice
675QXM4777 • $13

5528.

Baby's First Christmas
475QXM4027 • $13

5529.

Calamity Coyote
675QXM4467 • $11

5530.

Centuries of Santa 2
575QXM4789 • $17

5531.

Christmas Bells 1
475QXM4007 • $35

5532.

Cloisonne Partridge
975QXM4017 • $14

5533.

Coca-Cola® - Cool Santa
($N/E)QXC4457 • $12

5534.
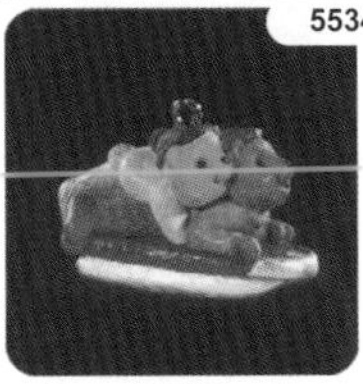
Downhill Double
475QXM4837 • $10

5535.

Friendship Duet
475QXM4019 • $8

5536.

Furrball
575QXM4459 • $10

5537.

A Gift From Rodney
($N/E)QXC4129 • $10

5538.

Grandpa's Gift
575QXM4829 • $11

5539.

Heavenly Praises
575QXM4037 • $10

5540.

Holiday Express Train Base
5000QXM5452 • $90
Re-issued from 1993 & 1994.

5541.

Joyful Santa
475QXM4089 • $10

5542.

Little Beeper
575QXM4469 • $11

5543.

March of the Teddy Bears 3
475QXM4799 • $12

5544.

Miniature Clothespin Soldier 1: British
375QXM4097 • $17

5545.

Miniature Kiddie Car Classics 1: Murray® Champion
575QXM4079 • $15

5546.

Miniature Kiddie Car Classics 1: Murray® Champion
($N/A)QXM4079C • $500
Edition Size - 64.

5547.

Miniature Rocking Horse 8
475QXM4827 • $16

5548.

A Moustershire Christmas
2450QXM4839 • $29 • Set/4

5549.

Nature's Angels 6
475QXM4809 • $14

5550.

The Night Before Christmas 4
475QXM4807 • $20

5551.
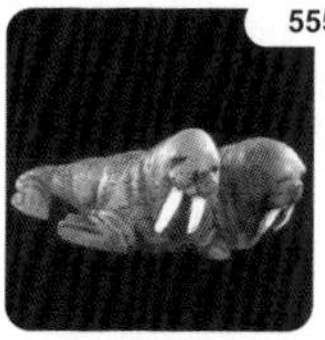
Noah's Ark: Merry Walruses
575QXM4057 • $20

5552.

Noah's Ark: Playful Penguins
575QXM4059 • $34

5553.

Noel RR 7: Milk Tank Car
675QXM4817 • $17

5554.

Nutcracker Guild 2
575QXM4787 • $16

5555.

Old English Village 8: Tudor House
675QXM4819 • $13

5556.

On the Road 3
575QXM4797 • $13

5557.

Pebbles and Bamm-Bamm™ - The Flintstones™
975QXM4757 • $16

5558.
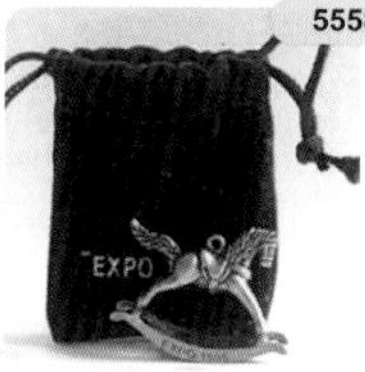

Pewter Rocking Horse
795(N/A) • $44

5559.

Precious Creations
975QXM4077 • $14

5560.

Santa's Club Soda: Cozy Christmas
($N/A)QXC4119 • $17

5561.

Santa's Little Big Top 1
675QXM4779 • $16

5562.

Santa's Visit
775QXM4047 • $12

5563.

Six Mice: Christmas Wishes
375QXM4087 • $14

5564.

Six Mice: Tiny Treasures
2900QXM4009 • $41 • Set/6

5565.

The Ships of Star Trek™
1995QXI4109 • $29 • Set/3

5566.

Starlit Nativity
775QXM4039 • $16

5567.

Sugarplum Dreams
475QXM4099 • $11

5568.

Tunnel of Love
475QXM4029 • $10

1996

5569.

Alice in Wonderland 2: Mad Hatter
675QXM4074 • $17

5570.

Baby Sylvester™
575QXM4154 • $14

5571.

Baby Tweety™
575QXM4014 • $20

5572.

Centuries of Santa 3
575QXM4091 • $20

5573.

A Child's Gifts
675QXM4234 • $10

5574.

Christmas Bear
475QXM4241 • $10

5575.

Christmas Bells 2
475QXM4071 • $20

5576.

Cloisonne Medallion
975QXE4041 • $10

5577.

Coca-Cola® - Cool Delivery
575QXM4021 • $11

5578.

Gold Rocking Horse
1295(N/A) • $60

5579.

Gone with the Wind™
1995QXM4211 • $49 • Set/3

5580.

Hattie Chapeau
475QXM4251 • $8

5581.
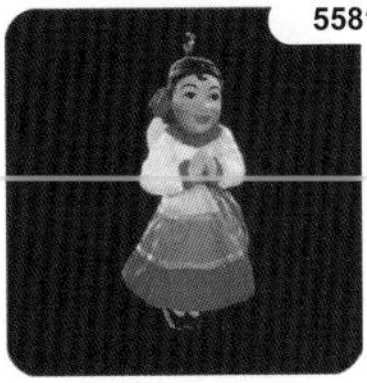
Joyous Angel
475QXM4231 • $10

5582.
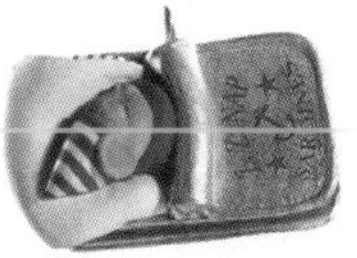
Long Winter's Nap
575QXM4244 • $13

5583.

March of the Teddy Bears 4
475QXM4094 • $12

5584.

Message for Santa
675QXM4254 • $13

5585.

Miniature Clothespin Soldier 2: Early American
475QXM4144 • $13

5586.

Miniature Kiddie Car Classics 2: Murray® Fire Truck
675QXM4031 • $13

5587.

Miniature Kiddie Car Classics 2: Murray® Fire Truck
($N/A)QXM4031C • $500
Edition Size - 256.

5588.
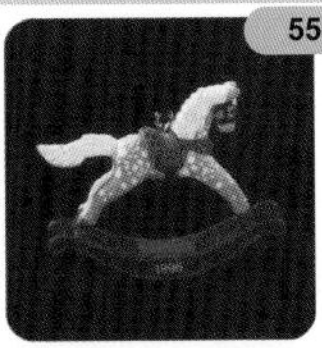
Miniature Rocking Horse 9
475QXM4121 • $17

5589.

Nature's Angels 7
475QXM4111 • $10

5590.
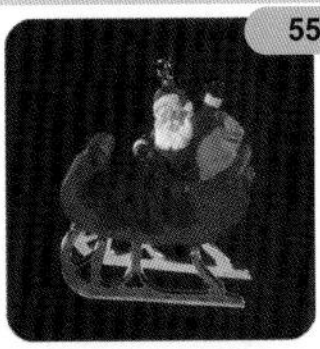
The Night Before Christmas 5
575QXM4104 • $14

5591.

Noah's Ark: African Elephants
575QXM4224 • $28

5592.

Noel RR 8: Cookie Car
675QXM4114 • $20

5593.

Nutcracker Ballet 1: Nutcracker Ballet
1475QXM4064 • $25

5594.

Nutcracker Guild 3
575QXM4084 • $20

5595.

O Holy Night
2450QXM4204 • $32 • Set/4

5596.

Old English Village 9: Village Mill
675QXM4124 • $23

5597.

On the Road 4
575QXM4101 • $13

5598.

Peaceful Christmas
475QXM4214 • $12

5599.

Rudolph's Helper
($N/E)QXC4171 • $10

5600.

Santa's Club Soda: Holiday Bunny
($N/A)QXC4191 • $12

5601.

Santa's Little Big Top 2
675QXM4081 • $17

5602.

Six Mice: Tiny Christmas Helpers
2900QXM4261 • $42 • Set/6

5603.

Sparkling Crystal Angel
975QXM4264 • $18

5604.

A Tree for Woodstock®
575QXM4767 • $17

5605.

The Vehicles of Star Wars™
1995QXM4024 • $42 • Set/3

5606.

Winnie the Pooh and Tigger
975QXM4044 • $20

1997

5607.

Alice in Wonderland 3: White Rabbit
695QXM4142 • $12

5608.

Antique Tractors 1
695QXM4185 • $17

5609.

C-3PO™ and R2-D2™
1295QXI4265 • $31 • Set/2

5610.

Casablanca™
1995QXM4272 • $24 • Set/3

5611.

Centuries of Santa 4
595QXM4295 • $11

5612.

Christmas Bells 3
495QXM4162 • $19

5613.

Coca-Cola® - Ice Cold Coca-Cola®
695QXM4252 • $11

5614.

Future Star
595QXM4232 • $8

5615.

He Is Born
795QXM4235 • $12

5616.

Heavenly Music
595QXM4292 • $8

5617.

Home Sweet Home
595QXM4222 • $11

5618.

Honey of a Gift
695QXD4255 • $13

5619.

Jolly Old Santa
($N/E)QXC5145 • $8

5620.

King of the Forest
2400QXM4262 • $47 • Set/4

5621.

Miniature 1997 Corvette®
695QXI4322 • $8

5622.

Miniature Clothespin Soldier 3: Canadian Mountie
495QXM4155 • $10

5623.
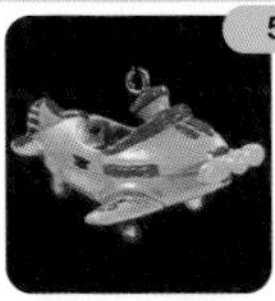
Miniature Kiddie Car Classics 3: Murray® Pursuit Airplane
695QXM4132 • $11

5624.

Miniature Kiddie Car Classics 3: Murray® Pursuit Airplane
($N/A)QXM4132C • $500
Edition Size - 320.

5625.

Miniature Rocking Horse 10
495QXM4302 • $10

5626.

Noah's Ark: Gentle Giraffes
595QXM4221 • $16

5627.

Noel RR 9: Candy Car
695QXM4175 • $13

5628.

Nutcracker Ballet 2: Herr Drosselmeyer
595QXM4135 • $13

5629.

Nutcracker Guild 4
695QXM4165 • $12

5630.

Old English Village 10: Village Depot
695QXM4182 • $11

5631.

On the Road 5
595QXM4172 • $10

5632.

Our Lady of Guadalupe
895QXM4275 • $9

5633.

Peppermint Painter
495QXM4312 • $10

5634.

Polar Buddies
495QXM4332 • $10

5635.

Ready for Santa
($N/E)QXC5142 • $7

5636.

Santa's Little Big Top 3
695QXM4152 • $13

5637.

Seeds of Joy
695QXM4242 • $10

5638.

Sew Talented
595QXM4195 • $11

5639.

Shutterbug
595QXM4212 • $10

5640.

Six Mice: Tiny Home Improvers
2900QXM4282 • $46 • Set/6

5641.

Snowboard Bunny
495QXM4315 • $7

5642.

Snowflake Ballet 1
595QXM4192 • $17

5643.

Teddy-Bear Style 1
595QXM4215 • $11

5644.

Victorian Skater
595QXM4305 • $8

5645.

Welcome Friends 1
695QXM4205 • $14

1998

5646.

Alice in Wonderland 4: Cheshire Cat
695QXM4186 • $13

5647.

Angel Chime
895QXM4283 • $16

5648.

Antique Tractors 2
695QXM4166 • $20

5649.

Betsey's Prayer
495QXM4263 • $7

5650.

Centuries of Santa 5
595QXM4206 • $17

5651.

Christmas Bells 4
495QXM4196 • $12

5652.

Coca-Cola® Time
695QXM4296 • $14

5653.

Ewoks™
1695QXI4223 • $25 • Set/3

5654.

Fishy Surprise
695QXM4276 • $12

5655.

Glinda and the Wicked Witch of the West™
1495QXM4233 • $30 • Set/2

5656.

Holly-Jolly Jig
695QXM4266 • $12

5657.

Kansas City Angel
($N/A)QXC4526 • $195

5658.

Kringle Bells
($N/E)QXC4486 • $10

5659.

Miniature Clothespin Soldier 4: Scottish Highlander
495QXM4193 • $13

5660.

Miniature Kiddie Car Classics 4: Murray® Dump Truck
695QXM4183 • $12

5661.

Miniature Kiddie Car Luxury Edition 1: 1937 Steelcraft Auburn
695QXM4143 • $11

5662.

The Nativity 1
995QXM4156 • $33

5663.

Noah's Ark: Peaceful Pandas
595QXM4253 • $14

5664.

Noel RR 10: Caboose
695QXM4216 • $16

5665.

Noel RR Locomotive 1989 - 1998
1095QXM4286 • $19

5666.

Nutcracker Ballet 3: Nutcracker
595QXM4146 • $14

5667.

Nutcracker Guild 5
695QXM4203 • $16

5668.

On the Road 6
595QXM4213 • $12

5669.

Pixie Parachute
495QXM4256 • $12

5670.

Sharing Joy
495QXM4273 • $13

5671.

Singin' in the Rain™
1095QXM4303 • $16 • Set/2

5672.

Snowflake Ballet 2
595QXM4173 • $20

5673.

Superman™
1095QXM4313 • $20

5674.

Teddy-Bear Style 2
595QXM4176 • $12

5675.

Tree Trimmin' Time
1995QXD4236 • $30 • Set/3

5676.

Welcome Friends 2
695QXM4153 • $20

5677.

Winter Fun with Snoopy® 1
695QXM4243 • $28

1999

5678.

Antique Tractors 3
695QXM4567 • $16

5679.

Betsey's Perfect 10
495QXM4609 • $8

5680.

Celestial Kitty
695QXM4639 • $13

5681.

Centuries of Santa 6
595QXM4589 • $12

5682.

Christmas Bells 5
495QXM4489 • $12

5683.

Classic Batman™ and Robin™
1295QXM4659 • $28 • Set/2

5684.

Crystal Claus
995QXM4637 • $16

5685.

Girl Talk
1295QXD4069 • $19 • Set/2

5686.

Gold Locomotive
1095(N/A) • $31

5687.

Holiday Flurries 1
695QXM4547 • $15

5688.
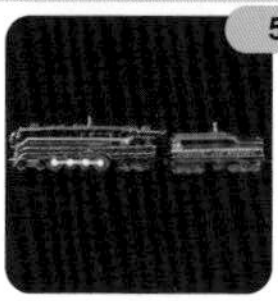
LIONEL® Norfolk and Western 1: Locomotive and Tender
1095QXM4549 • $25 • Set/2

5689.

Love to Share
695QXM4557 • $11

5690.

Marvin the Martian™
895QXM4657 • $14

5691.

Max Rebo Band™
1995QXI4597 • $26 • Set/3

5692.

Merry Grinch-mas
1995QXI4627 • $26 • Set/3

5693.

Miniature Clothespin Soldier 5: French Officer
495QXM4579 • $10

5694.

Miniature Kiddie Car Classics 5: Murray® Tractor and Trailer
695QXM4479 • $12

5695.

Miniature Kiddie Car Luxury Edition 2: 1937 Steelcraft Airflow
995QXM4477 • $12

5696.

Miniature Harley-Davidson® Motorcycles 1
795QXI6137 • $20

5697.

The Nativity 2
995QXM4497 • $22

5698.

Noah's Ark: Trusty Reindeer
595QXM4617 • $12

5699.

Nutcracker Ballet 4: Mouse King
595QXM4487 • $12

5700.

Nutcracker Guild 6
695QXM4587 • $12

5701.

Roll-A-Bear
695QXM4629 • $10

5702.

Santa Time
795QXM4647 • $13

5703.

Seaside Scenes 1
795QXM4649 • $14

5704.

Skating with Pooh
695QXD4127 • $12

5705.

Snowflake Ballet 3
595QXM4569 • $12

5706.

Snowy Surprise
($N/E)QXC4529 • $10

5707.

Taz™ and the She-Devil
895QXM4619 • $13

5708.

Teddy-Bear Style 3
595QXM4499 • $12

5709.

Travel Case and BARBIE™ Ornament
1295QXI6129 • $22 • Set/2

5710.
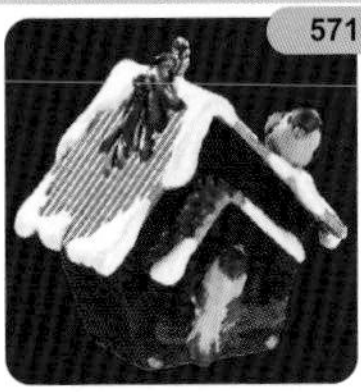
Welcome Friends 3
695QXM4577 • $12

5711.

Winter Fun with Snoopy® 2
695QXM4559 • $38

5712.

Wonders of Oz™ 1: Dorothy's Ruby Slippers™
595QXM4599 • $84

2000

5713.

Antique Tractors 4
695QXM5994 • $20

5714.

Bugs Bunny™ and Elmer Fudd™
995QXM5934 • $12

5715.

Catwoman™
995QXM6021 • $11

5716.

Celestial Bunny
695QXM6641 • $10

5717.

Christmas Bells 6
495QXM5964 • $23

5718.

Christmas Bells 6
($N/A)QXM5964C • $52

5719.

Devoted Donkey
695QXM6044 • $12

5720.

A Friend Chimes In
($N/E)QXC4491 • $17

5721.

Green Eggs and Ham™ - Dr. Seuss®
1995QXM6034 • $29 • Set/3

5722.

Holiday Flurries 2
695QXM5311 • $17

5723.

Ice Block Buddies 1
595QXM6011 • $9

5724.

Jedi™ Council Members
1995QXI6744 • $26 • Set/3

5725.

LIONEL® Norfolk and Western 2: Horse Car and Milk Car
1295QXM5971 • $18 • Set/2

5726.

Little Frosty Friends: Husky
($N/E)XPT1995 • $10

5727.

Loyal Elephant
695QXM6041 • $13

5728.

Mickey and Minnie Mouse
1295QXD4041 • $19 • Set/2

5729.

Miniature Clothespin Soldier 6: Sailor
495QXM5334 • $13

5730.

Miniature Kiddie Car Classics 6: 1968 Jolly Roger Flagship
695QXM5944 • $12

5731.

Miniature Kiddie Car Luxury Edition 3: 1935 Steelcraft by Murray®
695QXM5951 • $13

5732.

Miniature Harley-Davidson® Motorcycles 2
795QXI6001 • $17

5733.

Monopoly™: Advance to Go 1: Sack of Money
895QXM5341 • $12

5734.

Mr. Potato Head®
595QXM6014 • $13

5735.

The Nativity 3
695QXM5961 • $16

5736.

Noah's Ark: Kindly Lions
595QXM5314 • $12

5737.

Nutcracker Ballet 5: Sugarplum Fairy
595QXM5984 • $32

5738.

Nutcracker Guild 7
695QXM5991 • $12

5739.

Precious Penguin
995QXM6104 • $16

5740.

Santa's Journey Begins
995QXM6004 • $14

5741.

Seaside Scenes 2
795QXM5974 • $13

5742.

Silken Flame BARBIE™ Ornament and Travel Case
1295QXM6031 • $20 • Set/2

5743.

Star Fairy
495QXM6101 • $20

5744.

Teddy-Bear Style 4
595QXM5954 • $10

5745.

Welcoming Angel
595QXM5321 • $17

5746.

Winnie the Pooh: Tigger-ific Tidings to Pooh
895QXD4014 • $14

5747.

Winter Fun with Snoopy® 3
695QXM5324 • $17

5748.

Wonders of Oz™ 2: The Tin Man's Heart™
595QXM5981 • $10

2001

5749.

Antique Tractors 5
695QXM5252 • $16

5750.

Antique Tractors 5
($N/E)QXM5252C • $38

5751.

Battle of Naboo™
1495QXM5212 • $26 • Set/3

5752.
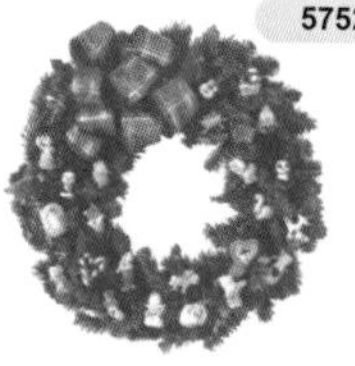
Celebration Wreath
6500QXC4572 • $127

5753.

Christmas Bells 7
495QXM5245 • $10

5754.

Christmas Bells 7
($N/A)QXM5245C • $35
Edition Size - 15000.

5755.

Cooking for Christmas: Sweet Contribution
495QXM4492 • $13

5756.

Cooking for Christmas: Sweet Contribution
($N/A)QXM4492C • $50
Edition Size - 5000.

5757.

Dashing Through the Snow
695QXM5335 • $10

5758.

Disney Birthday Bash - Fantasia
1495QXD4205 • $20 • Set/6

5759.

Gearing Up For Christmas
695QXM5352 • $8

5760.

The Glass Slipper - Cinderella
795QXD4182 • $13

5761.

Holiday Flurries 3
695QXM5272 • $12

5762.

Holiday Shoe
495QXM5365 • $7

5763.

Ice Block Buddies 2
595QXM5295 • $16

5764.

Jiminy Cricket - Pinocchio
795QXD4185 • $12

5765.

LIONEL® Norfolk and Western 3: Car Carrier and Caboose
1295QXM5265 • $24 • Set/2

5766.

Miniature Kiddie Car Classics 7: 1924 Toledo Fire Engine #6
695QXM5192 • $34

5767.

Miniature Kiddie Car Luxury Edition 4: 1937 Garton Ford®
695QXM5195 • $14

5768.

Miniature Rocking Horse
($N/A)QXC4592 • $10

5769.

Miniature Sky's the Limit 1: The Flight at Kitty Hawk
695QXM5215 • $22

5770.

Miniature Harley-Davidson® Motorcycles 3
795QXI5282 • $18

5771.

Monopoly™: Advance to Go 2: Race Car
895QXM5292 • $13

5772.

The Nativity 4
995QXM5255 • $17

5773.

Noah's Ark: Bouncy Kangaroos
595QXM5332 • $11

5774.

Radiant Christmas
795QXM5342 • $11

5775.

Ready for a Ride
695QXM5302 • $16

5776.

Santa-in-a-Box
695QXM5355 • $10

5777.

Scooby-Doo™
695QXM5322 • $12

5778.

Seaside Scenes 3
795QXM5275 • $12

5779.

Solo in the Spotlight Case and BARBIE™ Ornament
1295QXM5312 • $19 • Set/2

5780.

Starfleet™ Legends
1495QXM5325 • $34 • Set/3

5781.

Sweet Slipper Dream
495QXM5345 • $11

5782.

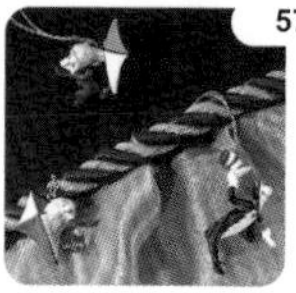

Thing One and Thing Two!™ - The Cat in the Hat™
1495QXM5315 • $22 • Set/3

5783.

Tweety™
695QXM5305 • $11

5784.

Winter Fun with Snoopy® 4
695QXM5262 • $16

5785.

Wonders of Oz™ 3: Toto™
595QXM5285 • $19

2002

5786.

Angel in Training
695QXM4403 • $17

5787.

Antique Tractors 6
695QXM4336 • $16

5788.

Antique Tractors 6
($N/A)QXM4336C • $35

5789.

Christmas Angel Display
1695QXM4573 • $26

5790.

Christmas Bells 8
495QXM4326 • $17

5791.

Enchanted Evening Case and BARBIE™ Ornament
1295QXM4383 • $26 • Set/2

5792.

Gift For Gardening
495QXM4463 • $15

5793.

Gifts of the Season
2800QXM4576 • $53 • Set/6

5794.

Ice Block Buddies 3
495QXM4356 • $17

5795.

Jingle Belle
595QXM4483 • $16

5796.

Lighted Display Tree
1495QXM4536 • $26
Re-issued in 2003.

5797.

Miniature Kiddie Car Classics 8: 1930 Custom Biplane
695QXM4333 • $17

5798.

Miniature Kiddie Car Classics 8: 1930 Custom Biplane
($N/A)QXM4333C • $35

5799.

Miniature Sky's the Limit 2: 1917 Curtiss JN-4D "Jenny"
695QXM4363 • $14

5800.

Miniature Harley-Davidson® Motorcycles 4
795QXI4346 • $20

5801.
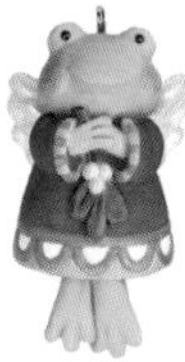
Mistletoad
495QXM4563 • $17

5802.

Monopoly™: Advance to Go 3: Locomotive
895QXM4353 • $22

5803.

Paintbox Pixies 1: Dream
695QXM4543 • $12 • Set/2

5804.

Raggedy Ann and Andy®
995QXM4496 • $17 • Set/2

5805.

Santa Jumping Jack
595QXM4473 • $23

5806.

Santa's Big Night: Five Tiny Favorites
($N/E)QXM4566 • $20 • Set/5

5807.

Snow Cozy 1
495QXM4546 • $17

5808.

Steam Locomotive & Tender - LIONEL®, The General
1295QXM4366 • $26 • Set/2

5809.

Sugar Plum Fairies
1495QXM4513 • $27 • Set/6

5810.

Sugar Plum Tabletop Topiary
1995QXM4506 • $36

5811.

Tin Man™
695QXM4556 • $11

5812.

Two Tiny Penguins
995QXM4413 • $18 • Set/3

5813.

Up to the Tweetop - Tweety™
595QXM4396 • $26

5814.

Winnie the Pooh: On the Slopes
695QXD4553 • $12

5815.

Winter Fun with Snoopy® 5
695QXM4343 • $17

5816.

Winter's Here!
695QXM4423 • $14

2003

5817.
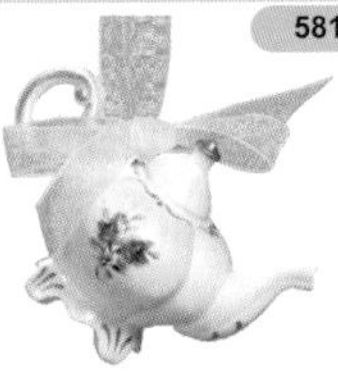
Afternoon Tea 1
695QXM4937 • $28

5818.

Antique Tractors 7
695QXM4889 • $16

5819.

Antique Tractors 7
695QXM4889C • $34

5820.

Bunny Skates - Maxine
595QXM4957 • $10

5821.

Charming Hearts 1
995QXM4939 • $13

5822.
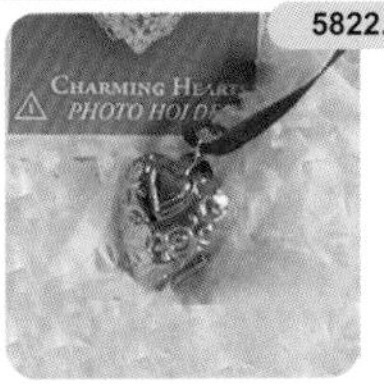
Charming Hearts 1
($N/A)QXM4939C • $49

5823.

Christmas Bells 9
495QXM4927 • $10

5824.

The Christmas Pageant
995QXM4406 • $17 • Set/3

5825.

Clever Cardinal
695QXM5019 • $12

5826.

Clone Troopers™
995QXM5127 • $19 • Set/2

5827.

The Cowardly Lion™
695QXM4219 • $11

5828.

Here Comes Santa
1495QXM4929 • $25 • Set/3

5829.

Ice Block Buddies 4
495QXM4899 • $12

5830.

Join the Caravan! - Corvette® 50th Anniversary
3000QXM4977 • $32 • Set/5

5831.

Jolly Li'l Santa
495QXM4433 • $10

5832.

Joy to the Birds! - Woodstock®
595QXM4967 • $11

5833.
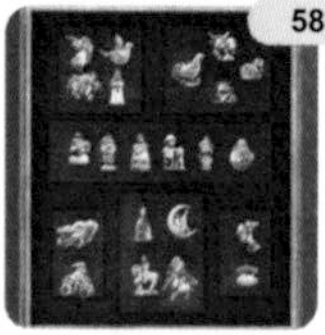
Keepsake Ornament Gallery Collection
7500QXC4609 • $109

5834.

Kitchen Angels
995QXM5029 • $22 • Set/3

5835.

Kitchen Angels Spoon Tree
1995QXM5027 • $29 • Set/6

5836.

Kitty Catch
495QXM4997 • $12

5837.

Lawn Patrol
595QXM4979 • $12

5838.

Lighted Display Tree
1495QXM4536 • $26
Re-issued from 2002.

5839.

Merrier by the Dozen
1495QXM5049 • $23 • Set/12

5840.

Miniature Kiddie Car Classics 9: Jingle Bell Express
695QXM4867 • $12

5841.

Miniature Ornament Display Window
1495QXC4687 • $28

5842.

Miniature Sky's the Limit 3: Curtiss R3C-2 Racer
695QXM4877 • $14

5843.

Miniature Sky's the Limit 3: Curtiss R3C-2 Racer
($N/A)QXM4877C • $35

5844.

Miniature Harley-Davidson® Motorcycles 5
795QXM4879 • $16

5845.

Mouse-Warming Gift
695QXM4999 • $12 • Set/3

5846.

Paintbox Pixies 2: Believe
695QXM4919 • $12 • Set/2

5847.

Puppies on the Doorstep
695QXM4989 • $14

5848.

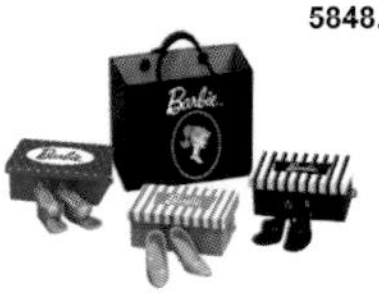

Shopping for Shoes BARBIE™
1495QXM4949 • $20 • Set/7

5849.

Snow Cozy 2
495QXM4917 • $16

5850.

Snow Cozy 2
($N/E)QXM4917C • $32

5851.

The Snowmen of Mitford
1295QXM4959 • $22 • Set/3

5852.

Steam Locomotive and Tender - LIONEL® Blue Comet
1295QXM4887 • $20 • Set/2

5853.

A Sweet for Tweety™
595QXM5057 • $10

5854.

Symbols of Christmas
1995QXC4597 • $34 • Set/6

5855.

Tinker Bell - Peter Pan
695QXM5097 • $15

5856.

'Tis the Season!
1495QXM5047 • $20
Re-issued in 2004.

5857.

Winnie the Pooh: Ring-a-ling Pals
1295QXM5077 • $15 • Set/3

5858.

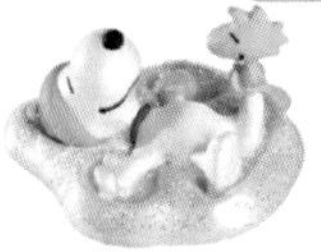

Winter Fun with Snoopy® 6
695QXM4869 • $12

2004

5859.

Adding the Right Touch BARBIE™ Ornaments
1495QXM5214 • $25 • Set/9

5860.

Afternoon Tea 2
695QXM5171 • $13

5861.

Antique Tractors 8
695QXM5154 • $13

5862.

Candy Cane Trio - Winnie the Pooh & Friends
1295QXM5114 • $19 • Set/3

5863.

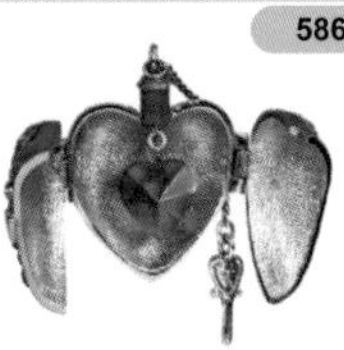

Charming Hearts 2
995QXM5194 • $14

5864.

Charming Hearts 2
($N/E)QXM5194C • $40

5865.

Christmas Bells 10
495QXM5134 • $13

5866.

Classic Red Riding Hood
795QXM5201 • $13

5867.

Cookies, Anyone?
695WD3037 • $13

5868.

Display Tree
1695QXM5254 • $30

5869.

Forever Friends 1: Santa Wanna-Be
595QXM5151 • $12

5870.

Holiday Bouquet
1995QXM5244 • $30 • Set/5

5871.

Ice Block Buddies 5
495QXM5141 • $13

5872.

Just for Santa
695WD3036 • $13

5873.

Let It Snow, Man!
695QXM5234 • $15

5874.

Miniature Fire Brigade 1: 1929 Chevrolet® Fire Engine
995QXM5164 • $15

5875.

Miniature Kiddie Car Classics 10: 1949 Gillham™ Sport Miniature
695QXM5161 • $13

5876.

Miniature Sky's the Limit 4: Spirit of St. Louis
695QXM5181 • $13

5877.

Miniature Harley-Davidson® Motorcycles 6
795QXM5191 • $13

5878.

Paintbox Pixies 3: Wish
695QXM5174 • $12 • Set/2

5879.

Pinocchio Marionette
795QXM5121 • $12

5880.

Prince Charming
595QXM5224 • $12

5881.

Purr-Fectly Contented
995QXM5241 • $19 • Set/3

5882.

Putting On The Glitz - Tweety™
995QXM5111 • $16

5883.

Santa's Balloon Tree
595QXM5221 • $11

5884.

Scarecrow™
695QXM5091 • $12

5885.

Snow Cozy 3
495QXM5144 • $11

5886.

Star Trek™ Insignias
1295QXM5211 • $20 • Set/3

5887.

Star-Spangled Banner
895QXM5204 • $13

5888.

Steam Locomotive and Tender
1295QXM5131 • $24 • Set/2

5889.

Sweeter By The Dozen
1495QXM5274 • $23 • Set/12

5890.

'Tis the Season!
1495QXM5047 • $20
Re-issued from 2003.

5891.

Welcome Sound - Mickey Mouse
595QXM5231 • $12

5892.

Who Goes There!
595QXM5094 • $10

5893.

Winter Fun with Snoopy® 7
695QXM5184 • $16

2005

5894.

Afternoon Tea 3
695QXM8955

5895.

Amazing No. 53 - Herbie, the Love Bug
695QXM8175

5896.

Angelic Trio
1295QXM8162 • Set/3

5897.

Antique Tractors 9
695QXM8992

5898.

Candy Cane Tweat - Tweety™
695QXM8752

5899.

Charming Hearts 3
995QXM8962

5900.

Christmas Bells 11
495QXM8975

5901.

Christmas Stocking Display
2495QXM8182

5902.

The Conductor's Watch – The Polar Express™
795QXM6472

5903.

Dancing Santa
595QXM8132

5904.

Dorothy - The Wizard of Oz™
695QXM8922

5905.

Forever Friends 2: Love to Shop!
595QXM8935

5906.

Holiday Headliner - Mickey Mouse
995QXM8942

5907.

Ice Block Buddies 6
495QXM8972

5908.

LIONEL® Steam Locomotive and Tender
1295QXM2075 • Set/2

5909.

Lucky Slot Machine
795QXM8135

5910.

Miniature Fire Brigade 2: American LaFrance 700 Series Pumper
995QXM2062

5911.

Miniature Kiddie Car Classics 11: 1935 Timmy Racer
695QXM8985

5912.

Miniature Sky's the Limit 5: GeeBee R-1 Super Sportster®
695QXM2072

5913.

Miniature Harley-Davidson® Motorcycles 7
795QXM2065

5914.

Peace, Hope and Joy - The Gifts of Christmas
1295QXM8172 • Set/3

5915.

Penguin Races
1295QXM8155 • Set/3

5916.
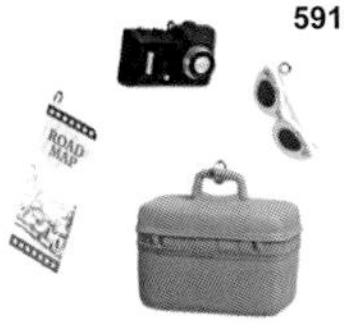

Road Trip BARBIE™ Ornament Set
1495QXM8982 • Set/4

5917.

Rosette Dreams Bride and Groom
1295QXM2082 • Set/2

5918.

The Royal Princesses
1995QXM8952 • Set/4

5919.

Rudolph the Red-Nosed Reindeer®
795QXM8995

5920.

See No Humbug!
1295QXM8152 • Set/3

5921.

Sleepy-Time Mouse
695QXM8145

5922.

Snow Cozy 4
495QXM8965

5923.

TIE Advanced x1™ and Millennium Falcon™
1495QXM2085 • Set/2

5924.

Tiny Ballerina
595QXM8142

5925.
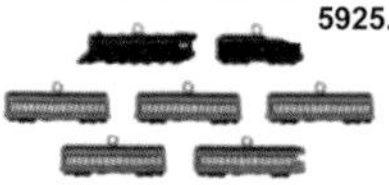
Train Set – The Polar Express™
2400QXM6475 • Set/7

5926.

Winnie the Pooh: Up for Adventure - Winnie the Pooh® and Tigger
1295QXM8945 • Set/2

5927.
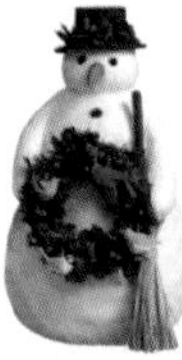
Winter Friends
2800QXM8165 • Set/5

5928.

Winter Fun with Snoopy® 8
695QXM2092

Easter/Spring Ornaments

Designed to brighten your spring, Easter/Spring ornaments are colorful and simply delightful. The Spring Ornament Line, first offered in 1991, offers variety ranging from religious to whimsical; there is something for everyone.

1991

5929.
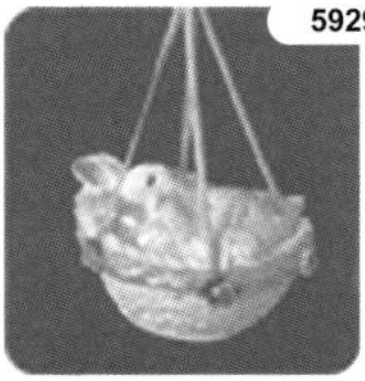
Baby's First Easter
875QEO5189 • $25

5930.

Daughter
575QEO5179 • $30

5931.

Easter Memories
775QEO5137 • $13

5932.
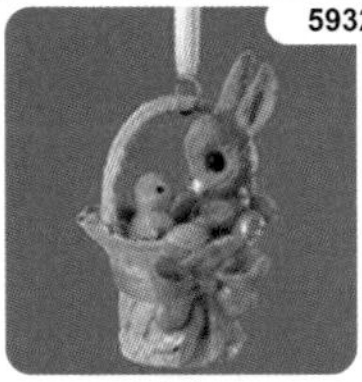
Full Of Love
775QEO5149 • $45

5933.

Gentle Lamb
675QEO5159 • $19

5934.

Grandchild
675QEO5177 • $22

5935.
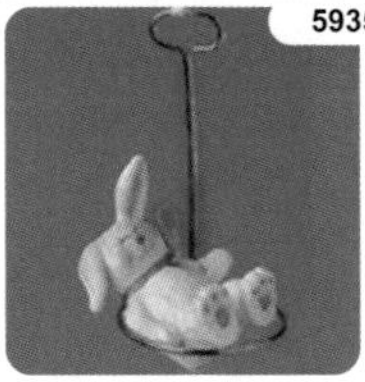
Li'l Dipper
675QEO5147 • $25

5936.

Lily Egg
975QEO5139 • $17

5937.

Son
575QEO5187 • $25

5938.

Spirit Of Easter
775QEO5169 • $29

5939.
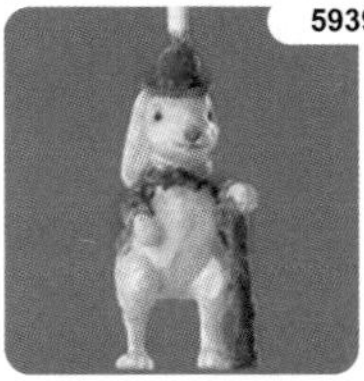
Springtime Stroll
675QEO5167 • $20

1992

5940.

Baby's First Easter
675QEO9271 • $20

5941.

Belle Bunny
975QEO9354 • $32

5942.

Bless You
675QEO9291 • $20

5943.
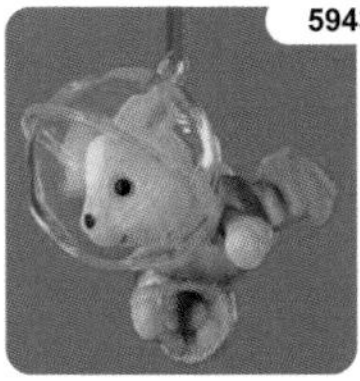
Cosmic Rabbit
775QEO9364 • $19

5944.

Crayola® Bunny
775QEO9304 • $35

5945.

Cultivated Gardener
575QEO9351 • $16

5946.

Daughter
575QEO9284 • $17

5947.
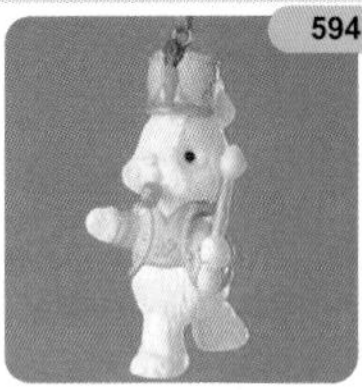
Easter Parade 1
675QEO9301 • $22

5948.

Eggs in Sports 1
675QEO9341 • $30

5949.

Eggspert Painter
675QEO9361 • $22

5950.

Everything's Ducky
675QEO9331 • $22

5951.
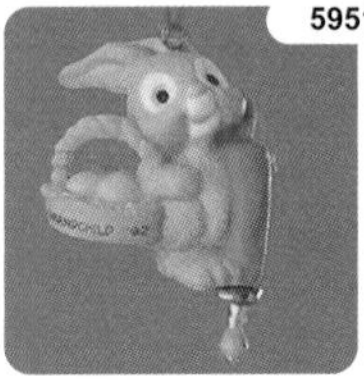
Grandchild
675QEO9274 • $17

5952.
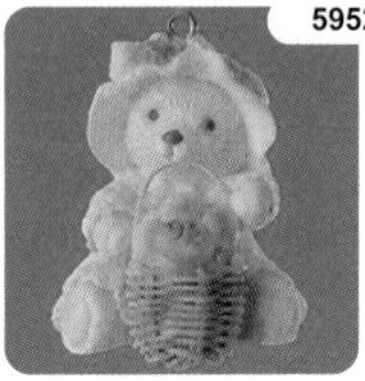
Joy Bearer
875QEO9334 • $22

5953.
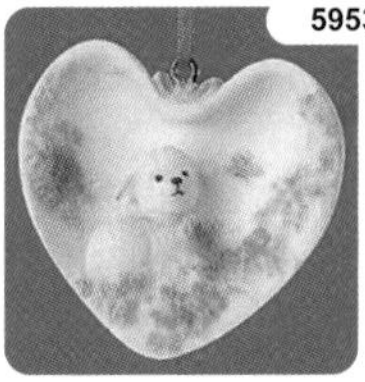
Promise Of Easter
875QEO9314 • $23

5954.
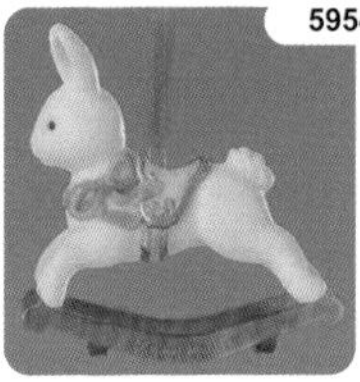
Rocking Bunny
975QEO9324 • $22

5955.

Somebunny Loves You
675QEO9294 • $37

5956.
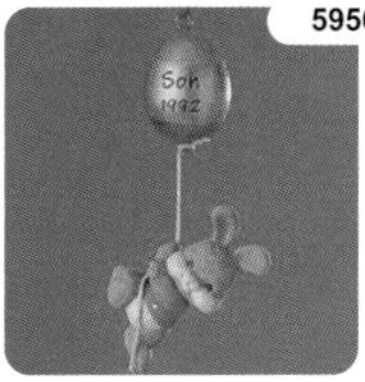
Son
575QEO9281 • $17

5957.
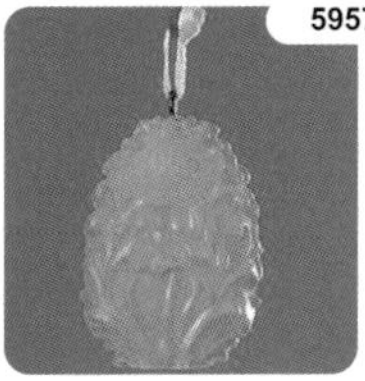
Springtime Egg
875QEO9321 • $20

5958.

Sunny Wisher
575QEO9344 • $17

5959.

Warm Memories
775QEO9311 • $13

1993

5960.
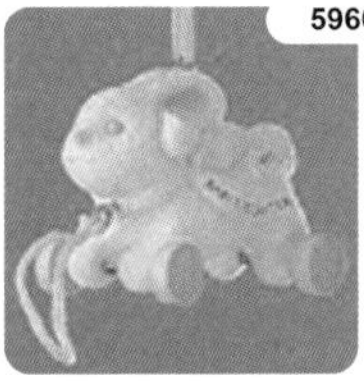
Baby's First Easter
675QEO8345 • $14

5961.
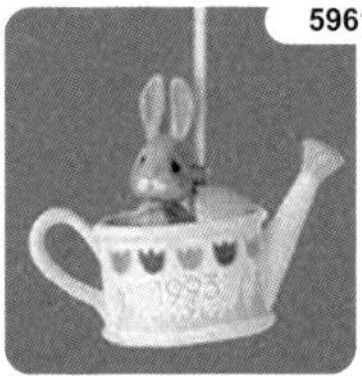
Backyard Bunny
675QEO8405 • $16

5962.

Barrow of Giggles
875QEO8402 • $22

5963.
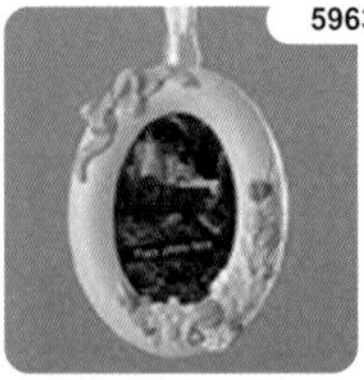
Beautiful Memories
675QEO8362 • $16

5964.
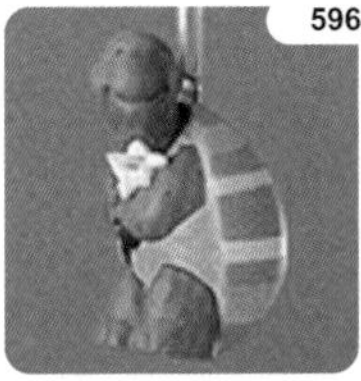
Best-dressed Turtle
575QEO8392 • $18

5965.
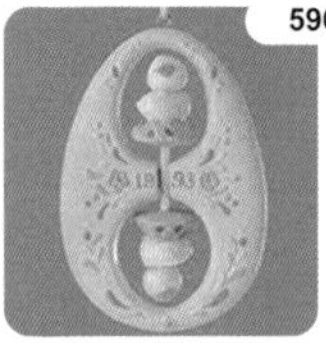
Chicks-on-a-Twirl
775QEO8375 • $14
Twirl-About

5966.

Daughter
575QEO8342 • $16

5967.

Easter Parade 2
675QEO8325 • $18

5968.

Eggs in Sports 2
675QEO8332 • $14

5969.

Grandchild
675QEO8352 • $14

5970.

Li'l Peeper
775QEO8312 • $20

5971.
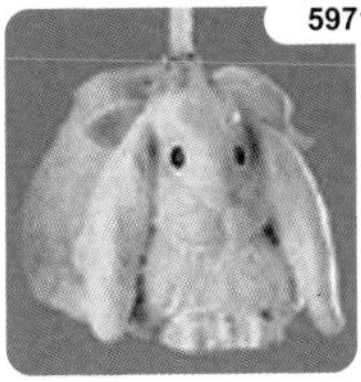
Lop-Eared Bunny
575QEO8315 • $18

5972.

Lovely Lamb
975QEO8372 • $20

5973.

Maypole Stroll
2800QEO8395 • $34 • Set/3

5974.

Nutty Eggs
675QEO8382 • $13

5975.

Radiant Window
775QEO8365 • $13

5976.

Son
575QEO8335 • $16

5977.

Springtime Bonnets 1
775QEO8322 • $25

5978.

Time for Easter
875QEO8385 • $18

1994

5979.

Baby's First Easter
675QEO8153 • $19

5980.
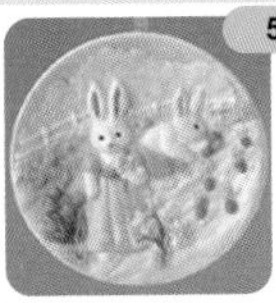
Collector's Plate - Easter 1: Gathering Sunny Memories
775QEO8233 • $28

5981.

Colorful Spring
775QEO8166 • $30

5982.

Daughter
575QEO8156 • $14

5983.

Divine Duet
675QEO8183 • $17

5984.

Easter Art Show
775QEO8193 • $17

5985.

Easter Parade 3
675QEO8136 • $23

5986.

Eggs in Sports 3
675QEO8133 • $17

5987.

First Hello
($N/A)QXC4846 • $40

5988.

Here Comes Easter 1
775QEO8093 • $34

5989.

Joyful Lamb
575QEO8206 • $23

5990.

PEANUTS®
775QEO8176 • $30

5991.

Peeping Out
675QEO8203 • $16

5992.

Riding a Breeze
575QEO8213 • $16

5993.

Son
575QEO8163 • $12

5994.

Springtime Bonnets 2
775QEO8096 • $32

5995.

Sunny Bunny Garden
1500QEO8146 • $31 • Set/3

5996.
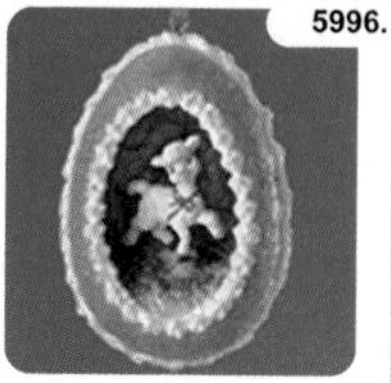
Sweet As Sugar
875QEO8086 • $17

5997.

Tender Touches: Sweet Easter Wishes
875QEO8196 • $26

5998.

Tilling Time
($N/A)QXC8256 • $35

5999.

Treetop Cottage
975QEO8186 • $17

6000.

Yummy Recipe
775QEO8143 • $17

1995

6001.

Apple Blossom Lane 1
895QEO8207 • $18

6002.

April Shower
695QEO8253 • $10

6003.

Baby's First Easter
795QEO8237 • $13

6004.

Bugs Bunny™
895QEO8279 • $16

6005.
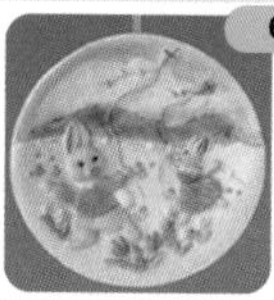
Collector's Plate - Easter 2: Catching the Breeze
795QEO8219 • $14

6006.

Daughter
595QEO8239 • $12

6007.

Easter Beagle
795QEO8257 • $26

6008.

Easter Eggspress
495QEO8269 • $11

6009.

Elegant Lily
695QEO8267 • $8

6010.

Flowerpot Friends
1495QEO8229 • $23 • Set/3

6011.

Garden Club 1
795QEO8209 • $18

6012.

Ham 'n Eggs
795QEO8277 • $11

6013.

Here Comes Easter 2
795QEO8217 • $19

6014.

May Flower
495QXC8246 • $36

6015.

Picture Perfect
795QEO8249 • $16

6016.

Son
595QEO8247 • $15

6017.
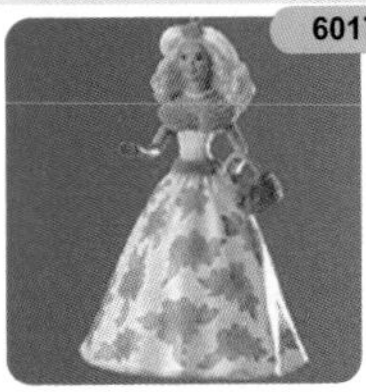
Springtime BARBIE™ 1
1295QEO8069 • $24

6018.

Springtime Bonnets 3
795QEO8227 • $14

6019.

Tender Touches: High Hopes
895QEO8259 • $17

1996

6020.

Apple Blossom Lane 2
895QEO8084 • $13

6021.

Beatrix Potter™ 1: Peter Rabbit
895QEO8071 • $78

6022.
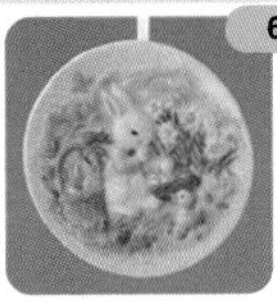
Collector's Plate - Easter 3: Keeping a Secret
795QEO8221 • $14

6023.

Cottontail Express 1: Locomotive
895QEO8074 • $32

6024.

Daffy Duck™
895QEO8154 • $26

6025.

Easter Morning
795QEO8164 • $14

6026.

Garden Club 2
795QEO8091 • $20

6027.

Here Comes Easter 3
795QEO8094 • $14

6028.
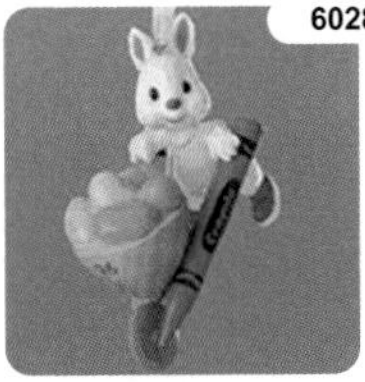
Hippity-Hop Delivery
795QEO8144 • $20

6029.

Joyful Angels 1
995QEO8184 • $23

6030.
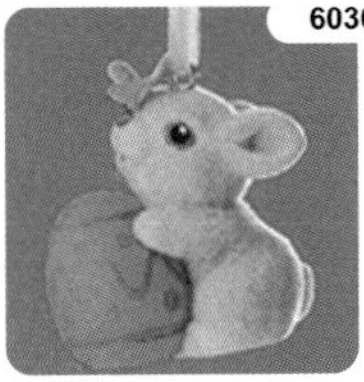
Look What I Found!
795QEO8181 • $22

6031.

Parade Pals
795QEO8151 • $32

6032.

Pork 'n Beans
795QEO8174 • $12

6033.

Springtime BARBIE™ 2
1295QEO8081 • $19

6034.

Springtime Bonnets 4
795QEO8134 • $19

6035.

Strawberry Patch
695QEO8171 • $16

6036.

Strike Up the Band
1495QEO8141 • $20 • Set/3

6037.

Tender Touches: Eggstra Special Surprise
895QEO8161 • $18

1997

6038.

Apple Blossom Lane 3
895QEO8662 • $12

6039.

Beatrix Potter™ 2: Jemima Puddle-duck
895QEO8645 • $18

6040.

Children's Collection 1: BARBIE™ as Rapunzel
1495QEO8635 • $20

6041.

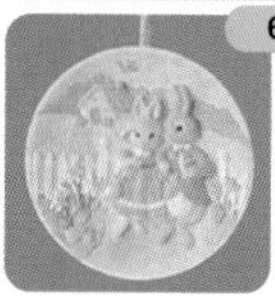

Collector's Plate - Easter 4: Sunny Sunday's Best
795QEO8675 • $14

6042.

Cottontail Express 2: Colorful Coal Car
895QEO8652 • $18

6043.

Digging In
795QEO8712 • $12

6044.

Eggs-pert Artist
895QEO8695 • $17

6045.

Garden Club 3
795QEO8665 • $13

6046.

Gentle Guardian
695QEO8732 • $8

6047.

Here Comes Easter 4
795QEO8682 • $14

6048.

Joyful Angels 2
1095QEO8655 • $20

6049.

Nature's Sketchbook: Garden Bunnies
1495QEO8702 • $23

6050.

A Purr-fect Princess
795QEO8715 • $11

6051.

Sidewalk Cruisers 1: 1935 Steelcraft Streamline Velocipede
1295QEO8632 • $23

6052.

Springtime BARBIE™ 3
1295QEO8642 • $19

6053.

Springtime Bonnets 5
795QEO8672 • $12

6054.

Swing-Time
795QEO8705 • $8

6055.

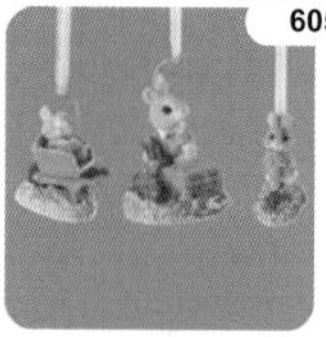

Tender Touches: Bumper Crop
1495QEO8735 • $23 • Set/3

6056.

Tender Touches: Farmer's Market
1500QXC5182 • $22

6057.

Victorian Cross
895QEO8725 • $12

1998

6058.

Bashful Gift
1195QEO8446 • $18 • Set/2

6059.

Beatrix Potter™ 3: Benjamin Bunny
895QEO8383 • $19

6060.

Bouquet of Memories
795QEO8456 • $12

6061.

Children's Collection 2: BARBIE™ as Little Bo Peep
1495QEO8373 • $22

6062.

Cottontail Express 3: Passenger Car
995QEO8376 • $17

6063.

Forever Friends
995QEO8423 • $16

6064.

Garden Club 4
795QEO8426 • $12

6065.

The Garden of Piglet and Pooh
1295QEO8403 • $19 • Set/2

6066.

Going Up? Charlie Brown®
995QEO8433 • $19

6067.

Happy Diploma Day!
795QEO8476 • $13

6068.

Joyful Angels 3
1095QEO8386 • $17

6069.

Midge™ - 35th Anniversary
1495QEO8413 • $20

6070.

Practice Swing - Donald Duck
1095QEO8396 • $16

6071.

Precious Baby
995QEO8463 • $14

6072.

Sidewalk Cruisers 2: 1939 Mobo Horse
1295QEO8393 • $22

6073.

Special Friends
1295QEO8523 • $17

6074.

Star Wars™
1295QEO8406 • $20

6075.

Sweet Birthday
795QEO8473 • $13

6076.

Tigger in the Garden
995QEO8436 • $17

6077.

Victorian Cross
895QEO8453 • $16

6078.

Vintage Roadsters 1: 1931 Ford® Model A Roadster™
1495QEO8416 • $20

6079.

Wedding Memories
995QEO8466 • $14

6080.

What's Your Name?
795QEO8443 • $14

1999

6081.

40th Anniversary Edition - BARBIE™ Lunchbox
1295QEO8399 • $20

6082.

Batter Up! Charlie Brown® and Snoopy®
1295QEO8389 • $22 • Set/2

6083.

Beatrix Potter™ 4: Tom Kitten
895QEO8329 • $14

6084.

Birthday Celebraton
895QEO8409 • $9

6085.

Children's Collection 3: BARBIE™ as Cinderella
1495QEO8327 • $24

6086.

Cottontail Express 4: Flatbed Car
995QEO8387 • $14

6087.

Cross of Faith
1395QEO8467 • $23

6088.

Easter Egg Nest
795QEO8427 • $12

6089.

Easter Egg Surprise 1: Duck
1495QEO8377 • $22

6090.

Fairy Berry Bears 1: Strawberry
1495QEO8369 • $15

6091.

Final Putt, Minnie Mouse
1095QEO8349 • $14

6092.

Friendly Delivery, Mary's Bears
1295QEO8419 • $18

6093.

Happy Bubble Blower
795QEO8437 • $10

6094.

Happy Diploma Day!
1095QEO8357 • $13

6095.

Inspirational Angel
1295QEO8347 • $22

6096.

Mop Top Billy
1495QEO8337 • $29

6097.

Precious Baby
995QEO8417 • $13

6098.

Sidewalk Cruisers 3: 1950 Garton® Delivery Cycle
1295QEO8367 • $24

6099.

Spring Chick
2200QEO8469 • $23

6100.

Springtime Harvest
795QEO8429 • $11

6101.

The Tale of Peter Rabbit - Beatrix Potter™
1995QEO8397 • $28 • Set/3

6102.

Tiggerific Easter Delivery
1095QEO8359 • $14

6103.

Vintage Roadsters 2: 1932 Chevrolet® Sports Roadster
1495QEO8379 • $23

6104.

Wedding Memories
995QEO8407 • $10

6105.

Winner's Circle 1: 1956 Garton® Hot Rod Racer
1395QEO8479 • $20

2000

6106.

Alice in Wonderland
1495QEO8421 • $35

6107.

Ballerina BARBIE™
1295QEO8471 • $32

6108.

Bar and Shield Harley-Davidson®
1395QEO8544 • $35

6109.

Beatrix Potter™ 5: Mr. Jeremy Fisher
895QEO8441 • $17

6110.

Bugs Bunny™
1095QEO8524 • $16

6111.

Cottontail Express 5: Caboose
995QEO8464 • $17

6112.

Easter Egg Surprise 2: Rabbit
1495QEO8461 • $26

6113.

Fairy Berry Bears 2: Blueberry
995QEO8454 • $17

6114.

Frolicking Friends - Bambi®, Thumper, and Flower
1495QEO8434 • $25 • Set/3

6115.

Happy Diploma Day!
1095QEO8431 • $13

6116.

PEANUTS® Lunchbox Set
1495QEO8444 • $26 • Set/2

6117.

Sidewalk Cruisers 4: Hopalong Cassidy Velocipede
1295QEO8411 • $35

6118.
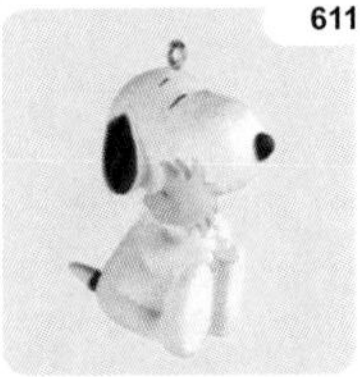
A Snug Hug
995QEO8424 • $28

6119.

Spring is in the Air 1: Eastern Bluebird
995QEO8451 • $28

6120.
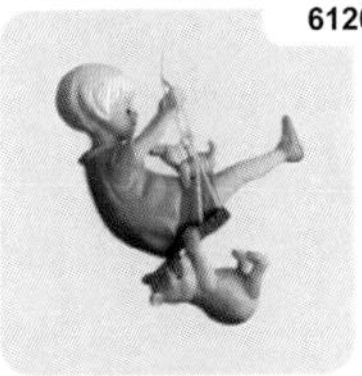
A Swing With Friends
1495QEO8414 • $26

6121.

Time in the Garden
1095QEO8511 • $17

6122.

Vintage Roadsters 3: 1935 Auburn Speedster
1495QEO8401 • $30

6123.

Winner's Circle 2: 1940 Garton® Red Hot Roadster
1395QEO8404 • $22

2001

6124.

Bashful Bunny
595QEO8502 • $10

6125.

Birthday Wishes BARBIE™ 1
1495QEO8575 • $25

6126.

Charming Chick
595QEO8515 • $10

6127.

Easter Egg Surprise 3: Chick
1495QEO8532 • $19

6128.

The Empire Strikes Back™ Lunchbox Set
1495QEO8585 • $24 • Set/2

6129.

Fairy Berry Bears 3: Raspberry
995QEO8565 • $12

6130.

Happy Hopper
595QEO8505 • $10

6131.

Lovely Lamb
595QEO8512 • $10

6132.

Peter Rabbit - Beatrix Potter™
895QEO8545 • $12

6133.

Riding on the Breeze
1095QEO8612 • $18

6134.

Sidewalk Cruisers 5: 1934 Mickey Mouse Velocipede
1295QEO8552 • $30

6135.

Spring is in the Air 2: American Goldfinch
995QEO8535 • $17

6136.

Taz™ Paint Egg!
1095QEO8572 • $16

6137.

Vintage Roadsters 4: 1930 Cadillac®
1495QEO8555 • $28

6138.

Winner's Circle 3: 1960 Eight Ball Racer
1395QEO8562 • $23

2002

6139.

Birthday Wishes BARBIE™ 2
1495QEO8513 • $26

6140.

Peek-a-Boo Egg: Bunny Business
995QEO8546 • $23

6141.
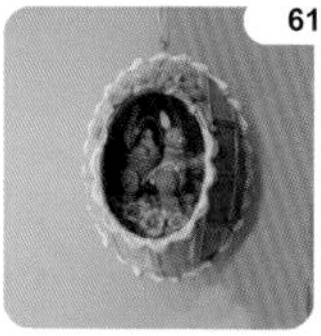
Peek-a-Boo Egg: Easter Egg-spress
995QEO8536 • $26

6142.

Peek-a-Boo Egg: Spring Peepers
995QEO8543 • $23

6143.

Sculpted Bunny Spring Ornament Tree
1495QEO8556 • $28
Re-issued in 2003.

6144.

Shimmering Carrot Trimmers
595QEO8563 • $10 • Set/8
Re-issued in 2003.

6145.

Shimmering Easter Eggs
1495QEO8553 • $19 • Set/4

6146.

Sidewalk Cruisers 6: 1937 Mickey Mouse® Streamline Express Coaster Wagon
1295QEO8516 • $28

6147.

Spring is in the Air 3: American Robin
995QEO8506 • $26

6148.

Vintage Roadsters 5: 1954 Buick® Wildcat II
1495QEO8526 • $36

6149.

Winner's Circle 4: 1941 Garton® Speed Demon
1395QEO8503 • $26

2003

6150.

Birdhouse Row
1295QEO8529 • $17 • Set/4

6151.

Birthday Wishes BARBIE™ 3
1495QEO8549 • $23

6152.
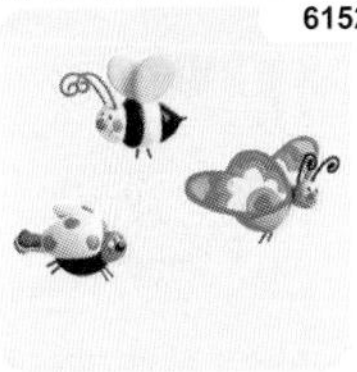
Buzz-A-Dee Bugs
795QEO8537 • $14 • Set/3

6153.

Keepsake Ornament Tree
1495QEO8547 • $22

6154.

Nature's Sketchbook: Around the Home
1295QEO8017 • $26

6155.

Nature's Sketchbook: Outdoor Dining
1295QEO8007 • $24

6156.

Nature's Sketchbook: Place in the Sun
1295QEO8019 • $22

6157.

Nature's Sketchbook: Rippling Dream
1295QEO8009 • $18

6158.

Nature's Sketchbook: Vine Ornament Display
995QEO8027 • $24

6159.
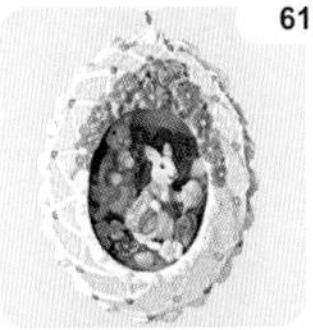
Peek-a-Boo Egg: Egg Hunt Hoppers
895QEO8039 • $18

6160.
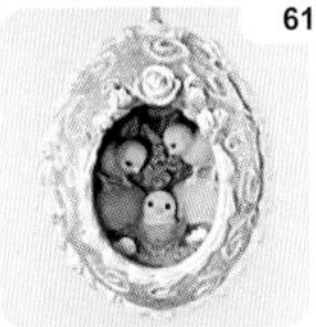
Peek-a-Boo Egg: Peep-a-Boo Chicks
895QEO8037 • $17

6161.

Peek-A-Boo Egg: Wheely Wonderful Easter
895QEO8029 • $18

6162.

Sculpted Bunny Spring Ornament Tree
1495QEO8556 • $28
Re-issued from 2002.

6163.

Shimmering Carrot Trimmers
595QEO8563 • $10 • Set/8
Re-issued from 2002.

6164.

Shimmering Easter Eggs (Pink)
795QEO8047 • $18 • Set/2

6165.

Shimmering Easter Eggs (Purple)
795QEO8049 • $18 • Set/2

6166.

Tweedle Dee Tweedle Deet: Friends of a Feather
995QEO8517 • $12

6167.

Tweedle Dee Tweedle Deet: Look Who's Here!
795QEO8509 • $12

6168.

Tweedle Dee Tweedle Deet: Treetop Duet
795QEO8507 • $14

6169.
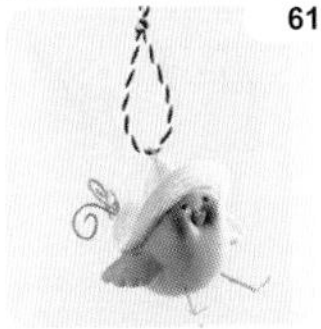
Tweedle Dee Tweedle Deet: Weatherbird
795QEO8519 • $12

2004

6170.
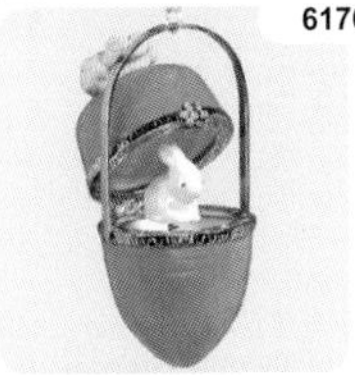
Bunny Found A Carrot
995QEO8574 • $17

6171.

Bunny's Dancing Eggs
795QEO8394 • $17

6172.

Chicky's Bouncing Daisies
795QEO8384 • $17

6173.

Hatched Before Your Eyes
995QEO8571 • $17

6174.

It's the Easter Beagle!
995QEO8361 • $28

6175.
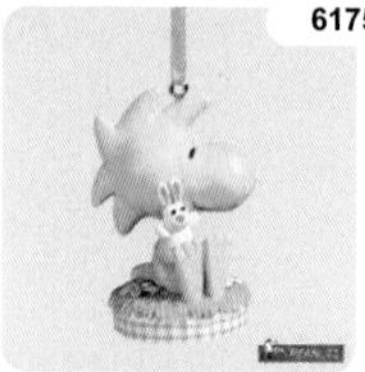
A Little Bunny Hug
995QEO8381 • $20

6176.

Nature's Sketchbook: Chatty Chickadees
1295QEO8311 • $18

6177.

Nature's Sketchbook: Curious Blue Jay
1295QEO8304 • $18

6178.

Nature's Sketchbook: Good Morning Doves
1295QEO8314 • $18

6179.

Nature's Sketchbook: Hide and Seek
1295QEO8324 • $18

6180.

Nature's Sketchbook: Relaxing Robins
1295QEO8321 • $18

6181.

Nature's Sketchbook: Thirsty Cardinal
1295QEO8301 • $18

6182.

A New Friend
995QEO8364 • $20

2005

6183.

Trellis Display
1495QEO8581 • $20
Re-issued in 2005.

6184.

Easter Parade: Brand New Wheels
795QEO8245

6185.

Easter Parade: Bunny Buggy
595QEO8232

6186.

Easter Parade: Here Comes the Band
995QEO8235 • Set/3

6187.

Easter Parade: Very Important Bunny
995QEO8242

6188.

Joyful Garden Set
1295QEO8252 • Set/3

6189.

Nature's Sketchbook: First Bouquet
1295QEO8282

6190.

Nature's Sketchbook: Garden Awakens
1495QEO8285 • Set/3

6191.

Nature's Sketchbook: Nature's Secret Artist
995QEO8272

6192.

Nature's Sketchbook: New Address
1295QEO8275

6193.

Nature's Sketchbook: New Joys
995QEO8265

6194.

Nature's Sketchbook: Spring's Peaceful Promise
995QEO8262

6195.

Springtime Inspirations
995QEO8255

6196.

Trellis Display
1495QEO8581
Re-issued from 2004.

Halloween Ornaments

Halloween is now the number two decorating holiday. The new Hallmark Halloween Line of ornaments and "haunted village" pieces make decorating quick and easy. They are fast becoming spook-tacular family favorites.

2002

6197.
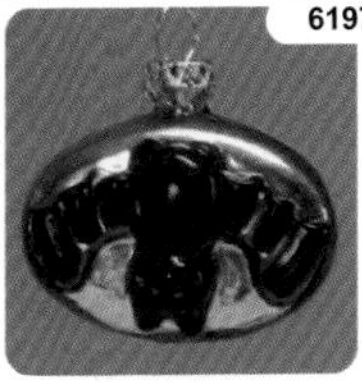
Bat
($N/E)(N/A) • $15

6198.
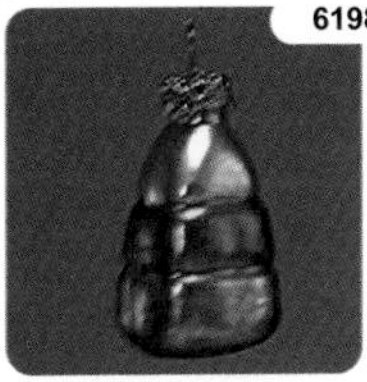
Candy Corn
($N/E)(N/A) • $15

6199.
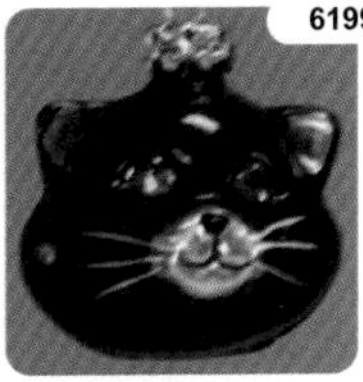
Cat
($N/E)(N/A) • $15

6200.

Ghost
($N/E)(N/A) • $15

6201.

Jack O'Lantern
($N/E)(N/A) • $15

6202.
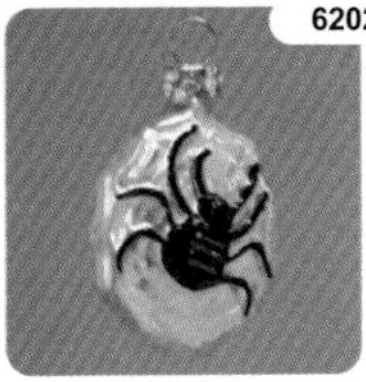
Spider
($N/E)(N/A) • $15

6203.

Witch
($N/E)(N/A) • $15

2003

6204.

1300 Old Oak Road
1295QFO6037 • $32

6205.
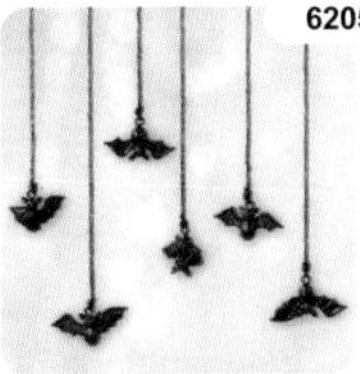
The Acrobats
495QFO6029 • $19 • Set/6

6206.

Mesmerelda
995QFO6039 • $18

6207.
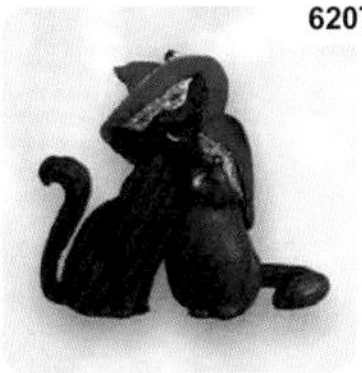
Midnight Serenade
695QFO6047 • $12

6208.
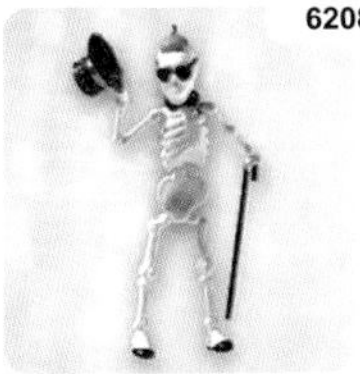
Mr. Tap Happy
695QFO6017 • $19

6209.

Sneakaboo
695QFO6009 • $12

6210.

Stack O'Lanterns
695QFO6049 • $12

6211.

Van Ghoul
695QFO6007 • $13

6212.

Zephyr
695QFO6019 • $12

2004

6213.

Bateson, The Butler
795QFO6054 • $14

6214.

Frederick O'Ghastly and Friends
1295QFO6061 • $19 • Set/3

6215.

Hugo, The Handyman
1295QFO6044 • $19

6216.

The Mansion on Ravenwood Lane
3995QFO6024 • $50

6217.

The Master
1295QFO6031 • $19

6218.

Matilda, The Cook
1295QFO6041 • $19

6219.

Old Ned, The Musician
1295QFO6034 • $19

6220.

Trick or Treat!
995QFO6051 • $16

2005

6221.

Hauntington: Bartholomew Hauntswell
1295QFO6322

6222.

Hauntington: Cass Taspell
795QFO6302

6223.

Hauntington: Deadwood Street Shops
3995QFO6325
MAGIC.

6224.

Hauntington: Grandma Tillie and Willie
1295QFO6335 • Set/2

6225.

Hauntington: Hauntington Town Hall
3995QFO6332
MAGIC.

6226.

Hauntington: Ivana Hacketoff
795QFO6305

6227.

Hauntington: Ms. Bonnie and Bones
1295QFO6342 • Set/2

6228.

Hauntington: Officer Rob Graver
795QFO6315

6229.

Hauntington: Scoops McGore
795QFO6312

6230.

Hauntington: The Old Oak
1495QFO6345

Special Issue Ornaments

Featured for the first time in a Hallmark value guide, these special issue ornaments are both hard-to-find and fun to collect. This section includes Hall Family Card Ornaments, The Ambassador Ornaments, and the Mayors Ornaments. See the editorial on page 14 for more details.

Ambassador Holiday House Collection

6231.

Angel
649QX3H • $75 • 1980

6232.
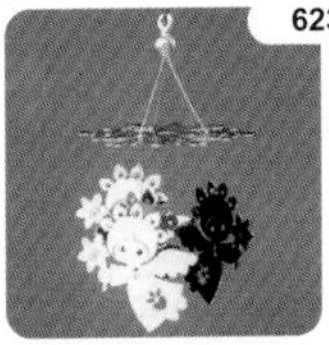
Angel Chimes
549QX23E • $500 • 1981
EXTREMELY RARE

6233.
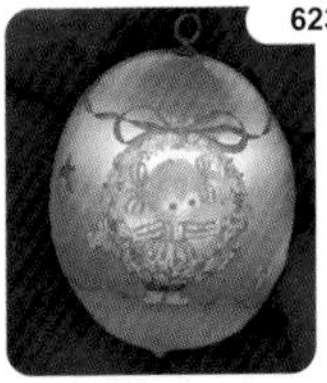
Angel Love
398QX14H • $35 • 1980

6234.
Have You Seen Me?
Angel Love
449QX43E • $35 • 1981

6235.
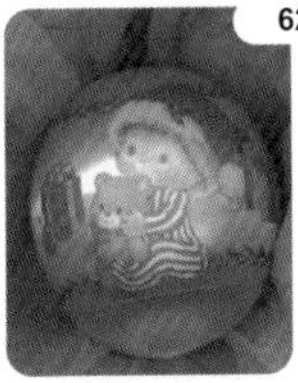
Baby's First Christmas
398QX8H • $45 • 1980

6236.

Baby's First Christmas
449QX38E • $45 • 1981

6237.

Baby's First Christmas
498QX48E • $200 • 1981
VERY RARE

6238.

Baby's First Christmas
($N/E)unknown • $400 • 1982
EXTREMELY RARE

6239.

Beauty of Christmas
398QX15H • $35 • 1980

6240.

Birds of Winter
449QX41E • $45 • 1981

6241.

Carousel Angel #2
649QX45G • $750 • 1979
EXTREMELY RARE

6242.

A Christmas Treat
498QX42G • $200 • 1979
VERY RARE

6243.

Colors of Christmas: Cardinal
449QX33E • $100 • 1981

6244.

Colors of Christmas: Joy
398QX19H • $45 • 1980

6245.

Colors of Christmas: Merry Christmas
449QX34E • $100 • 1981

6246.

Colors of Christmas: Partridge
($N/E)unknown • $100 • 1979
RARE

6247.

Colors of Christmas: Wreath
349QX35G • $100 • 1979
RARE

6248.

Colors of Christmas: Wreath
398QX18H • $45 • 1980

6249.

Disney
449QX37E • $45 • 1981

6250.

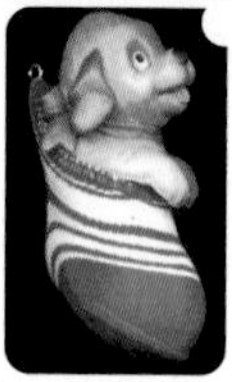

Dog in Stocking
499QX49F • $15 • 1982

6251.

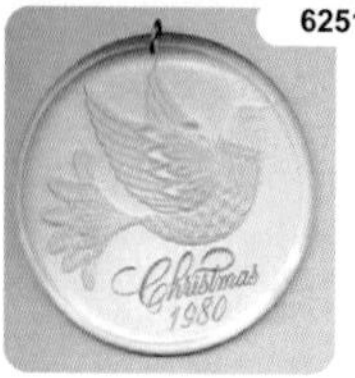

Dove
398QX20H • $45 • 1980

6252.

First Christmas Together
398QX9H • $45 • 1980

6253.

First Christmas Together
449QX45E • $40 • 1981

6254.

Have You Seen Me?

Heaven on Earth
449QX46E • $35 • 1981

6255.

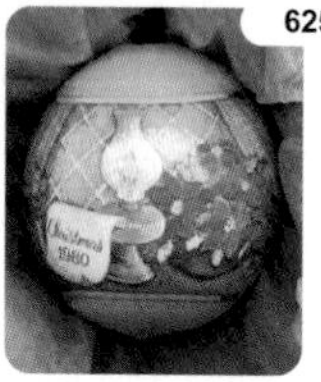

Home
398QX16H • $40 • 1980

6256.

Home
449QX45E • $35 • 1981

6257.

Little Blessing
398QX17H • $35 • 1980

6258.

Little Redbird
398QX4H • $35 • 1980

6259.

Love Heart
498QX32E • $150 • 1981
RARE

6260.

Matchless Christmas
398QX41G • $200 • 1979
VERY RARE

6261.

Mickey Mouse
398QX6H • $50 • 1980

6262.

Mouse and Candlestick
398QX21H • $45 • 1980

6263.

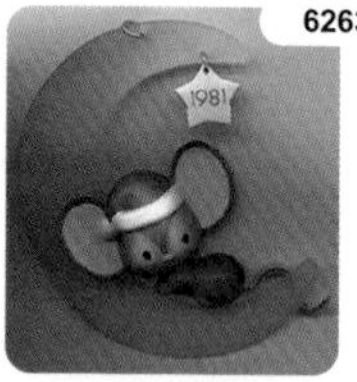

Mouse on Moon
698QX30E • $75 • 1981

6264.

Nativity
498QX31E • $150 • 1981
RARE

6265.

Night Before Christmas
398QX11H • $35 • 1980

6266.

Night Before Christmas
449QX40E • $35 • 1981

6267.

PEANUTS®
398QX10H • $50 • 1980

6268.

PEANUTS®
449QX35E • $50 • 1981

6269.

Pink Panther™
349QX49G • $150 • 1979
VERY RARE

6270.

Have You Seen Me?

Pink Panther™
398QX13H • $100 • 1980
RARE

6271.

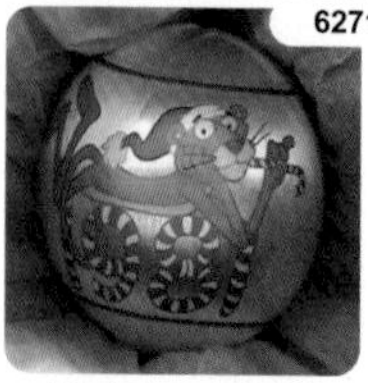

Pink Panther™
449QX36E • $40 • 1981

6272.

Raccoon on Candycane
698QX29E • $300 • 1981
VERY RARE

6273.

Rocking Horse
549QX1H • $75 • 1980

6274.

Santa
398QX2H • $48 • 1980
Re-issued in 1981.

6275.

Santa
498QX2H • $48 • 1981
Re-issued from 1980.

6276.
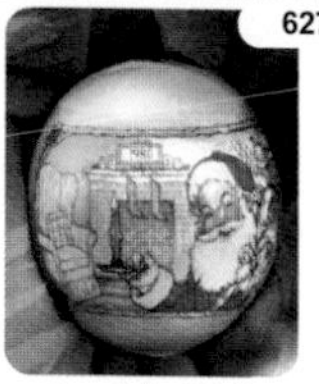
Santa's Visit
398QX12H • $35 • 1980

6277.

Scooby-Doo™
349QX48G • $150 • 1979
VERY RARE

6278.
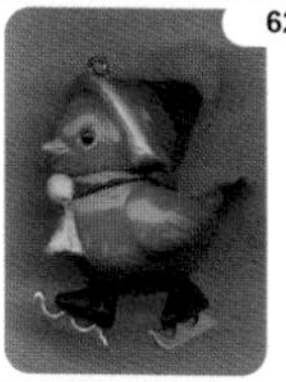
Skating Redbird
498QX26E • $200 • 1981

6279.

Snowflake
349QX37G • $100 • 1979
RARE

6280.

Soldier
498QX25E • $100 • 1981

6281.

Sparrow on Holly Twig
349QX38G • $75 • 1979
RARE

6282.
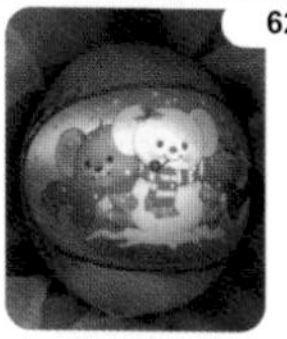
Together Times Friendship
449QX44E • $30 • 1981

6283.

Train
649QX5H • $75 • 1980

6284.
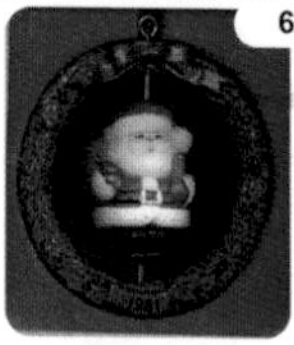
Twirl-About Santa
698QX27E • $175 • 1981
RARE

6285.

White Mouse
449QX47E • $400 • 1981
RARE

6286.
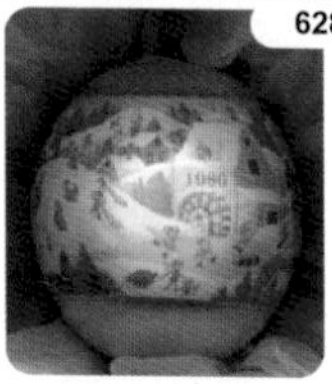
Winter's Gift
398QX7H • $40 • 1980

Hall Family Ornaments

6287.
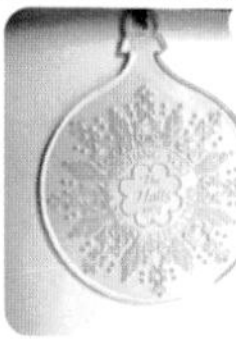
1974 - Acrylic Disc
($N/A)(N/A) • $473
RARE

6288.

1975 - Stained Glass Angel
($N/A)(N/A) • $348
RARE

6289.

1976 - Acrylic Star
($N/A)(N/A) • $348
RARE

6290.

1977 - Acrylic Dove
($N/A)(N/A) • $263

6291.

1978 - Tree & Birds
($N/A)(N/A) • $105

6292.
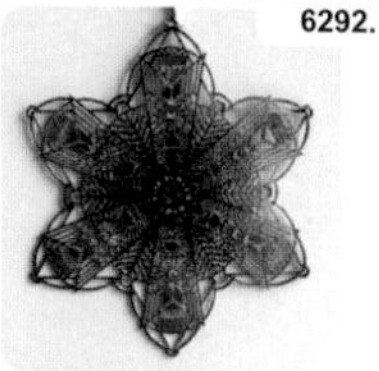
1979 - Snowflake
($N/A)(N/A) • $110

6293.

1980 - Acrylic Bell
($N/A)(N/A) • $103

6294.

1981 - Angel in Blue Star
($N/A)(N/A) • $93

6295.

1982 - Brass Nativity
($N/A)(N/A) • $103

6296.

1983 - Three Kings
($N/A)(N/A) • $63

6297.

1984 - White Bisque Angel
($N/A)(N/A) • $110

6298.

1985 - Mary & Joseph
($N/A)(N/A) • $93

6299.

1986 - Brass Nativity Tree
($N/A)(N/A) • $63

6300.

1987 - Angel with Harp
($N/A)(N/A) • $85

6301.
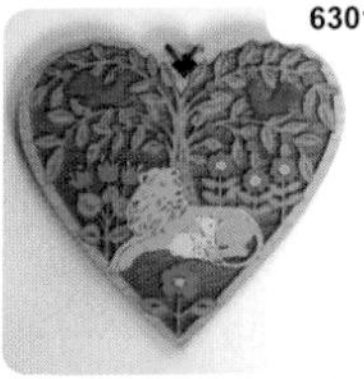
1988 - Lion & Lamb
($N/A)(N/A) • $88

6302.
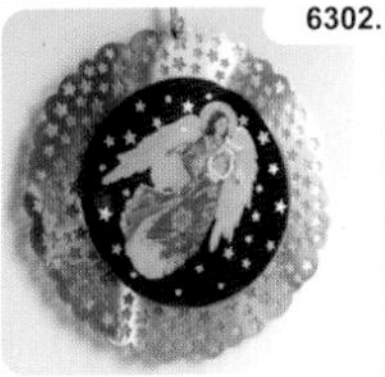
1989 - Silver Angel
($N/A)(N/A) • $80

6303.

1990 - Brass Star with Dove
($N/A)(N/A) • $113

6304.
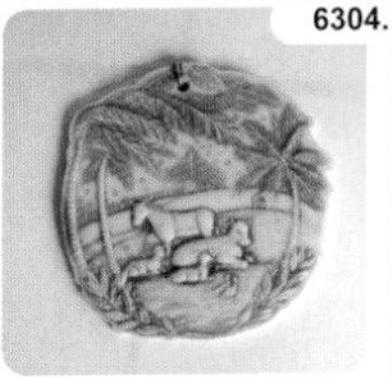
1991 - Nativity
($N/A)(N/A) • $90

6305.

1992 - Madonna & Child
($N/A)(N/A) • $160

6306.

1993 - Mary Hamilton Angel
($N/A)(N/A) • $175

6307.

1994 - Acrylic Poinsettia
($N/A)(N/A) • $93

6308.

1995 - M. Bastin Birdhouse
($N/A)(N/A) • $113

6309.

1996 - Christmas Tree
($N/A)(N/A) • $150

6310.

1997 - Brass Manger
($N/A)(N/A) • $135

6311.

1998 - Laser Cut Wreath
($N/A)(N/A) • $150

6312.

1999 - Tiffany Angel
($N/A)(N/A) • $175

6313.

2000 - Silver Dove
($N/A)(N/A) • $135

6314.

2001 - Magi Scene
($N/A)(N/A) • $135

6315.

2002 - Mary with Lamb
($N/A)(N/A) • $175

6316.
Have You Seen Me?
2003 - Brass Filigree Wreath
($N/A)(N/A) • $135

6317.

2004 - Brass Filigree Stocking
($N/A)(N/A) • $145

Mayor's Tree Ornaments

6318.

1981 - Five Pointed Acrylic Star
($N/E)(N/A) • $195

6319.
Have You Seen Me?
1982 - Triangular Shape Acrylic Tree
($N/E)(N/A) • $295

6320.
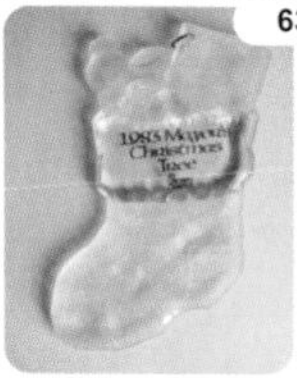

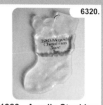

1983 - Acrylic Stocking
($N/E)(N/A) • $295

6321.

1984 - Acrylic Bear
($N/E)(N/A) • $245

6322.

1985 - Acrylic Mug
575(N/A) • $149

6323.
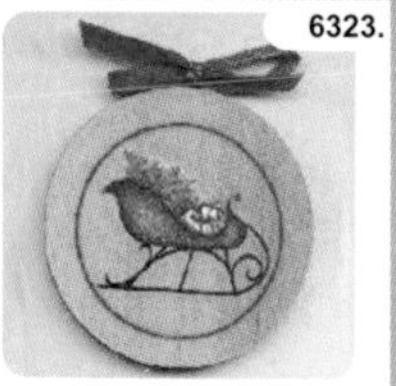

1986 - Wood Sleigh
($N/E)(N/A) • $N/E

6324.
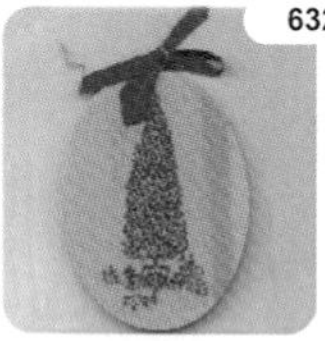

1987 - Oval Tree
($N/E)(N/A) • $500
RARE

6325.
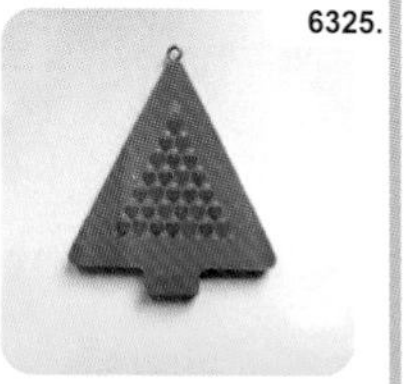

1988 - Triangular Tree
600(N/A) • $59

6326.

1989 - Shaped Tree
750(N/A) • $49

6327.

1990 - Tree on Round Disk
750(N/A) • $59

6328.

1991 - Holiday Pinecone
($N/E)(N/A) • $468
RARE

6329.

1992 - Christmas Wreath
($N/E)(N/A) • $415
RARE

6330.

1993 - Toy Soldier
($N/E)(N/A) • $600
RARE

6331.

1994 - Rocking Horse
1000(N/A) • $300

6332.
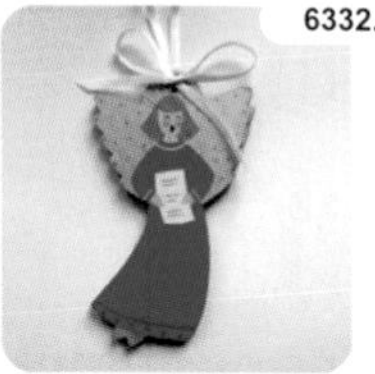

1995 - Caroling Angel
1000(N/A) • $89

6333.

1996 - Locomotive
1200(N/A) • $67

6334.

1997 - Holiday Homestead
1200(N/A) • $313

6335.
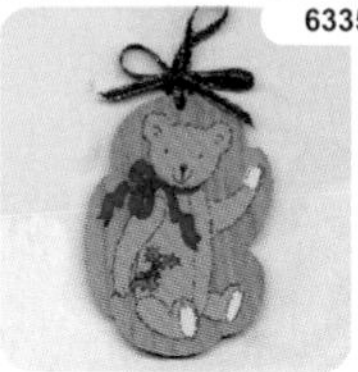

1998 - Teddy Bear
1200(N/A) • $42

6336.

1999 - Snowflake
1200(N/A) • $40

6337.
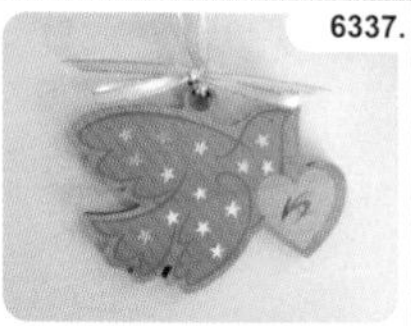

2000 - Dove with Heart
1250(N/A) • $39

6338.

2001 - Glittery Reindeer
1250(N/A) • $38

6339.

2002 - Teddy Bear
($N/E)(N/A) • $35

6340.
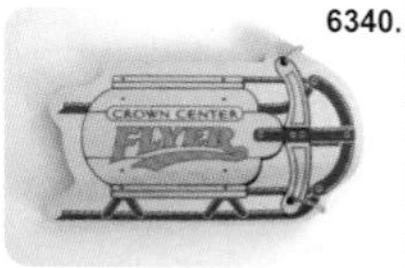

2003 - Nostalgic Sled
($N/E)(N/A) • $39

6341.

2004 - Snowman
($N/E)(N/A) • $30

Tree Toppers

The perfect way to top your Hallmark Ornament tree is with a Hallmark Tree Topper. With many different styles and materials from which to choose, there is one that would be perfect for any style or size tree.

Full Size

6342.
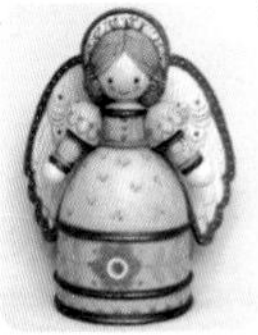
Angel
900HSD2302 • $168
1977

6343.

Angel
2450QTT7101 • $46
Issued 1984 & 1985.

6344.

Angel
($N/E)XXA9155 • $N/E

6345.

Angel Baby
($N/E)unknown • $N/E

6346.

Angel of Light
3000QLT7239 • $48
Issued 1991 & 1992.

6347.

Angel Snowman
($N/E)XBH4315 • $N/E

6348.

Brass Angel
($N/E)unknown • $N/E

6349.

Brass Star
2500QX7054 • $80
1980

6350.

Chris Mouse
($N/E)CA16294 • $N/E
1999

6351.
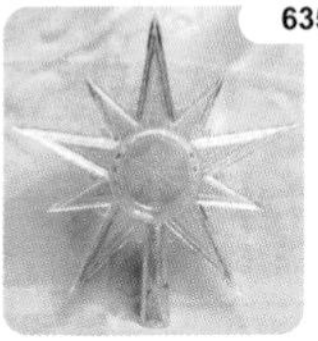
Christmas Star
750QX7023 • $42
1978

6352.

Christmas Star
695XXA9149 • $N/E
1991

6353.

Country Holiday Goose
1400QTT7123 • $35
1986

6354.

Frostlight Faeries: Queen Aurora
3500QP1662 • $56
2001

6355.

Gentle Angel
1400QTT7126 • $28
1987

6356.

Homespun Angel
1600QTT6252 • $N/E
1985

6357.

Maxine
1695ZXS6002 • $N/E
1997

6358.

Mitford Snowman
($N/E)unknown • $N/E
2000

6359.

Santa
1800QTO7006 • $29
1986

6360.

Santa
995XPF4253 • $N/E
1988

6361.

Santa Bear
1600XXA8259 • $N/E
Issued in 1991 & 1992.

6362.

Santa with North Pole
($N/E)XXA4152 • $N/E
1994

6363.

Shining Star
1750QLT7096 • $50
1986

6364.

Snowman
($N/E)XPF3209 • $N/E

6365.

Star
3500XXA7139 • $N/E
Issued 1991 & 1992.

6366.

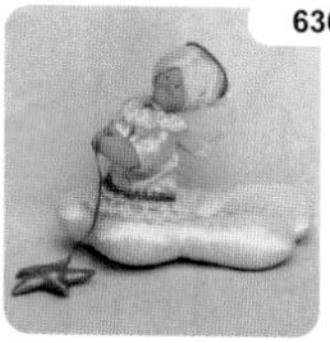

Starry Angel
1700QTT7116 • $24
1986

6367.

Tiffany Angel
1000QX7037 • $40
1979

Miniature

6368.

Beautiful Angel
1295QXM4987 • $18
2003

6369.

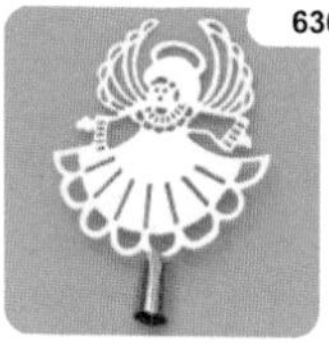

Brass Angel
($N/E)QXM5671 • $N/E
Ultra-miniature. 1988

6370.

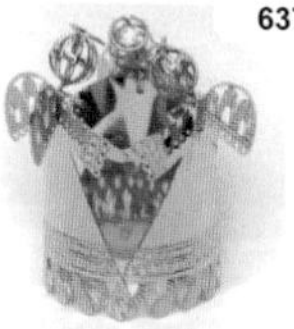

Dancing Angels
975QXM5891 • $17
Issued 1992, 1993 & 1994.

6371.

Festive Angel
975QXM5783 • $26
Issued 1990 & 1991.

6372.

Graceful Angel
1295QXM5385 • $22
2001

6373.

Heavenly Glow
975QXM5661 • $22
Issued 1988 & 1989.

6374.

Shining Star
995QXM4141 • $22
Issued 1995, 1996 & 1997.

6375.

Victorian Angel
1295QXM4293 • $19
Issued 1998, 1999 & 2000.

ALPHABETICAL INDEX

Below is an alphabetical listing of all the Ornaments and Tree Toppers featured in this Value Guide. Series and Collections are in bold type with all their items listed alphabetically beneath the title.

Keepsake Christmas Ornaments

Miniature Ornaments

Easter/Spring Ornaments

Name .... Page

Halloween Ornaments

Special Issue Ornaments

Ambassador Holiday House Collection

Name .... Page

Name .... Page

Colors of Christmas

Hall Family Ornaments

Name .... Page

Mayor's Tree Ornaments

Tree Toppers

SERIES INDEX

Below is a page index of all the series ornaments featrued in this value guide, including their colorways and complements. Colorways and complements are designated as follows: ■ Colorway ■ Complement

Nina Aube

Title: Sculptor IV
Started: Hallmark 7/81; Keepsakes 11/94
Hometown: Chicago, Illinois

Nina Aube started telling people she was going to be an artist from the day she first learned to talk.

Nina doesn't remember doing it, but her sisters say she once sculpted a perfect ear of corn out of modeling clay. Their appreciation of her effort stayed with her and encouraged her. In fact, an appreciation of art was even part of the games they played. They especially loved a game Nina called "Draw in the Dark." They'd turn off the lights and draw something, then turn the lights back on and giggle over the drawings.

Nina was also known for her artistic talent at school, which proved to be a problem at times. Some of the boys tried to get her to do their art assignments for them. She also had a habit of drawing in the margins of her papers during math class.

Then, as well as now, Nina always enjoyed adding touches of fashion sense to her artwork. She especially liked drawing girls wearing the trendy clothes of the '60s and '70s. That's why you'll sometimes find some unique clothing touches added to the signature sweetness of Nina's Keepsake Ornament designs.

Katrina Bricker

Title: Artist III
Started: Hallmark 3/94; Keepsakes 2/95
Hometown/state: Erie, Pennsylvania

Katrina Bricker always knew that art was what she wanted to do. There was never a question of anything else. She credits her mother, an art teacher, with instilling the joy of the artist in her.

Of course, knowing exactly what you want to do at such a young age can pose some concentration problems at school. Katrina remembers having a particularly hard time learning states and capitals. She once had to stay after school to do a special worksheet on the subject and got into trouble with her teacher for spending time doodling in the margins of the paper. The same teacher later gave Katrina her first public recognition as an artist – a prize for creating a Thanksgiving bulletin board display that was judged the best display in school.

Katrina first tried sculpting in the third grade with a rendering of the comic strip character, Garfield. Later, in her senior year of high school, she did a project involving another of her lifelong interests – horses – which helped her to realize her passion for sculpting.

Robert E. Chad

Title: Senior Sculptor
Started: Hallmark 3/87; Keepsakes 3/87
Hometown/state: Fair Lawn, New Jersey

Chad, as he's called by all who know him, has had a knack for drawing throughout his whole life. Even his fifth grade teacher – a cartoonist on his own time – noticed Chad's talent and moved him to a desk right in front of his own. He made sure that Chad kept up with his art.

Chad's favorite subject in those days was a character he created called "Surfer Joe" – a long-haired, big-nosed, cartoon wave rider. Chad says every artist has a "Surfer Joe" in his or her past: one thing they remember drawing almost constantly early on.

Three-dimensional art eventually got Chad's attention. It even turned up in his drawing style. He began drawing with the goal of making his images look like they were coming right off of the page. He tried some actual three-dimensional pieces but wasn't happy with them. The most memorable of those was the face of a bear carved into a bar of soap for a Boy Scout project.

Today, he makes rough sketches of Keepsake Ornaments jump off the page and onto people's Christmas trees.

Ken Crow

Title: Master Artist
Started at Hallmark: 8/79
Started in Keepsakes: 11/83
Hometown/state: Long Beach, California

Ken Crow's talent became apparent in 11th grade history class, where he discovered that a picture truly is worth a thousand words. The teacher, Mr. Ciriello, allowed Ken to use creative illustration in his class notes.

When Mr. Ciriello spoke about the Civil War, Ken would draw his teacher into war scenarios being discussed. When Mr. Ciriello explained how an economy works, Ken drew him on a treadmill that was turning the cogs that make an economic engine run.

Ken calls Mr. Ciriello's encouragement the "green light" that told him he had an aspect to his artistic sensibility that set him apart. Where many people could draw and sculpt, Ken could put ideas and art together to communicate.

Ken first used that skill professionally as an editorial cartoonist for a newspaper. He now uses it to communicate a sense of history and emotion in the expressive and complex work he does with Keepsake Ornaments.

But how did Ken go from drawing to becoming an expert in mechanical Christmas ornaments? As a child, he tore apart every toy he ever had to see how it would work. He even made other toys out of the spare parts.

Joanne Eschrich

Title: Master Sculptor
Started: Hallmark 9/81; Keepsakes 1/96
Hometown: Westport, Massachusetts

Joanne Eschrich knew she had talent in third grade, when classmates would ask her to draw for them. In high school, she got a similar reputation as a science illustrator. She illustrated several reports for friends until the biology teacher caught on.

As a young artist being raised on a farm, Joanne had no shortage of animal friends to pose for her. Joanne's particular creative talents also lent themselves to just about any game. She built dollhouses with her sisters and spaceships with her brothers.

When college came along, Joanne knew she was going for art. Nothing else was as important. Despite her parents' attempts to talk her out of an art career, she persevered and got an interview with Hallmark in her senior year. A job offer soon followed.

Joanne had never even considered sculpting when she was asked to try doing a piece for the Hallmark Merry Miniatures line. She created a basset hound named Sebastian for that assignment and discovered that she was a sculptor as well as an illustrator.

Julie Forsyth

Title: Sculptor IV
Started: Hallmark 1979; Keepsakes 4/98
Hometown: New Jersey

One of Julie Forsyth's first memories of art is the time she spent as a preschooler copying the projects her mother would bring home from an art class she was taking.

In the first grade Julie sculpted a dog and started showing it around. The response she got was so overwhelming that she knew she had found what she wanted to do with her life.

Dogs remained a favorite subject for a long time, as did cats and horses. Julie preferred the movement of living things over still-life art.

Julie had another significant experience with three-dimensional art when she was eleven. After seeing a poster of a woman in head-to-toe body paint, Julie sculpted a woman and painted her head-to-toe in hippie colors. The image was so strong that, years later, she painted a doll in similar colors for an art show at Hallmark.

Julie also studied pottery but didn't have what she calls "a feel" for the potter's wheel. Her teacher encouraged her to create a bust instead. It was another success, proving once again that Julie's first grade intuition was right all along.

John "Collin" Francis

Title: Artist IV
Started: Hallmark 10/66; Keepsakes 10/85
Hometown: Casper, Wyoming

John "Collin" Francis took an aptitude test in high school that said he would be good at art. He liked art, but never thought himself very good at it.

As John tells it, his earliest efforts ranged from "sloppy" in kindergarten to "stiff" in high school. In fact, his kindergarten teacher couldn't even read the name on one assignment and returned the paper to him.

Good at it or not, John kept on having fun with art. War was going on overseas at the time, and the imaginations of boys across the country were wandering. John remembers drawing airplanes with friends when they should have been listening to their teachers.

Art didn't become a goal until college, where John majored in pre-engineering. His roommate had an art minor and would bring projects home with him. Deciding he liked what his roommate was doing better than engineering, John changed his major.

Influenced largely by a sculpting teacher named Gary Coulter, John strove throughout college to become an artist. As collectors will attest, he has succeeded.

Steve Goslin

Title: Tech Artist III
Started: Hallmark 6/78; Keepsakes 10/95
Hometown: Shawnee, Kansas

Steve Goslin jokes that he learned to be creative "through osmosis." Both of his parents were career artists at Hallmark.

Steve's first job with Hallmark was in the mailroom. He also worked in the manufacturing department, and then as a security guard.

It wasn't until his parents retired and moved to France that Steve began to experiment with his artistic skills. He had created a portfolio by buying Hallmark cards and mimicking their artistic styles. He started whittling and carving things, such as the bedtime story squirrel he made for his children. He was thrilled when a position opened up with Keepsake Ornaments.

In Keepsakes, Steve says, you learn as you go. A lot of his work involves computers, which always means experimenting and trying new things. He finds great inspiration in watching other Keepsake artists at work. He also loves that his children enjoy thinking up ornament ideas and sharing them with him.

Tammy Haddix

Title: Senior Sculptor
Started: Hallmark 6/88; Keepsakes 11/96
Hometown: Kansas City, Missouri

Tammy Haddix has been drawing for as long as she can remember. Her earliest work was done on countertops and inside closets. Once her mother discovered them, the countertop projects disappeared immediately. The closet drawings were another story. Mom, an artist herself, was so proud of them that it was only recently that she painted over them.

Tammy is proud of her mom as well. After Tammy told colleagues about the finely detailed cake decoration in which her mother specializes, some of those designs were featured in Spring Keepsake Ornaments.

Hallmark caught Tammy's eye early on. When she was five years old, her mother took her to a Hallmark store. Tammy was so impressed by all the beautiful artwork surrounding her that she declared her intention to work for Hallmark

Several years later, she began work in the company's illustration studio. She also began developing an interest in sculpture – something she had tried in school but never pursued seriously. In addition to illustrating, Tammy did freelance work for Keepsake Ornaments that eventually won her a spot on the Keepsakes staff. Her work can still be found in closets – stored after Christmas.

Kristina Kline

Title: Senior Designer
Started: Hallmark 5/95; Keepsakes 5/95
Hometown: Osceola, Iowa

Kristina Kline has been around art for as long as she can remember. Her mother was well known as an artist in their local community, so art was just a natural part of life.

Kristina's first memory of getting a response to her own art was from the sixth grade, when her class had an assignment to write a daily journal entry. Feeling that she wasn't communicating everything she wanted to say, she started adding little drawings to her entries. Combining words with images completed the thoughts she wanted to put down.

Kristina's teacher wrote a comment in the journal along the lines of, "Nice drawings. But let's concentrate on the writing part." She tried, but the journal just didn't make sense to her without the drawings, and the assignment didn't seem complete. She kept on drawing until the teacher finally realized what Kristina was doing. The messages behind the drawings came through loud and clear.

From illustration to three-dimensional art, Kristina's talent continued to evolve until she became the fine sculptor she is today. She credits much of her success to her mother, who always encouraged her to try something new with her talent.

Joyce Annette Lyle

Title: Sculptor IV
Started: Hallmark 9/79; Keepsakes 8/84
Hometown/state: Tulsa, Oklahoma

Joyce Lyle had two distinct advantages as a childhood artist: her mother, who always encouraged artistic pursuits; and her older brother, Jerold. An accomplished artist, he made himself available to critique her work.

All that coaching paid off in the fifth grade when some of Joyce's drawings won first prize in a school art contest. Joyce continued to have the benefit of Jerold's mentoring for many years – even in high school, where he became her classroom art teacher.

Joyce's first three years in the Keepsake Ornaments studio were spent expertly painting completed sculpts and creating original drawings that were made into brass ornaments. Later, she began studying the craft of sculpting, where mentoring once again played an important role. Joyce credits colleagues Ken Crow and Linda Sickman, as well as now-retired artists Donna Lee, Ed Seale, and Duane Unruh, with providing the same sort of nurturing she received from her brother.

Tracy W. Larsen

Title: Sculptor IV
Started: Hallmark 10/87; Keepsakes 8/95
Hometown: North Ogden, Utah

Tracy Larsen, like most preschoolers, spent a lot of time with cartoons, but instead of just watching them, Tracy drew them. He has wonderful memories of copying characters from The Flintstones and Peanuts.

He also copied newspaper comic strips. But at the mature age of eight, Tracy moved to the more sophisticated material on the editorial page. The Nixon vs. Humphrey presidential race of 1968 became a favorite subject.

While looking through newspapers and magazines, Tracy started noticing the differences among artists' styles; another aspect of the knack for art he talks about discovering.

Tracy's first sculpting was done with clay-like kneaded erasers. He wishes the sort of arts & crafts sculpting material available to his kids today had been available in his childhood.

His first serious sculpture was the bust of Muhammad Ali he did in high school. Tracy credits his junior high and high school art programs with helping him hone his skills.

Mr. Lynn A. Norton

Title: Technical Artist III
Started: Hallmark 7/66; Keepsakes 3/87
Hometown: Saint Joseph, Missouri

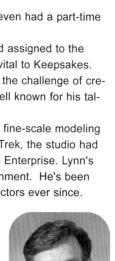

Lynn Norton was drawing by the time he was seven years old. His parents knew he had talent and displayed his work proudly. They nurtured his ability, as did his teachers, throughout his school years.

Far ahead of many art students in high school Lynn was given such independent assignments as building sets for school plays and making signs for school activities. He even had a part-time job with a sign painting company.

Lynn was hired by Hallmark right out of high school and assigned to the Engraving Studio, where he honed the skills that make him vital to Keepsakes.

Calling himself "more artisan than artist," Lynn relishes the challenge of creating the perfect likeness of a popular subject. He is most well known for his talents as a fine-scale model-maker and technical artist.

Lynn credits the Star Trek television show with bringing fine-scale modeling to Keepsakes. For the 25th anniversary celebration of Star Trek, the studio had an opportunity to create an ornament version of the Starship Enterprise. Lynn's interest in both flying ships and Star Trek won him the assignment. He's been crafting aircraft and spacecraft for Keepsake Ornament collectors ever since.

Don Palmiter

Title: Senior Sculptor
Started: Hallmark 1967; Keepsakes 1987
Hometown: Kansas City, Missouri

Don Palmiter's earliest artistic achievement came when he won a fourth grade drawing contest. The subject of his drawing will come as no surprise to people familiar with Don's work. It was a 1950s sedan with tail fins.

Cars weren't Don's only fascination. He also loved architecture and drawing buildings, houses and bridges, with an eye toward becoming an architect.

During Don's senior year of high school, he attended a student assembly hosted by Hallmark. Growing up in Kansas City, Don had always admired the work of Hallmark artists, so the assembly was a special treat for him. An instructor confident in Don's ability encouraged him to apply for a job at Hallmark. In April of 1967, Don graduated. In June, he started working for Hallmark.

He was immersed in three-dimensional work from day one, starting out in artistic engraving, where he made embossing plates for greeting cards. Eventually, he began taking various sculpting assignments, honing his abilities and developing a great love for the craft. When an opportunity to join the Keepsake Ornament studio came along, Don found a home that continues to challenge and fascinate him every day.

Anita Marra Rogers

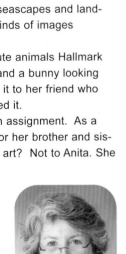

Title: Senior Sculptor
Started: Hallmark 3/87; Keepsakes 3/85 (two years of freelance)
Hometown: Kansas City, Missouri

Anita Marra Rogers used to draw a lot of horses, dogs, and unicorns as a child. Her mother was so impressed with those drawings that she signed Anita up for oil painting lessons. At nineteen, she applied for a job with Hallmark. Even though her paintings were very good, she was turned down. A few years later, a Hallmark sculptor looked at those same paintings. What he saw were a lot of beautifully rendered seascapes and landscapes. He told Anita that she simply wasn't painting the kinds of images Hallmark wanted.

He invited her to come in and see the sort of small, cute animals Hallmark artists were sculpting. Anita tried her hand at one: a deer and a bunny looking sweetly at each other over a snow bank, she then showed it to her friend who told her then that she had a career in sculpting if she wanted it.

Hallmark wasn't Anita's first experience of sculpting on assignment. As a child, she used to sculpt cotton candy into animal shapes for her brother and sisters to eat. A sacrifice of sugary sweetness for the sake of art? Not to Anita. She has never liked cotton candy.

Linda Sickman

Title: Master Artist
Started: Hallmark 3/63; Keepsakes "From the beginning, whenever that was..."
Hometown/state: Clinton, Missouri

Linda Sickman has two distinct memories of her beginnings as an artist. The first pieces that come to mind are some beaded felt angels she made for friends in her Campfire Girl group. She also remembers working hard on a classroom art assignment, a paper Halloween mask. Her determined goal was to add dimension to that flat piece of paper. She accomplished that by using smaller pieces of paper, folded accordion style, as attachments to her mask.

Little did that young Missouri mask-maker know that she would earn quite a reputation for her ability to enhance things with dimension.

From felt and beads to folded paper, even then, Linda liked to stretch herself. She can well be described as a lifelong student of art. In order to stay fresh, she's always on the lookout for a medium with which she hasn't worked before, or a new way to apply a familiar medium. Working her way through those self-directed challenges has resulted in a lot of happy results for her and for collectors who admire her work.

Susan Tague

Title: Master Sculptor
Started: Hallmark 10/87; Keepsakes 8/95
Hometown: Lynbrook, L.I., NY

Sue Tague started sculpting as a little girl, but she didn't call it sculpting at the time. She would sit in the family garden, rubbing soft stones against the ground until she had formed them into interesting shapes.

Sue always liked working with her hands and enjoyed helping her father with carpentry projects. But her dad would never let his little girl touch power tools. To this day, they make her nervous.

Sue's art talents were many, so people often turned to her for help. She made posters for school activities, decorated menus for a local luncheonette, and even painted an ice skating scene on the wall of an ice cream parlor. While she never studied sculpting, Sue did have a college design teacher who liked to assign toys as projects. Sue's first three-dimensional piece was a marionette she made for that class.

Sue interviewed with Hallmark because her parents were concerned that she hadn't had many job interviews after graduation. She got the job, thinking she'd work for awhile and then travel to London to study print-making. Sue never made it to London, however. Shortly after moving to Kansas City, she met her husband.

Sharon Visker

Title: Artist IV (Sculptor)
Started: Hallmark 9/83; Keepsakes 5/00
Hometown: Colorado Springs, Colorado

Sharon Visker grew up in an atmosphere where art was a natural part of life. Both her mother and brother were artists. Watching her mother take classes and do various projects played a very early role in piquing Sharon's own interest in art. Her admiration for her brother, "who seemed to be able to draw just about anything," spurred her on as well.

When she tried it, she loved it, and found that she was good at it. She discovered others thought so too, when some friends offered to buy some bubblegum cards Sharon had copied. She didn't make a cottage industry out of it, but the reaction she got from the few cards she did made her realize that she was indeed an artist who could make people notice her work.

Throughout grade school and high school, Sharon put together creative bulletin board displays, designed yearbooks, and won various art contests.

Her ability as an illustrator eventually brought Sharon to Hallmark. She was an illustrator for about fifteen years until a woodcarving she made in a workshop led her to discover a whole new side of her artistic ability. She's been sculpting ever since.

LaDene Votruba

Title: Sculptor IV
Started: Hallmark 12/73; Keepsakes 8/83
Hometown: Wilson, Kansas

LaDene Votruba's earliest memories of creating art are blended with childhood daydreams inspired by newspaper reports about World War II. She remembers drawing pictures of the airplanes she imagined streaking across the skies overseas.

Later, she moved on to a gentler subject, inspired by her grandfather. Happy hours spent listening to him read the story of Bambi sparked a love for deer and nature that inspires much of LaDene's art to this day.

What about sculpting? Well, a lot of farm-bred artists have claimed to draw inspiration from the soil, but none more literally than LaDene. Some of her earliest sculpting was done with clay she dug out of the ground on her family's Kansas farm. As LaDene was an aspiring cowgirl at the time, horses featured prominently in those pieces.

Much of LaDene's work is still based on reflections of what matters to her personally. Whether she's adding to her book and magazine collection or making a mental note on the run, when something touches her heart, she holds onto it. Later, she creates from it, as she has done all her life.

Christopher Webb

Title: Tech Artist III
Started: Hallmark 8/97; Keepsakes 8/97
Hometown: St. Louis, Missouri

Chris Webb started drawing in grade school as a cheap way to satisfy his urge to create. Paper and pencils weren't too big a load on his young budget. He soon became known as "the artist" in school, with all around him assuming that he would one day make his living that way.

While Chris took art in school, his instructor knew that the school's limited program wouldn't be enough. He suggested trying the Kansas City Art Institute. In the Institute's wood shop, Chris first got his hands on real sculpting and woodworking tools. It was the first time he had the opportunity to use high-quality tools to explore his ideas. Every student was required to study in the shop, but most took the course and never came back. Chris practically never left, discovering talents there that he didn't know he had.

And where did Chris get the interest in motor vehicles that is apparent in much of his Keepsakes work? Chris has been finding his way around the inside of automobiles since he was fifteen. His uncle also owned a motor parts store where Chris spent a lot of his time.

Charles Nello Williams

Title: Sculptor IV
Started: Hallmark 7/95; Keepsakes 7/95
Hometown: Safford, Arizona

Nello Williams grew up drawing anytime and anyplace he could, even in school and not just in art class. On more than one occasion, he found drawing in the margins of papers a lot more interesting than listening to his teachers.

Nello's earliest sculptures were of ships and robots from the television program Lost in Space. Sculpting was a talent that came in handy for a nine-year-old. Once, he saw a scary dungeon set advertised in a comic book. He couldn't afford to send for it, so he sculpted it himself.

Popular culture has always been a favorite subject for Nello. In high school, he and a friend sculpted masks of characters from Planet of the Apes – a big movie of the day. Little did he know that pop culture would one day build a large part of his Keepsake Ornament reputation.

Nello is also a musician. He remembers designing album covers and t-shirts for his high school garage band. He even designed a guitar for himself. Twenty years later, he actually built it. Nello sees guitar design as a place where his two great loves, sculpture and music, meet. He's currently building his fourth instrument.

COPYRIGHTS AND TRADEMARKS

© Simon & Schuster, Inc. Licensed by United Media. Raggedy Ann and Andy and associated characters are trademarks of Simon & Schuster, Inc.

From an original illustration by Norman Rockwell in the Hallmark Fine Art Collection.

© 1993 Hallmark Cards, Inc. Marty Links™ designs.

Rudolph the Red-Nosed Reindeer © and ® The Rudolph Co., L.P. "Rudolph the Red-Nosed Reindeer" animated program © 1964, renewed 1992 Classic Media, Inc. All rights reserved. Under license to GT Merchandising & Licensing LLC.

© Disney

PEANUTS ©United Feature Syndicate, Inc.

© Joan Walsh Anglund

© Disney Based on the "Winnie the Pooh" works by A.A. Milne and E.H. Shepard.

© The Jim Henson Company. JIM HENSON'S mark & logo, MUPPETS mark & logo, MUPPET, characters and elements are trademarks of The Jim Henson Company. All rights reserved.

© The Coca-Cola Company. All Rights Reserved.

Mary Emmerling © 1986 Mary Emmerling

© 2005 Binney & Smith.

TM & © 2005 Dr. Seuss Enterprises, L.P. All Rights Reserved.

OREO® Sandwich Cookie Trademark used under license from Nabisco, Inc.

Chevrolet, Corvette Emblems and Body Design are General Motors Trademarks used under license to Hallmark Cards, Inc.

© PAWS

™ & © 2005 Paramount Pictures. All Rights Reserved.

© Ford used under license from the Ford Motor Company.

Elvis Presley and Elvis are trademarks of Elvis Presley Enterprises, Inc. Copyright 1993 and/or Trademark Service Mark of Elvis Presley Enterprises, Inc.

LIONEL® Licensed by Lionel LLC.

LOONEY TUNES, characters, names and all related indicia are trademarks of and © Warner Bros. Entertainment Inc. (s05)

BARBIE and associated trademarks and trade dress are owned by, and used under license from, Mattel, Inc. © 2005 Mattel, Inc. All Rights Reserved.

© 1993 Mary Engelbreit

SUPERMAN, characters, names and all related indicia are trademarks of and © DC Comics. (s05)

BATMAN, characters, names and all related indicia are trademarks of and © DC Comics. (s05)

BEATLES™ PRODUCT © Apple Corps LTD & ™. Licensed by: Determined Productions, Inc.

© 1994 Family of Babe Ruth & Babe Ruth Baseball League, Inc. Used under license authorized by Curtis Management Group, Indianapolis, Indiana, 46202, USA.

Also from Bangzoom

Boyds Tracker Plush & Resin Second Editions

Retail: $21.95 books
$29.95 software programs

Over 150 expert contributors helped produce the Second Editions of the world's most complete Boyds guides to secondary market prices. Both books include new releases, early pieces, and variations. Full color photographs and identifying data are provided for all entries. The software catalogs inventory and enters values automatically.

Ty Beanies Tracker

Retail: $16.95 book
$16.95 software

A full year to prepare with dozens of contributors, the Second Edition of the Ty Beanies Tracker is by far the most comprehensive guide to secondary market pricing ever produced. The software catalogs inventory and enters values automatically.

The Birth of Christmas

by Clifford F. Boyle

COMING IN SEPT. 2005

Retail: $18.95 book

Mr. Boyle captures the essence of this most solemn and joyous event in poetic language that is both traditional and relevant.

The greatest gift one can give this season is the miracle of Christmas.

For more information or to order, please go to our web site:

www.bangzoom.com

or call: **800-589-7333**

Bangzoom